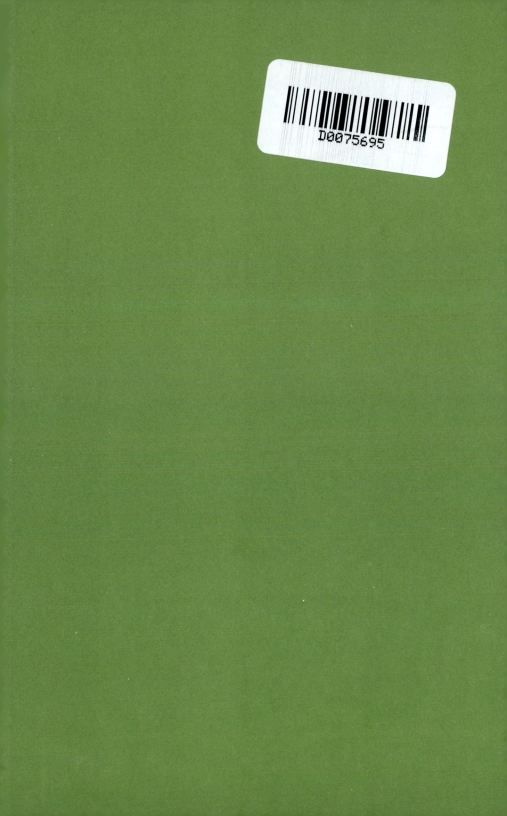

LETTERS AND DOCUMENTS

KIERKEGAARD'S WRITINGS, XXV

KIERKEGAARD

LETTERS AND DOCUMENTS

Translated by

Henrik Rosenmeier

with Introduction and Notes

PRINCETON UNIVERSITY PRESS
PRINCETON, NEW JERSEY

Library of Congress Cataloging in Publication Data will be
found on the last printed page of this book

Editorial preparation of this work has been assisted by a
grant from Lutheran Brotherhood, a fraternal benefit society,
with headquarters in Minneapolis, Minnesota

Designed by Frank Mahood

Printed in the United States of America
by Princeton University Press, Princeton, New Jersey

CONTENTS

CORRESPONDENCE REGISTER
vii

CHRONOLOGY
ix

FOREWORD, by Howard V. Hong and Edna H. Hong
xvii

TRANSLATOR'S PREFACE
xxvii

Documents Relating to the Life of Søren Kierkegaard
1

Letters
35

Dedications
427

EDITORIAL APPENDIX

Acknowledgments
441

Key to References
443

Notes
445

vi

APPENDICES

I. Kierkegaard Family
501

II. Maps
503

BIBLIOGRAPHICAL NOTE
507

INDEX
511

CORRESPONDENCE REGISTER

(The references are to the letter numbers in the text.)

LETTERS FROM SØREN KIERKEGAARD TO:

Agerskov, C., 7
Algreen-Ussing, T., 178
anonymous, 302, 310, 312
Boesen, E., 8, 49, 50, 54, 60, 62, 68,
    69, 72, 79, 80, 82, 86-106, 176,
    232, 233, 245, 263, 265
Bojesen, E. F. C., 48
Bremer, F., 204
Caroline Amalie, 295
Clausen, H. N., 159, 288
Collin, J., 294
de Bretteville, L., 271
Eiríkson, M., 164
Fabricius, F., 12
Giødwad, J. F., 111, 131
Heiberg, J. L., 9, 134, 136, 281, 282
Heiberg, Joh. Luise, 283
Hohlenberg, M. H., 11
Ibsen, P. D., 109, 151
Iversen, A. C. D. F. G., 298
Kiellerup, C. E., 218
Kierkegaard, H. P., 47, 113, 114, 196
Kierkegaard, H., 112, 150, 161, 167
Kierkegaard, M. A., 299a
Kierkegaard, P. C., 1, 2, 70, 73, 74,
    75, 77, 83, 84, 108, 115, 116, 117,
    118, 133, 149, 166, 194, 240
Kofoed-Hansen, H. P., 139
Kold, O., 120a
Kolderup-Rosenvinge, J. L. A., 180,
    184, 186, 188, 189, 190, 211, 214,
    217
Krieger, A. F., 81
Levin, I., 122-30

Library, Royal, 110
Lind, P. E., 5
Lund, C., 52, 59, 65, 147, 303, 304
Lund, Henriette, 53, 56, 71, 85, 120,
    137, 140, 141, 165, 306, 307, 308,
    309
Lund, Henrik, 244, 276, 305
Lund, M., 58, 63, 67
Lund, P. W., 3
Lund, S., 64
Lund, W., 57, 168
Luno, B., 119
Molbech, C., 169
Mynster, F. J., 299
Mynster, J. P., 191, 243, 286
Møller, P. L., 121
Nathanson, M. L., 76
Nielsen, M., 107
Nielsen, N. P., 170
Nielsen, R., 183, 210, 213, 219, 220,
    222, 224, 226, 228, 231, 253-59
Olsen, R., 15-46
Philipsen, P. G., 154, 156
Phister, J. L., 193, 274
Reitzel, C. A., 152, 157, 300
Schlegel, F. and R., 235-39
Sibbern, F. C., 55, 132
Spang, C. P., 142, 143, 144, 146, 301
Spang, P. J., 51, 61
Stilling, P. M., 241
Thomsen, J., 148, 195, 197
Trier, S. M., 192
Werliin, J. C., 171
Zeuthen, F. L. B., 175

LETTERS TO SØREN KIERKEGAARD FROM:

Andersen, H. C., 206
anonymous, 78, 268, 277, 278, 292,
   311
Bang, O., 242, 267, 284
Boesen, E., 250, 272, 285
Bremer, F., 201, 203
Clausen, H. N., 158, 287
de Bretteville, L., 270
Eiríkson, M., 163
Fibiger, I., 289
Gyllembourg, T., 138
Hauch, C., 207
Heiberg, J. L., 6, 135
Kierkegaard, E. P., 10, 14, 66
Kierkegaard, H. P., 202
Kierkegaard, M. A., 13
Kierkegaard, M. P., 4
Kofoed-Hansen, H. P., 279, 293,
   297

Kolderup-Rosenvinge, J. L. A., 160,
   172, 173, 181, 185, 187, 216, 221,
   264
Lund, Henrik, 198, 246, 248, 251,
   262, 266, 273, 275
Lund, M., 199
Nielsen, R., 177, 179, 182, 208, 209,
   212, 215, 221, 223, 225, 227, 229,
   230, 247, 249, 252, 260, 261, 291,
   296
Paludan-Müller, F., 205
Petersen, F. C., 162, 234
Philipsen, P. G., 153, 155
Reitzel, C., 290
Ross, P., 280
Rudelbach, A. G., 269
Schmidt, A. T., 200
Spang, C. P., 145, 301
Zeuthen, F. L. B., 174

CHRONOLOGY

1756	Michael Pedersen Kierkegaard, S. K.'s father, born in Sæding, Jutland, Denmark.
1768	M.P.K. leaves Sæding for Copenhagen.
1777	M.P.K. released from serfdom.
1788	M.P.K. receives royal permit to deal in goods from the Far East.
1794	M.P.K. marries Kirstine Røyen.
1796	M.P.K. inherits uncle's estate; Kirstine Røyen Kierkegaard dies childless.
1797 Apr. 26	M.P.K. marries Ane Sørensdatter Lund.
1813 May 5	Søren Aabye Kierkegaard born at Nytorv 2 (now 27), Copenhagen, son of Michael Pedersen Kierkegaard and Ane Sørensdatter Lund Kierkegaard.
June 3	Baptized in Vor Frue Church congregation (meeting in Helliggeistes Church) in Copenhagen.
1821	Enrolled in Borgerdydskolen in Copenhagen.
1828 Apr. 20	Confirmed in Vor Frue Church congregation (meeting in Trinitatis Church) by Pastor J. P. Mynster (later Bishop of Sjælland).
1830 Oct. 30	Registered as a student at University of Copenhagen.
Nov. 1	Drafted into Royal Guards, Company 7.
Nov. 4	Discharged as unfit for service.
1831 Apr. 25	Finishes first part of second examination (Latin, Greek, Hebrew, and history, *magna cum laude*; mathematics, *summa cum laude*).

Oct. 27	Completes second part of second examination (philosophy, physics, and mathematics, *summa cum laude*).

1834

Apr. 15	Entry I A 1 of journals and papers.
July 31	Mother dies.
Dec. 17	Article "Yet Another Defense of Woman's Eminent Talents," *Kjøbenhavns flyvende Post*, no. 34.

1835	Summer in north Sjælland.

1837	Between May 8 and May 12. On a visit to the Rørdams in Frederiksberg meets Regine Olsen for the first time (*JP* V 5219-20; *Pap*. II A 67, 68).
Autumn	Begins teaching Latin for a term in Borgerdydskolen.
Sept. 1	Moves from home to Løvstræde 7.

1838	"The Battle between the Old and the New Soap-Cellars" (a philosophical comedy drafted but not completed or published; *Pap*. II B 1-21).
May 19	About 10:30 A.M., S. K.'s entry concerning "an indescribable joy" (*JP* V 5324; *Pap*. II A 228).
Aug. 8/9	Father dies, 2:00 A.M.
Aug. 14	Father buried in family plot in Assistents Cemetery.
Sept. 7	Publication of *From the Papers of One Still Living, published against his will by S. Kierkegaard*. (About H. C. Andersen as a novelist, with special reference to his latest work, *Only a Fiddler*.)

1840

Feb. 1	Census list gives address as Kultorvet 132 (now 11).
Apr. or Oct.	Moves to Nørregade 230 A (now 38).
June 2	Presents his request for examination to theological faculty.
July 3	Completes examination for degree (*magna cum laude*).
July 19– Aug. 6	Journey to ancestral home in Jutland.
Sept. 8	Proposes to Regine Olsen.
Sept. 10	Becomes engaged to Regine.

Oct. 8   First number of *Corsaren* (*The Corsair*) published by M. Goldschmidt.

Nov. 17   Enters the Pastoral Seminary.

1841

Jan. 12   Preaches sermon in Holmens Church (*JP* IV 3915; *Pap.* III C 1).

July 16   Dissertation for the *Magister* degree, *The Concept of Irony, with Constant Reference to Socrates*, accepted.

Aug. 11   Returns Regine Olsen's engagement ring.

Sept. 11   Dissertation printed.

Sept. 28   10 A.M.–2:00 P.M., 4:00 P.M.–7:30 P.M. Defends his dissertation. (In 1854, Magister degrees came to be regarded and named officially as doctoral degrees.)

Oct. 11   Engagement with Regine Olsen broken.

Oct. 25   Leaves Copenhagen for Berlin, where he attends Schelling's lectures.

1842

March 6   Returns to Copenhagen.

Nov. 11   S. K.'s brother Peter Christian Kierkegaard ordained. *Johannes Climacus, or De omnibus dubitandum est* begun but not completed or published.

1843

Feb. 20   *Either/Or*, edited by Victor Eremita, published.

May 8   Leaves for short visit to Berlin.

May 16   *Two Upbuilding Discourses*, by S. Kierkegaard, published.

July   Learns of Regine's engagement to Johan Frederik Schlegel.

Oct. 16   *Repetition*, by Constantin Constantius; *Fear and Trembling*, by Johannes de Silentio; and *Three Upbuilding Discourses*, by S. Kierkegaard, published.

Dec. 6   *Four Upbuilding Discourses*, by S. Kierkegaard, published.

1844

Feb. 24   Preaches terminal sermon in Trinitatis Church.

March 5	*Two Upbuilding Discourses*, by S. Kierkegaard, published.
June 8	*Three Upbuilding Discourses*, by S. Kierkegaard, published.
June 13	*Philosophical Fragments*, by Johannes Climacus, published.
June 17	*The Concept of Anxiety*, by Vigilius Haufniensis; and *Prefaces*, by Nicolaus Notabene, published.
Aug. 31	*Four Upbuilding Discourses*, by S. Kierkegaard, published.
Oct. 16	Moves from Nørregade 230 A (now 38) to house at Nytorv 2, Copenhagen.

1845

Apr. 29	*Three Discourses on Imagined Occasions*, by S. Kierkegaard, published.
Apr. 30	*Stages on Life's Way*, edited by Hilarius Bogbinder, published.
May 13–24	Journey to Berlin.
May 29	*Eighteen Upbuilding Discourses* (from 1842–43), by S. Kierkegaard, published.
Dec. 27	Article "The Activity of a Traveling Esthetician. . . ," containing references to P. L. Møller and *The Corsair*, by Frater Taciturnus, published in *Fædrelandet*.

1846

Jan. 2	First attack on S. K. in *The Corsair*.
Jan. 10	S. K.'s reply by Frater Taciturnus in *Fædrelandet*.
Feb. 7	Considers qualifying himself for ordination (*JP* V 5972; *Pap.* VIII¹ A 4).
Feb. 27	*Concluding Unscientific Postscript*, by Johannes Climacus, published.
March 9	"Report" (*The Corsair*) begun in first NB Journal (*JP* V 5887; *Pap.* VII¹ A 98).
March 30	*Two Ages: the Age of Revolution and the Present Age. A Literary Review*, by S. Kierkegaard, published.
May 2–16	Visit to Berlin.

June 12 Acquires Magister A. P. Adler's books: *Studier og Exempler, Forsøg til en kort systematisk Fremstilling of Christendommen i dens Logik*, and *Theologiske Studier*.

Oct. 2 Goldschmidt resigns as editor of *The Corsair*.

Oct. 7 Goldschmidt travels to Germany and Italy.

1847

Jan. 24 S. K. writes: "God be praised that I was subject to the attack of the rabble. I have now had time to arrive at the conviction that it was a melancholy thought to want to live in a vicarage, doing penance in an out-of-the-way place, forgotten. I now have made up my mind quite otherwise" (*JP* V 5966; *Pap.* VII¹ A 229).

Date of preface to *The Book on Adler*, not published; ms. in *Papirer* (*Pap.* VII² B 235-70; VIII² B 1-27).

Drafts of lectures on communication (*JP* I 649-57; *Pap.* VIII² B 79-89), not published or delivered.

March 13 *Upbuilding Discourses in Various Spirits*, by S. Kierkegaard, published.

Sept. 29 *Works of Love*, by S. Kierkegaard, published.

Nov. 3 Regine Olsen marries Johan Frederik Schlegel.

Dec. 24 Sells house on Nytorv.

1848

Jan. 28 Leases apartment at Rosenborggade and Tornebuskegade 156 A (now 7) for April occupancy.

Apr. 19 S. K. notes: "My whole nature is changed. My concealment and reserve are broken—I am free to speak" (*JP* V 6131; *Pap.* VIII¹ A 640).

Apr. 24 "No, no, my reserve still cannot be broken, at least not now" (*JP* V 6133; *Pap.* VIII¹ A 645).

Apr. 26 *Christian Discourses*, by S. Kierkegaard, published.

July 24-27 *The Crisis and a Crisis in the Life of an Actress*, by Inter et Inter, published.

Aug. Notes that his health is poor and is convinced that he will die (*JP* VI 6229; *Pap.* IX A 216).

Reflections on direct and indirect communication (*JP* VI 6231; *Pap.* IX A 218, 221-24).

Sept. 1	Preaches in Vor Frue Church (*JP* IV 3928-32; *Pap.* IX A 266-69, 272).
Nov.	*The Point of View for My Work as an Author* "as good as finished" (*JP* VI 6258; *Pap.* IX A 293); published posthumously in 1859 by S. K.'s brother, Peter Christian Kierkegaard.
	"Armed Neutrality," by S. Kierkegaard, written toward the end of 1848 and the beginning of 1849 (*Pap.* X^5 B 105-10) but not published.

1849

May 14	Second edition of *Either/Or*; and *The Lily of the Field and the Bird of the Air*, by S. Kierkegaard, published.
May 19	*Two Minor Ethical-Religious Essays*, by H. H., published.
June 25-26	Councillor Olsen (Regine's father) dies.
July 30	*The Sickness unto Death*, by Anti-Climacus, published.
Nov. 13	*Three Discourses at the Communion on Fridays*, by S. Kierkegaard, published.

1850

Apr. 18	Moves to Nørregade 43 (now 35).
Sept. 27	*Practice in Christianity*, by Anti-Climacus, published.
Dec. 20	*An Upbuilding Discourse*, by S. Kierkegaard, published.

1851 | *Veiviser* (directory) listing for 1851: Østerbro 108 A (torn down). |

Jan. 31	"An Open Letter . . . Dr. Rudelbach," by S. Kierkegaard, published.
Aug. 7	*On My Work as an Author*; and *Two Discourses at the Communion on Fridays*, by S. Kierkegaard, published.
Sept. 10	*For Self-Examination*, by S. Kierkegaard, published.

1851-52	*Judge for Yourselves!* by S. Kierkegaard, written. Published posthumously, 1876.
	Veiviser listing for 1852-55: Klædeboderne 5-6 (now Skindergade 38).

1854

Jan. 30	Bishop Mynster dies.

Apr. 15   H. Martensen named Bishop.

Dec. 18   S. K. begins polemic against Bishop Martensen in *Fædrelandet*.

1855

Jan.-
May   Polemic continues.

May 24   *This Must Be Said; So Let It Now Be Said*, by S. Kierkegaard, advertised as published.

First number of *The Moment*.

June 16   *Christ's Judgment on Official Christianity*, by S. Kierkegaard, published.

Sept. 3   *The Unchangeableness of God. A Discourse*, by S. Kierkegaard, published.

Sept. 25   Ninth and last number of *The Moment* published; number 10 published posthumously. S. K. writes his last journal entry (*JP* VI 6969; *Pap.* XI² A 439).

Oct. 2   Enters Frederiks Hospital.

Nov. 11   Dies.

Nov. 18   Burial in Assistents Cemetery, Copenhagen.

Kierkegaard in His Letters

"I do not know what is the matter with Søren. I cannot make him write to you. I wonder whether it is intellectual poverty that prevents him from thinking of something to write about or childish vanity that keeps him from writing anything except that for which he will be praised, and, inasmuch as he is unsure about it in this case, whether that is why he will write nothing."[1]

The sixteen-year-old Søren Kierkegaard himself had to copy this criticism of himself after dutifully transcribing his seventy-three-year-old father's letter to his brother Peter, who was studying abroad, into a copybook (a common procedure in pre-carbon-copy days). To his father's oblique rebuff, Søren appended: "I (Søren) will soon write to you so that I may be able also to gainsay Father."

This volume of letters by and to Søren Kierkegaard, translated and published in English for the first time almost a century and a half after the date of the first extant letter, is indeed a gainsaying of Michael Pedersen Kierkegaard, who seemed to have forgotten—or perhaps never realized!—that a teenage son is loathe to write letters under his father's scrutiny and to an elder brother whom everyone is hoping he will emulate in every way. Once he got away from their well-meaning, scrutinizing solicitude, Søren abandoned the schoolboy's pedantic and informatory style of letter writing and began to write letters that revealed powers and perceptions far beyond his years.

Such a letter is the long one (Letter 3) Kierkegaard wrote to Peter Wilhelm Lund on June 1, 1835. Although it does not dance dialectically in what Frithiof Brandt calls "his own lan-

1. *Breve og Aktstykker vedrørende Søren Kierkegaard*, I-II, ed. Niels Thulstrup (Copenhagen: Munksgaard, 1953-54), II, p. 24.

guage, the language of Kierkegaard,"[2] it demonstrates that the young man born with so much talent, and standing "not at a crossroads—no, but at a multitude of roads," is achieving literary style. True, its prose does not sparkle, and it is elaborately and unripely weighty, but it hints of skills already on the way—poetic imagery, subtle irony, and an exuberant vocabulary that suggests an inordinate infatuation with words. Even more so, the letter indicates that the young Kierkegaard's imagination has been fired by the brilliant young natural scientist, his sister Petrea's brother-in-law. Undoubtedly the conversations Kierkegaard heard in his sister's home between his brother Peter, a theologian, and Wilhelm were mind-expanding, but Wilhelm Lund's temperament and love of life seemed to have made a much greater impact upon him. In a way the letter signals the young Kierkegaard's coming out of the greenhouse of his father's home into the exciting, unexplored world represented by Wilhelm Lund. Even more important, it gives a clue to his central concern, his "desire to clarify and solve the riddle of life," which led him on an "inland journey"[3] as part of his search "to find the idea for which I am willing to live and die."[4]

The letter (Letter 5) Kierkegaard wrote a month later to Peter Engel Lind, a fellow student at the University of Copenhagen, was written from Gilleleje, a fishing village on the north coast of Sjælland, where the elder Kierkegaard had wisely sent his son for what Eduard Geismar has called a "summer vacation of self-knowledge."[5] Alone at Gilleleje, taking many solitary walks along the sea and the lakes of that region, Kierkegaard struggled to find the direction for his life.

2. Frithiof Brandt, *Søren Kierkegaard* (Copenhagen: Det danske Selskab, 1963), p. 27.

3. *Søren Kierkegaard's Journals and Papers*, I-VII, ed. and tr. Howard V. Hong and Edna H. Hong (Bloomington: Indiana University Press, 1967-78), V, 5726 (*Pap*. V B 47:13).

4. *JP* V 5100 (*Pap*. I A 75). This much-quoted "Gilleleje entry" in Kierkegaard's journal (August 1, 1835) is a companion piece to the letter to Wilhelm Lund.

5. *Søren Kierkegaard*, I-VI (Copenhagen: Gads Forlag, 1927-28), I, p. 29.

At this place he received "the very first and hitherto only letter that I have received from any of my acquaintances." Confessing in his prompt reply (Letter 5) to enjoying attention and craving reciprocation to what he always knew to be a scintillating personality, Kierkegaard declares that the silence of all his friends who had volunteered to write is teaching him to focus upon his inner life: "it spurs me on to comprehend myself, my own self, to hold it fast in the infinite variety of life, to direct toward myself that concave mirror with which I have attempted until now to comprehend life around me." Here in this letter we also find an enunciation of one of his first principles of letter writing—not to bind the recipient to the obligation of answering. Seven years later he repeats his principle (Letter 61): "My letters also have this negative characteristic: they do not require a reply"—however great the desire to receive a reply.

Other principles of letter writing evolved and were borne out in the brilliant correspondence Søren Kierkegaard carried on until his death. After his first somewhat discursive letters, it became one of his firm principles to steer straight into an idea, subject, theme, or event, and not to stray from it. He reminded a nephew (Letter 63) that "it is always beneficial to practice writing about some event, and that in this I am a good correspondent. . . ." A delightful example of Kierkegaard's wit doing a dialectical dance without moving from the spot is Letter 81, describing the accidental stopping of a railroad train on a journey to Berlin. The higher his estimate of the intellect of his correspondent, the more he seemed to hold to this principle.

Perhaps more attitude than principle is Kierkegaard's feeling that a letter was equivalent to a visit: "a note in my language is the same as a visit in that of others"(Letter 114). "If it should seem to you at some point that the door to your room were opening and as if my thin self with my thin stick were entering, then please permit this little letter to constitute an attempt to recompense you for a moment, if for a moment you should miss something because the door did not open"

(Letter 61). "Goodbye—for it seems to me as if I have been talking with you" (Letter 161).

Indeed, as Kierkegaard confessed to his cousin Julie Thomsen (Letter 148), he preferred writing letters to paying visits: "My d[ear] J., all this may seem rather strange to you. Perhaps you are thinking as follows: 'The time he uses to write a letter could just as well be used to pay a visit—and used far better.' I concede it, I concede everything, I make every concession—in order to do something, at least, and I prefer to do it in writing, for to do it in conversation would really mean defeat. The fact is that I am actually in love with the company of my pen . . . indeed, it even prevents me from seeking the company of anybody else."

Kierkegaard's love affair with his pen produced his published works, from which the world has built the image of a gifted theologian, philosopher, psychologist, and prescient prophet of the cultural disintegration of the life without absolutes and the Absolute. But the love affair also produced his journals and letters. With the almost simultaneous completion of the publication of the *Journals and Papers of Søren Kierkegaard* by Indiana University Press and the publication of the *Letters* by Princeton University Press, the English-reading world now has access to the man who was Søren Kierkegaard as well as to his mind. One has no hesitancy in conjecturing that reading the journals and the letters together will be a powerful gainsaying of a selectively overpublicized and often distorted image of both man and thought.

Kierkegaard's letters to his four nephews and two nieces, the children of his sisters Nicoline and Petrea, who had married Lund brothers, are an indisputable gainsaying of the distorted image of a man who supposedly was born unsympathetic, somber, and sarcastic. Such a splenetic uncle could never have penned these letters, nor would "the little correspondence club" have responded to such an uncle. "Uncle Søren" was an affectionate, gay, teasing uncle who did not talk or write down to them.

Kierkegaard's detractors might argue that the letters from Berlin to his nieces and nephews were all part of the dissembling to Regine, intended to convince her, through information innocently relayed by his nieces and nephews, that in far-away Berlin he was happy, busy, and not at all shattered. But if there was any point or plot to this correspondence, it was poignant rather than perfidious. Kierkegaard in Berlin still cherished the wild hope that he might return to Regine, and if so, "then I would wish to include those few creatures whom she has learned to love through me, my four nephews and two nieces. To that end I have kept up, often at a sacrifice of time, a steady stream of correspondence with them" (Letter 68). The fact that the letters continued after that particular point was no longer valid indicates no self-centered schemer and perennial misanthrope but a man of feeling who could write, "I find my position in life as an uncle a gratifying employment" (Letter 108).

There are scores of letters in this volume that gainsay the image of Kierkegaard as an insensitive, caustic recluse, unwilling or unable to feel compassion for his fellow beings. There are "condolence letters" that are as wise as they are tender. "To my way of thinking there is nothing worse than that hustling sympathy that seeks in clichés and stock phrases—yes, one might best put it like that—seeks to burden him who is distraught" (Letter 109). There are letters on behalf of some of his more humbly stationed acquaintances, notably the carpenter F. C. Strube (Letter 192). There is a delightful letter to his cousin Julie accompanying a gift to her small son: "It is obvious that we wronged your little son today, for we walked too fast, and we, or I, am to blame for his beginning to cry, which from a child's point of view he was completely justified in doing. It is for this reason that I am writing and sending the accompanying parcel" (Letter 195).

But the most gainsaying of all these letters are his letters to his severely crippled-from-birth second cousin, Hans Peter Kierkegaard, and to his sister-in-law Henriette Kierkegaard, who suffered severe mental depressions and spent much of her adult life in bed. He wrote firmly but tenderly to Hans Peter: "Above all do not forget your duty to love yourself; do not permit the fact that you have been set apart from life in a way, been prevented from participating actively in it, and that you are superfluous in the obtuse eyes of a busy world, above all, do not permit this to deprive you of your idea of yourself, as if your life, if lived in inwardness, did not have just as much meaning and worth as that of any other human being in the loving eyes of an all-wise Governance, and considerably more than the busy, busier, busiest haste of busy-ness—busy with wasting life and losing itself" (Letter 196). His letters to Jette reveal an uncanny psychological perception of her inner state and a concern that she be healed of her hypochondria— and he advises practically: "*Above all, do not lose your desire to walk; every day I walk myself into a state of well-being and walk away from every illness; I have walked myself into my best thoughts, and I know of no thought so burdensome that one cannot walk away from it*" (Letter 150). But Henriette did not take her brother-in-law's advice, and he tried once again, this time more passionately and much more directly. "*To have faith is constantly to expect* the joyous, the happy, the good. . . . You are in some measure always suffering—hence the task lies right here: Divert your *mind, accustom yourself by faith to changing suffering into expectation of the joyous. It is really possible*" (Letter 167). —And this from a person who himself was not unacquainted with despondency and is dismissed by some as a complainer and self-tormentor.

The Kierkegaard—Kolderup-Rosenvinge correspondence alone would make a gem of a small book that could easily stand on its own two pens. Apparently the friendship germinated suddenly from an earlier acquaintance, and soon the law professor and Kierkegaard were going for long walks together on Monday afternoons. When the walks were interrupted by Professor Kolderup-Rosenvinge's summer vacation in the country, Kierkegaard wrote: "As with G. W.'s need to talk, so also with my longing for and need to walk with you, sir. And since that is not possible, there is no other way than to teach myself to walk with you in writing"(Letter 180). Thus began this all too brief (the first "walking letter" was dated July 1848; K.-R. died in 1850) exchange of letters in

Attic style and sparkling with Attic wit between two peerless peers in the art of letter writing—or rather, the art of walking and talking together. Needless to say, these "walking letters" (they can scarcely be called pedestrian) are a piquant gainsaying of Fredrika Bremer's assessment of Kierkegaard (Letter 204 and note).

In a way, Kierkegaard's letters to Emil Boesen from Berlin ("I confide only in you" [Letter 60]—"Of course, you are the only person to whom I write in this manner" [Letter 69]) gainsay Kierkegaard himself. So sure that breaking the engagement with Regine was going according to brilliant plan and that it was all having a salutary effect upon him ("Nothing, after all, so develops a human being as adhering to a plan in defiance of the whole world" [Letter 5]), Kierkegaard betrays the tortured treadmill of his thoughts in these long, hastily written responses to his friend's letters from Copenhagen. Although he maintained that he was being completely open to at least one person in his life, the letters nevertheless reveal that he kept much from his only confidant. So sure that it was all over between himself and Regine, Kierkegaard responds to Emil's report that Regine is not looking well with an abrupt decision to leave Berlin and return to Copenhagen, although he couches his decision in cautionary instructions and does not directly reveal his true feelings. "For safety's sake I want you to make it generally known that as soon as Schelling has finished I am coming home. That was always my plan [the plan was to stay a year and a half; he stayed five months]. My intention was to have another look at the affair then" (Letter 68).

Although the letters to Boesen reveal much more than Kierkegaard probably intended, they will not stop the debate over whether Kierkegaard compassionately broke the engagement for Regine's sake (as he claimed) or selfishly for his own (as his detractors claim). In that paper war there is substance for both sides in these letters. "Just as strongly as I feel that I am an exceptional amorist, I also know very well that I would be a bad husband and always will remain so" (Letter

62). "I have no time to get married" (Letter 54). What they reveal most poignantly, perhaps, is that Kierkegaard himself did not fully understand the complexity of his own motives, and his later statements about clearly understanding them were formulated in recollection.

In addition to being significant contributions to an insight into the Søren-Regine relationship, the letters to Boesen provide a lively running report on Kierkegaard's leap into authorship, for *Either/Or* was begun in Berlin in 1841-42 and was finished in Berlin during a very brief second visit in the spring of 1843. Writing again to Emil Boesen, Kierkegaard says: "In my indolence during the past months I had pumped up a veritable shower bath, and now I have pulled the string and the ideas are cascading down upon me: healthy, happy, merry, gay, blessed children born with ease and yet all of them with the birthmark of my personality" (Letter 82).

Despite all the research and speculating and writing that has been devoted to Kierkegaard's relationship to Regine (his own "explanation" can be said to embrace his published works and unpublished writing), the love letters have not been available in their entirety to English readers. Anyone who knows anything about Kierkegaard knows about the "tall palisander cupboard"[6] he had custom-made to treasure their love letters and other documents related to "Her." Regine's letters to him were burned by her own hand when the contents of the shrine were given to her after his death. Kierkegaard's very first letter to Regine (Letter 15) is a clear signal that his letters were not going to conform to the ordinary amorous epistles. Well along in the correspondence (Letter 31), after some penetrating comments on love and love letters, he writes, "My letters are not a gradually exhausting bleeding to death." Indeed, there is no bleeding of any kind in these letters, no indication whatsoever of the forging of the iron will to renounce her love. However, his reference to David's ability to banish Saul's black mood (Letter 32) may be

6. *JP* VI 6472 (*Pap.* X⁵ A 149); "her tall cupboard," *JP* VI 6762 (*Pap.* X⁴ A 299).

significant: "David was able to banish Saul's black mood, and yet I have never heard that he was a particularly great artist. I imagine it was his young, joyful, fresh spirit that helped so much, and you possess yet something more—a love for which nothing is impossible. . . ." Kierkegaard might well have been thinking that the renunciation was necessary, for it would be impossible for him to keep from making this "joyful, fresh spirit" unhappy. Or was he recognizing that his black mood, which Regine had the power to banish, was one of the forces that would drive him to produce his lifework?

As the massive lifework of Kierkegaard's short life clearly reveals, the relationship, but not the love, was renounced. Kierkegaard's love for Regine was forced down into himself, where it became a perennial fresh spring for a variety of themes in the Kierkegaard literature. To gainsay any charge that Kierkegaard made this love subserve his writing, selfishly used Regine as a poetic subject, there are his words (Letter 50) to Boesen: "I do not turn her into a poetic subject . . . I think I can turn anything into a poetic subject, but when it is a question of duty, obligation, responsibility, debt, etc., I cannot and will not turn those into poetic subjects. If she had broken our engagement, my soul would soon have driven the plow of forgetfulness over her, and she would have served me as so many others have done before her—but now, now I serve her."

The most eloquent gainsaying to any such charge is in one of the shortest but most pathos-filled of Kierkegaard's letters (Document XXI), a letter he intended as his last will and testament.

Dear Brother,

It is, of course, my will that my former fiancée, Mrs. Regine Schlegel, inherit without condition whatever little I may leave. If she herself will not accept it, she is to be asked if she would be willing to administer it for distribution to the poor.

What I wish to give expression to is that to me an engage-

ment was and is just as binding as a marriage, and that therefore my estate is her due, exactly as if I had been married to
her.

Your brother
S. KIERKEGAARD

Howard V. Hong
Edna H. Hong

TRANSLATOR'S PREFACE

This volume contains all the known correspondence to and from Søren Kierkegaard, a number of Kierkegaard's letters in draft form, and documents and records pertaining to his life and death. Because of the paucity of extant material, brief notes (for example, those to and from his lifetime friend, Emil Boesen), which are a token of a relationship, have also been included. The present volume is a translation of Volume I of *Breve og Aktstykker vedrørende Søren Kierkegaard*, edited by Niels Thulstrup, plus a few recently discovered letters and dedications. The notes form Volume II of the Danish edition.[1]

Breve og Aktstykker is a compilation from numerous public and private sources and collections, the three principal ones being the holdings of the Royal Library in Copenhagen, *Søren Kierkegaards Papirer*,[2] and *Søren Kierkegaards Efterladte Papirer*.[3] The reader who wishes to consult the originals is referred to the Thulstrup notes, in which the location of each letter is indicated.

The Danish text attempts faithfully to record every possible textual correction, deletion, and marginal or linear insertion. For purposes of translation, I thought that practice neither practicable nor valuable, but wherever an alteration might indicate something about Kierkegaard's thinking, whether a second thought or a change in the thrust of meaning, or the care with which Kierkegaard strove to make himself clear, I have indicated the change in square brackets. In his preface,

1. Ed. Niels Thulstrup, under the auspices of the Søren Kierkegaard Society, the text edited with the assistance of Carl Weltzer, I-II (Copenhagen: Munksgaard, 1953-54).
2. Ed. P. A. Heiberg, V. Kuhr, and E. Torsting, I-XI³ (Copenhagen: Gyldendal, 1909-48); 2 offset edition, ed. Niels Thulstrup, I-XI³ + XII-XIII (Copenhagen: Gyldendal, 1969-70), XIV-XV, Index A-F, G-Q, by N. J. Cappelørn (1975-76).
3. Ed. H. P. Barfod and H. Gottsched, I-VIII (Copenhagen: 1869-81).

Niels Thulstrup comments on the difficulties of establishing a reliable text. Kierkegaard's handwriting is not always easy to decipher, and at times the punctuation is "faltering and unsure."[4] I have accordingly tried to read for meaning, and have sometimes modified the syntax by inserting periods, while retaining Kierkegaard's unorthodox use of colons and dashes. Walter Lowrie once remarked on "Kierkegaard's use of the dash, which he employed more frequently than any other author I can think of—for the most part appropriately. . . ."[5] Although Lowrie replaced multiple dashes with three periods, I have sought to retain them, omitting only those that seemed to obscure the meaning, with the justification that private letters are substantially different in kind from prose intended for publication.

In preparing the notes, I have freely adapted those by Thulstrup: a few have been translated in their entirety, some have been contracted, and some omitted. Other notes, principally dealing with Danish phenomena, such as topography, history, and customs have been added, and I have sought to expand the references to Kierkegaard's works as well as to his private papers wherever I was able to do so. Still I must emphasize that without the use of the Thulstrup notes and without the generous assistance of Howard and Edna Hong, the critical apparatus would have been inadequate, indeed.

Henrik Rosenmeier

4. *Breve og Aktstykker*, I, pp. ix-x.
5. Translator's Preface, *Attack upon "Christendom"* (Princeton: Princeton University Press, 1944), p. vi.

DOCUMENTS
RELATING TO THE LIFE OF
SØREN KIERKEGAARD

I. Baptismal Certificate

Anno 1813, June 3 (written, the year eighteen hundred and thirteen, the third of June) Mr. Michael Petersen Kirkegaard, former hosier, and his wife, Mrs. Ane Sørens^{dr}[1] Kirkegaard, née Lund, residing at 2 Nyetorv, had a son, born May 5, baptized in Helliggeistes Church and named Søren Aabÿe.[2] I certify that this is in accordance with the baptismal records of the Church.

Copenhagen, April 21, 1818.   R. GYLCHE
                                               Sexton.

II. Copy from the Baptismal Records [1813]

June 3: Mr. Mikael Petersen Kierkegaard, former hosier, and his wife, Mrs. Ane Sørensd^r-Kierkegaard, née Lund, residing at 2 Nyetorv, their son, born May 5, named *Søren Aabye*. The sponsors:[1] the mother and Mrs. Abelone Aabÿe, Mr. Anders Kierkegaard, vendor of silk and fabrics, Niels Aabÿe, Christen Aggerschou, Otto Møller, Peter Aabÿe, and the father himself.

III. Certificate of Vaccination

R[1]
F   Certificate of Cowpox Inoculation.
VI

Søren Aabye Kierkegaard
born in Copenhagen and residing in Copenhagen, was at the age of three months inoculated with cowpox by me, the undersigned, on September 23, 1813. Upon careful examination between the seventh and ninth days after the inoculation, I have found all those symptoms that prove them to be genuine cowpox: for they were unbroken and undamaged, filled with clear liquid, depressed in the center, and surrounded by a red

circle. Thus he has been duly subjected to genuine cowpox, which in the future will protect him from infantile smallpox. Upon my honor and conscience I certify this to be so.

Copenhagen, April 25, 1818.   G. F. DØRGE
                                            County Surgeon.

IV. *Copy from the Confirmation Records and Certificate of Confirmation*

(a)

[1828] April 20: Comfirmed by Dr. Mynster[1] on the Second Sunday after Easter: Boys: . . . No. 20. Søren Aabÿe Kierkegaard. [*grade*] . . . mg.[2]

(b)

I hereby certify that
Søren Aabÿe Kierkegaard
was confirmed by me in the
Parish of Frue Church, April 20, 1828.

Copenhagen, April 21, 1828   MYNSTER

V. *School Evaluation*[1]

Søren Aabye Kierkegaard, Michael Petersen Kierkegaard's son, born May 5, 1813 (Baptismal Certificate no. 2), entered the preparatory class of this school in 1821.

Quick-headed, receptive to everything that requires exceptional interest, but for a long time he was extremely childish and wholly devoid of seriousness; and a taste for freedom and independence, which also manifest themselves in his behavior as a good-natured, occasionally amusing lack of constraint, prevented him from entering too deeply into any subject or from embracing it with so much interest that he would not be able to pull back again in time. When this impetuousness, which rarely allowed him to bring his good intentions to fruition or to persist in pursuing a set goal, abates with time; when more seriousness enters his character, in which respect there has been notable progress, especially during the past year; and when his good intellect can develop more freely and without encumbrance at the University, he will surely be counted among the able and in many ways come to resemble his older brother.[2] His personality is lively, like Anger's,[3] but even merrier, and although cleverer, still open and unspoiled. Of several brothers and sisters who have all enjoyed an excellent upbringing, he is the youngest. A couple of years before he entered school, he lost his next to youngest brother,[4] whose illness may have been brought about when his head struck that of another boy while they were playing in the schoolyard. This, coupled with the fact that he is of small physical stature, may have had some influence on his upbringing for several years thereafter. He has read and presents: In Latin: by Horace: the *Odes*, the first three books of the *Epistles*, and *Ars Poetica*; by Vergil: the first six books of the *Aeneid*; by Terence: *Andria* and *Phormio*; by Cicero: *De officiis*, the first two books of *De oratore*, the Catilinean orations, "Pro Roscio Amerino," "Lege Manilia," "Archia poeta," "Milone," "Ligario," "Dejotaro," the first forty letters in the Weiske edition; the first *Pentade* by Livy; *Bellum civile* by Caesar; both *Wars* by Sallust; Cornelius Nepos. In Greek: by Homer: Books 3, 4, 5, 8, 9, 10, 11, 12, and 22 of the *Odyssey* and the first seven books of the *Iliad*; *Crito* and *Euthyphro* by Plato; *Memorabilia Socratis* by Xenophon; *Urania* and *Calliope* by Herodotus; the Gospel of St. John. In Hebrew: Genesis; Exodus, chapter 15. He used the following textbooks:[5] Fogtmann's textbook on religion; Hersleb's larger *History of the Bible*; Kall and Kofoed's *History*; Riise's *Geography*; Ursin's textbooks; Lindberg's Hebrew, Tilemann's German, and Deichman's French grammars.

VI. *School Testimony.*

Rector Magnificus!

Respected and excellent Professors!

Cicero says that above all the citizens ought to be persuaded that the gods govern and rule everything; that all events occur by virtue of their divine power; that they are the benefactors of mankind; that they observe the character of everyone, how he acts, how he errs, and how he practices piety in religion by worshiping the gods; and that they reward the good and punish the evil. The annals of the Roman people and the monuments of antiquity testify that those persons whose minds were permeated by those thoughts in no manner deviated from the true, useful wisdom, indeed that they who obeyed the gods were given all manner of prosperity, while those who defied them were afflicted with adversity. The most worthy young *Severinus Aabye Kierkegaard* early became accustomed to seeking the basis for his life in this persuasion and to judging the outcome of events thereby. For from the outset he was, by the earnestness of his parents and by their good example, imbued with the strongest feeling of religious reverence, devotion to God, and moral responsibility, which were then subsequently nourished by the instruction of his first childhood teachers, who had been carefully chosen for this purpose. As a nine-year-old, when he was first entrusted to our care, he did not allow himself to be confused by those who do not know how they should behave but who, like those who swim against the current, are swept along by bad companions as if by a strong torrent; on the contrary, he showed all of us his ability and eagerness to learn, no less his readiness to obey, and his utterly modest and moral way of life, so that it is certainly to be hoped that he will become the equal of his brother, as he is like him in talents. —The root of these virtues are the pure devotion to God that was already sown in his mind from the outset of his life. For his father has acted as a merchant in conformance with the prescriptions of philosophy and, in the conduct of his business, has united the reading of works on theology, philosophy, and the fine arts; and his wisdom and goodness are evident in all his circumstances and especially in the rearing of his children, from whom he himself has also received great benefit with respect to the education of his mind and spiritual enjoyment. Inasmuch as the father's home is thus a model of diligence, patience, and frugality, and is established in conformance with those doctrines by which children are taught divine virtue and wisdom, so he has instructed his son to view everything in the light of love for God and duty and to seek the author of everything in God as the source of all wisdom. He has taught him on the one hand that God does not reward the idle, yet on the other hand that without prayer intelligence can accomplish nothing, lest the mind be led into error; and he has done everything to awaken the boy's love for a scholarly education, the foundation of all respectable efforts. This young man, who has thus been reared and educated in accordance with the custom of his parents and with the discipline that serves the welfare of the state, and not in the frivolous and contumacious spirit in which many exist, and who possesses precious and pleasing characteristics, is warmly recommended to *you, O learned men*.

Written in Copenhagen, October 3, 1830.

M. NIELSEN,[1]

Principal of the school

that is called the Borgerdyds School.

VII. *Transcript of artium examination* [1]

Søren Aabÿe Kierkegaard has presented himself for the *artium* examinations in October, 1830, and on the basis of individual grades in

Written work in his native tongue	Laud p.c.
Latin	Laud
Written translation into Latin	Laud
Greek	Laud p.c.
Hebrew	Laud
Religion	Laud
Geography	Laud
History	Laud p.c.
Arithmetic	Laud
Geometry	Laud
German	Laud
French	Laud p.c.

has achieved the overall grade of *Laudabilis*.

Copenhagen, October 30, 1830.
  This is hereby certified by the undersigned

J. W. HORNEMANN[2]
Dean of the Faculty of Philosophy.

VIII. *Letter of Admission to the Academic Community*[1]

The Rector of the University of Copenhagen
with
The Faculty Senate
[*seal*]
May this bring happiness and good fortune! Upon examination, in which he demonstrated his skill in the liberal arts
with the grade of *Laudabilis*,

Søren Aabÿe Kierkegaard
from the Borgerdyds School in Copenhagen

has been enrolled as a member of the academic community of
the University of Copenhagen. He has promised conscientiously to observe the laws according to the precepts presented to him.
  In testimony and as confirmation, this letter is signed,

Copenhagen, October 30,1830.
J. W. HORNEMANN.
At present Rector of the University.

IX. *Certificate of Medical Discharge from the Military*

Having been appointed a member of the seventh company
of His Majesty the King's Guards on November 1, 1830, the
bearer,
Søren Aabÿe Kierkegaard, a student,
did not serve in the above-mentioned company because he is
unfit for service according to a certificate from the army sur-

geon, wherefore he is deleted from the rolls of the Guards at his own request.

Copenhagen, November 4, 1830.

> [*wax seal*]
>
> HEGERMANN LINDENCRONE.
> By His Royal Majesty, the King of Denmark etc.,
> Lord Chamberlain, Colonel and Commander
> of the above-mentioned Guards and of the 2nd In-
> fantry Regiment. Commander of *Dannebrog* and Mem-
> ber of *Dannebrog*.

X. Transcript of the Second Examination,[1] Parts One and Two

Søren Aabÿe Kierkegaard.		Søren Aabÿe Kierkegaard	
The Second Examination		The Second Examination	
Part One		Part Two	
April 25, 1831.		October 27, 1831.	
Latin,	Laudabilis[2]	Philos. Theor.,	Laud. p.c.
Greek,	Laudab.	Philos. Pract.,	Laud. p.c.
Hebrew,	Laudab.	Physics,	Laud. p.c.
History,	Laudab.	Math. Sup.,	Laud. p.c.
Math. Inf.,	Laud. p.c.		
	Søeborg.		Søeborg.

XI. Petition for Examination[1]

Søren Aabye Kierkegaard respectfully greets the Very Reverend Professors of the Theological Faculty of the University of Copenhagen.

I was born on May 5, 1813. My father was the late Michael Petersen Kierkegaard, a former merchant, whose memory I venerate. I was graduated *cum laude* from a private school in Copenhagen, and when I had passed the preliminary examinations at our University with a first with honors, I directed my soul and mind to theology and decided that I would put special emphasis on the mastery of the exegetical and historical disciplines. Therefore I diligently attended the lectures here at our University, and today I must with gratitude remember the profit and assistance which at that time fell to my lot from those lectures. But inasmuch as I daily grew farther and farther away from theology and in the course of time with all sails set slipped into the study of philosophy, which then had won special acceptance among us, I became certain that I could not satisfy the demands of theology nor it mine, and I left it completely. I freely admit that under such circumstances, had I not in a certain sense felt myself bound by a promise on account of my father's death, I would never have been able to bring myself to continue in this direction, which I had long ago abandoned, and resume the studies I had already consigned to oblivion. Accordingly, as I who once made a more fortunate beginning now try to swim my way back through the waves, I return more happily to you, Very Reverend Professors, and commend my studies to you as best I may.

Copenhagen, June 2, 1840.

I have studied Genesis, sixteen psalms from the first Book of Psalms, Book four from the Book of Psalms, the first nine chapters of Exodus in the Old Testament.

XII. *From the Theological Examination Records*[1]

Examen theologicum
July 3, 1840

Candidati: 1. Kjerkegaard, Søren
         2. Kruse, Jørgen Hermann
Examen exorsus est S. V. Prof. Dr. Scharling.[2]

Symbolic writings, how are they to be interpreted?	*rsp.*
Which derivation of the word "symbolum" is a false one?	*mod. Ex. rsp.*

The development of symbolism, is it
ancient?   *rsp.*
What characterizes this scholarly field in
recent times?   *rsp. (em. Ex.)*
Who was the first to emphasize its purely
historical character?—subsequent account?   *rsp.*
Ecumenical symbols, how are they to be   *rsp. non*
interpreted?   *accurate.*
Which origin has been attributed to the
apostolic symbol?   *rsp.*
What might be the intention of such a
gathering of the apostles?   *rsp.*
Reasons against this?   *rsp.*
In which apostle might one expect reference
to such authority?   *adj. Ex. rsp.*
In which Epistle does Paul inform us about
his relationship with the other apostles?   *(mod. Ex.) rsp.*
What historical proof does Paul furnish for
his independence from apostolic teaching?   *(adj. Ex.) rsp.*
What is related in Galatians about that
conference with the apostle? When?   *rsp.*
Which journeys to Jerusalem are mentioned?   *rsp. (corr.*
Which others?   *Ex. et add.)*
St. Athanas. Whence the name? Related to
the dispute?   *rsp.*
The symbolic books of the Danish Church?
(*repetitio* [Augsburg] Conf[ession])[3]   *rsp.*
The date of the Augsburg Confession?   *rsp. add. Ex.*
Authentic copy, if extant?
What was Melancthon's opinion of this
work?   *rsp.*
What changes were made in it?   *rsp. (non*
                                                       accuratissime)

How did the enemies of Protestantism seek
to exploit that change?   *rsp. (add. Ex.)*
What argument for Christendom was from
the first considered to be of greatest
significance?   *adj. Ex. rsp.*

How did the early apologists demonstrate
the proof of the prophesies of the Old
Testament?   *rsp.*
What was the consequence of this
misconception?   *rsp.*
Whereby such an argument of necessity
must be modified?   *rsp. add. Ex.*
What is the apologetic significance of this
proof?   *rsp.*

The Very Reverend Professor Dr. Engelstoft[4] continued the
examination.

Genesis 9:16-29.

How do you distinguish between this and
other covenants?   *rsp.*
How do you distinguish between those
covenants?   *rsp. add. Ex.*
What sections of the covenant can be found
in the beginning of the chapter?   *rsp. add. Ex.*
What is granted man for the sustenance of
life?   *rsp.*
What opinion does the author leave unstated
in this distinction?   *rsp. (add. Ex.)*
How does the Golden Age come to an end?   ——
What is the distinction between this
covenant and the subsequent one with
Abraham?   *rsp. add. Ex.*
With respect to the contents of the covenant?   *rsp.*
What is required of man?   —— *adj. Ex.*
                                                        rsp.

Traces of the precepts of the Noachites?   *rsp. add. Ex.*
The Hebrew name for proselytes?   *rsp.*
Were the precepts of the Noachites adopted
by the Christians?   *rsp.*
Was the covenant with Abraham the last
one? The distinguishing characterstic of this
covenant? Was it adopted in the Mosaic
covenant?   *rsp. add. Ex.*

How are the differences in living habits of the proselytes of the gate and of justice manifested?	*r. corr. Ex.*
What is this called in Greek? The etymology? בְּרִית	*rsp. (add. Ex.)*
The derivation of the Hebrew noun בָּרַת [to cut]?	*rsp.——*
What is the parallel in Noah's account of the origin of man?	*rsp.*
The reason for the spread of such an account?	*——adj. Ex.*
What is the reason for the assumption that different phenomena may have been the cause?	*(adj. Ex.) rsp. (add. Ex.)*
How does it present itself, if one such phenomenon is assumed?	*rsp. (mod. Ex.)*
The customary grounds for this assumption?	*rsp.*
As the first farmer and the first to cultivate wine, with whom must Noah be compared?	*rsp.*
What is the origin of Dionysius' name? Who were the mothers of Dionysius and Noah?	*rsp.*
What is the basic idea behind any attempt to establish a moral precept?	*rsp.*
Is a moral precept from all points of view equally necessary now?	*rsp.*
How does one represent the moral precepts as the goal?	*rsp. em. Ex.*
Primary characteristics of a *eudaim* system?[5]	*rsp. (mod. Ex.)*
What principal thought is the point of departure?	*rsp.*
In which moral precepts does it manifest itself?	*rsp.*
Kant's argument against that?	*rsp.*
Kant's and Fichte's views of morality?	*rsp.*
Accordingly, how must we consequently conceive of the principle of moral precepts?	*rsp.*
The relationship to religion?	*rsp.*

How does the categorical imperative lead to religion?	*rsp. add. Ex.*
How is the philosophical position distinguished from the Christian positive one?	*rsp. add. Ex.*
Where in particular? —How were positive laws viewed in Luther's system?	*mod. Ex. rsp.*
How is the necessity of duty regarded? By Lutheran theology?	*rsp.*
How could it be regarded in a different way?	*rsp. (adj. Ex.)*

. . . The Very Reverend Professor Dr. Hohlenberg[6] concluded the examination.

Romans 1:1-13.

What was the disagreement in the Arian dispute? The terminology?	*rsp.*
What was the occasion for Paul's going to Rome?	*rsp.*
The occasion for this Epistle? Were the Christians in Rome formerly pagans or Jews?	*rsp.*
Why were the Jews expelled from Rome in the reign of Claudius?—"Because they were disruptive at the urging of Chrestus."	*rsp. em. Ex.*
How did the Gospel travel to Rome? Can this be verified historically?	*rsp.*
What is the probable assumption about it?	*rsp.*
What persuaded Paul to write the Epistle? From where?	——
Who are the Romans mentioned in the Epistle?	*rsp. aliq.*
What do the first seven verses contain?	*rsp.*
How does this introduction differ from the others by Paul? Why?	*rsp. add. Ex.*
Did Paul write epistles to other congregations he did not know?	*rsp. (Eph.)*
At the time, had Paul been to Ephesus?	*(adj. Ex.) rsp.*

Which congregations founded by Paul
received epistles from him?   *rsp. (add. Ex.)*
What is understood by κλητος et
ἀφωρισμενος?   *rsp.*
ὁ ἐπαγγ. δια προφ.—Why does he not
recollect the way the Christian religion was   *(adj. Ex. et*
transmitted to the gentiles?   *exp.)*
γραφαι αγιαι, which are they? Why several?
What is meant by ἡ γραφη?   *rsp. (corr. Ex.)*
ἐν δυναμει? To be interpreted adverbially?   *adj. Ex. rsp.*
κατα σαρκα et κατα πνευμ? Why both?   *aliq.*
ἐξ ἀναστασεως νεκρων. In what two ways
can this be understood?   *(add. Ex.)*
Why is it maintained that this knowledge is
proof of the Resurrection?   *rsp.*
χαρις κ. ἀποστολη ἔλαβομεν? *rsp.*   *rsp.*
Elsewhere, did Paul place "the Call" before
the authority of Christ?   *rsp.*
Why especially in Galatians? *rsp.* And in
Corinthians?   *rsp.*
From the very beginning, what was the
relationship of the Bishop of Rome and of
the congregation to the rest of
Christianity?What was it that caused it to be
thought especially important?—   *rsp. add. Ex.*
How do Tertullian and Irenaeus speak of it?   *rsp. (mod.*
    Ex.)

The importance of the apostolic tradition?   *rsp.*
Which other bishops enjoyed preeminent
respect?   *rsp. (add. Ex.)*
The title of Patriarch?   *rsp.*
The usual reason why such individual
bishops were singled out?   *rsp. (add. Ex.)*
How did the Synods increase respect for the
bishops? *In specie* the Bishops of Rome?   *rsp.*
When does the Bishop of Constantinople
attain greater respect?   *rsp.*
What other bishops submitted to him?   *rsp.*

What contributed to Rome's ascendency
over Constantinople?   *rsp.*
What prerogatives did Leo the Strong
receive? from whom?   *rsp.*
When did the Popes especially increase their
prerogatives? Defy the emperors?   *rsp.*

XIII. *Recommendation by Michael Nielsen* [1]

Mr. S. A[a]bÿe Ki[e]rkegaard, *candidatus theol.*, distinguished himself in this school by virtue of diligence, intellect,
and brilliant comprehension of the subjects taught in general,
and of the form and spirit of languages in particular. Already
at that time he aroused great expectations of that uprightness,
independence, and skill, of that penetrating, lucid, and comprehensive view, of that profound, vivid, and earnest mind,
and of that skill in representation, superb in all respects,
which he has subsequently demonstrated. Even though circumstances have not made it mandatory for him to teach, he
has often felt the urge to do so. Accordingly, for several years
he has, at my request, assisted me with the weaker students in
their written Latin translations and has worked effectively to
awaken them to thought, which was not merely aimed just at
their examinations but continued to be effective in their subsequent lives. For a couple of years, when I myself was unable
to correct the written translations of the senior class on account of bad eyesight, he performed this task for me with that
insight into language, now more mature, which I recognized
in him when he was a student. Throughout one school year,
at his own request, he taught Latin to the second form and
brought it far in Latin and in its whole intellectual development; some of them were graduated this year, when he again
kindly assisted me with Latin and written translation for the
senior class during the busiest period, and he did so as well as
I myself could have done. —Accordingly, insofar as I am able

to judge, he has uncommon mastery of both spoken and written use of the Latin language.—

The Borgerdyds School in Copenhagen, November , 1840.

M. NIELSEN.

XIV. *From the Records of the Pastoral Seminary*[1]

Record
of
the homiletic and catechetic exercises
at the Pastoral Seminary
commenced on January 22, 1833.

Winter semester 1840/41.

Pursuant to the notice published in *Adresseavisen*, the graduates listed below presented themselves at the Seminary on Tuesday, November 17, 1840:
Newcomers to report were:
S. Kierkegaard, July, 1840.
Summer semester, 1841.
Wishing to continue from the winter semester 1840/41:
. . . S. A. Kierkegaard.

On that day [*Tuesday, December 1, 1840*], a sermon by Mr. Wittrock[2] on the text of Romans 13:11 *ad fin*[3] was criticized. It had been delivered the preceding Sunday at Vartou Church. The critics were Messrs. S. Kierkegaard and G. Strøm.[4]—

The delivery was praised. The voice was somewhat weak, but otherwise a pleasant and calm presentation.—Concerning the sermon as a whole: it displayed a Christian spirit suitable for edification.

The author's *thema* was: "The night is spent, the day is at hand!"[5] Against the theme and its development, it was argued that it was a good deal too discursive and that the author had elaborated on these two phrases as an image, which was scarcely Paul's intention. There is a call and an admonition in it, which are not sufficiently maintained in the sermon itself. Mr.Kierkegaard read his criticism aloud, in which, from the point of view of a listener, he had found himself unable to discern that rhythm in the sermon that was undeniably contained in the text;[6] Mr. Kierkegaard proposed the theme: "Awaken from sleep." This might be outlined as follows:

(1) "Awaken from sleep" is a serious phrase; many may not be in need of hearing it, but nonetheless everybody ought to take it to heart.

(2) The sleep of apathy and indifference exists; fight against them!

(3) There exists a sleep of certainty, a hardening in sin—he who fails to reflect on judgment and reckoning must be opposed.

Conclusion: Awaken! Christ is now returning (an allusion to the new Church Year). Christ demands open ears and willing hearts!—

It would be possible to outline the author's theme as follows (on purely historical grounds):

(1) This is the jubilant cry at the birth of Christ.

(2) Many nations have subsequently repeated it.

(3) Your people have also proclaimed it. (The introduction of Christianity.)

(4) Hence I am a Christian; I shall walk in that way; and although it may still be night in many places, I shall pray for enlightenment for those places.

(5) One day there will be a day of light for all nations.—

With respect to *details*: *the prayer*: in this the outline is too much *in nuce*,[7] "so the Prophets foretold," etc., for here there is a double meaning, both against the enemies of Israel and the opponents of Christianity, and one ought to hold fast to one (the latter) interpretation; p. 5: it was thought that one ought not to say from the pulpit that the Apostles expected the return of Christ during their lifetime; that one ought to be careful about this frequently misunderstood doctrine of the return of Christ on the last day.—The author calls Advent a day filled with seriousness; it is rather a day of joy.—Some beautiful passages, pp. 11-12, were read aloud.—Overall, the language was found to be very suitable.—

. . . Wednesday, December 9. Mr. Kierkegaard catechized on the words, "Thy will be done," and Mr. Wad[8] on "God's Unchangeableness."

Tuesday, January 12, [1841] . . . On that day Mr. S. Kierkegaard's first sermon, delivered at noon in Holmens Church, was criticized. The text was Philippians 1:19-25. The critics were Messrs. Fenger[9] and Linnemann.[10]—

The delivery: The sermon had been very well memorized, the voice was clear, the tone dignified and forceful.—On the whole the sermon had been written with great thought and sharp logic. But it was somewhat difficult and certainly far too exalted in tone for the average person.—The author's theme: "For to me to live is Christ, and to die is gain!" "We shall consider in what sense it may be said, 'For to me to live is Christ,' in order to make it possible to add, 'to die is gain.' "—

The development of the argument is reproduced exactly in Mr. Fenger's criticism (see the enclosed).—With respect to the design of the sermon, it was pointed out that it was the great wealth of thought and richness of idea that made the sermon relatively incomprehensible and unsuitable for retention by the average person, for otherwise it must be conceded that the thought pattern was consistent, the tone biblical, and the form not lacking in popular appeal.—The preacher's objection that he had not deviated from the text was met as follows: that it is not *necessary* to take up and treat the text in its entirety, but occasionally even more important simply to exhaust *one* aspect, primarily the principal aspect.—The main objection was directed at the conclusion of the sermon, which is that death is a gain only for those by whom the eternal and concealed life has already been comprehended here below and who "have grown to the fullness of Christ's manhood." This is to deprive the great majority of people of the sole comfort they have from death, for the concealed life has not been revealed to them in this manner. We ought to preach that death is usually a gain for humanity at large, for otherwise, what comfort have we left for the dying Christian who still believes in grace and mercy? The theme has this formulation: "In what sense may it be said that," but the sermon is not didactic in declaring "in this or that sense," etc., for on the contrary the author has presented several situations in which "it may be said that" (see the theme).—Mr. Fenger missed that fresh vitality in the sermon that he believes it ought to exude in order for it truly to summon mankind from the world to God, and objects that the author has depicted the struggles of the soul as far too difficult for them to have any appeal to the average person who is unfamiliar with such matters.—The critic also felt that the author moves in too mystical a sphere in his conclusion ("the blessing of silent prayer," "the joyousness of contemplation," "God's presence in us") instead of discussing what lies closer to hand, the Word and the Sacraments.—The author defended himself against these two objections.—As to specific details, only a few were mentioned, for the language won *great* praise.—*The prayer* was *particularly beautiful*. A very beautiful passage from the beginning was read aloud as well. "Heaven far less petty" (probably incomprehensible).—Here and there the sentences were also a little difficult. "To unquiet," preferably: "to disquiet."—The closing words won much praise.

Thursday, March 9 [1841] a sermon written by Mr. T. Thomsen[11] on I Thessalonians 4:1-7 and delivered on Sunday the seventh in Vartou Church was criticized. The critics were Messrs. S. Kierkegaard and E. Hagerup.

   The sermon was a homily on the text. The language dignified with genuine Christian spirit. However, the sermon topic had not been completely exhausted, and the details not adequately developed. *The prayer* very beautiful, but the critics disagreed completely in their views of the relationship of the prayer to the sermon.—The remark that our age yields to that of the apostolic congregation when it comes to the fervor of faith was one which Dr. Münter wished omitted.—"A wide demand" was emended to "a widespread demand." "The world is called frail," is, however, acceptable, when it pertains to mankind. Mr. Kierkegaard further documented his opinion that there was *no* relationship between the prayer and the sermon by remarking that the prayer could just as well be about faith and hope as about charity, but the reply was that the sermon is a homily and thus it speaks in general terms.—Furthermore, a prayer usually ought to contain only an allusion to the sermon.—Kierkegaard thought that one ought to have the whole sermon in mind as one writes the prayer, but that he has virtually confined himself to the latter aspect. But Thomsen did think that he had spoken about sanctification in general and that this had been the subject of the allusion. "The law is given sword in hand" (disapproved). Also the expression "period." The author argued vehemently against fornication and adultery. Although it is proper to speak without reserve from the pulpit, one must be reasonable and acknowledge the claims of decency. Kierkegaard remarked that it was unsuitable to develop a homily upon this text, because the particular points do not stand out with equal emphasis; hence the particular aspect of fornication ought not to be treated on its own. Agreement was reached on this point.—

The distinction between the magnitude of this sin in comparison with others, gluttony, for example—as if fornication corrupts everything while the other sins do so only in particular ways—was rejected.—An admonition to indecent old men not to reflect on the sins of their youth is probably less warranted than one not to conjure up new images. Concerning "transgressions," the author had failed to go into sufficent detail with reference to everyday life.—The expression "outwardly and inwardly" was a little too modern for the pulpit. Dr. M.[12] proposed the inclusion of the way in which God punishes with the sword of secular authority.

On the same day (May 18) Mr. Chievitz[13] preached in Holmens Church. Messrs. Kierkegaard and Licht[14] were the critics. The text: I Peter 4:7-11. The theme: How God may be glorified in all things through Jesus Christ. The introduction: Not until a dear friend has been called from us do we remember his last words. Thus, not long ago (at Easter!) we remembered Christ's last words before he died. That which he spoke about, "the end of all thing is at hand," must also be included here. These words are now interpreted as an intimation of the Feast of the Pentecost, when it is said that the end of all things is at hand for all of us, which is to be taken to mean that the end of the old man must be at hand. We can only prepare ourselves for the Feast by putting on the new man and surrendering ourselves to God. Therefore the author wishes to consider *how we may glorify God in all things*. This is then developed in three sections: (1) by doing our duty, (2) through charity that promises us that it will heal everything, (3) through the help of God, prayer, etc. The introduction seemed indescribably strained to Dr. M. and vague (to Kierkegaard).

Dr. Münter proposed the following outline: We glorify God (1) by deed, (2) in communication with others, (3) in prayer, (4) in joys and sorrows, (5) by our death. "In all things" and "through Jesus Christ" might in particular be emphasized here. With each of these points the words of the text might suitably be employed.

Mr. [*deleted*: Dr.] Kierkegaard proposed the use of amphibole in the expression to *glorify God*, that is, (1) by our faith and love, (2) by glorifying God for everything. The outline was found extremely forced. On the whole, the particular points do not cohere properly. Within the confines of the text, the last aspect is not warranted. "The spiritual gift" (p. 4, from I Corinthians 12) is given another meaning than the Apostle's. What is said about art and science is not very well suited for the average person.

Otherwise there were in the sermon a certain simplicity and purity that make the overall impression one of edification. The delivery was good. The sermon had not been completely memorized.

XV. *Petition to the King*[1]

Copenhagen, June 2, 1841.

Søren Aabÿe Kierkegaard, Graduate in theology cum laude in June, 1840, most humbly petitions for permission to submit his dissertation written for the Magister degree,[2] *On the Concept of Irony with Constant Reference to Socrates*, in his native tongue, but furnished with a Latin summary and with the oral defense to be conducted in Latin.

To the King!

The undersigned hereby ventures to apply to Your Majesty with his most humble petition for permission to submit his dissertation written for the Magister degree, *On the Concept of Irony with Constant Reference to Socrates*, in his native tongue, but furnished with a Latin summary and with the oral defense to be conducted in Latin.

In venturing most humbly to call Your Majesty's exalted attention to my present petition, it is primarily the idea that through Royal favor a similar concession has been granted to both Mag. Hammerich and Mag. Adler[3] that gives me the courage to hope, and this all the more so because the external circumstances seem completely identical. For, with respect to the subject matter I have chosen to treat, although the concept of irony belongs to antiquity in a manner of speaking, yet it also really belongs to it only to the extent that the modern age thereby commences, so that the understanding of this concept in the strictest sense must be claimed for more recent times. To this must be added that this concept, again in the period that lies closest to us, has manifested itself in abundant individual profusion. This, its appearance in our age, must also be taken into proper regard. In consideration thereof, I permit myself most humbly to call to the exalted attention of Your Majesty how difficult, indeed almost impossible, it would be to deal exhaustively with this subject in the language that has hitherto been that of the learned without its causing the free, personal presentation[4] to suffer unduly. But just as the nature of the subject matter must recommend my present petition, so I hope that through my examinations, which have all been completed with the highest grades, and the philological-philosophical examination with distinction, that I have furnished evidence that I possess so much knowledge of the learned languages that I cannot be considered as having rendered myself unworthy of such a favor. To this must be added that for a considerable period I have been engaged in teaching the Latin language and have thereby had occasion not to forget what I have learned and perhaps to learn more. With respect to this, I permit myself most humbly to include a copy of a recommendation[5] from the headmaster of the Borgerdyds School, Professor Nielsen:

"Mr. S. Aabÿe Kierkegaard, *Candidatus Theol.*, distinguished himself in this school by virtue of diligence, intellect, and brilliant comprehension of the subjects taught in general, and of the form and spirit of languages in particular. Already at that time he aroused great expectations of that uprightness, independence, and skill, of that penetrating, lucid, and comprehensive view, of that profound, vivid, and earnest mind, and of that skill in representation, superb in all respects, which he has subsequently demonstrated. Even though circumstances have not made it mandatory for him to teach, he has often felt the urge to do so. Accordingly, for several years he has, at my request, assisted me with the weaker students in their written Latin translations and has worked effectively to awaken them to thought, which was not merely aimed just at their examinations, but continued to be effective in their subsequent lives. For a couple of years, when I myself was unable to correct the written translations of the senior class on account of bad eyesight, he performed this task for me with that insight into language, now more mature, which I recognized in him when he was a student. Throughout one school year, at his own request, he taught Latin to the second form and brought it far in Latin and in its whole intellectual development; some of them were graduated this year, when he again kindly assisted me with Latin and written translation for the senior class, and he did so as well as I myself could have done.—Accordingly, insofar as I am able to judge, he has uncommon mastery of both spoken and written use of the Latin language.

The Borgerdyds School in Copenhagen, November , 1840.   M. NIELSEN."

That this may most graciously be granted is the petition of
the most humble
SØREN AABŸE KIERKEGAARD
Graduate in theology.

XVI. *Certificate from the Pastoral Seminary*

It is hereby certified that Mr. Søren Aabÿe Kierkegaard, *Mag. Artium*,[1] participated in the homiletic and catechetic exercises in the Royal Pastoral Seminary during the winter semester of 1840/41.

Copenhagen, October 1, 1841.   B. MÜNTER.[2]

XVII. *Magister Diploma*[1]

May the all-benevolent, almighty God grant this undertaking happiness and good fortune! On the authority of our most high, most gracious lord, Christian VIII, King of the Danes, the Vends, and the Goths, Duke of Slesvig, Holsten, the Ditmarshes, Lauenburg, and Oldenburg,[2] whose most gracious consent has been communicated through the Royal College governing university and school affairs, the faculty of philosophy of the University of Copenhagen under the rector, Hans Christian Ørsted,[3] Doctor of Philosophy, Professor in Ordinary of physics, the rector of the Polytechnical Institute, *Conferentsraad*,[4] Commander of *Dannebrog*[5] with the silver cross, Knight of the *Légion d'Honneur*, through Frederik Christian Sibbern,[6] Doctor of Philosophy, Professor in Ordinary and Knight of *Dannebrog* with the silver cross, at present dean of the faculty of philosophy, confer on the most learned man, Søren Aabye Kierkegaard, the title of *Magister Artium* and all the rights and dignity pertaining thereto. In addition to the other proper specimens of learning, he has written and on September 29, 1841, publicly defended his inaugural dissertation "On the Concept of Irony with Constant Reference to Socrates."

Copenhagen, October 20, 1841. Under the University Seal.

XVIII. *Excerpt from the Examination Record of the Pastoral Seminary and Certificate for the Homiletic Test*[1]

(a)

The Record of the Theological Examinations with Distinction [1830—1861], *p. 151*: [S. A. Kierkegaard:] February 24, 1844: *Laudabilis.*[2] I Corinthians 2:6-9.

C. E. Scharling[3]

J. H. Paulli.[4]

(b)

Magister S. Kierkegaard, candidate for the holy ministry, received the grade *laudabilis* for the graduation sermon he delivered on this day in Trinitatis Church on the text: I Corinthians 2:6-9.

Copenhagen, February 24, 1844.

C. E. Scharling   J. H. Paulli.

XIX. *Decision about Burial Plot*[1]

This spring I would like to have our burial plot repaired as follows:

The small upright column (which carries the text about Father's first wife)[2] should be removed. The fence should be closed behind it.

The fence should be nicely repaired.

Just inside the fence, where the small column stood, a carved tombstone with a marble cross should be placed. The face of this tombstone should carry the words that formerly were on that small column.

Leaning against this tombstone should be placed that tablet with Father's and Mother's names together with the rest, which was of course drawn up by Father himself.

Then another tablet corresponding with this tablet should be made and on it written (but in smaller letters so that there is additional space left) what is now written on that large flat stone that covers the grave, and aforementioned large stone removed altogether. This tablet should also lean against the tombstone.

The whole burial plot should then be leveled and seeded with a fine species of low grass, but a very tiny spot of bare soil should show in the four corners, and in each of these corners should be planted a little bush of Turkish roses, as I believe they are called, some very tiny ones, dark red.

On the tablet (on which is written what stood on the large flat stone, that is, the names of my late sister and brother)[3] there will thus be sufficient space so that my name can be placed there as well:

Søren Aabye, born May 5, 1813, died — .

And then there will be enough space for a little stanza, which may be done in small letters:

> In yet a little while
> I shall have won;
> Then the whole fight
> Will all at once be done.
> Then I may rest
> In bowers of roses
> And perpetually
> And perpetually
> Speak with my Jesus.

(By Brorson,[4] no. 231, no. 1 in the section about constancy and growth in the faith.)

XX. *Hospital Record*[1]

Journal of sickness and death.

† 11/11   '55. 9 p.m.   Paralysis—(tubercul?)
                                        [*Deleted*: Hemiplegia]
                                        no autopsy.

Dr. Søren Kjerkegaard
Age 42
Admitted 10/2   '55
Cond[ition]
Prev[ious] dis[eases]   } *v* [*ide*] *infr* [*a*]
Cause
M[edication] adm[inistered]

When young the patient suffered from the usual childhood
diseases, but since that time he has as a rule been in good
health. However, he did suffer for a considerable time from
constipation, but lately movements have been daily and natural. He cannot offer any specific reason for his present sickness. However, he does associate it with drinking cold seltzer
water last summer, with a dark dwelling, together with the
exhausting intellectual work that he believes is too taxing for
his frail physique. He considers the sickness fatal. His death is
necessary for the cause which he has devoted all his intellectual strength to resolving, for which he has worked alone,
and for which alone he believes that he has been intended;
hence the penetrating thought in conjunction with so frail a
physique. If he is to go on living, he must continue his religious battle; but in that case it will peter out, while, on the
contrary, by his death it will maintain its strength and, he believes, its victory.

For some time he has had a cough, which in the beginning
brought up a creamlike expectorate, later a serous one, clear
with yellow clots. Initially the cough gave him some pain in
the front part of his chest; it is now painless although very
exhausting.

About two weeks ago as he was sitting on a sofa and leaning forward in it, he slid to the floor and raised himself with
difficulty.[2] After that he stayed up for some time, but the next

day as he was about to get dressed he fell once more. There was no dizziness, cramp, nor loss of consciousness, only a feeling of utter weakness. He could not raise himself, his legs failed him for a while, yet he did manage to get up again.

That was the way it was for some days; at times he would collapse, and if he walked, it was with uncertainty; he could not step where he wanted, but usually came up short; he did not stumble. Now formication also began to set in, numbness, at times shooting pains from the loins down through the legs. Sensation remained unimpaired. Urination was either obstructed or involuntary (yet it must be noted that he had suffered previously from a difficulty in passing his water, yet only when he thought that he was or might be observed as he was urinating. When he was alone the urine was passed without obstruction). He became constipated. There was no headache or dizziness. The upper extremities unimpaired in every respect; good appetite; mental abilities completely unimpaired.

10/4 '55. During the last few days he has been completely unable to stand on his legs or to get up. If supported, he can move his legs forwards, but not place his feet properly on the ground; they fall, heels first. For a short period he can hold himself upright, but not steadily. If he sits up, he can neither twist nor turn. He slumps to the left side, where he complains of some pain, on account of this, he believes. Lying down, he can pull his legs up a little, but cannot raise them. Sensation is still unimpaired; formication and pain occur more often, as do the urinary difficulties. There is no fever.

The chest gives clear percussion everywhere. In front the expiration is protracted, otherwise nothing abnormal; auscultation has not been carried out on his back. There is no soreness along the spine nor in any particular place nor otherwise anything abnormal.

He has taken *Inf. Valerian. Paresis* D[aily] c[are], 1/2 of best ration.

10/5 The urine contains a considerable amount of phosphates, is clear, cloudy.

Last night only little sleep. The cough is fairly frequent.

The expectorate as described. Yesterday *Inf. Saleb.* was prescribed.

Today he has to pass his water very frequently, perhaps on account of the previously mentioned aversion to passing water in the presence of others (the night nurse), and he is almost constantly thinking about it. He even believes that this flaw has had a decided effect on his life and has made him an eccentric.

10/6 He is even less able than before to support himself on his legs. He is to be rubbed along the spine with *ol. tebinth* morning and evening. *Rp. Ess. valerian. ammon gtt.* XXV four times daily. 1/2 bottle of beer.

10/7 Because of his religious convictions he has asked for discontinuation of beer. *Rp. Hb. trifol. fibr. Flos chamom* $\bar{a}$ $\bar{a}$ 2 ounces. *Flos arnicæ* 1/2 ounce in one cup of tea morning and evening.

10/10 At present his strength seems to decrease more and more. He cannot stand on his legs or help himself. Yet he can sit up and speaks fairly well. He is constipated.

10/11 W[ith] E[ffect]   *F. eccoprot. mit.*

10/12 He passes the urine quite involuntarily when coughing or moving. He is now completely unable to move his left leg and feels weaker. He continues to insist that his death is near.

10/13 He continues to cough and to expectorate a clear serous liquid with loose yellow clots.

He is given only tea in the morning. He is not rubbed with medication, because it causes him discomfort.

The urine continues to be passed involuntarily, as for instance last night in bed.

10/14 The condition is not materially changed. He has been constipated for three days. *Ol. ricini* 1/2 ounce.

10/15 No effect, therefore this morning *repetat.*

He has no strength to support himself at all with his arms, because he cannot contract the muscles in his back; he is able to move his arms freely.—

When he attempted to get up, the patient complained of pain in his left hip, which he claims he has suffered from for several days but has not mentioned. He keeps his left leg in a bent position at hip and knee and tilted over the right leg, but without any particular contraction of the muscles. The least motion causes him considerable pain in the hip, also some in the knee, where, incidentally, nothing abnormal is to be observed, as is true of the hip.

10/16 The urine continues to be passed involuntarily and very frequently. Therefore, by request, discontinuation of the tea.

10/18 No particular change in condition. He has been constipated for three days.

10/19 On closer examination of the leg, a fairly considerable contraction of biceps, semitendinosus, and membranosus is found after all.

Yesterday he was given *clysma sapon*, w[ith] g[ood] effect.

10/21 Little change in condition in recent days. Yesterday he voided after *Inf. sennæ*, which he himself believes to be the result of having eaten rye bread.

10/22 Constipated yesterday. The urine continues to be passed involuntarily, mostly at night. The patient himself thinks that his strength is decreasing more and more. He also seems to collapse more. P[ulse] 100.

10/23 Today he is lying with his leg stretched out, slightly turned inwards. Movement still causes him a great deal of pain in the hip. These days he looks a bit more lively. The cough continues to trouble him. The expectorate consists of purulent clots, a few of which are closely mixed with light red blood.—

10/25 Yesterday the patient was given *Inf. sennæ*, after which he voided, which he himself believes the result of some pears. His condition is unchanged.

10/29 The patient's strength seems to decrease more and more. He sits up during the day, but is very slumped. Sometimes the cough plagues him a great deal. His mental abilities are still unimpaired. Voiding must always be brought about by *clysma* after other means have been tried. The urine continues to be passed involuntarily.

11/1 For the last few days his lower extremities have been treated with electricity every evening, but the effect has only been very slight. The contractions feeble, and he hardly feels it. The day before yesterday he received *Inf. sennæ*, after which he voided three times. —Otherwise the condition is unchanged. Discontinuation of *Tra. Valerian ammon. Rp. Inf. ton. nervin.* Half an ounce three times daily.

11/4 Yesterday an examination of his posterior revealed a not inconsiderable number of excoriations, some large, some small, on both *nates* and *os sacrum*, some of them rather unclean in appearance. There are also small blisters on the *tronchanteres*. Daily change of bedding. On the sores: wet compresses. Last night when he was treated with electricity, the effect on the leg muscles was not inconsiderable.

11/6 Constipated. *Inf. sennæ*. His strength is now decreasing more and more, and he cannot bring up the expectorate. But his appetite is quite good. The electricity treatments are now working well.

11/7 Still without result.

11/8 Subsequent voiding.

11/9 In recent days the patient's strength has visibly decreased. He is lying quietly dozing (stuporous), says nothing, and ingests nothing. His face seems a little distorted, for the left corner of his mouth appears to be pulled slightly upwards. The p[ulse] was close to 100 the day before yesterday, steady, weak. Urine continues to be passed involuntarily, is fairly clear; excrement is also passed involuntarily—the excoriations have not healed, but they look cleaner. The p[ulse] is 130 today, less steady, weak.

11/10 The patient continues to lie in the same stuporous condition. The p[ulse] is 130, still fairly steady, but less so than yesterday, irregular. If one raises his arms, they fall back again heavily and are somewhat stiff in the elbows. He can raise both eyelids, and the distortion in his face is not markedly pronounced. His *habitus* is very collapsed, he breathes rapidly, noiselessly.

11/11 The patient is in the same condition. The p[ulse] is slower, his breathing heavy and short.

11/12 He continued in the same condition, died last night at 9 p.m.

XXI. *Will*[1]

Dear Brother,

It is, of course, my will that my former fiancée, Mrs. Regine Schlegel, inherit without condition whatever little I may leave. If she herself will not accept it, she is to be asked if she would be willing to administer it for distribution to the poor.

What I wish to give expression to is that to me an engagement was and is just as binding as a marriage, and that therefore my estate is her due, exactly as if I had been married to her.

Your brother
S. KIERKEGAARD.

[*Address:*]
To Dr. Kierkegaard, pastor.
To be opened after my death.

LETTERS

1. S. K.—*March 8, 1829*—*P. C. Kierkegaard.*[1]

Dear Brother,

Were you to draw conclusions about how I live on the basis of what I write, you might easily decide that I am dead and gone, but Father's letters do not allow you to entertain any such thought. Had I only written as often as you have admonished me, something would have come of it, but you have not yet seen any fruits from your encouragements nor the reward that ought to follow your encouragements. Most of your letters to Father have usually concluded with a reminder to write you. You must in truth have great patience, for you have never tired of reminding me. When you noticed that all those encouragements to write contained in your letters to Father were of no avail, you decided to remind me of my duty through somebody else, Oldenburg,[2] and he did indeed bring me the message that you were expecting a letter from me every postal day. Furthermore, he reminded me that Fenger's brothers[3] were writing to Fenger.[4] So I, too, decided to write to you, if for no other reason than to let you know that I am alive. If I were to offer excuses now for not having written to you for so long, I would be wasting your time, for they could never be valid excuses. I might tell you that I have been somewhat ill, but what would that prove, what would that procure other than an excuse for not writing on those days when I was ill, and they cannot exceed five or six in number. That I have not had time will not help me either, for you know yourself from your own school days that there is always some time when it is unnecessary for one to do anything. So I will offer no excuses at all but directly beg your pardon for having neglected to do my duty.

I suppose that you learned long ago that Henrichsen[5] has left the Borgerdyds School and been transferred to Elsinore. When he left, our class presented him with a snuffbox, for we had learned he wanted one. For this not exactly grandest of presents he sent us his thanks through Mr. Warncke the following day. He is the first of the masters at the Borgerdyds

School to have left during your absence. Ludvig Møller has taken over his Hebrew class while Bojesen has his Latin class.

For some time the Professor[6] has been bothered with a bad leg, which troubled him a good deal, for he could not supervise the running of the school himself and had to turn it over to Mr. Bang. All the while he was unable to walk, we had to go to his place where we recited our lessons, and he also assigned us so many written translations into Latin that in the end even he could not sort them out. At last he was on his feet again and worked with us for some time, but then the same leg gave him trouble once more. A fire had broken out in his stove, and as he hurried to put it out he accidentally injured the leg, which then became much worse. Nevertheless, he chose to hold classes with the B section of the first-year Latin class whose door is next to his room, and thus he was able to be with us in a step or two. He entered by that door every day wearing one slipper and one boot. However, the news that he hurt himself while extinguishing the fire in his stove I have only from Peer, his servant, who usually is very reliable. Lately it has been said several times that Professor Thune has died, but this has not yet come true. Still, these rumors show that he must be very ill. Each time such a rumor spread, it caused general grief among those young people who want to graduate next time and fear that Ursin might replace him, which seems very likely, and he does have a reputation for badgering. At least they prefer someone who in order to get a precise answer to his precise question repeats it, rather than one who does not repeat his question and even phrases it vaguely.

I said earlier that Henrichsen was the first master to leave the school, from which you may gather there must be several, as indeed there are. The second is in fact Friedenreich, who has been appointed an assistant principal at the Efterslægts School,[7] where he replaces Bentzen, who in his turn has become a minister, but in a calling that will not put so much in his pocket as did his post at Efterslægten, which, as far as I know, pays 800 *rdl.*[8] a year. To replace Bentzen three new masters have joined the school: Krøyer, a small person no

bigger than I (I am no bigger than I was when you left), and
Zager and Bergenhammer. This is probably a heavy loss for
the school, for Friedenreich has the greatest knowledge of history and geography of all the masters at the school; yet
Warncke boasts that the school could not survive without
him, but that is probably mere boasting, and I for one believe
that it is more likely that Warncke cannot survive without the
school. Father is working on a letter to you, but you know
Father and realize how much time he needs to write a letter,
since he is able to write for only one or two hours every
morning. I hope you are well. Nicoline's arm is on the mend,
but the finger she crushed gives her great pain and will probably heal slowly. Do write her again so she may have some
comfort in adversity. Henrich is well, but Michael is ailing.
Father, Mother, Nicoline, Petrea, Christian, Ferdinand, Mrs.
Lund, and Niels[9] all send you greetings. Most loving greetings to you

from your devoted brother,
SØREN.

Copenhagen, March 8, 1829.
    [*Address in another hand*:]

Herrn	[*Postmark*:]
Cand. Theol: P. C. Kierkegaard	Hamburg
Unter Linden 20 drey Treppen	3/13
in	N. 3/15 2.
Berlin	
postage paid Hamburg	

2. *S. K.—March 25, 1829—P. C. Kierkegaard.*

Dear Brother,

    Your reply arrived long before I had expected it. I waited
for your letter for less time than you had to be in suspense for
mine, and I am pleased that you liked it. As to your belief that
I have read Cicero's letters, this is not so at all; I have not read
a single one of them. I suppose that I shall get to read them

next year. It is true that the *artium*[1] has not yet become particularly difficult, but it may become so by the time I have to take my exams, for a man by the name of Asp, *cand. theol. et juris,*[2] has written a book about increasing the *artium* requirements. He demands, for example, that solid geometry and trigonometry be made mandatory subjects for this examination, and he demands that there be written translations in German and French[3] and that the English language not be neglected as it has been until now, but that it be taught and that there be written translations in this language as well. He also proposes that anyone who fails any subject pass another exam in that discipline the following spring. One thing he complains of in his book is the slighting of the university-trained graduates in medicine in favor of apprentice barbers.[4] I really hope that his proposals are not adopted, as it would be extremely unpleasant for me to have to tackle the English language in my last year of school. It was already decided at the time of the last exams that I not be examined until 1830 because I am, after all, a bit young. Bindesbøll teaches religion and New Testament; Warncke is my history teacher, of course; Marthensen is my mathematics teacher; and Ursin has left the school for good. I am studying Greek with the Professor, something I did not expect, inasmuch as he became quite fed up last year with teaching Greek to the A section of the first class.

Incidentally, you must not think that the Professor's sickness has been a particularly dangerous one, for he has in fact been teaching us for a long time now, and his leg is completely healed. When you write to him, do not go into too much detail about the cause of his being laid up, for, as you know, I only heard about it from his servant.

If you could find something out about Fritz Lange,[5] whether his eyes are better or are even worse, I would appreciate it. What I have heard here is that where he was staying he started wearing thick glasses on doctor's advice but that he fell in the street and got splinters in his eyes and because of that went completely blind, but this I neither credit nor hope.

I have indeed found the book you requested, and Father has also fulfilled your wish and bought you a Danish Bible. These books will, as you request, be sent along, tied and sealed in a small canvas-covered box. Greetings have been conveyed to Mrs. Fenger,[6] as you requested in your letter, and she returns most loving greetings to you. She had obtained one of the books, P. Hald's dissertation, and it has already been sent. She promised to see if she could get hold of the other, the Bishops' Pastoral Letter of 1817, and if she does, it will be sent with the others.

I hope you are as well as most of us here are, with the exception of Petrea, who has been unwell for some time. Nicoline is mending, and her finger is nearly cured, but it is still somewhat sore.

Everybody sends you greetings: Father, Mother, Nicoline, Lund, Petrea, Niels, Mrs. Lund, and Ole Lund's daughters,[7] but above all, greetings   from

Your affectionate brother,
SØREN.

Copenhagen, March 25, 1829 [*in M. P. Kierkegaard's*[8] *handwriting:*] Probably Ferdinand will write a few words on the back of this.

M. P. Kierkegaard—July 15, 1829—P.C.K.

P.S. Just as Søren is about to enter this letter in the copy book, Lorentzen is paying me a visit, and he asks most emphatically that his warmest greetings be sent to you. I (Søren) will soon write to you so that I may be able also to gainsay Father.

3. *S. K.—June 1, 1835—P. W. Lund*.[1]

Copenhagen, June 1, 1835.

You know how inspiring I once found it to listen to you and how enthusiastic I was about your description of your stay in Brazil, although not so much on account of the mass of detailed observations with which you have enriched yourself and your scholarly field as on account of the impression your first journey into that wondrous nature made upon you: your paradisical happiness and joy. Something like this is bound to find a sympathetic response in any person who has the least feeling and warmth, even though he seeks his satisfaction, his occupation, in an entirely different sphere, but especially so in a young person who as yet only dreams of his destiny. Our early youth is like a flower at dawn with a lovely dewdrop in its cup, harmoniously and pensively reflecting everything that surrounds it. But soon the sun rises over the horizon, and the dewdrop evaporates; with it vanish the fantasies of life, and now it becomes a question (to use a flower metaphor once more) whether or not man is able to produce—by his own efforts as does the *nereum*—a drop that may represent the fruit of his life. This requires, above all, that one be allowed to grow in the soil where one really belongs, but that is not always so easy to find. In this respect there exist fortunate creatures who have such a decided inclination in a particular direction that they faithfully follow the path once it is laid out for them without ever falling prey to the thought that perhaps they ought to have followed an entirely different path. There are others who let themselves be influenced so completely by their surroundings that it never becomes clear to them in what direction they are really striving. Just as the former group has its own implicit categorical imperative, so the latter recognizes an explicit categorical imperative. But how few there are in the former group, and to the latter I do not wish to belong. Those who get to experience the real meaning of Hegelian dialectics in their lives are greater in number. Incidentally, it is altogether natural for wine to ferment before it becomes clear; nevertheless this process is often disagreeable in its several stages, although regarded in its totality it is of course agreeable, provided it does in the end yield its relative results in the context of the usual doubt. This is of major significance for anybody who has come to terms with his destiny by means of it, not only because of the calm that follows in contrast to the preceding storm, but because one then *has life* in a quite different sense than before. For many, it is this Faustian element[2] that makes itself more or less applicable to every intellectual development, which is why it has always seemed to me that we should concede cosmic significance to the *Faust* concept. Just as our ancestors worshipped a goddess of yearning, so I think that Faust represents doubt personified. He need be no more than that, and Goethe probably sins against the concept when he permits Faust to convert, as does Mérimée when he permits Don Juan to convert.[3] One cannot use the argument against me that Faust is taking a positive step at the instant he applies to the Devil, for right here, it seems to me, is one of the most significant elements in the Faust legend. He surrendered himself to the Devil for the express purpose of attaining enlightenment, and it follows that he was not in possession of it prior to this; and precisely because he surrendered himself to the Devil, his doubt increased (just as a sick person who falls into the hands of a medical quack usually gets sicker). For although Mephistopheles permitted him to look through his spectacles into man and into the secret hiding places of the earth, Faust must forever doubt him because of his inability to provide enlightenment about the most profound intellectual matters. In accordance with his own idea he could never turn to God because in the very instant he did so he would have to admit to himself that here in truth lay enlightenment; but in that same instant he would, in fact, have denied his character as one who doubts.

But such a doubt can also manifest itself in other spheres. Even though a man may have come to terms with a few of these main issues, life offers other significant questions. Naturally every man desires to work according to his abilities in this world, but it follows from this that he wishes to develop his abilities in a particular direction, namely, in that which is best suited to him as an individual. But which is that? Here I am confronted with a big question mark. Here I stand like Hercules—not at a crossroads—no, but at a multitude of roads, and therefore it is all the harder to choose the right one. Perhaps it is my misfortune in life that I am interested in far too many things rather than definitely in any one thing. My

interests are not all subordinated to one but are all coordinate.
I shall attempt to show how matters look to me.

1. *The Natural Sciences*. (In this category I include all those
who seek to explain and interpret the runic script of nature,
ranging from him who calculates the speed of the stars and, so
to speak, arrests them in order to study them more closely, to
him who describes the physiology of a particular animal,
from him who surveys the surface of the earth from the
mountain peaks to him who descends to the depths of the
abyss, from him who follows the development of the human
body through its countless nuances to him who examines in-
testinal worms.) First, when I consider this whole scholarly
field, I realize that on this path as well as on every other (but
indeed primarily here) I have of course seen examples of men
who have made names for themselves in the annals of
scholarship by means of enormous diligence in collecting.
They master a great wealth of details and have discovered
many new ones, but no more than that. They have merely
provided the substratum for the thought and elaboration of
others. These men are content with their details, and yet to
me they are like the rich farmer in the gospel;[4] they have
gathered great stores in their barn, yet science may declare to
them: "Tomorrow I demand your life," inasmuch as it is that
which determines the significance of each particular finding
for the whole. To the extent that there is a sort of unconscious
life in such a man's knowledge, the sciences may be said to
demand his life, but to the extent that there is not, his activity
is comparable to that of the man who nourishes the earth by
the decay of his dead body. The case differs of course with
respect to other phenomena, with respect to those scholars in
the natural sciences who have found or have sought to find by
their speculation that Archimedean point that does not exist
in the world and who from this point have considered the totality and seen the component parts in their proper light. As
far as they are concerned, I cannot deny that they have had a
very salutary effect on me. The tranquility, the harmony, the
joy one finds in them is rarely found elsewhere. We have
three worthy representatives here in town: an Ørsted,[5] whose

face has always seemed to me like a chord that nature has sounded in just the right way; a Schouw,[6] who provides a study for the painter who wanted to paint Adam naming the animals; and finally a Horneman,[7] who, conversant with every plant, stands like a patriarch in nature. In this connection I also remember with pleasure the impression you made upon me as the representative of a great nature which also ought to be represented in the National Assembly.[8] I have been and am still inspired by the natural sciences; and yet I do not think that I shall make them my principal field of study. By virtue of reason and freedom, life has always interested me most, and it has always been my desire to clarify and solve the riddle of life. The forty years in the desert before I could reach the promised land of the sciences seem too costly to me, and the more so as I believe that nature may also be observed from another side, which does not require insight into the secrets of science. It matters not whether I contemplate the whole world in a single flower or listen to the many hints that nature offers about human life; whether I admire those daring designs on the firmament; or whether, upon hearing the sounds of nature in Ceylon,[9] for example, I am reminded of the sounds of the spiritual world; or whether the departure of the migratory birds reminds me of the more profound yearnings of the human heart.

2. *Theology*. This seems to be what I have most clearly chosen for my own, yet there are great difficulties here as well. In Christianity itself there are contradictions so great that they prevent an unobstructed view, to a considerable extent, at any rate. As you know, I grew up in orthodoxy, so to speak. But from the moment I began to think for myself, the gigantic colossus began to totter. I call it a gigantic colossus advisedly, for taken as a whole it does have a good deal of consistency, and in the course of many centuries past, the component parts have become so tightly fused that it is difficult to come to terms with them. I might now agree with some of its specific points, but then these could only be considered like the seedlings one often finds growing in rock fissures. On the other hand, I might also see the inconsistencies in many specific

points, but I would still have to let the main basis stand *in dubio* for some time. The instant *that* changed, the whole would of course assume an entirely different cast, and thus my attention is drawn to another phenomenon: rationalism, which by and large cuts a pretty poor figure. There is really nothing to object to in rationalism, as long as reason consistently pursues its own end and—in rendering an explanation of the relation between God and the world—again comes to see man in his most profound and spiritual relation to God; and in this respect, rationalism from its own point of view considers Christianity that which for many centuries has satisfied man's deepest need. But then it is in fact no longer rationalism, for rationalism is given its real coloring by Christianity. Hence it occupies a completely different sphere and does not constitute a system but a Noah's Ark (to adopt an expression Professor Heiberg[10] used on another occasion), in which the clean and the unclean animals lie down side by side. It makes roughly the same impression as our Citizens' Volunteer Company of old would have made alongside the Royal Potsdam Guards. Therefore it attempts essentially to ally itself with Christianity, bases its arguments upon Scripture, and in advance of every single point dispatches a legion of Biblical quotations that in no way penetrate the argument. The rationalists behave like Cambyses, who in his campaign against Egypt dispatched the sacred chickens and cats in advance of his army, but they are prepared, like the Roman Consul, to throw the sacred chickens overboard when they refuse to eat. The fallacy is that when they are in agreement with Scripture, they use it as a basis, but otherwise not. Thus they adopt mutually exclusive points of view.

[Part of the letter is missing.]

As to minor discomforts I will merely say that I am now studying for my theological qualifying examinations, an occupation that holds no interest for me at all and which accordingly does not proceed with the greatest efficiency. I have always preferred the free and thus perhaps somewhat indefinite course of study to that service offered at a pre-set table where one knows in advance the guests one will meet and the food one will be served every single day of the week. Nevertheless, it is a necessity, and one is scarcely permitted out onto the scholarly commons without having been branded. In my present state of mind, I also consider it useful for me to do so and furthermore, I also know that in this way I can make Father very happy (for he thinks that the true land of Canaan lies beyond the theological qualifying examinations, but at the same time, as Moses once did, he climbs Mount Tabor and reports that I will never get in—but I do hope that his prophecy will not come true this time), so I suppose I must get to work. How fortunate you are to have found in Brazil a vast field of investigation where every step offers strange new objects and where the cries of the rest of the learned republic cannot disturb your peace. To me the learned theological world seems like the Strandvej on a Sunday afternoon in the season when everybody goes to Bakken in Dyrehaven:[11] they tear past each other, yell and scream, laugh and make fun of each other, drive their horses to death, overturn, and are run over. Finally, when they reach Bakken covered with dust and out of breath—well, then they look at each other—and go home.

As far as your returning is concerned, it would be childish of me to hasten it, as childish as when the mother of Achilles attempted to hide him in order that he might avoid a speedy, honorable death.—Take care of yourself!

4. *Michael Pedersen Kierkegaard—July 4, 1835—S. K.*[1]

My dear Son,

I send you these few lines in my own hand in order to lessen your worry about my letting Peter answer your letters instead of writing myself. Thank God, there is no other reason, internal or external, than that which you know about and suppose: my ever increasing difficulty in writing, with which you are quite familiar. Besides, in the past few days, I have been plagued more than usually by my colic.

Your letter says nothing about how you are, and from this I

conclude that you are well, which makes me very happy. Your brother is also in good health, and so are your brothers-in-law and their children.—

Please give affectionate and friendly greetings to Mr. Mentz[2] and his wife from us, and especially from me.

> Your most loving and wholly
> devoted father,

Copenhagen, July 4, 1835.   M. P. KIERKEGAARD.

[*Address:*]

To S. A. Kierkegaard, Student in Theology
at the Inn at Gilleleje.[3]

5. *S. K.—July 6, 1835—P. E. Lind.*[1]

July 6, '35

Dear friend,

I received your letter of June 27 on July 1. How welcome and unexpected. Not that it was unexpected in itself to find a letter from you, but I did not expect it to be the very first and hitherto only letter that I received from any of my acquaintances, partly so because I have called on you so rarely of late and because my visit to you the day before I left[2] probably seemed to you like a notification that I wished to take your hermeneutical lectures[3] along with me to the country rather than like a farewell visit, and partly also because you promised to write to me but did not say when, whereas others who volunteered to write as soon as possible have been silent so far. This last circumstance leaves me with mixed feelings. While I was in town I became accustomed to enjoying a certain amount of attention from a number of students, which really pleased me and was necessary for me personally. I cannot deny that this betrays a weakness and that it shows greater strength to be able to remain in the depths of the sea, as many fish do, rather than frequently to feel the need, as does the sunfish, to display one's silvery light on the surface. Nor do I believe myself so weak that I would go under if this element were denied me: the sap and the strength would remain the same, but the shape would change; constantly to meet resistance, to be honed on sharp rocks, must no doubt furrow one's face, but it also robs one of a certain elasticity. Yet, just as I now believe on the one hand that such external circumstances may be beneficial for many people and that they have been so for me *in specie* [in this case], on the other hand they might lead to many wild shoots and growths on the Tree of Life, since the personalities that most need this sort of external favor are precisely those who within themselves have not definitely and clearly marked off the path they must follow, at whose cradle nature did not place a *port epée* [scabbard], but who in the course of the dialectics of life must labor towards an awareness of their destiny. Those external circumstances might then further serve to bring out human powers, for everywhere there are lantern carriers who beckon one now hither now yon.—Consequently, this circumstance is to my advantage, for it teaches me to focus upon my inner self, it spurs me on to comprehend myself, my own self, to hold it fast in the infinite variety of life, to direct towards myself that concave mirror with which I have attempted until now to comprehend life around me. It pleases me because I see that I am able to do it, because I feel I have strength enough to hold the mirror, whether it shows me my ideal or my caricature, those two extremes between which life constantly moves, as H. Steffens[4] says; and it saddens me because it teaches me how much to rely on people, because it shows me that that attention was perhaps based on fear of me rather than on love for or interest in me. Therefore, should you happen to meet one or another of my acquaintances, please give him my regards, but in no way request him to write to me, for just as pleasing as every letter is to me, just as displeasing would it be for me to know that I myself possibly prompted it. Enough of this. I return to the contents of your letter.—

I am sorry that you have a headache, but hope that it is long since gone by the time you receive this. However, the very circumstance that it is your "headache that gives you occasion to write" ought to make you less strict in your demand for a reply. Well, never mind. I am positive that my reply would not have remained unsent—even without such an earnest reminder. I suspect that in this I would have behaved like one of the sons in the gospel.[5]

Next, concerning those things you were not sure you should write to me about, I am sure I ought not to reply to them.

As to your squabble with Ussing:[6] I have not been able to familiarize myself with the issue, for I have not seen a newspaper all the while I have been here. However, I am pleased that you have taken him to task, for I was annoyed at the way he replied to Brøndum's[7] first defender. It is true that the latter deserved a little slap for his pathetic defense, but Ussing merited a serious drubbing for the cunning manner in which he dealt with the case. Hence I intended to write against him, but my journey prevented me, and an acquaintance whom I put in a frame of mind to write more or less what I wanted written has presumably not done so. I wanted to show him that the whole secret lies in his silently ignoring part of the preceding speech. But anyway, this is of no importance, since you have brought him to the point where he admits he is wrong. It is perhaps best to pay no attention to his subsequent behavior.

Inasmuch as my letter permits me to write no more and I do not want to spoil you by writing two letters at once, I will cease for now. It is true, though, that I did want to write a good deal more about the conclusion of your letter—but about this on another occasion, and perhaps I will also change my attitude towards it. Thank you for your letter, and take care of yourself.

Yours,   S. A. Kierkegaard.

[*Address*:]
To
Mr. Lind, Student in Theology
St. Giertrudstræde
in Copenhagen

6. *J. L. Heiberg—March 16, 1836—S. K.*

Enclosed please find six special reprints of the *Flyvepost*,[1] no. 82 & 83. I suppose you already know from Mr. Langhoff[2] that the delay is not my fault.

Once more, my thanks for your essay. It pleased me even more on this new reading.

Respectfully, J. L. HEIBERG

March 16, 1836

7. *S. K.—December 7, 1837—Christian Agerskov.*[1]

December 7, '37

Dear Sir:

Herewith I send you at last (*tandem aliquando*) the money[2] you once (*olim*, in the past) [lent me], for which I hereby thank you very much. Furthermore, I beg you to forgive me for taking so long, and I am sure you will, for your delicacy as a creditor might almost tempt people to remain your debtors. For this I send you especial thanks.

Yours, S. KIERKEGAARD.

P.S. Please give my messenger a slip of paper with some hieroglyph or other as a token that you have received this. I shall soon call on you in person, but I did not want to pay a visit while trotting on a business errand.

8. *S. K.—July 17, [1838]—Emil Boesen.*[1]

Dear Emil!!

You, my friend, *the only one*, through whose intercession I endured the world that in so many ways seemed unbearable, the only one left when I let doubt and suspicion like a violent storm wash away and destroy all else—*my Mount Ararat*, where is it? Do you think the weather is now such that I may go ashore, that I may now leave my ark, or rather my poorly manned vessel (there is only one man aboard, myself, and a feeble one at that, and practically comparable to that sailor at

Gilleleje who had but 1½ arms and yet always sailed *alone*)—my faithful stablemate who at times did not shy from bending your own back to relieve me when my mind like my back was bent from carrying like Atlas the world, which my imagination let me think I could carry and a Hercules tricked me into taking upon myself. It is this same world I now see crashed at my feet, destroyed for me as I am for it—my συζυγε [comrade], have you straightened yourself to your full height, to that posture one must assume *over* the world in order neither to break one's back lifting its copper coins nor to miss out entirely on its splendors—have you gained such balance face to face with the world that you are able to thrust your head into the world, so to speak, and look around, just as a life-size human head is represented in a copper engraving as looking on amidst a dance of gnomes and fairy maidens?—Answer, I beseech you, within the magic circle of our friendship! Speak, loudly "that I may see you"[2] . . . . . These and similar exclamatory epistles, addresses of gratitude, and provocative petitions have been conceived in my brain at the dictation of my heart under the seal of my character, but hitherto I have always waited in vain for the regular mail service, that is, that consistency of mood without which they could not possibly reach your *hand* and through *goodness* continue—to the heart. However, so that these letters to you as you are—written, as St. Paul says, not with pen and ink, but inscribed in my heart (cf. II Cor. 3:2)—might become something more, or, if you wish as I do, something less—in brief: so that my thought of you may not vacillate uncertainly between an ecstatic *exacerberatio* [exacerbation][3] and a *Somnambüle*, a drugged sleep, an *emolities cerebri* [softening of the brain], do accept these lines.

How everything has changed since the time I so often visited you, since that time when all those transactions occurred, the consequences of which amount to a deposit in our *fiscus* [treasury], an unsettled account, which I think we both will remember with pleasure for some time to come, an unsettled *account* which separates only to the same extent that it unites, an unsettled account, which, like the vertical line joining the common base line, forms *adjacent angles* with frequently changing sizes. The world has taken much from me, very much indeed, but, God be praised, not any more than it has given. I have learned *eminus* (in fencing: at a distance) that it can take away more, much more, if one is not careful to join betimes that company that has never had a shortage of funds and has not yet failed to meet its obligations. Do you remember when I once sang these lines in your room with singular premonition:

> I have seen you in the emperor's lofty halls,
> And faithfully I share your poverty and need,[4]

and you tried to dismiss it as a joke? It turned out to be only too true. I know that *you* have remained faithful to me, that you are still my συζυγος [comrade] and have not become one who has been unequally yoked together with unbelievers [ετεροζυγων απιστοις],[5] but also I know that I have been dethroned, become an ex-monarch. Could any dethroned prince,[6] strictly speaking, be said to be *without a country* any more than a twenty-five-year-old man without expectations; could any exiled king more absolutely feel himself deprived of every prospect of ever again setting foot in his *inherited realm* enlarged by conquest than I do? Or can any exiled prince more bitterly feel the faithlessness of his subjects than a poor author without readers? And what is more preposterous than an *homme de lettres* studying for his final examinations? And is not my whole life so bungled that it cannot acquire meaning unless it were simply to happen, *quia absurdum est*—much less that I myself could give meaning to it. I have taken Hoffmann's *Wercke*[7] along, and although I do feel that I am related to him in many ways, my grief about the world and in the world has not yet despairingly swung around to its opposite; nor has my grief for the world completely dissolved itself in a Hoffmanesque proliferating realization of the wish that the whole world be damned to Bloksbjerg,[8] and conceived with such indignation that one personally has to spend most of one's time in the same place to make sure that the world is properly tortured and plagued; and finally in destructive fury one feels all alone in a life-and-death waltz with witches and trolls, tortured by the thought that *this* was not the right point from which to shake the world, for it is certainly true that wherever the devil the Archimedean point lies, it is *not* at Bloksbjerg.—I need a voice as piercing as the glance of *Lynceus*, as terrifying as the groan of the giants, as sustained as a sound of nature,[9] extending in range from the deepest bass to the most melting high notes, and modulated from the most solemn-silent whisper to the fire-spouting energy of rage. That is what I need in order to breathe, to give voice to what is on my mind, to make the *viscera* of both anger and sympathy tremble. Therefore I write to you, and the more I think about our motto: "*A church stands in the distance,*"[10] the more I also feel the truth of what you once remarked, that it had come considerably closer, but still I can never become more than one who primarily *listens*. My speech is not suitable for it;[11] it is uncircumcised, unevangelical, night-hoarse like the scream of the gull, or vanishing like the blessing on the lips of the mute. Therefore, you must speak.

July 17.   Eternally yours,   S. K.

Postscript: I would ask you first and then again once more to read the preceding signature. It has no upward stroke by which to hold you, but perhaps a simplicity that may attract you. Thus you may make it into a sort of refrain and so come to see the whole letter, as it were, within this parenthesis, the sign for which you need not shape out of a simple curved line, but out of ☾ ☽, an a- or de-scending moon, or the *vice a vice* of my own character, a parenthesis in which you are in truth included and in which I hope you also feel at home.

9. *S. K.—July 28—J. L. Heiberg.*

                                             July 28, '38
Honored Professor:
    I received your letter last night. Only one point in it troubles me somewhat. I am afraid that it may seem in some way

as if I almost tried to get around that warning contained in
your first letter by employing those same ordinary and im-
precise phrases in which you orally stated your stylistic requirements.[1] On this occasion, I cannot refrain from asking
you, sir, to remember, as far as you are able to do so, those
remarks I then made, which I think contained an Amen that
was modified in several ways.—Unless, that is, I have been so
unfortunate as to have expressed myself incomprehensibly,
just as I see from your letter that I must have misunderstood
you.

As for my essay and its fate, I will, sir, take the liberty of
visiting you in this connection very soon.

Yours respectfully,
S. KIERKEGAARD

[*Address:*]
To
Professor Heiberg.

10. *Else Pedersdatter Kierkegaard—September 4, 1838—
P. C. Kierkegaard and S. K.*[1]

Dear honored nephews,

We have with pleasure received your honored letter of August 12. We read it mostly with tears in our eyes, with longing and sad hearts. For we gather from it the touching news
that my dear, now departed Brother, the noble old man, has
found Rest in the Lord at the summons of Death.[2] The
thought that my dear brother is no more on this earth and that
his body has been given to the silent hiding place of the grave
moves me and fills me with longing, yet not only me, but
also my husband, my daughter, and my son-in-law. However, the beautiful consolation that you gave us in your most
honored letter, my dear nephews, that I in a little while may
expect to see him transfigured next to God in a better native
land: that thought consoles and calms our longing and depressed hearts somewhat. Peace be to his dust, the noble de-

parted one; may God give joy to his soul in the Highest; we hope, we pray, we implore the All-Benevolent One that we may meet. Thanks to you, dear nephews, for your kind offer that you, as my dear brother's two sons and sole surviving children, will continue whatever assistance I may now and then have had from my dear brother. For this shows clearly that you are endowed with the spirit of true benevolence, just like your dear father and mother, and likewise that you keep before your eye the wondrous words of Our Savior when He says, "What you have done towards the least of my Brethren, that you have done towards me."[3] What is of further concern in my letter is my heartfelt wish and cordial request to you, if the occasion should ever permit you to do so, that you make a journey over here to Jutland to visit us, for it would be inexpressibly dear to me and all my family to see and speak with you, the dearest and most precious treasure my beloved brother left behind him here below. I suppose my last letter to your dear Father came too late, but I expect you have received it. Had not the distance been so great, I might have wished for some small thing of his as a remembrance of him. Next, I ask you to greet your brothers-in-law and the beloved little ones, but especially are you, dear nephews, both greeted in the friendliest way by me, my husband, daughter, and son-in-law.

Your devoted,

ELSE PEDERS DATTER

Sedding Kierkegaard,[4] September 4, 1838.

P.S.

I would very much like to know something of your situation if you have a little time to write.

[*Address:*]
S.T.
Mr. Dr. P. Chr. Kierkegaard
in Copenhagen
Free postage
Varde.

11. *S. K.—no date—M. H. Hohlenberg.*[1]

Dear Sir:

There must be infinite coherence in the world, an inexhaustible *quantum satis*, one might say, of reason and digestive power. Indeed, I feel at this moment that I could present the physico-teleological[2] proof of God's existence with great energy, for my life is so lacking in coherence, so confused, so dependent on my galoshes (said *in parenthesi*: I believe that rubber makes one melancholy)—and on my brain (said *in parenthesi*: there has never been a time when my brain has been so terribly unmanageable as now) that I really do not know what I am doing; and if somebody were to ask me what I intended to do a moment from now, he could easily embarrass me. Yet, when I look back on my *vita ante acta* [earlier life],[3] I am often shocked to find in it a unity, a continuity, a skillfulness in plan and execution that owe nothing at all to me. That is the way it is: some people act coherently whereas I succeed in figuring out the coherence only afterwards. If I were to imagine a child, alternating between predominant abandon and childish dejection, jotting down on paper all kinds of lines, incomplete creations, deformed monstrosities, and a great artist were to stand at his side and with his overwhelming imagination and sureness were able to transform the most insignificant line of the most worthless *Phratze* [sketch] into a beautiful simplicity and work everything into a harmonious whole—I feel just as that child must feel. I know nothing of what is to come, and as yet I have not succeeded in boarding the future, nor even managed to get hold of it with grappling hooks. Just as a spider[4] flinging itself from a fixed point down into the coherent consequences of its own productivity and seeing before it an empty space with no possibility of gaining a foothold is unable, no matter how much it might jerk, to make use of what lies right beside it, unless it concentrates more and more upon itself and gradually gains possession of it by means of the consequence that lies behind it—so is my whole life turned around; yet it is no more of a turning around—(*Umgekeerheit*;[5] I write in German and simple German at that, but I hope that my thought does not suffer thereby; it is said that a beautiful girl looks her best in simple clothing, in a negligée, and indeed nymphs are spied upon in their bath)—than is characteristic of all speculative thought, according to Daub.[6] But to the point: I do not write this in order to plague you with explanations about myself—why I write it I shall really not be able to explain for another half year or more—but to call your attention to what you may already have noticed, the incomprehensible fact that I do not come to visit you at all, that while my thoughts have traveled to Jutland several times, my body has not gotten itself to Frederiksberg. For me it is quite in order that I do not understand this, for later on I will realize that this *was* quite all right because I understand it. And this consideration has something encouraging about it insofar as unity is achieved, and something humiliating about it insofar as I feel that I myself do not accomplish it, but that I only create confusion.

Yours,   S. K.

12. *S. K.*—[1838]—*F. Fabricius.*

Honored Sir:
   Please accept this.

Yours respectfully,
S. KIERKEGAARD.

[*On an enclosed slip of paper*:]
Kierkegaard, S., From the Papers of One Still Living, published against his will. [August] 8, 1838. Reitzel, X and 79 pp., 48.[1]

The Author.

[*Address*:]
To
Mr. Secretary Fabricius
Regentsen.[2]
[*in red crayon*: Kjerkegaard.]

13. *M. A. Kierkegaard*[1]—*March 16, 1839—P. C. Kierkegaard and S. K.*

Since the executors of your late father's[2] estate in accordance with his will have awarded each executor a 200 *rdl.* fee from the estate for this legal transaction, I wish hereby to serve notice that I wish to give up my fee. However, it is my request and wish that you distribute said sum in three equal shares to the following families who in the past have maintained an especially close connection with your father although they were only distantly related to him. These are: the widow Mrs. Røjen,[3] the widow of my late blessed brother, Anders Kierkegaard, and Mrs. Agerskov.[4]

I hope that my request and wish will have your approval and be in accordance with your wishes. And I entertain the happy conviction that if this had been known to your father while he was alive and had taken effect after his death, it would surely have given him great pleasure, and that for the families listed it will now become a loving memory of your father—my blessed departed cousin.

Copenhagen, March 16, 1839. With respect I sign myself
your devoted uncle.—
M. A. KIERKEGAARD.

To
Doctor P. Chr. Kierkegaard
and Søren A. Kierkegaard

14. *Else Pedersdatter Kierkegaard—March 24, 1840— P. C. Kierkegaard and S. K.*[1]

To the gentlemen, my dear nephews,

We have intended to write for a long time, but this has been postponed by accidental and demanding circumstances, but I see from your dear letter that your journey[2] went amusingly and happily and that you have come back safe to Copenhagen and your dear family and friends.

I have been very weak throughout this winter, and my
husband has been confined to his bed a good deal of the time.
The words of Our Lord Jesus when he himself says, "See, I
am with you always"³ have not proved wrong, but we ought
to enter God's kingdom through many tribulations.⁴ And my
daughter was confined on October 21 and gave birth to a
daughter who is called Else Marrie, and I was hoping it would
be a boy so that I could have it named after your blessed
father. And there was much I would have liked to talk with
you about, but the time was so short for both you and me.
Still, might it not be possible that your dear brother would
give us the pleasure of traveling here to our home. It is not for
the grand manner of living you may expect with us but for
Christian love and talk with one another as friends and rela-
tions.

The Mercy, Peace, and Blessing of God and Our Lord Jesus
Christ be in and upon all of you.   A loving
greeting to you and all your dear family and friends. We ask if
you would not have the goodness to answer in a couple of
words about that when occasion arises. We ask you not to
scorn this poorly written and very bad [letter]. I ask you to be
so good as to send my very cordial greetings to Cousin Mik-
kel Kierkegaard⁵ in Købmagergade.

I am and remain your loving and grateful aunt

                ELSE PEDERS DATTER KIERKKEGAARD

Sedding, March 24, 1840

[*Address*:]
Dr. P. Chr. Kierkegaard who resides
at 2 Ny Torv
in Copenhagen
ad
postage via   /Copenhagen
    Varde

15. *S. K.—no date—Regine Olsen.*[1]

My Regine!

To

<u>Our own little Regine</u>

S. K.

Such a line under a word serves to direct the typesetter to space out that particular word. To space out means to pull the words apart from one another. Therefore, when I space out the words above, I intend to pull them s o v e r y f a r a p a r t that a typesetter presumably would lose his patience for he would very likely never get to set anything else in his life.

Your   S. K.

16. *S. K.—no date—Regine Olsen.*

My Regine!

How beautiful the face with a meaningful expression, how enchanting the eye that understands every hint! It is as if one read with his eyes what the other wrote with his eyelid. And yet the eye has its limits and the writing of the eyelid cannot be read from a distance; it can only be understood close up. But how quick is the thought when it is sent winging with all the might of the tensed spirit like an arrow from the drawn bow, and how surely it strikes its target! How lightly and beautifully it rises like the falcon, hovers over its prey, lights on it, holds it fast, so that nothing can tear it away.

It is Indian summer, towards evening. —The little window is open, the moon swells, outdoing itself in splendor so as to eclipse the mirror image in the sea, which seems to outshine it, almost audibly—it is that wonderful. The moon flushes with rage and conceals itself in a cloud, the sea shivers—You sit on the sofa, your thoughts float far afield, your eye is fixed on nothing, infinite thoughts fade away only in the infinity of the wide heavens, everything in between is gone, it is as though you sailed in the air. And you summon the fleeting thoughts that show you an object, and if a sigh had propulsive force, if a human being were so light, so ethereal that the compressed air released by a sigh could carry him away, and indeed the more quickly the deeper the sigh—then you would be with me in that very instant.

————But how quick is the thought when it is sent winging with all the might of the tensed spirit like an arrow from the drawn bow, when yearning is the bowstring, joyful certainty the arm that draws it, and unfailing hope the eye that takes aim.

A hieroglyph[1] is enclosed; it may be argued that it is a rosary, but the reference is not so much an allusion to the rose blossom as to the string of beads and to the meditative quiet solemnity with which its owner is accustomed to let it pass through his hands link by link and to name the name.

Your   S. K.

17. S. K.—no date—Regine Olsen

My Regine!

This is Knippelsbro.[1] I am that person with the spyglass. As you know, figures appearing in a landscape are apt to look somewhat curious. You may take comfort, therefore, in the fact that I do not look quite that ugly and that every artistic conception always retains something of the ideal, even in caricature. Several art experts have disagreed as to why the painter has not provided any background whatsoever. Some have thought this an allusion to a folk tale about a man who so completely lost himself in the enjoyment of the view from Knippelsbro that at last he saw nothing but the picture produced by his own soul, which he could just as well have been looking at in a dark room. Others have thought that it was because he lacked the perspective necessary for drawing—houses. But the spyglass itself has a unique characteristic about which tradition tells us the following: the outermost lens is of mirror glass so that when one trains it on *Trekroner* and stands on the left side of the bridge at an angle of 5° off Copenhagen, one sees something quite different from what is seen by all the other people about one; thus, in the midst of a friendly chat about the view of the ships, one sees or thinks that one sees, or hopes to see, or wishes to see, or despairs of seeing that which the secret *genie* of the spyglass reveals to him who understands how to use it correctly. Only in the proper hands and for the proper eye is it a divine telegraph; for everybody else it is a useless contrivance. Yesterday your brother[2] scolded me for always speaking of *my* cobbler, *my* fruit dealer, *my* grocer, *my* coachman, etc., etc., etc. By this means he seems to have accused me of a predominant use of the first-person possessive pronoun. Only you know of *your* faithful friend that I am not extensively but intensively much more given to the use of the second-person possessive pronoun. Indeed, how could he know that, how could any person at all—as I am only yours

Yours eternally.

In testimony whereof I permit my *eternalized* P. Moller[3] to stand as witness.

Granted in *our* study.

[*Address:*]
To
Miss R. Olsen.

18. *S. K.—no date—Regine Olsen.*

My Regine!
Es endet Schmerz
So wie der Scherz
So wie die Nacht
Eh' man's gedacht.[1]

The other day when you came to see me you told me that when you were confirmed your father had presented you with a bottle of lily of the valley (*Extrait double de Muguet*). Perhaps you thought that I did not hear this, or perhaps you thought that it had slipped by my ear like so much else that finds no response within. But not at all! But as that flower conceals itself so prettily within its big leaf, so I first allowed the plan of sending you the enclosed to conceal itself in the half-transparent veil of oblivion so that, freed from every external consideration, even the most illusive, rejuvenated to a new life in comparison with which its first existence was but an earthly life, it might now exude that fragrance for which longing and memory ("from the spring of my youth")[2] are rivals. However, it was nearly impossible for me to obtain this essence in Copenhagen. Yet in this respect there is also a providence, and the *blind* god of love always finds a way. You happen to receive it at this very moment (just before you leave the house), because I know that you, too, know the infinity of the moment. I only hope it will not be too late. Hasten, my messenger, hasten my thought, and you, my Regine, pause for an instant, for only a moment stand still.

Yours eternally, S. K.

[Address:]
To
Miss R. Olsen.

19. *S. K.—no date—Regine Olsen.*

My Regine!

Three weeks ago today you were expecting a letter from me, but I did not write. Alas, to whom could I have entrusted that letter? Do you remember the poem, "The Fiddler at the Fountain"?[1] Much of it is very beautiful, but what appeals to me most is that he confides only in "the light dancer of the woods": the fish, the bird, the mouse, etc. Of course, I know that this is not really in the poem, and that if some people were to see these lines, they would accuse me of having read much more into the poem than was there originally. So be it. Why should that concern me as long as you understand me, as long as we have a secret bond that remains a mystery to everyone else, not only because it is confided mutely, but because it speaks a language that you alone understand, and I, when you have understood me. But three weeks ago you expected me to write and not to come calling—and today you expect me to come calling and not to write. What if I were to do both! (However, I shall probably not call until twelve o'clock in order to escort you to my aunt's in Gothersgade.) In truth, I come, I write, I think, I speak and falter and sigh, and my room resounds with my monologues, and in you alone, my sole confidante, dare I confide what it is that now boisterously wells up in me and then again is lost in silent reverie—in you alone dare I confide—what you have confided in me. For know that every time you repeat that you love me from the deepest recesses of your soul, it is as though I heard it for the first time, and just as a man who owned the whole world would need a lifetime to survey his splendors, so I also seem to need a lifetime to contemplate all the riches contained in your love. Know that every time you thus solemnly assure me that you always love me equally well, both when I am happy and when I am sad, most when I am sad—most when I am sad—because you know that sorrow is divine nostalgia and that everything good in man is sorrow's child— know that then you are rescuing a soul from Purgatory. You know that the Catholic Church teaches that the prayers of the faithful succor the souls in Purgatory; I know that this is true, and each time you speak of your love, I cease to hear the rattling of the chains; then I am free [*in the margin*: "He (*Eros*) brings peace to mankind, rest to the stormy sea; he bids the winds be silent, and he lulls sorrow into slumber."],[2] infinitely free like a bird on the wing; then I am free, and happy in my freedom, and am myself a witness to my own happiness, while formerly I was both prisoner and my own jailer.

Yours eternally,   S. K.

Whenever you catch a breath of that heliotrope at home, which is still fresh, please think of me, for truly my mind and my soul are turned toward this sun, and I have a deep longing for you, thou sun amongst women.[3]

20. *S. K.—[October] 28, [1840]—Regine Olsen*.

Wednesday, the 28th.
4 p.m.

My Regine!

. . . . . And winter came, and the flowers withered, but some he took in and saved from the cold. And he sat by the window and, filled with yearning, held them up. But the life in them was too weak, and in order to preserve it if possible, he crushed them in his hand, and they died; but one drop remained, which, born in pain, has an immortality that only the fragrance of flowers and old melodies have.

Take at once my letter on its long journey!
Genie of the Ring:
Thou never hadst such quick conveyance![1]

Yours eternally,   S. K.

21. *S.K.—no date—Regine Olsen*.

My Regine!

I have now read so much by Plato on love,[1] but still there is one encomium on it that I value more highly than the *summa summarum* of all those by the competitors in the *Symposium*, or, rather, there is a love upon which I will deliver an encomium, not at any symposium but in the stillness of the night when everybody sleeps or in the midst of noisy uproar when nobody understands me. —In the stillness of midnight, for the day does begin at midnight, and at midnight I awoke and the hours grew long for me, for what is as swift as love? Love is the swiftest of all, swifter than itself.

> Zwei Musikanten ziehn daher,
> Vom Wald aus weiter Ferne,
> Der eine ist verliebt gar schr,
> Der andre wär' es gerne.[2]

What is here separated in two, love unites; he is in love, and yet at the same time he is constantly wishing to be so: a restiveness, a yearning, a longing make him wish at every moment to be what he already is at that very moment. It constantly outbids itself without taking notice of the fact that the only other bidder is itself, so that in a manner of speaking, it is the only bidder. In a state of blissful impatience it bids higher and higher all the time, because possession of its object is incommensurable with any worth. Like that merchant, it sells everything in order to buy the field in which the precious pearl lay buried, and it wishes always to possess more in order to pay more dearly for it. Just as the merchant[3] sighs to himself each time he contemplates his treasure: "Why could not the whole world be mine, so that I might give it away in order to acquire the treasure I won?"—so love never possesses its object in a dead and impotent way but strives at every moment to acquire what it possesses at that very moment. It never says, "Now I am safe, now I will settle down," but runs on forever, more swiftly than anything else, for it outruns itself. But this haste, this hurry, this restiveness, this yearning, this wishing, what is it but the power of love to drive out forgetfulness, stupor—death? And what would even heavenly bliss be without wishing, without the wish to possess it, for only sober understanding thinks it foolish to wish for what one possesses. But this wish is also clamoring or whispering, depending on circumstances, but never many-tongued; for if I dared to wish, then I certainly know what I would wish for, and if I dared to wish for seven things, yet I would have only one wish, notwithstanding the fact that I would gladly wish it seven times, even though I knew that it had been fulfilled the first time. And that wish is identical with my deepest conviction: that neither Death, nor Life, nor Angels, nor Principalities, nor Powers, nor the present, nor that which is to come, nor the Exalted, nor the Profound, nor any other creature may tear me from you, or you from me.[4]

> Die stehn allhier im kalten Wind,
> Und singen schön und geigen:
> Ob nicht ein süssverträumtes* Kind
> Am Fenster sich wollt' zeigen?[5]

Your   S. K.

Postscript: When you have forgotten everything that lies between, I would only ask you to read the salutation and the signature, for as I myself have become aware, it has the power to calm or to excite as have but few incantations.

22. *S. K.—no date—Regine Olsen.*

My Regine!

It is winter now, but therefore the very season to think of summer. My horse neighs, the reins are loose in my hand, nature awakens, and in the first chill of dawn each tree bends forward to see if its neighbor is still in the same place, a solitary bird takes flight and proudly lets its song echo in the whispering woods, a deer breaks in terror, peers about, and vanishes into the secrecy of the woods. —Farewell! It happened more quickly than I have told it and is perceived more quickly than it happened. —Accept my thanks, thou wondrous nature! Accept my thanks, thou mother of us all, whose

* I hope this phrase may be applied to you and that you have not become too anxious at the thought that I might suddenly measure one foot between the eyes.

rich womb conceals more, much more than your children can devour with their insatiable eyes—my horse foams, it barely touches the ground—the trees stir uneasily, they shiver with yearning, and they sadly bow their heads to look at one another for yet a moment.

It is winter now, but the Feast of Tabernacles was celebrated in winter. So then I too shall build my leafy bower. I sit quietly within, a solemn air pervades it, which nature does not possess, for recollection sanctifies it; but nature is without a past, a child who does not know the pain of life nor its pleasure, a child who smiles innocently but can tell nothing. —Should you wish to see this leafy bower of mine, a drawing is enclosed.[1] Customarily one uses young, fresh, pliable shoots, not dry twigs without fragrance and without suppleness.

Your   S. K.

23. *S. K.—no date—Regine Olsen.*

My Regine!

This letter has no date nor will it get one, for its principal content is the consciousness of a feeling that probably is present in me at every moment, albeit in all the different musical keys of love, and that is precisely why it is not present at any particular moment as opposed to others (not exactly at ten o'clock or at eleven sharp, not on November 11[1] as opposed to the tenth or the twelfth). For this feeling is constantly rejuvenating itself; it is eternally young, like those books transmitted to us from the Middle Ages, which although several hundred years old are always "printed this year." —Today I stood on the Knippelsbro, and this day does not have a date either, as there is no day when I do not undertake that expedition.

On St. Martin's Eve when I failed to come at eight o'clock, I was at Fredensborg, but I cannot say yesterday or the day before yesterday, for I have no today as a point of departure. People were surprised that I drove alone. Formerly, as you know, I never drove alone, for sorrow, worry, and sadness were my faithful companions. Now those in the traveling party are fewer in number. They are memory and recollection of you when I drive out, and longing for you when I drive home again. And at Fredensborg[2] these companions of mine meet, embrace, and kiss.[3] This is the moment I love so much, for you know that I love Fredensborg indescribably for a moment, for one moment, but only for one moment that is priceless to me.

As this letter is undated and consequently might have been written at any time, it also follows from this that it may be read at any time, and if any nocturnal doubt should assail you, you may read it even at night; for truly, if I ever doubted for a moment that I dared call you "mine" (you know how much I associate with this expression; you know this, you who wrote me yourself that your life would be *concluded* with me if I were to become separated from you; Oh, do then let it be *included* in me as long as we are united, for until then we are not truly *united*), I have never doubted for a moment, no—I write this out of the deepest conviction of my soul—indeed not even in the most obscure corner of the world shall I doubt that I am yours,

Yours eternally,   S. K.

24. *S. K.—no date—Regine Olsen.*

My Regine!

Today is Saturday and I shall not visit you. But because my voice, regardless of how loudly I were to speak here at home, would be too weak to reach your ear unless it echoed there, as I hope it does (and should you not be aware of it at some point, you must believe that this is because it slumbers, but it will soon wake again), I send you this little picture which, however silent it may be, yet surely will not only speak but also appeal to you. It shows an old woman reading. It is apparent that she is reading aloud, but the reason is not so much that someone is listening as that when a person wants to master the finest he craves not only to see but also to hear it. (You yourself may conduct an experiment; I doubt that you would be satisfied with letting your eye fleetingly glance at the words "My Regine" or with staring at them for a long time; for my own part at least I say them aloud again and again.) —In order that I might also have something, I have kept your knitting. I sit and look at it. I have pushed aside the little table in front of my sofa, and your knitting lies by my side. I read aloud, then comes silence, and I turn to rest my weary head at your bosom. —The doorbell rings—I put on my *glasses* to go and open the door. I return once more to sign this letter, and that which I received from my father I surrender to you:

"Your most loving and wholly devoted"[1]

S. K.

9:30 a.m.

25. *S.K.—no date—Regine Olsen.*

1 p.m.

My Regine!

Even at this very moment I am thinking of you, and if at times it seems to you that I am avoiding you, this is not because I love you less, but because it has become a necessity for me to be alone at certain moments. But you are by no means excluded from my thoughts and forgotten; on the contrary, you are present in a most vivid way. And when I think of your faithful heart, I become happy once more; then you are hovering about me, then everything else vanishes from my horizon, which expands infinitely and knows only one limitation. (The enclosed drawing[1] will give you an idea of this.) Then I return to you once more and the hovering thought finds rest in you.

Your   S. K.

26. *S. K.—December 9, [1840]—Regine Olsen.*

Wednesday, December 9.

My Regine!

> He sealed the maiden's ears,
> He sealed her lips so red;
> Then to the ocean floor
> With the maiden fair he sped.[1]

That is just about what I have done, for my real life is not in the external and visible world but deep down in the secret chambers of my soul (and what image could be more beautiful and fitting for that than the sea?), hence I know of nothing with which to compare myself but a merman; hence it also became necessary to seal "her ears and seal her lips so red," that is to say, for the duration of the descent, because down there it is unnecessary, as we learn in the "mouth upon mouth" of the next stanza. Thus it is not necessary to seal her ears down there, for they are closed, or, to state more exactly how surely they are closed—they are open only to his voice. There are many small but cosy rooms down there, where one may safely sit while the ocean storms outside. In some one can faintly hear the din of the world, not anxiously clamoring but quietly dying away and really irrelevant to those who inhabit the rooms. You will find one of these rooms, which functions both as living room and festival hall, reproduced on the enclosed sheet of paper. Still, why all this description of places you already know and already have taken possession of and own so that I myself only own them insofar as I am

Yours
your   S. K.

27. *S. K.—no date—Regine Olsen.*

My Regine!

Am I dreaming, or "comes a dream from the spring of my youth here to my easy chair"?[1] —This picture[2] belongs to you, and yet it is here now. But it finds no rest, no abiding place with me *any longer*; it yearns impatiently to take the message to you and to remain with you. She holds a flower in her hand. Is it she who gives it to him, or has she received it from him only to return it to him in order to receive it once more? No outsider knows. The wide world lies behind him; he has turned his back upon it. Stillness prevails throughout as in eternity, to which such a moment belongs. Perhaps he has sat like this for centuries; perhaps the happy moment was only a brief one and yet sufficient for an eternity. With the picture my thought also returns to its beginning, and I tear myself away, flee from everything that would imprison me in chains of sorrow, and I cry out louder than the sorrows . . . . . yet, yet, yet in all of this I am happy, indescribably happy, for I know what I possess. And when it storms and roars in the workshop of my thoughts, I listen for your voice; and when I stand in a crowd amidst noise and uproar that do not concern me, then I see the open window, and you stand in your summer dress—as once at the Schlegels[3]—and you look and look, and the surroundings become alien to you and only contribute towards directing your attention, your soul to one point, unwaveringly with no thought for anything else, and the distance between us vanishes and you are mine, united with me, though a whole continent were to separate us.

I am enclosing a scarf. I ask you to accept it and desire that *you alone* may know that you own this trifle. When you are festively dressed (you know my opinion of that) and you sit alone waiting for me, then please indicate to me that you own it and that possession of it is not unwelcome to you.

Your   S. K.

[*On the back of the enclosed picture*:]

> Es vergeht keine Stund in der Nacht,
> Da mein Herze nicht erwacht,
> Und an dich gedenkt,
> Dass du mir viel tausendmal
> Dein Herze geschenkt.
>
> *des Knaben Wunderhorn.*[4]

[*In Regine Olsen's handwriting*:]

> And if my arm doth give such pleasure,
>   Such comfort and such ease;
> Then, handsome merman, hasten;
>   Come take them both—oh, please.[5]

28. *S. K.—no date—Regine Olsen*

My Regine!

> Was passt, das muss sich ründen,
> Was sich versteht, sich finden,
> Was gut ist, sich verbinden,
> Was liebt, zusammen sein.
> Was hindert, muss entweichen,
> Was krumm ist, muss sich gleichen,
> Was fern ist sich erreichen,
> Was keimt, das muss gedeihn.[1]

Today is Tuesday. As you know. But Christmas comes before New Year; that is, the Church year precedes the secular, and so also the poetical precedes the actual, which is not to say that the poetical ceases where the actual begins, but that the former is older than the latter and delimits the latter as the eternal always delimits the temporal.

Your   S. K.

[Address:]
To
Miss Regine Olsen.

29. *S. K.—December 30, [1840]—Regine Olsen.*

My Regine!   Wednesday, December 30.

In order to convince you that your box is not used for tobacco but rather serves as a sort of temple archive, I send you the enclosed document.

Today I reminded you of that Wednesday when I *approached* you for the second time in my life. Even the weather recalled that memory to my soul, just as a winter day occasionally may evoke the thought of a summer day quite vividly by virtue of a certain similarity that has its basis in dissimilarity. I felt so unspeakably lighthearted. I drove to Lyngbye,[1] not as I usually do, somber and dejected, carelessly flung in a corner of the carriage seat. I sat in the middle of the seat, uncommonly straight, not with my head bent low, but looked about me happily and confidently. I was immensely pleased to see everybody. I greeted them with mingled feelings, as if each person possessed at once both the sacred solemnity of old friendship and the seductive charm of new acquaintance. In the parsonage I heaped flattery on everybody; we swam in a surfeit. I enjoyed being extravagant, because I felt myself stirred by something far exalted above flattery. . . . . . But today this recollection affected you painfully. You misunderstood me. Allow me then to relate another old tale that also took place on a Wednesday. The event occurs in historical time, and therefore I shall date it. It was on Wednesday, November 18, 1840, that you told me that you had expected a letter from me. At first I only wanted to reply in kind by saying that it was really more appropriate for me to receive than to write a letter. Your remarks about the difficulty in getting to write and having your letter posted came as pure and good seed sown in soil that had been properly weeded (for you remember that I said that the thought of those difficulties had suddenly occurred to me and that this thought instantly became my best, most faithful companion who would never leave my side), and now a rich (the Latinist says *læta*, that is, joyful) abundance bloomed where formerly a cold wind had swept across naked fields. You told me that you had thought of bringing the letter yourself. Then I saw you, and I see you just as clearly, just as vividly at this moment. You walk quietly and meekly, your eyes on the ground, and only occasionally do you lift your gaze filled with peace and bliss to heaven. You walk unperturbed and undisturbed by your wordly surroundings with your thought focused on only one object, as a devout pilgrim in the service of love. Unnoticed you make your way (I see everything in the mind's eye), nobody bows respectfully to the halo around your head, but neither does anyone compassionately pity you (perhaps you remember that you spoke about Alberg's family);[2] only one person sees you, only one understands you, but neither will he permit you to undertake this pilgrimage, not even in the spirit. And when you sometimes bow your head sadly, then he knows that the spirit is willing, then he hastens to meet you, then he feels, my Regine, that you have conquered him, then he wishes to try you no more; and although the struggle was very brief and although he may with a slight change say like Caesar, "I came, I saw, *she* conquered," the joy shall be no less long-lasting.

Your   S. K.

The enclosed manuscript depicts a wreath and an eye that looks at that wreath.

30. *S. K.*—*[New Year, 1841]*—*Regine Olsen.*

My Regine!

May God grant you a Happy New Year: many smiles and few tears!

I send you a handkerchief with this. I have had it placed under your pillow. If at some point you suddenly awaken frightened by a painful dream and cannot hold back your tears, do wipe them away with this "linen cloth." Then you will remember that I sent it to you and that I myself would like to stop them. But when happy and contented, rich like the poor widow[1] who gave away everything she possessed, richer than the world, you lay your head upon the same pillow, then this linen cloth will remind you of me once more and that you have wiped away my tears, the only person who has ever done so, as you are the only one who has seen them. Then, whenever you want to do so, you will easily see my picture in this cloth. St. Veronica wiped away the sweat of Christ with a precious linen cloth, and as a reward his image remained in it, and when she had folded it five times she owned five likenesses of him. In order to see my picture in this cloth you have to call it forth yourself, but I know that you are able to do so. But, oh, do not summon me when I am uneasy and worried, someone denied peace by his dark thoughts, haunted by secret grief as a fitful spirit fleeing hither and yon, but when I am gentle and friendly and filled with hope and confidence. In any case, I desire that this linen cloth may not leave your bed.

Your   S. K.

31. *S. K.—no date—Regine Olsen.*

My Regine!

Perhaps you were also expecting to receive, along with *Old Memories*,[1] a potential memory in the form of a letter. It did not turn out that way, so please accept these lines, which may—who knows—soon become a representative of a time gone by. It is fine that you should be expecting a letter from me, and especially so when your expectation does not take the form of an intense disquiet that needs to be calmed, but is a devoted, quiet longing that does not devour the external manifestation in order to be sated, as it were, but rather conceals it as Mary did, deep in her heart—that does not devour it, for it is self-sustaining, because it feels within itself a blessed certainty, a capacity for growth into eternal life. The reverse of this is that I, on the other hand, at every moment feel within myself a mood that makes a letter imminent even though circumstances constantly set it aside, and therefore, no matter how much time passes between each letter, whenever I do write, I find that it is as natural as though I had done the same thing the day before. But freedom is love's element. And I am convinced that you honor me too much to want to see me as a diligent *kammerjunker*[2] who carries out the ministerialia of love with the zeal of an accountant, or to want me to compete for a medal of endurance in oriental arts and crafts. And I am convinced that *my Regine* is too much of a poet, whenever a letter does not come, to consider this as neglect of "dutiful attention," to use an official expression—too much of a poet, even if a letter were never to arrive, to long to return to the fleshpots of *Egypt*[3] or to wish always to be surrounded by a lovesick suitor's enamoured treading of the mill. My letters are not a gradually exhausting bleeding to death. Each letter is the fruit of a visit with which the god of Love favors me and which, by my letter, I confide in that person from whom the god always brings greetings and in whose name he comes. For love is nothing, or insipid flattery, when it does not have a definite form. That form is assumed by the god, or rather, he lets a holy sleep fall upon you and leads you to me, and you do not know it until my letter tells you that you have visited me, and both of us thank him, the god, to whom we owe so much, who grants so much to all those who ask but do not *demand*.

Your   S. K.

At this moment I walk past your window. I look at my watch, and that signifies that I have seen you. If I do not look at my watch I have not seen you.

32. *S. K.—no date—Regine Olsen.*

My Regine!

Because all writing is merely a faint whisper, I have pronounced this salutation aloud to myself and, insofar as I can judge, with that voice which I have less in my power than it has me in its or, I might say, that you have in yours, regardless of the fact that you are silent and it is I who speak.

Inasmuch as you have given up your higher musical studies (please do not imagine that I am pursing my mouth in a sarcastic smile or that my lips are flippantly aquiver, for if they are quivering, it is because they are still trembling from the last time I spoke), you will have to be satisfied with a little subsidy for the dissemination of music in the living room. There, too, you will find no lack of opportunity for musical study whenever you attempt to chase away my dark moods with the aid of music. So, although your playing may not be perfect in the artistic sense, in this you will, regardless, be able to succeed. David was able to banish Saul's black mood,[1] and yet I have never heard that he was a particularly great artist. I imagine it was his young, joyful, fresh spirit that helped so much, and you possess yet something more—a love for which nothing is impossible.

Your   S. K.

33. *S. K.—no date—Regine Olsen.*

Tuesday evening-Wednesday morning

My Regine!

No more will I tempt you, for now I know your mind;
Christ grant that every maiden were of your faithful kind.
Reward you—that I will: you spoke in pleasing way.
God's Peace! Farewell! Tomorrow dawns another day.[1]

The ballad does not inform us in what manner Wolmer rewarded her, and however noble this may sound from the mouth of King Wolmer, "I will reward you," the maid is apparently so *lofty*, so *rocklike* (and rocks are not usually found in bogs)[2] that any royal gift would be much too small. Hence poetic balance is not achieved until we assume that King Wolmer and a certain other person are basically identical. Thus when the tempestuous King Wolmer reins in his unruly horse, storms away like an autumnal gale, and, wishing to comfort her, says, "Tomorrow dawns another day," this is not really so. No, not at all.

But o'er the fence now vaulted her true-love so sweet,
With joyful steps he hastened, the maid's embrace to meet.

And although it seems to me that the reward fails to appear in this case as well, the maid may find herself so contented that she thinks herself rewarded inasmuch as she assures herself that he was present and yet was *not* present in that precipitous gale[3] but rather in the soft breeze.

Your   S. K.

34. *S. K.—no date—Regine Olsen.*

I enclose a picture,[1] which I do not wish to have hanging neglected in an uninhabited room.

Your   S. K.

Ich dein
Du mein
Du mein' Friede
Klang im Liede
Trost im Leide
Brunnquell aller Lebens-Freude.[2]

[*Address*:]
To
Miss Regine Olsen.

35. *S. K.—[January 23, 1841]—Regine Olsen.*

My Regine!   12 o'clock.
Here you have the manuscript[1] that caused me to leave you
just then. I assume—do you not agree?—that you will concede that if the learned world were allowed to see it, they
would declare it the most foolish thing I have yet written, indeed, completely void of meaning.

Please accept then my congratulations or rather the sum of
those wishes that have been set in motion towards you at different times and days; accept them all combined in a single
wish: may God grant that nobody will take your joy away
from you—not you yourself by restless yearning, by un-
timely doubt, by self-consuming despondency—not I by my
heavy bent of mind and my self-made worries—not by the
smile of prosperity—not by the tears of adversity—not by the
impatient haste of longing—not by the disappointing delu-
sions of recollection. Accept this wish! And if it seems to you
for a moment that I have grown so old that my wish resembles a prayer and my expression of it a blessing, do nevertheless accept it and accept it with as much feeling as I impart it,
for then I know that the time will come when once again with
blessing I shall ascertain that you have preserved your happiness. But then my blessing will become a thanksgiving, for I
would see the fulfillment of that which of all things is most on
my mind.

                                              Your   S. K.

Of springtime will I not remind,
Nor of the dreams gone by;
But I shall teach you how to find
The joys that near you lie.
Do not lament the joys of spring
That slumber far from sight,
For in that tear which so doth sting
There lies yet some delight.[2]

This is the first birthday at which I am present and presumably it will be some time before I do this again. Therefore, if you can use it, please accept this paint set. I hope you can use it. And just as you rescue the modest flower from the night of death and oblivion, so my grateful memory walks once more in the harvested field and always finds something new to preserve. Accept these candlesticks, and let them shine for you just as your music has so often lightened my dark spirit. Probably there is no need for me to ask you to think about me during all of this, but if it will give you pleasure, if your thoughts of me will be easier, freer, more expansive when you are firmly persuaded that I share your satisfaction with these occupations, then please be unalterably assured thereof.

Some time ago you sent me some wildflowers. You had not forgotten what I had said earlier. My taste is still the same. In the meantime, I have tried in vain to get hold of some specimens; still, to some extent I have succeeded, as you will find out when I call on you.

Your   S. K.

36. *S. K.—no date—Regine Olsen*

My Regine!

This very moment I have finished the critique[1] I have to turn in today. But you must not believe that it is because I happen to have a pen in my hand that I take this occasion, as it were, to write *on occasion*. If you could only see the illegible scrawl that is on its way in a messy envelope to His Honor, the Very Reverend Dr. Münter,[2] Preacher to the Royal Court, Knight and Member of *Dannebrog*, member of the Board of Governors of the Pastoral Seminary, etc., etc., and were you next to see what pains I take to write legibly, with how much pleasure my hand delineates each letter, if you could only see how lightly it rests upon the paper, and how deliberately it hesitates now and then, and with what abandon it sometimes executes a curve and yet does not go astray but returns and rounds off the word—then you would know that I am thinking of you and that I read far more significant gestures into the movements of the pen.

My Regine, you want so much to hear this name, and I want so much to use it, and yet we do perhaps have different associations with it. Perhaps you associate the modest thought with it that you are, as I want you to be, the very model of that picture which my yearning sought—and I, I associate the proud thought with it that you belong to me, not for a fleeting moment, not partially, but completely and forever. But then again I am not proud, for what do I have but what has been given me? If it had been possible for me to "enchant" you, if in egotistical smugness I could call you mine, oh, how impoverished would I not be in my wealth, and how vain would not my happiness be. For only he who is free is able to give of himself, and the freer he is, the more extravagant he can be. Therefore, whenever I call you "mine," it is because I reassure myself once more of the abundance I possess; for a moment you have torn yourself away from me, only to rejoin me yet more closely. He who possesses himself possesses the greatest riches; and even though somebody possessed the whole world, he could not be as extravagant as he who gives of himself. There are many who might not be able to understand this, but in my eyes you are richer than the whole world and have greater abundance than an oriental potentate—you, my Regine, are more extravagant and happier in extravagance than anybody else can be.

Perhaps you are thinking of me at this very moment, and perhaps I do not emerge clearly and definitely before you, but your awareness dawns in feeling. And in that I am also present. Jupiter metamorphosed himself into a cloud so that he might visit Io, and so too when you volatilize me into a cloud, then I am as well

Your   S. K.

37. *S. K.—no date—Regine Olsen.*

My Regine!
Wir haben uns bedacht [We have reconsidered[1]]. Do come to 7 Store Kiøbmagergade[2] on your way back from your music lesson. I promise to meet you there.

Your   S. KIERKEGAARD.

[Address:]
To
Miss R. Olsen.

38. *S.K.—no date—Regine Olsen.*

My Regine!

> Whom most they love they most chastise:
> 'Tis folly in the whole world's eyes.
> Both walk as one to death and grave:
> The world thinks "madly" they behave.[1]

When I have spoken with you as I did today, not coldly and severely (I would never be able to do that) but seriously, albeit mildly and tenderly, I should not like you to think for a moment that I feel myself superior at such times; and to show you that I chastise myself in the same way, I send you as a remembrance of this morning a copy of the New Testament and thank God that I became the person charged with providing you with that which we all need. You know that the angels in heaven rejoice[2] in your every victory, but surely their joy is not diminished by the presence of one person on earth, an insignificant being to be sure, who humbly shares their joy.

Your   S. K.

39. *S. K.—no date—Regine Olsen.*

My Regine!

The moment will not favor us. All right, let us recollect instead. Recollection is my proper element,[1] and my recollection is ever fresh, and like a brook it winds its way through the moor of my life, murmuring and speaking, speaking and murmuring always the same, assuaging grief, beckoning and tempting me to follow it all the way back to its source where it wells up from the shadowy memories of childhood. Therefore my recollections come to life not only when conflicting moods come into contact with each other—as green wreaths although withered will smell fresh again when there is a change in the weather (although all recollections smell sweetest and most indescribably when it rains)—but indeed are alive constantly, and the more adversity in the world, the more intensely I recollect. However, with respect to my recollection I am still young, as you may conclude from the fact that I am unlike old people who recall very well what is most remote in time but not what is closest. For me every harmonious contact with an idea and with life instantly clarifies, transfigures itself into a recollection, and while it brings close to me what happened long ago, it pushes what happened most recently far back in order to call it forth in the light-dark [*hell-dunkel*] of recollection. Regardless of the fact, then, that on this particular day the moment has denied us its assistance and regardless of the fact that as I write this the hour has not yet come, I recollect all this as something long past, and thus it loses its painful sting and retains its nostalgic sweetness.

Your S. K.

40. *S. K.—no date—Regine Olsen.*[1]

My Regine!

Thank you for all the time you spent on my lettercase; thank you for all the mental embroidery your mind has magically wrought while your hand cunningly formed visible pictures in pearls, visible but hence temporal and not eternal like that labor of mind. Thank you for the lettercase; thank you for your wish Sunday afternoon; thank you for your wish Tuesday morning; thank you for coming; thank you for coming early; thank you for coming alone; thank you for your happiness; thank you for your anxiety.

I send you a rose with this. Unlike your present, it has not blossomed in my hands in all its splendor but has withered in my hands; unlike you I have not been the happy witness to all its unfolding; I have been the sad witness to its gradual decay. I have seen it suffer; it lost its fragrance, it hung its head, its leaves drooped in its struggle with death, its blush faded, and its fresh stem dried. It forgot its magnificence, thought itself forgotten, and did not know that I always had it in mind, nor did it know that together we both preserved its recollection. —In truth, had it known, then it would have revived with joy, and when its time had once more come, it would have had only one wish, and that wish I hereby fulfill, for it would have wished to remain with you. It would have said: "You saw me every day, and although I thank you for not forgetting me, I am not surprised by this; but she did not see me and yet she did not forget me." So I am hereby executing its last will: it returns to you to whom it first belonged. Its tomb is white and pure and your seal is upon it. Perhaps you do not remember it, but that is because it is invisible. In *A Thousand and One Nights*[2] a girl is described who in addition to other virtues also had a mouth like the seal of Solomon. Thus, when I press my lips to this sheet of paper, I am placing not my but your seal upon it. I know very well that border disputes may easily arise here if anywhere, but I have settled them. The seal is yours, but I keep it. But in a seal, as you know, the letters are reversed, and from this it follows that the "yours" by which you validate the certainty of possession appears as a "mine" from my side. Herewith have I sealed this parcel, and I would ask you to do likewise with the enclosed rose before it is put away in the temple archive.

Your   S. K.

With this is enclosed a tracing of the seal.

41. *S. K.—September 11, 1841—Regine Olsen.*[1]

My Regine!

Are you going to Ordrup[2] today? If your answer should be "No!" you might perhaps, since you did not write to me yesterday, send me your "No" of today. However, I only ask about this in order to know if I may call on you today.

September 11.

Your   S. KIERKEGAARD.—

[*Address:*]
To
Miss R. Olsen.

42. *S. K.—no date—Regine Olsen.*

My Regine!

You may remember that about a year ago[1] I sent you a bottle of this essence, adding that I had deliberately let some days go by after you had mentioned your fondness for it in order to conceal that fine flower in the veil of recollection. Now I recollect this once more. In other words, I recollect that you then mentioned that which I recollect, that I recollected that you mentioned it. Thus the recollection of it has become even more precious to me, not retrospectively but progressively. That is the blessing of time. I send you then a bottle of it enveloped in an abundance of leafy wrappings. But these leaves are not the kind one tears off hastily or throws aside with annoyance in order to get to the contents. On the contrary, they are precisely of that kind that gives pleasure, and I see with how much care and solicitude you will unfold every single leaf and thereby recollect that I recollect you, my Regine, and you will yourself recollect

Your   S. K.

[*Address:*]
To
Miss Regine Olsen

43. *S. K.—no date—Regine Olsen.* [1]

My Regine!
You must not expect me this afternoon, as I find myself prevented from coming until this evening.

Your   S. K.

[*Address:*]
To
Miss Regine Olsen.

44. *S. K.—no date—Regine Olsen.*

My Regine!
You are not to expect me this evening, as I find myself prevented from coming.

Your   S. K.

[*Address:*]
To
Miss Regine Olsen

45. *S. K.—no date—Regine Olsen.*

I would like to put something fragrant in the box, but as I have nothing at hand except the enclosed letter, I hope you will be content with that.

[*Address:*]
To
Miss Regine Olsen.

46. *S. K.—no date—Regine Olsen.*

My Regine!
Just now I walked past the theater. [1] I bought two tickets; one is for you, and at six o'clock sharp when I shall call to

give you yours, you will know for whom the other is intended. Are you going to your music lesson after all? And do you want me to meet you there? Or would it not be best for you to stay at home? In any case, I would like your reply by my messenger.

Your   K.

[*Address on the envelope:*]
To
Miss Regine Olsen

47. *S. K.—[1841]—Hans Peter Kierkegaard.*[1]

Dear Peter,

I assume that your messenger brought back a card from me the other day in which, if I do not misremember, owing to too much distracting business, I asked you to forgive me for having forgotten to get hold of your books on account of "too much business." This must, however, be amended: on account of too much business I had forgotten that I had remembered to do what was required of me to obtain them. The fact is that I have lent them to Mrs. Rørdam's four daughters[2] (do not be alarmed, for the rest of the tale will show that they are not reading all of them at once; indeed, sometimes for long intervals *none of them at all*), and of these the two who have read them the most have gone to the country, and out of concern for the books, they have put them under lock and key. (You see, then, that there has been some time when none of them at all has been reading them.) That is the trouble. Incidentally, I believe that they will return on Monday, and the books will then be sent to you without delay and with the appropriate thanks for the loan and a small request that you forget my negligence and forgive it, if for no other reason, then for the sake of the piquancy of the situation.

Your   S. KIERKEGAARD.

[*Address:*]
To
Mr. Peter Kierkegaard.

48. *S. K.—[September 1841]—E.F.C. Boiesen.*

Dear Professor Boiesen:[1]

Above all, please do not read yourself into exhaustion in the enclosed book,[2] do not permit the heavy book to become an encumbrance in any way upon this little note, for the facts are as stated on the outside: it is the book that accompanies the letter, not the letter that accompanies the book. The letter is quickly read and nevertheless the main thing, while the book is mere freight, scarcely palatable, much less something to get your teeth into. In other words: without any obligation or request whatsoever "to read" (Prof. Nielsen),[3] please accept what in all respects is a complimentary copy, with the note as a small expression of my regard for the good will and interest with which I believe you have sometimes followed my efforts.

No reply is necessary. What you probably still say many times a day, as you used to at the Borgerdyds School, I will say here: "That will do," and my intention is not to make you "the next" who "continues."[4]

Sincerely,
Your devoted
S. KIERKEGAARD.

[*Address:*]
To
Professor Boiesen
at Sorøe.
Accompanying parcel with a book marked "B."

49. *S. K.—[October 31, 1841]—Emil Boesen.*

Dear Emil,

I have arrived in Berlin[1] as you may already have learned from my letter to Peter, which I wrote very quickly but mailed somewhat late. It is still my unalterable opinion that travel is foolish. But I hope that my stay will not be without significance for me when I have settled down a bit. I have

much to think about and am suffering from a monstrous productivity block. I have as yet no occasion to let its *nisus*[2] wear
off (and it has already for some time been true of my countenance what was said about that emperor, *"vultus erat niten-
tis"*).[3] I have begun to attend lectures. I heard one by
Marheineke[4] with which I was quite pleased, for although it
did not contain anything new, it was very nice to hear much
of that which one is accustomed to seeing in print. Schelling[5]
has not yet begun.

How are things with you at home?—and how is that person
whose name I will not mention, although I hope your letters
will contain something enlightening for me? Provide me with
news. But the deepest secrecy must prevail. Do not let anybody suspect that I want it. Hitherto I have firmly adhered to
the principle according to which I have decided to act. In this I
had the encouragement, if you please, and I think of it mostly
from that point of view, of having Professor Sibbern[6] look
for me the day before I left "in order to give me a thorough
dressing down," since he too had now become convinced that
I was an egotistical and vain man, an ironist in the worst
sense. When he did not find me, Peter became the victim; he
grew angry and replied that it was none of Sibbern's business.
I suppose Sibbern has spoken with the family. I could only
wish that he had also spoken with her, for then I would have
attained my goal. Meet her without being observed. Your
window can assist you. Mondays and Thursdays from 4 to 5
p.m., her music lessons. But do not meet her in the street except Monday afternoons at 5 or 5:30, when you might meet
her as she walks from Vestervold via Vestergade to Klæde-
boderne,[7] or on the same day at 7 or 7:30, when she and her
sister are likely to go to the Exchange by way of the arcades.
But be careful. Visit the pastry shop[8] there, but be careful. For
my sake practice the art of controlling every expression, of
being master of any situation, and of being able to make up a
story instantaneously without apprehension and anxiety. Oh,
one can fool people as much as one wants, as I know from
experience, and at least with respect to this I have unlimited

recklessness. But she must not suspect that I am concerned about her, for she might misunderstand and become dangerously ill. Also, sound out Peter a little. I wrote nothing at all to him, or at least I did so very guardedly. I trust nobody. He used the opportunity provided by Sibbern's visit to try to penetrate my shell but met only my ironic laughter. For I am afraid that somebody or other might take it upon himself to tell her that I am still thinking about her. That would be quite a rewarding role, which might be tempting.

I can well imagine that many of my good friends will use my absence to malign me, but do not defend me—I beg of you. Still, write to me so that I may surmise whence animosity comes.

As for yourself: work—write—forget. Those stubborn thoughts must be made to obey. Acquire a wider circle of acquaintance in order to learn better how to be self-contained. I am sitting here in a hotel at a noisy dinner table where every possible language is spoken, where everybody is very busy, and for a moment I am silent in order to allow this noise to compel my thought inwards. "Cheers for me and you, say I; that day will never be forgotten."⁹ And so I live every day. I have in fact decided to eat at the hotel. It is not much more expensive. The food is good, and I do not care to eat with the Danes (this last is a secret note for you alone). In case anyone asks you where I eat, reply that the hotel keeper had offered me such reasonable rates before I had spoken with the Danes that I preferred to eat here. Incidentally, I feel inner strength within me, and so, period.

Take care of yourself!

Your   S. KIERKEGAARD.

Please do me the favor of sending a little note of greeting to Henrich, Michael, Carl, Sophie, Jette, Wilhelm.¹⁰ You can send it to 7 St. Kjøbmagergade.
My address is:

Mittelstrasse 61
eine Treppe hoch.

[*Address*:] *An dem Herrn, Cand. der Theologie*
E. Boesen
Copenhagen
Philosophgangen

[*Postmarks*:]
Berlin   Hamburg
10/31   3–4   11/2

50. *S. K.—November 16, 1841—Emil Boesen.*

Dear Emil,   November 16, '41
   Please accept my thanks for doing what your letter declares
and shows—for thinking of me. And truthfully, in spite of *all*
that egotism that *all* the world attributes to me, I do think that
I deserve this from a few people, and from you I desire it, for
my heart has also opened itself to you and is even opening itself at this moment as I think about you. Can you doubt that?
—And yet, a small reproof seems hidden somewhere in your
letter because I used the phrase, "I trust nobody," as though
you were included in that. If I really did not trust you, do you
not think I would be prudent enough to avoid telling you that
I trusted absolutely nobody? You are perhaps the only person
I have told that, for I pretend to trust the others, and in consequence my sources of information are always all the more
immediate, and my opinion then emerges as a calculated result of them. By the way, I may have used the expression
rather impetuously, for what I wanted to say was that I did
not believe you had sufficient practice to undertake observations,[1] and since it was important to me that she be deprived
of any opportunity for the least suspicion, since it was so important to me, so immensely important that I would despair
only at the moment that happened, then you will easily be
able to explain that phrase to yourself, all the more so when
you reflect on the skill I rightly or wrongly consider mine in
this matter. Please do not be angry about this. The matter was
so much on my mind that I would do anything to test you;
indeed, had you been the most accomplished observer the

world had ever known, I might still perhaps have said something similar. In return for this slight apology, I must now take the field with a little outburst that I shall render to you as spontaneously as I possibly can. The occasion was a statement in your letter to the effect that it would perhaps be most proper not to give me any information at all about her, and this despite the fact that I had most earnestly requested it. "Death and Pestilence![2] Does he want to be my guardian, would he make me his ward, would he make a spoiled child of me, and then on top of this tell me so to my face?" You may well imagine the rhythm in this lecture delivered in my room with unusual energy, and all the more so as on that very day I had put away my heavy, cork-soled boots, was walking around in my thin ones, and accordingly could more easily manage the high tragical pace, easy and powerful at the same time. In other words, you would leave me to my daydreams! In this you are wrong, for I do not dream; I am wide awake and alert. I do not turn her into a poetic subject, I do not call her to mind, but I call myself to account. This is as far as I can go: I think I can turn anything into a poetic subject, but when it is a question of duty, obligation, responsibility, debt, etc., I cannot and I will not turn those into poetic subjects. If she had broken our engagement, my soul would soon have driven the plow of forgetfulness over her, and she would have served me as so many others have done before her—but now, now I serve her. If it were in her power to surround me with vigilant scouts who always reminded me of her, still she could not be so clearly remembered as she is now in all her righteousness, all her beauty, all her pain. So just keep me informed. In the course of these recent events my soul has received a needed baptism, but that baptism was surely not by sprinkling, for I have descended into the waters; everything has gone black before my eyes, but I ascend again. Nothing, after all, so develops a human being as adhering to a plan in defiance of the whole world. Even though it were something evil, it would still serve to a high degree to develop a person. So just write, and please do write, if you would, a little more clearly, whenever you have an intelligence report. I do not shy away from the thought of her, but whenever I think of the poor girl—and yet she is too good to be called a poor girl—and yet she is a poor girl—and yet my strength of mind has been guilty and has broken the proudest of girls. —As you see, I am on a treadmill, and I only need to tread the mill in this manner for one hour every day, and then let my hypochondria be the surly coachman who always cries "giddyap" and strikes the sorest spots with his whip, for then I have had sufficient exercise for that day, and then I need all my strength of mind to say, "Stop! Now I will think of other things." And yet my soul is sound, sounder than ever before.

This is how matters now stand. Let the town gossip. Let Christian,[3] my brother-in-law, and other nitwits prattle on and on. Anyone who thinks it too much to designate his own wife as residuary legatee would really think me mad if he were to hear that I would gladly place my whole estate in her hands if she so wished—oh, my! You say that you find it scarcely bearable to have the whole town talking like this. To me it is indescribably gratifying, for it is the only thing that may help her. ———Among all the things you write about, there is only one that worries me a little, and that is that she has invited Henrich, Michael, etc., to visit her. She is clever, and one year under my auspices has not exactly made her more naïve; among other things it has taught her that I notice even the most trivial triviality. My procedure with respect to the children must be altered. I regret to say it, but I trust nobody, although this is not to say that it would ever occur to me to say anything to them, but feeling emotional about them she might perhaps see something more in it, etc. With considerable caution you have managed to avoid everything. As you know, the last evening before I left, she was probably at the theater,[4] and you also know how I avoided her. It would always have been wrong to meet her, for surely she would always have assumed that some feeling for her remained.

And now about you. Do you have any responsibility, have you broken any obligation, and does it really upset you if you walk past her window and see her laughing? Write about her, for then she will sit even more prettily inside, and laugh and cry and do whatever you please. My dear Emil, let me say this to you: if you get angry, please do not hide it from me. You ought not to give in to that type of thing. Whether my soul is too egotistical or too great to be troubled by such matters, I do not know, but it would not disturb me. Nobody takes care of you, nobody has a valid claim on you, nobody cares whether you disintegrate in doubt or are transfigured in the clouds, except that one or those few persons who are close but demand nothing of you except that you feel well, that you feel at one with your soul. If my presence has sometimes been damaging to you, allow my absence to benefit you all the more, but above all let it have one result: that we may meet even more intimately, with greater sympathetic harmony, when the time comes. I have lost much or robbed myself of much in this world, but I will not lose you; I have kicked the world, I mock it; I wish to God that I did not, in some sense, have so much right to do so. But I shall hold on to you, and precisely by doing that, I shall prove that I am

Your S. K.

Greetings to your father and mother.

[*Address*:]
An
dem Herrn Cand. theol. E. Boesen
Copenhagen
Philosophgangen
fr.

[*Postmarks*:]
Berlin   Hamburg
11/18   5–6   11/20

51. *S. K.—November 18, 1841—P. J. Spang.*[1]

Dear Pastor Spang,

I suppose the town has not yet given you the opportunity to forget the name of Kierkegaard, even though his character as represented by the town is so altered, so unrecognizable, that you would scarcely acknowledge him. This being so, it is really against my principles to write now, for one should not do so until one can assume that one is beginning to be forgotten. Besides, I had counted on forgetfulness for another reason, for I flattered myself that tonight, especially in your room, I might now and then be summoned forth by your art in poetic form in a lonely, idle moment—after having probably all too often been conjured up with malevolence: "To the eternal shame of the traitor,"[2] etc.—I say "probably," for one would think that *I* would know it better than anyone else, that in every such operation something would have to happen inside me to indicate that it was taking place. But this is not so at all. For no matter how willing I am to be summoned, how sympathetic my response to even the most distant sympathetic touch—nay, thought—I cannot be persuaded when I am not willing. I would not have gone away had there not been other things to determine me, for it is not my habit to avoid confrontation with a crowd. For two weeks I flouted the town in all ways, but not a soul dared utter the least word to me. When I left, the sluice gates of conversation opened, and it is probably still dripping from the roofs. What is Sibbern[3] doing? For I do assume that the sane and lofty in him have prevailed once more, or has he really placed himself at the head of the gossipmongers at tea parties? If so, what danger is there in that? I am no longer in town, and if I were, Sibbern would be man enough to prevent my approaching any girl, at least according to his own conceited idea of himself. And should there be more of my evil kind, Sibbern might of course resign his chair and let himself be hired as an "uncle" or family protector for a small fee. He might be mounted on horseback to enable him to get around more quickly. Then he could let me have his chair, and thus all would be well served, and I rendered harmless, for as Sibbern knows, a professor of philosophy ought not to do that sort of thing. If he has come to his senses, please give him my regards. Otherwise, should you meet anybody who, whether he knows me or not, is busily engaged in spoiling my good name and reputation, please greet him from me and tell him that I have asked you to say hello to everybody who remembers me. Do this with sufficient irony, and the situation could be quite amusing.

Here in Berlin I live with extraordinary punctuality. Punctually at ten o'clock I go to a certain nook to pass my w. . . . For this is the only one in a vast territory where there is no notice posted to remind one of what one must but may not do. This reminds me of *Justitsraad* Hiorthøy,[4] in Copenhagen, who at a certain hour always stood in a certain spot to pass his w. . . . Yet he did this mainly out of his conscientiousness in general; here it is sheer necessity. In this moral town one is almost forced to keep a bottle in one's pocket, even though this is otherwise deemed immoral; but clearly it may be done for many different reasons. I could become quite expansive on this subject, for it intervenes in and disrupts all human affairs. When two people go for a walk in the Thiergarten and one of them says, "Please excuse me for a moment," that is the end of that excursion, for then he must go all the way home. Almost everybody in Berlin performs these necessary errands. When I have taken care of this, I visit my coffee shop, the best I have found in Berlin. A coffee shop with better coffee than in Copenhagen, more journals, excellent service. As long as the owner remains in Berlin, I cannot suffer from homesickness. But already I am thinking about our separation. He will probably remain, but I shall have to leave him at some point. That is life. We meet, become acquainted, learn to appreciate each other (as Sparganapani—that is his name—understands very well), and then we must part and nothing remains between us. —The streets are too broad for my liking and so are Steffens' lectures. One cannot see from one side to the other nor keep track of the passersby, just as with Steffens'[5] lectures; but of course the passersby are exceedingly interesting, just as Steffens' lectures are. I think Steffens resembles Reitzel.[6] Have you ever seen him? —I do not mean Reitzel, but Steffens.

Schelling[7] has commenced, but amidst so much noise and bustle, whistling, and knocking on the windows by those who cannot get in the door, in such an overcrowded lecture hall, that one is almost tempted to give up listening to him if this is to continue. I happened to sit between notable people—Prof. Werder[8] and Dr. Gruppe[9]. Schelling himself is a most insignificant man to look at; he looks like a tax collector, but he did promise to assist science, and us with it, to the flowering it has long deserved, to the highest it can attain. This would be gratifying enough for an old man, but for a young man it is always problematical to become contemporary with that rare flower at such an early age. However, I have put my trust in Schelling and at the risk of my life I have the courage to hear him once more. It may very well blossom during the first lectures, and if so one might gladly risk one's life.

How are you? Are you well, healthy, strong? If you have the opportunity, please let me know.

Please take care of yourself.

Your   S. K.

52. *S. K.—December 8, 1841—Carl Lund.*[1]

Berlin   December 8, '41

My dear Carl,

It probably cost you a certain effort before you could make up your mind to write to me, because you were afraid that you had nothing to write about, or did not write well enough, or did not spell correctly. You must not worry about all that, just write. Indeed, you write very well, and with the exception of one word, everything is so grammatically and calligraphically sound that a *magister artium* [Master of Arts] would be pleased to sign his name to it. But it is precisely because you may have more obstacles to contend with that you should also be allowed to see a spur to continue in the pleasure with which I receive your epistle.

Time changes everything, and as I see from your postscript in which you have noted what is most important, it has also changed you: *Carl* in a shirt and pants! When all is said and done, you may be the one who has changed most by the time I hope to be home. I may not even be able to recognize you, for by then you will probably have begun wearing a vest. From this you may also gather how pleased I am that despite this total change, this metamorphosis (a word you may have learned in natural science), you remain unchanged in your relationship with me. If I stay abroad long enough, you may even have tails on your coat. Alas! Alas! Alas! If you should refuse to acknowledge me, how shall I then recognize you?

But before I proceed to this or that little item of news, I want once and for all to ask you and the others to let me know whether the letters I write have in fact reached those for whom they were intended. I have written both Henrich and Michael, but have not learned whether these letters have arrived safe and sound in Copenhagen.

What shall I now tell *tuis auribus dignum* [worthy of your ears]? Shall I tell you that the dogs here in Berlin perform a very different role from that in Copenhagen? They are used to pull carriages. One, two, or sometimes three big dogs are hitched up to one of the little carriages used for transporting milk to the capital from the country. When there is only one dog, the man or his wife usually join in pulling, but when there are two, the driver usually walks calmly along on the pavement, with his dogs and the cart in the middle of the street. But one day I saw a little boy employed as a driver for such a cart, and he sat in it and drove along at full speed with his milk. The dogs are harnessed just like horses, but usually somewhat more loosely so that when they stop they may sit and rest. Usually these dogs are very steady and sedate, and one seldom sees a dog determined to go in a direction other than that which his driver chooses.

In the Thiergarten great numbers of squirrels with their noise and racket make it very entertaining to roam about, especially in the remoter parts. Like the Frederiksberg Gardens, the Thiergarten is intersected by a canal, but the water is cleaner than at home. In the water are innumerable goldfish. I am sure you know them; if not, you can see them at any rate in the grocer's window in Nørregade diagonally opposite my old apartment. When the sun shines and the water is clear and quiet, it looks very pretty.

Now I have no more space to write, for the last page belongs to Sophie. As I said, it was good of you to write, my dear Carl. Please accept my greetings with this, as well as greetings that you must give Henrich, Michael, Sophie, Jette, Wilhelm. Please give my regards to your father. Please give my regards to the housekeeper.

Your   uncle K.

53. *S. K.—December 13, [1841]—Henriette Lund.*[1]

My dear Jette,   December 13.

Berlin.

Your letter of November 25 has arrived safely and I see by its date that it was finished long ago. This pleases me very much, my dear Jette, and if as a result of my letter to her, Sophie should in any way admonish you about writing to me, you know—just as I know—that in a good sense it comes after the fact.

Just as your letter pleased me in its own right, I am also pleased that it is written so neatly and prettily that it almost encourages me to take pains with my own handwriting.

I am writing this letter on an unusual kind of paper—not, however, because I want to make amends for my handwriting but because I know that you have had a birthday while I have been absent from Copenhagen. Had I been in town that day, in all likelihood I would have brought you a little gift. But I cannot do that now. This very day I walked about in Königstrasse and looked at all the beautiful things the merchants display in their windows, but it is always a precarious matter to send such things by post if one really wants them to reach Copenhagen safe and sound. Hence I have given up that plan. Therefore you will please accept my congratulations on a special kind of paper. And is it not true, little Jette, that getting a letter like this from Berlin is quite a remarkable thing for you, one which you at least have never before experienced? I imagine you playing in your living room at home now, and suddenly the doorbell rings, and in steps a man in a red coat with a silver badge on his chest and takes out a lot of letters, and among them there is also one for Jette Lund, and he adds that it costs three *sks.*, whereupon your father kindly advances the three *sks.*; and now you get the letter, and now you are allowed to break the sealing wax yourself, and now you are diligently and carefully trying to read what I am writing to you.

The border around this letter represents three large buildings in Berlin about which you know almost as much as I do. In Berlin there is a place, Unter den Linden, where one may travel at bargain rates in all three parts of the world.[2] With these pictures you will get an even better bargain in your own living room at home and be able to travel in Berlin. From the drawing you will see that in front of the museum there are some trees. It is a rather poor little park. But close by the door of the museum there is a gigantic stone basin, much larger than the one you see every day at the fountain in Gammel Torv. It is made of stone but is as smooth as a mirror and very beautiful.

You tell me, as I have already learned from all the letters from the little correspondence club, that Troels Lund[3] has become engaged. I have been waiting for your letter in order to give you the opportunity to congratulate him on my behalf.

Dear Jette, please accept my greetings, and also accept my greetings to Henrich, Michael, Carl, Sophie, Wilhelm,[4]

from your uncle.   S. K.

54. *S. K.—December 14, [1841]—Emil Boesen.*

My dear Emil,   December 14.
Thank you for your letter, and shame on you for letting me wait so long. After all, it has been almost a month. Furthermore, as my bootblack had mailed it for me, I was afraid that

he had been responsible in some manner for its not reaching you. But when he assured me repeatedly that he had indeed taken care of it, I was left in my solitude to pour out my faithful Danish heart in Danish on the subject of Danish faithlessness; I would even have written you a sermon upon this text: "I have learned to have abundance and to do without."[1] This sermon would presumably have contained a multitude of lies, in which all preternatural moods abound, among them the fundamental lie that I had learned to do without a letter from you. True enough, a letter is not a conversation, and the only thing I can say I miss now and then are my *colloquia*. How good it was to talk myself out once in a while, but, as you know, I need a rather long time for that even though I talk fast. Still, a letter always means a lot, especially when it is the only means of communication.

Should I tell you that you are fortune's child in finding news that is of interest to me, or should I admire your talent? Bærentzen,[2] the painter, must be a good source. One of the daughters there was also engaged; her fiancé left and let it be rumored that he had died (but be very discreet with this story, for the person in question probably still knows no better than that he is dead). But inasmuch as that young girl whose name I will not mention declines an invitation, then perhaps I ought to see genuine tact in this, proof that she fears to walk arm in arm with companions in misfortune, and that is good. That her family hates me is good. That was my plan, just as it was also my plan that she, if possible, be able to hate me. She does not know how much she owes me on that score, and I have left nothing untried (from which you may conclude that a good deal of what the family says is true), and I intend to go on leaving nothing untried. Even here in Berlin, my unfortunately all too inventive brain has not been able to refrain from planning this or that. She must either love me or hate me; she knows no third way. Nor is there anything more corrupting for a young girl than the stages in between. If she suspected how subtly everything was planned, after I had convinced [her] that it had to be broken, well then—then she would probably be right in seeing proof in it that I loved her. I have almost sacrificed my good name and reputation for her sake. For that was why I was defiant, that was why I spent two weeks in Copenhagen outdoing myself in effrontery, that is why I shall always try to appear in such a light that she may truly succeed in having me in her power. Believe me, I know how to be consistent.—But meanwhile please continue to provide me with whatever news you can find out about her.—

You seem to be afraid that I want to consign you to the idyllic, not as a place for frolicking but for grazing and grubbing about in the pond. How could you get such an idea? Have I not said and written that you are consigned to yourself, which is precisely why you can frolic about lyrically on your own, do whatever you want with the world, forget it, remember it, hate it, love it. Be glad that no other human destiny is tied to yours. Get into your kayak (surely you know those Greenland boats), put on your swimming suit, and be off with you to the ocean of the world. But that is certainly no idyll. If you cannot forget her, cannot write poetry about her, all right then, set all sails. Become all attentiveness. Let no opportunity to meet her pass you by. Always be on the lookout for the accidental; make use of it. You must be the one who makes it meaningful or the one who reduces it to nothing. If you sense that she wants to draw nearer, then break off, brush her aside; but next time you meet, cast her a meaningful glance. Death and Pestilence! Why all this fuss for the sake of a girl? Still, I want in no way to deny that your position is awkward. In that respect we are opposites. I always seem to behave actively, you passively. You lack one thing which I possess: you have not learned to despise the world, to see how trivial everything is: you break your back lifting its copper coins.

You write that you are gathering material for a new treatise.[3] Last time you were working on a short story. What is the meaning of this? How will it all end? Please be good enough to keep yourself in check a little. You know that I usually say of myself that I started out by biting off more than I could chew, but what are you doing right now?

Finish your short story whatever the cost. Or, and this would be my advice, write some critical essays first, for those are jobs you can finish quickly. I am writing furiously. As of now I have written fourteen printed sheets. Thereby I have completed one part of the treatise which, *volente deo* [God willing], I shall show you some day. This last week I wrote nothing. I am lying fallow, gathering strength, but already I feel something stirring within me. Please show me that you are careful about your tempo, which consists of *ein*, *zwei*, *drei*, etc. (Of course the deepest secrecy must prevail about my writing activity. You must not say a word about it.)

Schelling[4] is lecturing to an extraordinary audience. He claims to have discovered that there are two philosophies, one negative and one positive. Hegel is neither one nor the other; his is a refined Spinozaism. The negative philosophy is given in the philosophy of identity, and he is now about to present the positive and thereby assist scholarship to its true eminence. As you see, there will be promotions for all those with degrees in philosophy. In the future not only the lawyers will be *doctores juris utriusque* [the doctors of civil and canon law]. We, the magisters, are now *magistri philosophiæ utriusque* [the Masters of Arts in both kinds of philosophy], now, but not quite yet, for he has not yet presented the positive philosophy.[5]

By the way, what I write to you concerning this young girl must remain between us, and you must not with a single word in any way interfere with my tactics. What does it matter if people believe that I am a deceiver? I am just as able to study philosophy, write poetry, smoke cigars, and ignore the whole world. After all, I have always made fun of people, and why should I not continue to do so to the last?—Of course I have my painful moments when I regret that I became engaged, not that I broke the engagement. For only by virtue of the fact that I did become engaged to her did she gain any power over me. Had this not been the case, then my philosophy would soon have swept this actuality aside, however beautiful and interesting it was. Now in the event she does gain sufficient strength truly to hate me, it would be an exceedingly curious relationship if I should ever meet her again in this life. If so, I shall take care not to rob her of the sole benefit, which I have done my best to provide her with, for without my assistance she would never have had the strength to hate me. From the remarks you quote in your letter I gather that she must have confided in her sisters. That was what I wanted. For they will now fan the flames, and, while every remark I make is always of such a nature that I may give it another meaning whenever I choose, now that her sisters are her tutors in reading, everything will necessarily be understood as I want it to be understood.

And now, God be with you. Please write soon. My regards to your father and mother. Greetings to Henrich, Michael, Carl, Sophie, Jette, Wilhelm. NB. Please send me *The First Love*[6] in Heiberg's translation as soon as you can. It is in the theater repertoire and is available at Schubothe's;[7] but do not let anyone suspect it is for me.

> Your sincerely devoted
> S. KIERKEGAARD
> [Deleted: Farinelli][8]

[On an enclosed slip:]

I have no time to get married. But here in Berlin there is a singer from Vienna, a *Demoiselle* Schulze. She plays the part of Elvira and bears a striking resemblance to a certain young girl, so deceptive that I was extraordinarily affected to see her in the very part of Elvira.[9] When my wild mood sweeps over me, I am almost tempted to approach her and that not exactly with the "most honorable intentions." Usually it does not matter much about a singer, and she does look like her. It might be a small diversion when I am tired of speculation or sick of thinking about this and that. She lives nearby. Well, probably nothing will come of this. You know so well how I talk that you know what such stuff means, and it means no more now that I am writing about it. But meanwhile I do not want you to mention to anybody that there is such a singer in Berlin, or that she is playing Elvira, or etc.

[*Address:*]
An dem Herrn Cand. theol. E. Boesen
Copenhagen
Philosophgangen.

[*Postmarks:*]
Berlin   Hamburg
12/16 2-3   12/17 4-6

55. *S. K.—December 15, [1841]—F. C. Sibbern.*

Dear Professor: December 15 [*added in pencil:* 1841]
   Today, through my nephew Henrich Lund, I received the
greetings you expressly requested him to convey. I am so
pleased to have those greetings that it would never occur to
me to return my own greetings by the same medium. On the
contrary, I consider them a poetic summons (*poscimur*) to
reply in what may be a rather discursive manner.[1]
   Even now when I cannot personally ascertain it for myself
every day, I have never doubted that you would maintain
some of that interest with which you have always honored
me, especially after Poul Møller's death.[2] Therefore, when I
did not receive greetings of any kind from you until now, I
easily explained this to myself by saying that circumstance
had not brought you into contact with anybody whom you
knew to be writing to me.
   So here I am in Berlin going to lectures. I am attending lectures by Marheineke, Werder, and Schelling.[3] I have heard
Steffens[4] a few times and have also paid my fee to hear him,
but oddly enough, he does not appeal to me at all. And I, who
have read with such great enthusiasm much of what he has
written, *Karrikaturen des Heiligsten*, to mention just one example, I, who had really looked forward to hearing him in order
to ascertain for myself what is usually said about him, that he
is matchless when it comes to monologue—I am utterly disappointed. His delivery seems so uncertain and hesitant that

one begins to question what progress one is making, and when a flash of genius transfigures him, I miss that artistic awareness, that oratorical brilliance I have so often admired in his writings. He lectures on anthropology,[5] but the material is essentially the same as that contained in his published book. So I prefer to read him. But his *Anthropologie* will always make fairly heavy reading for anybody not well versed in the natural sciences. —I am, by the way, sorry to find myself disappointed in this respect. That's why I have not called on him either. On the whole I live as isolated as possible and am withdrawing more and more into myself.

Werder[6] is a virtuoso; that is all one can say about him. I suspect that he must be a Jew, for baptized Jews always distinguish themselves by their virtuosity and of course do participate in all fields nowadays. Like a juggler, he can play and frolic with the most abstract categories and with never so much as a slip of the tongue even though he talks as fast as a horse can run. He is a scholastic in the old sense; as they did in Thomas Aquinas, so he has found in Hegel not only the *summa* and the *summa summae* but the *summa summarum*. In this respect he is almost a psychological phenomenon for me. His life, his thought, the richness of the outside world almost seem meaningful to him only when they have reference to Hegel's *Logik*. It is, however, very advantageous for the young people studying at the University to have such a man.

Schelling[7] lectures to a select, numerous, and yet also an *undique conflatum auditorium* [audience blown together from everywhere]. During the first lectures it was almost a matter of risking one's life to hear him. I have never in my life experienced such uncomfortable crowding—still, what would one not do to be able to hear Schelling? His main point is always that there are two philosophies, one positive and one negative. The negative is given, but not by Hegel, for Hegel's is neither negative nor positive but a refined Spinozaism. The positive is yet to come. In other words, in the future it will not be only the lawyers who become the doctors of civil and canon law [*doctores juris utriusque*], for I venture to flatter myself that without submitting another dissertation I shall become a *magister philosophiae utriusque* [Master of Arts in both kinds of philosophy].

The longer I live here in Berlin the more I realize the truth of the advice you have given me again and again out of regard for both me and my dissertation: that it be translated into German. I will wait and see about that. If it does happen, I can honestly say that you are responsible. If any good comes of this, it will be a pleasure for me to think that in this I have once more an occasion to thank you.

Berlin is probably the only place in Germany worth visiting for scholarly reasons. Therefore I really hope to benefit from this semester. The stay here is helping me to concentrate and limit myself. Otherwise, God be praised, I am fairly well. From my native country I hear little. The Danes here do get the newspapers, but I do not read them as I do not have enough time, yet time enough and time sufficient to think about a man like you, dear Professor, who by your conduct towards me have always obliged me and entitled me to call myself

Your devoted
S. KIERKEGAARD.

[*Address:*]
An dem Herrn Prof. Dr. Sibbern
Ritter der D.O., *und* D.M.
Copenhagen

[*Postmark:*]
Berlin
12/16 2-3.

56. *S. K.—[towards the end of 1841]—Henriette Lund.*

My dear Jette,

You hope that I will forgive you your silence, and your hope shall not be in vain, all the more so because in the letter in which you tell me of that hope, in that very letter you assure yourself of it and make impossible for me what would otherwise have been impossible anyway.

I am glad the little scarf pleases you. You may thank Miss Dencker[1] for its being a "pretty little scarf," and you may thank Henrich for its coming as an agreeable surprise. From this you will see, my dear Jette, not only how much I want to do you a favor but also how willingly everyone lends me a helping hand. I know that you would also do the same if I were in need of your assistance to surprise any of the others. Perhaps you would almost prefer to be the one to assist me in giving pleasure to somebody else rather than be the object yourself of the combined efforts by me and the others. And that is as it should be, and it is indeed a beautiful secret when everybody may thus be made happy at the same time, even though in different ways.

A letter from Michael informs me that you have not been altogether well, but as you yourself do not mention this, I conclude that it cannot have been very serious.

My time is pretty well taken up, especially since *Geheimeraad*[2] Schelling is pleased to lecture for two hours every day, giving me much to attend to. That is why you are getting a brief reply from me. If this seems to you to be a change, yet that which I consider the principal object of a correspondence will remain unchanged: my greetings. My dear Jette, please convey my greetings to H., M., C., S., W.,[3] and accept my greetings for yourself.

Your uncle.

57. *S. K.—[autumn 1841]—Wilhelm Lund.*

My dear Wilhelm,

In your case there cannot as with Jette be a question of the non-arrival of a reply. Your reply was unexpected, but it is no less welcome on that account. That is the way to do it, my good Wilhelm! If you consider it an honor to write to me, why should you be excluded? If you consider it a task, why should you not be considered as capable of it as the others?

After all, you write neatly, clearly, and grammatically correctly except for a few errors (for example, you wrote: reladed[1]—you are probably well acquainted with the meaning of that double underlining). But we two have something to talk about, for like you I spend a good part of my day on the schoolbench, do not have afternoons off, nor even dancing and gymnastic lessons.

I was pleased with your letter not merely for its own sake but for its contents. You do not send love from H., M., C., S., J., but you do send greetings from Christian, Peder, and Ferdinand. Thank you for that. Hereby appointing you the *dux* [leader] of the class, I authorize you to greet them in return, and you may do so in whatever manner you please. I suppose you play soldiers with them now and then, and so take the opportunity to make them fall in line, and then deliver my greetings with the dignity of a general. Or you may use my name as the password of the day, for as you know, such a little word is also used in peacetime. Do as you please; when one is as far away as I am, one must depend on the inventiveness of others. Please give my greetings to Christian, Peder, and Ferdinand, and accept my love, dear Wilhelm, for yourself.

Your uncle.

58. *S. K.—[December 28, 1841]—Michael Lund*.

My dear Michael,

Your letter arrived safely some time ago. I say "some time ago," for several days have already gone by, and contrary to habit, I have not replied at once. My address is now 57 Jägerstrasse and you are hereby authorized and urged to bring this news forcefully to the attention of everybody concerned. By "everybody concerned" I mean not only the little coachman's guild[1] of which you are so fortunate as to be an honored member, but also Uncle Peter and Emil Boesen.

Per tot discrimina rerum [after so many dangerous troubles] I have, then, like unlucky game pursued by a cunning keeper, escaped to Jägerstrasse.[2] I hope the name of the street is not an unlucky omen. As is appropriate for a poet, I thrust you roughly *in medias res*, and as is typical for me, I tear you away from it just as precipitately, because presumably it cannot interest you.

I assume that you had a Merry Christmas and trust that my modest contribution played some part in your merriment. Please let the next person who writes to me describe how you celebrated this festive season. Here in Berlin all the Danes, whose number is as incredible as that of the grasshoppers in Egypt,[3] gathered for supper at the Belvedere, where we usually eat. We especially tried to cheer ourselves up and to bring back memories of home by eating apple dumplings. We also had a Christmas tree, and I believe I found as many presents on it as I have had delivered to you. The proprietress at the Belvedere is Danish and she honored us with her company for a few moments. She has a little daughter who also understands a bit of Danish. I enjoy seeing her once in a while and speaking a few words with her.

There are plenty of exhibitions in Berlin. The entrance fee is five silver groschen, which is always plenty for what one gets to see. Faust's *Wintergarten* plays an important part in the imagination of the people of Berlin. One Berliner said that it was really *grossartig* [splendid].[4] But that I cannot say. As the conscientious traveler should, I have of course also paid my entrance fee in order to see—and to see that there was not very much to be seen. It is a two-story building on the ground floor of which there are a lot of big trees, oranges, etc.; lamps have been hung in the trees, and upstairs there are little refreshment rooms where the Berliners amuse themselves *göttlich* [divinely]. In a few places Tyroleans play and sing.

You may already have been spoiled by my punctuality and may have grown lean with impatience over not having had a reply to your letter. Now please see to it, my dear Michael, that you grow fat again, and do not always depend on my being so punctual. I have a lot to do and must write to five, while the five or six of you continue to have only one.

Happy New Year, my dear M. Happy New Year to H., C., S., J., W. This letter will probably reach you New Year's Eve.

My love to you and the others.

from Your uncle.

[*Address:*]
An dem Herrn Michael Lund
Copenhagen
Store Kjøbmagergade 7

[*Postmarks:*]
Berlin 12/28 2-3
Hamburg 12/30

59. *S. K.—December 31, 1841—Carl Lund.*

My dear Carl,　　　　　　　　　　December 31, 1841.

Your letter has arrived safely, and I see from it that in the "Bryn"[1] establishment (alias the Brønd establishment) a number of shops have opened. We have plenty of those in Berlin. Otherwise there is no news from Copenhagen.

If I wanted to answer you in the same way in which you wrote to me, then I would end my letter at just about this point. Is this worthy of a rational creature in shirt and pants, especially during vacation? Or would you perhaps have written at greater length if you were still wearing a smock? And just because your coattails are presumably not very long, is this any reason for your letters not to be so? Just write freely about whatever occurs to you; do not be shy. Your letters are always welcome, and indeed all the more welcome the more I see on the one hand that you consider it an honor that the task of writing to me has been entrusted to you as well,[2] and on the other that you take pleasure in doing so.

From my letter to Michael[3] you will have learned that I have moved. The change is in all ways for the better. But regardless of the fact that the change is so complete, one thing is as good as unchanged and that is my bootblack, I mean my new bootblack, who in appearance is exactly like the old one: a big, stout, Royal Prussian, serious man, as was the former, but in addition a very careful and attentive man, as the former was not.

You probably had many presents on the Christmas tree. Please tell me next time what you got and among other things, what came from me, for I do hope you have received it.

Here in Berlin everything, even the weather, is regimented. We had indescribably bad weather on Christmas Day and especially the day after. Today, New Year's Day, it has really begun to freeze for the first time, and that is also as it should be. I suppose there has already been frost in Copenhagen for a long time, and by now you must have been out on the ice several times. All that kind of thing interests me. This you might tell me about.

Take care of yourself in the new year, my dear Carl. I send you good wishes and greetings, and please give my regards to H., M., S., W., J. from

Your uncle.

60. *S. K.—January 1, 1842—Emil Boesen.*

My dear Emil,   January 1, '42.
Happy New Year! Thank you for the old one. Thank you for your letter, which in a manner of speaking belongs to both, since I received it in the old and reply in the new.

However, please permit me to make a general remark concerning your handwriting. You write so illegibly that it is terrible. Each letter flows so indistinctly into the next that everything flows together, but such a confluence is not the total impression one might wish.

You ask whether my Elvira[1] is just as interesting close up. In a way I am somewhat closer to being able to answer that question, for this evening I sat in a box unusually close to the stage. You may be dissatisfied with this answer, but I can say no more. Besides, one ought not to make light of such matters, for it is well known that passion has its own special dialectic.

Incidentally, with respect to that affair in which I play the leading role in a manner of speaking (I refer to the one in Copenhagen), it was not terminated in this way, as you surely realize. I have certainly acted responsibly, or perhaps more correctly, chivalrously, and only to that extent perhaps irresponsibly. Surely you understand that I did not intend to make her unhappy. I have never told a single person how the whole business really fits together nor what my intention was. I shall certainly not readily forget that you have been decent enough not to pry, decent enough to remain steadfast, to believe even though you could not understand. In spite of all the attacks by the world, which have left me unaffected, or have merely brought a smile to my lips or a sarcasm, you have always been far closer to my true self, for you admonished me constantly to be more considerate of myself. From this it was clear to me that although you could not really figure the whole thing out, certainly you would never accuse me of [*deleted*: exaggerated] egoism but rather of exaggerated sympathy. Not even to you have I wanted to express myself, because I did not consider the matter as settled in any way, and my chivalry forbids me to speak to a third party about my true relationship with a girl. I see from one of your previous letters that she has apparently confided in her sisters. That is her affair. This can neither tempt me to become annoyed with her nor to follow her example, not to the former because in a certain sense I might want it this way, nor to the latter because I am always myself. Through me she has gained a power over me that she never would have gained on her own; I have confided in her the means most likely to bind me, and I have permitted her to employ those means against me. Certainly I need not have done all this, and yet in no way do I regret it. It is and always will be a difficult matter to understand my motives, for I have, perhaps unfortunately, such mastery over my feelings when I want to conceal them that my motives are not easily discovered. It was never my intention to leave her standing between 11 and 5 o'clock[2] for the rest of her life. If she can hate me, so be it, then she is saved, speaking in human terms. She does not know and never will be told that she may thank me for this. If she cannot, if she still has a glimmering of hope, so be it, then we shall wait and see. I intend to find out about it personally when I have the chance. As I said in a previous letter: to deceive the whole world is a matter of indifference to me, but honestly I do not pride myself on deceiving a young girl. To allow her to sense my enormously tempestuous life and its pains and then to say to her, "Because of this I leave you," that would have been to crush her. It would have been contemptible to introduce her to my griefs and then not be willing to help her bear the impact of them. She is proud; so is her family in the highest degree. To awaken that in her, to throw her into the arms of her family, to arrange everything so that she came to interpret it as desperate, was the only possible thing to do. To do it is not so easy, and I dare say that my practiced dissembling, my familiarity with passion, etc. are required for it.—This is as much as I shall tell you. I cannot and I will not go into detail here. You have been faithful to me when you really knew nothing and you will surely be no less so now that you see that I, insofar as I think I dare, am opening myself to you. Of course my letters to all other people seem to come from a very different quarter, which is to say that they do not mention her and are always written with cheerful exuberance, with all possible irony. Whatever I want to hide, I hide, and not even absence and all sorts of mixed feelings produced by absence, etc., can manage to pry me open. I confide only in you. I am used to doing that and I depend on your silence. For heaven's sake do not say a word to anybody about what I have written here; at the same time I also want to ask you to forgive me for not having told you or written you about it earlier. Once when I was talking with you I dropped a few veiled hints, which you certainly noticed but did not heed sufficiently. I must act as best I can. I confide in no one but you, because I know you can be silent. Suppose some outsider knew my feelings, then all would presumably be lost. Then I would not find out whether she is capable of hating me. I am not now nor have I ever been the issue. That is what you really reproach me for, but let that be. I am accustomed to mastering my feelings, and they must be silent. I am working, and so, period. I will only say this, that I shall never do anything for her out of pity; she is too good to be treated with pity. Silence! I do understand if you are not really surprised by what I am writing you. If you have anything to say, please write, for you are and always will remain the only person who has a seat and a vote in the council of my many and various thoughts. Write vigorously—and legibly—and quickly—

You ask what I am working on. Answer: it would take too long to tell you now. Only this much: it is the further development of Either Or.

Be strong, my dear Emil! Far be it from me to present myself as a model; but please believe me, I have many sorrows, many difficult moments, but I have not yet despaired. However, the time will come when I must drop the mask before the world as well, must reveal what dwells within me. Surely this will not be a period without trial and tribulation. With God's help I am not afraid of it. But it was also necessary that I stand alone so that the person in question would first get another impression of me.

Once more, be strong! You have asked me to sustain you. That I cannot do, nor is it perhaps necessary, but still my letters cannot weaken you.

Remember me to your father and mother. My greetings to you, my dear Emil.   Your   S. K.

My address is 57 Jägerstrasse, second floor. It would take too long and be too boring to tell you of all the plagues I have suffered with my fraudulent landlord. Now I am living in a good place, spaciously and elegantly, with the French doors open to my sitting room, and, God be praised, as always, open to my mind as well.

[*Address*:]
An dem Herrn Cand. theol. Emil Boesen.
Copenhagen
Philosophgangen.[3]

[*Postmarks*:]
Berlin   Hamburg
1/2 2–3   1/4

61. *S. K.—January 8, 1842—P. J. Spang.*

Dear Pastor Spang,   January 8, 1842.

Happy New Year! *Item* [Further], I wish for you that the sum of your uncertain income may be in direct proportion to my letters but otherwise be as different as possible from them. For my letters resemble uncertain income, do they not? Uncertain they are, that you will not deny; income they are, but so uncertain that one easily becomes uncertain (is this not true?) whether it is an income—so one may call this uncertain income. In this respect I hope that your uncertain income may not resemble my letters. On the other hand, it is possible that you were not expecting another letter from me now. In this respect I hope that the uncertain income may resemble my letters.

I have been sitting at home all morning, have read several learned and curious pamphlets, it is almost one o'clock, I shall not eat my dinner until a quarter to two, I have put my book aside and lit a cigar, and then it occurs to me that it might be an opportune moment to pay a visit to Pastor Spang. The scene remains, I regret to say, not your room but mine. This is the vantage point from which you must view my letter and all my other letters. In this respect I believe that I am a fairly good correspondent: my letters have all sorts of beneficial negative characteristics, and when you see my seal on a letter you are quite safe in accepting it. When postage on a letter has not been paid, one may occasionally be at a loss as to whether or not the post office should be allowed to keep it, whether its contents are worth the expense.—I always pay the postage, and in this I not only attempt to model myself after but even to outdo that great sage Socrates, who never accepted a fee for his tutorials. I say that I outdo him, although this is really incorrect, for I [outdo] his ideality merely by putting out money; for inasmuch as what I have to say cannot be compared with what Socrates had to say, I would not only [not] outdo him but not even model myself after him, if I were to apply the same criterion. In other words, I outdo him in that I do put out money, but this outdoing is really only an expression of my attempt to imitate. God knows whether my efforts in that respect will succeed and if I do not get off all too easily merely by paying the postage.—Everybody knows the trouble with paying the postage, but experienced people like you and me know yet another. When I receive a letter, even one with postage paid, but about which I judge or sense that it is a letter that will require a reply, then I am easily at a loss, and presumably it is the same with you: do you want to accept it or would it not be better to let the post office keep it? As the world becomes more civilized, I imagine it will become customary to be permitted to inspect the letters in order to see whether or not they require a reply, and thereupon to decide whether or not one wishes to accept them. Or one might introduce a stamp to be placed on the outside of envelopes. My letters also have this negative characteristic: they do not require a reply, and thus you may safely accept them.

As you see, my journey is developing and educating me; as you see, a great change has taken place in me, to wit: I remain unalterably the same.

"What news?"—you might presumably ask. We do not have much literary news except for Schelling's performance, which still continues unceasingly to maintain the interest of novelty. The second volume of Hegel's encyclopedia[1] has just been published, and Michelet has taken the liberty of writing a preface without showing it to the Society.[2] In it he attacks Schelling fairly sharply. This occurred just before Christmas. I had expected Schelling, who is very polemical in his lectures, to drop a few remarks about him, but this has not happened. Schelling's position is not a comfortable one. He has become involved with Court interests, which makes his conduct rather detested and is, of course, as is every external consideration, detrimental at all times. The Hegelians are fanning the flames. Schelling looks as sour as a vinegar brewer. To get an idea of his personal indignation you need only hear him say, *"Ich werde morgen fortfahren"* [I shall continue tomorrow]. (Unlike the Berliners who pronounce the *g* as a very soft *g*, he pronounces it as a very hard *k*: *morken*.) The other day he was half an hour late. Jacob von Thyboe[3] cannot have made a more terrible face at the siege of Amsterdam than

Schelling did as he vented his anger in a number of attacks upon the management of Berlin because there are no public clocks. In order to make up for it he wanted to lecture a little past the hour. That is not tolerated in Berlin, and there was scraping and hissing. Schelling became furious and exclaimed, "If my audience of gentlemen object to my lecturing, I should be glad to stop. *Ich werde morken fortfahren.*" Such little incidents are trivial, but what I write is trivial as well.—In a letter it is impossible to give any idea of his doctrine and the modifications his system of identity has acquired.

Werder[4] juggles with the categories as the strong man in Dyrehaven juggles with balls weighing twenty, thirty, forty pounds. It is terrifying to watch, and as in Dyrehaven one is sometimes tempted to believe they are paper balls. He is not only a philosopher but a poet as well. He has written a monstrously long play called *Christopher Columbus*,[5] and notwithstanding the censor's having deleted 600 lines, it still lasts from 5:30 to 10 p.m. In another sense as well it lasts even longer, for it spans fourteen years, and that being so, one should praise his brevity. It was performed for the first time last night, but it was impossible to get a ticket.

My time is up, and I do have Werder's example warning me to strive for brevity.

I am in good health, and from the bottom of my heart I wish you the same. If it should seem to you at some point that the door to your room were opening and as if my thin self with my thin stick were entering, then please permit this little letter to constitute an attempt to recompense you for a moment, if for a moment you should miss something because the door did not open. In any case, let this little letter be tangible proof that I exist, and that I think of you, and that I remain

Your devoted
S. KIERKEGAARD.

62. *S. K.—January 16, [1842]—Emil Boesen.*

My dear Emil,   Jan. 16, 1842
    Your letter arrived and was welcome, as is everything that
comes from you. However, there is something in it that I do
not understand, something that shows that you do not understand me. You say that there was conflict and discord in my
letter, but in what way I do not know. My view is unchanged, inflexibly unchanged, the same as it was that day,
the date of which I do not remember, and even long before
then. If you can succeed in showing me any deviation in my
compass or demonstrate that any faint puff of air, any squall,
or any mood has rippled the surface of my soul, let alone
stirred its depths, then I will pledge myself to give you not
only the gold of Peru but the girl you love into the bargain.
The matter remains unchanged. Just as strongly as I feel that I
am an exceptional lover, I also know very well that I would
be a bad husband and always will remain so. It is all the more
unfortunate that the former is always or usually in inverse
proportion to the latter. I am capable of tempting a girl, of
making an impression on her, and that I have done altogether
too often here [*may be read as*: formerly]. Her soul must have
acquired resilience through contact with me, and I dare say
that for a young girl it cannot have been a joking matter to
have contended with me. Either this resilience must elevate
her higher than she would ever have risen otherwise—and
that will happen if she is able to hate me; everything has been
directed towards that—or it will bring her down. If so, I stand
prepared, even if I am a bad husband and even if my soul is
preoccupied with far too many other things, for then she will
be just as well off with me. In saying this I am not under-
estimating myself, but my spiritual life and my importance as
a husband are irreconcilable entities.
    But you go on to ask if her image looms before me again.
Death and Pestilence! Would you make me a child once more
as if I did not know what I want, one who sits and sings in the
dark and sees ghosts and is afraid? Did I not tell you in my very
first letter that forgetting her is still out of the question? As

yet I have neither taken out the stylus of oblivion in order to efface, nor have I mixed the colors on my poet's palette in order to paint a portrait of recollection for myself. That I will not do; that would be irresponsible. I am not the issue. I realize very well what I have possessed, and my spirit is not yet extinct, my soul is not yet powerless, my thoughts still abound. I will certainly persevere, but she is the issue and how she takes it. That remains to be seen before I place the final period. And what is it you want now? Should I now vacillate, should I now fear that the effect of the broken engagement could not be overcome if she were to return to me? I do not fear that kind of thing, and moreover I am not permitting her to return because of promises of gold and greenwoods. There will always be enough pain, but I am only saying that she will be better off than if standing alone. I do not ask for more than that. I have far too much sense of and reverence for what stirs in a human being not to guard it with just as much esthetic as ethical earnestness. Therefore, get thee far behind me with such notions as that of her image probably looming before me again. You are not (I think you will agree with me and not be offended by my saying it) accustomed to holding your life poetically in your hand the way I am. So far I have managed that, and I still do so. Until now there has been no deviation. Everything has been so directed that she will come to see me as a deceiver; if this succeeds, then she has been helped, then she is afloat once more. But if she cannot do so, then I always have a ship at sea with a captain who knows his duty very well. I do not regret what has happened, and if you are able by the harshest torture to wring a single groan of that kind out of my letter, then in the future you may smile at my childishness. I do not regret it, least of all for my own sake. You ought to know enough about my relationship to be able to see the consistency with which I have steered towards the point where I now am. My life divides itself into chapters, and I can provide an exact heading for each as well as state its motto. For the present it proclaims: "She must hate me." No human being has been permitted to probe too deeply, and in the unanimous condemnation of the town you also see that I have proof that I acted correctly. I shall only give you one little example to convince you that I am the same. In the company of the Danes here in Berlin I am always cheerful, merry, gay, and have "the time of my life," etc. And even though everything churns inside me so that it sometimes seems that my feelings, like water, will break the ice with which I have covered myself, and even though there is at times a groan within me, each groan is instantly transformed into something ironical, a witticism, etc., the moment anybody else is present. I do this partly because I never became used to grabbing other people by the arm, and partly because my plan demands it. Here a groan which might, after all, possibly mean something entirely different, might reach the ear of a Dane, he might write home about it, she might possibly hear of it, it might possibly damage the transitional process, the result of which I intend to ascertain for myself in the fullness of time. Do you already see the great difficulty here? I must decide when that time is, however difficult it may be here once more to steer between the esthetic and ethical in the world. I have been ill; that is to say, I have had a lot of rheumatic headaches and have often not slept at night. I could call a doctor; perhaps something might be done about it. But if I called a doctor, the Danes would know about it at once. Perhaps it might occur to one of them to write home, it might reach her ear, it might be disturbing—ergo, I do not call a doctor, and I feel better because I remain faithful to my principle, and in spite of all his skill a doctor might do me harm because I would come into conflict with my principle. Do I need to feel ashamed when I compare myself with other people? Do I need to blush when I claim to know how to act and how to act consistently? What is more, I lack diversion. Absence from home practically always makes an impression on a person, and especially so under such utterly singular circumstances. The last day before I left, you accompanied me and got some idea of the many kinds of enjoyment always at my disposal. In Berlin I have nothing of the kind. I miss my hired coachman, my servant, my comfortable landau, my light-hearted flight through the lovely regions of our

Sjælland, the merry smiles of the young girls, which I knew how to turn to my advantage without doing them any harm. I am working hard. My body cannot stand it. So that you may see that I am the same, I shall tell you that I have again written a major section of a piece, "Either/Or." It has not gone very quickly, but that is due to its not being an expository work, but one of pure invention, which in a very special way demands that one be in the mood. I hold my life poetically in my hand, but from this follows that which I cannot get away from: that between two poetic possibilities there lies a third, that of actuality and contingency. Suppose she were taken ill. I have weighed that eventuality carefully, and obviously illness cannot be taken into account when it is a question of an entire life, but still this is a very special matter. But please note once more how faithful I am to my principle. I thought this matter over before I left home; a golden key opens all doors, and I believe you know that I understand the uses of money. For a moment it occurred to me that here again I might attempt bribery. It would have been easy for me. Moreover there was one person who I was certain could provide me with absolutely reliable information, but then I would have had to show him my hand. I dare not do that, and accordingly I remained faithful to my principle. You are the only one from whom I get an occasional bit of information about this affair, and surely you cannot complain that I am impatient in demanding it of you. And yet it is the only thing of importance at the moment. As to the rest, only I myself can gather the intelligence.

I hope you see that it provides an occasion for misunderstanding when you bring your own love affair into this. I know nothing of these sentimental palpitations. My relationship with her has a far different reality from that and has been appealed to a far more exalted forum, and if I had not had the courage myself to bring the case before that forum, I would consider myself a soft, esthetic, semi-human person, a worm. For it would be terrible to play for such high stakes merely because of a whim. Apparently you are a novice: you have feeling, I have passion. But my understanding is enthroned

above my passion; yet in its turn my understanding is passion. Here let me draw my sword from its scabbard. Is it
seemly to devote oneself in this manner to feeling? I do not
understand you. Once a girl has made such a strong impression on me as she has on you, then I declare war, and then I
am in my element, and war itself is my delight. That a girl
should be unconquerable, that thought has never yet been entertained in my recalcitrant, if you will, or proud head. Do
you not hear martial music, is not your soul all emotion? —It
is incomprehensible. And moreover, is not the world open to
you? My Emil, do learn a little from my example. Or do you
have the *idée fixe* that this girl can only be happy with you?—
eh bien! Still, you have no responsibility. Imagine what it
means to have lured a girl out into the mainstream and now to
be sitting and waiting to see how it will end. Should I not
have sunk deep into the earth; and yet I carry my head high.
And what are you doing to banish [*may be read as*: change] it?
Are you working, writing poetry, exposing your breast to
danger? You want to get away. There is no worse way. I
knew that before I went abroad, and I would not have gone if
it had not been out of consideration for her. I would have
spent the winter in Copenhagen. In the first place I wanted to
meet public opinion head on, and I believe that my presence
would have meant a lot, and second, I was aware of that
which we already spoke about at the time, that such a stay
might well have its own difficulties. But if the whole thing
was to have any meaning for her, I had to leave; ergo, I left. I
keep watch over myself. No miser could brood more anxiously over his treasure. I watch every word, every facial expression, every *Anspielung* [allusion]. Moreover, I keep up
my interest in scholarship, in art, and even—with God's
help—in my own productivity. That is the way things stand
with me, and so they must remain until the moment arrives.
As far as I am concerned, then, it cannot be a question of my
calming down, for I am calm; but, as there is a point outside
myself, I must wait for it to be clarified. I could of course fling
myself into my carriage at once and travel to Copenhagen and
see for myself, but I will not do that. It makes it all the worse

that Schelling's most recent lectures have not been of much significance. That being so, I could very well do it, but I will not do it because I do not want to, because it would only make me lose confidence in myself if I were to do it prior to the moment I decided upon when I left home. In this respect as well I have special signs to go by. Incidentally, I could wish I had my papers with me, for I do miss them also. What I have written here up to now is probably not bad, and I believe it will find favor in your eyes. So I also long, as St. Paul says, to present my charismatic gift to you. My Emil, would that I could shout these words so loudly that I might summon you from the hyperborean twilight of soul in which you live. And if you were to lose this girl now, is there then nothing else for you to do? That is the way it usually is for a young girl, but you, you can work, can bring joy to others, can fetch old and new things from your storeroom, can comfort; in short, you can become a pastor, and that is the only thing worth the trouble in this world. Note in this also my own misfortune, imagine the tempests that I have to endure, now more than ever, and now more than ever without having deserved them. For I have wanted to keep her out of this, too, not because of excessive stress, but for far more profound reasons.

Here you have my contribution in this matter. It will have to suffice; I can say no more. When that moment arrives when I say "Period," I shall tell you more, but I never communicate what does not belong to me. I know my own nature, and I have betrayed to her how one gains power over me. I did it painstakingly, and it would have been easy to prevent. But I do not want to steal away from it, for I have not wanted to provide myself with an opportunity for self-deception.

So you want to become a missionary? And you do not wish me to dismiss the matter lightly. All right then, why do you want to be one? If it is for your own peace of mind, I dare say that would be a most indefensible reason, and it does not exactly give one an idea of what is called "the call," for then one ought rather to say, "Physician, heal thyself." Or is it for the sake of others? To be honest, I do not believe it. You who are still suffering from such an affair, you would hardly be up to that. If you want to get away, all right then, travel, but do not take upon yourself such a serious responsibility. Or is it a legitimation, as though one could do no less? Am I right? If it offends you to have me speak like this, please forget it is I, imagine an older person, think of everything that might distort the impression of my words as separate from me, and retain only my friendship and its influence. Travel, if you want to; my purse is always open to you. But above all, work, set yourself a definite goal, and stick to it. If you so desire, I shall be happy to renounce my authority to say this, but it is nonetheless true.

You are getting a fairly long letter from me. I wanted to correct your ideas about me. I am glad to learn from your letter that she is well; that she is cheerful is an ambiguous matter. The Olsen household has great ability in dissimulation, and surely association with me has not diminished that virtuosity.

And now, my dear Emil, my greetings, my friendship, my devotion to you. I sing that little song from *The White Lady*[1] (the tenant farmer's lines to the officer at the very beginning): "Take my hand, take my hand; in this breast dwells honesty."

Greetings to your father and mother.
Your S. K.

I do not need to tell you that in regard to all my letters the deepest secrecy must prevail.

[*Address:*]
An dem Herrn Cand. theol. E. Boesen
Copenhagen
Philosophgangen

[*Postmarks:*]
Hamburg   Berlin
1/18   1/17 2-3

63. *S. K.—January 16, 1842—Michael Lund.*

My dear Michael,[1]   January 16, '42.

Your letter has arrived safely, and I am beginning my reply on this page because an artist has let *das unvordenkliche Seyn, das allem Denken zuvorkommt* [the unimaginable being that precedes all thinking] precede. As you probably do not understand what I mean, please be good enough to show this quotation to Uncle Peter and tell him that it is *Geheimeraad* Schelling's favorite expression and that I hope that on the basis of this he will be able to imagine the progress S. believes he has made beyond the philosophy of identity.

I am glad that the Christmas present selected for you after careful deliberation has arrived safely and that you are pleased with it. My wish, which should have accompanied the present, comes somewhat late, but I hope in time it will catch up with it, for you did get quite solid things. —Please accept my thanks for having promptly notified Uncle Peter and E. B.[2] of my new address. I am glad to know that when I ask for help from my good Michael, I ask for help from a reliable person.

After some days of terrible cold we now have beautiful winter weather, and just as the cold then was of a severity I have not experienced in Copenhagen, so these last days have been more pleasant than winter days in Copenhagen.

We ride in sleighs, which is delightful. Coaches and almost all carriages are converted to sleighs, although usually so short-legged that they look ridiculous.

Were the Christmas holidays so devoid of pleasure for my good Michael that he does not have some little event to tell me about? May I remind him that it is always beneficial to practice writing about some event and that in this I am a good correspondent, because I am interested in the same things as he.

Did either you or Henrich speak with Prof. Sibbern[3] during the holidays? Please find out if he has received a letter from me.

Did Jette not get my letter? At any rate I have not seen a

reply from her. Please tell the next one who writes me to let me know about this.

Take care of yourself, my dear Michael. Please convey that with which I entrust you: greetings to H., C., S., W., J., and accept what you may keep for yourself, my greeting to you

from

Your uncle.

[*Address*:]
An dem Herrn Michael Lund
Copenhagen
7 Store Kjøbmagergade.

[*Postmarks*:]

Berlin	Hamburg
1/16 2–3	1/18

64. *S. K.—January 22, 1842—Sophie Lund*.

My dear Sophie,   January 22, '42
Your letter of the fifteenth has arrived safely, and I gather from it that "you are almost ready to go to a ball," but what I do not gather, or rather, do not quite understand is how you can add "that you cannot allow this occasion to pass without thanking me, etc." Is the moment before a ball such an opportune occasion to write me? Or do you thereby mean to tell me that you thought it would be great fun if I were now to walk in the door and see you in your dancing finery? Enough of this. I am pleased that you used the occasion, just as I also hope the occasion caused you no inconvenience, such as, for example, getting ink too close to your white dress, etc. So you went to a ball! If I had been present on that *occasion*, then I might, just as you were walking out the door, have said, "Be careful! See to it that your back is straight and upright, not leaning to either side!" It is too late now, but perhaps you will go to other balls.

So you are the person from whom one may get news, and I am glad of that. Sibbern did get my letter[1] after all.

I hope you had a good time at Mrs. Eckard's ball, and I hope for you that it is not the last.

Take care of yourself, my dear Sophie. My affectionate greetings.

Your uncle.

65. *S. K.—January 22, 1842—Carl Lund.*

My dear Carl, [*Written on the back of a letter to Sophie Lund.*]

You write that you cannot thank me enough for the two books; I am so pleased, for then there will always be some portion left for me after Henrich has received his share, for he chose them. I was not particularly lucky with the New Year's present I intended to give myself. For a long time I had in passing admired a slender cane in a wood turner's shopwindow, but I could not really make up my mind to buy it. One day my desire finally reached such heights that I entered the shop. What happens next is that in closing the door I smash a large pane of glass, whereupon I decided to pay for the pane and not buy the stick.

I am happy to see that your letter is a little more discursive than last time. Usually one does not encourage a writer to be discursive, but in your case I must continue to urge it.

My bootblack (not my "bootblak") is well and most likely would be even better if he knew you were asking how he was.

"You must owing to lack of time finish your letter as my devoted nephew." This phrase is not felicitous, and I am convinced that it is not only when you are in a tight spot that you will continue to be that.

Although it does not freeze very hard here, it freezes steadily, so the skaters can always have what they want. I suppose it is the same with you, and although you are not yet an artist, you are nevertheless an "amateur" and an admirer of Henrich and Michael (Not "Micarl").

Because the border around this letter will probably appeal

to you, I have arranged it so that you will be able to cut it out.[1]

Take care of yourself, my dear Carl. My affectionate greetings.

Your uncle.

66. *Else Pedersdatter Kierkegaard—January 24, 1842—*
P. C. Kierkegaard and S. K. [1]

Sædding, January 24, 1842

The Honorable and Learned
Gentlemen

P. Ch. Kierkegaard	and	S. A. Kierkegaard
Doctor.		Magister.

My beloved Nephews,

Once more my heart prompts me to write to you, my dear, blessed brother's beloved sons, for I am convinced that you will grant me the satisfaction now and then of venturing to make inquiries about your welfare and likewise also of telling you how my family and I are doing. This my conviction I dare hold since I have seen both of you show me the great attention of honoring me with a visit for the sake of your dear immortal father, my good brother. Perhaps I ought not to have bothered my honorable gentlemen nephews with my insignificant letter before I had received a reply to my last, but in the first place, my heart always yearns to thank you for the present[2] I enjoy annually from your good father's and, equally unforgettable, generous mother's hands, said present which was especially welcome this year as we were able to use it to buy grain after a crop failure here; and in the second place, I am not wholly free of longing to know if my letter and the four small cheeses which I sent last summer in June with the recruits[3] did arrive safely.

I find it quite natural that you have hesitated in answering my insignificant letter. You have both had much of importance to do last summer, so important that even our distant provincial newspapers have reported some of it. —For you, Doctor, have married,[4] and you, Mr. S. A. Kierkegaard, have taken your Magister degree.[5] —But whether the latter Mr. Nephew—who had the courtesy to inform me of his engagement—is married now: that I long to know.

Our state is as usual: increasing infirmity. This winter my husband often has to stay in bed; I myself can barely leave the parlor, for the smallest cold develops into sickness—yes, even our daughter is often ailing; our little granddaughter is the only one who is lively and gay.

In conclusion, you are hereby asked to accept my, my husband's, and our daughter's and other relatives' respectful greetings and congratulations upon the changes and progress [*the paper is torn here*] you have made with God's help.

The Blessing and Grace of God and Our Lord Jesus Christ be with all of you. That is the wish and prayer for you from your always

loving and devoted aunt
ELSE PEDERSDATTER KIERKEGAARD.

S. T.
Doctor P. Chr. Kierkegaard
in
Copenhagen

[*Address:*]
S. T.
Doctor P. Chr. Kierkegaard
in
Copenhagen

67. *S. K.—January 31, 1842—Michael Lund.*

My dear Michael,   January 31.

Your letter has arrived safely and now I hasten to reply. I say "now" because I have not had an opportunity to do so for the past few days.

Probably you will not object if the paper I write on also reminds you that I am in Berlin, and therefore I have once again chosen something of a similar kind. But what is the reason you are writing this time? Was it not Henrich's turn, or has he written and has his letter been lost? I do not have all the letters by me at the moment, but if Henrich has received replies to all his letters, then it was his turn to write to me. Will you please tell me about this next time, for you seem to be a reliable person.

I already knew about Lehmann's[1] sentence from the ballads, although with a few omissions the whole affair has been dealt with in the Prussian papers. However, I was happy to read your account of it, for I have found many little details in it, which always mean more to somebody who has been as well acquainted with domestic political matters as I have been.

It has been rather cold in Berlin, and the east wind has been particularly relentless. Now it is milder again, or rather very mild. There is a thaw and we have a westerly wind. As a rule Berlin either has cold weather of 14°F and a biting east wind or a west wind, thawing, and an unpleasant fog. Berlin is located in a swamp, and to find water you have only to poke your finger in the ground.

Your letter has made me happy. You have really made progress, and it is not only the longest letter you have written, as you yourself point out, but also the best.

You are wrong if you think that I myself go sleighriding. I leave that to the Berliners. I have always found riding in a sleigh too cold. Furthermore, although they usually drive uncommonly fast in Prussia (thus I myself, for example, traveled from Stralsund to Berlin, a matter of 144 miles, in twenty-two hours), they drive very sedately in sleighs, and usually there is only one horse to pull a whole family. From this you can see how much a single horse is able to pull. I have seen one horse pulling a carriage with eleven people to Charlottenburg.

Otherwise, everything is as usual. I attend lectures, and the *Geheimeraad*[2] has decided to lecture for two hours at a time in order to finish if possible before the semester ends.

Please greet H., C., S., J., W.

Take care of yourself, my dear Michael. Affectionate greetings.

Your uncle.

[*Address:*]
An Dem Herrn Michael Lund
Copenhagen
7 Store Kjøbmagergade.

[*Postmarks:*]
Berlin   Hamburg
2/1   2-3   2/3

68. *S. K.—February 6, [1842]—Emil Boesen.*

My dear Emil,   Feb. 6,
   I did receive your letter. You seem to hint in it that there is
some inconsistency between my last and next-to-last letters,
inasmuch as in the earlier one I urge you to be seated in the
council, and in the later one become a little vehement, almost
as if I wanted to dismiss you again. You are not completely
wrong about that. The fact is that when I assured you in my
first letter that you held a seat in the council of my thoughts,
that was true enough, but that means primarily that I often
include you in my thoughts, that you really do have a seat and
a vote in many aspects of my life, but especially with respect
to all of my modest production. However, in this matter I feel
that I must rely wholly upon myself, and there it was apparent to me at once that I had said too much and all the more so
when I read your letter. You miss the point, but you do so
because you do not know the true situation, primarily because you do not know my motives. This became even more
apparent to me in your letter, and perhaps I did react a bit
vehemently. It must have seemed especially so to you, although there really was not an untrue word in anything I said.
I have often said that I am born to intrigues, but in another
sense I can say that I am born to intrigues, entanglements,
peculiar relationships in life, etc., all of which perhaps would

not be so peculiar if I had not been so peculiarly constituted, primarily if I had not possessed what I might call that passionate coldness with which I rule my moods, that is, every determination of them *ad extra* [from the outside]. From the development of this argument you will see that I cannot add much to my previous letter. The affair, which by now has been dealt with often enough, has two sides: an ethical and an esthetic. Were she able to take the affair less to heart, or, if it might even become an impetus for her to rise higher than she otherwise would have, then the ethical factor is cancelled— then only the esthetic remains for me. Then I am your man, then I am in my element, equally much whether it is a question of forgetting or of conquering. She was an exceptional girl, as I have always said, and in that sense I have never cooled towards her. Nor do I believe that she would in that sense have been hurt by having been engaged to me. What is then to be done: I open the gates of oblivion, I fling myself into the stream[1] of life, and I believe that I am too good a swimmer to go under just because I am tossed by a little rolling swell. The esthetic is above all my element. As soon as the ethical asserts itself, it easily gains too much power over me. I become a quite different person, I know no limit to what might constitute my duty, etc. There you see the difficulty: if I had broken the connection for my own sake because I believed that the esthetic factor that constitutes something so essential in every character and required it in mine chiefly because I felt that my whole spiritual life was almost at stake (which would have been a most respectable reason and something quite different from the reason people usually have for breaking up, that there is somebody they like better, etc.)— then the ethical would have crushed me. I have been rather ill while I have been in Berlin, but now I am quite well again. Nobody will be told what goes on inside me, and now I am of course quite pleased with the thought that I held back about this. The cold is not so bad in Berlin, but the east wind is awful when it gets going, and often I have had the experience of not once being warm for a whole week in a stretch, not even at night. Cold, some insomnia, frayed nerves, disap-

pointed expectations of Schelling,[2] confusion in my philosophical ideas, no diversion, no opposition to excite me—that
is what I call the acid test. One learns [to] know oneself. It
was a godsend that I did not break the engagement for my
own sake; then it would have overwhelmed me. All that
which I wanted to save by breaking the engagement was in
the process of fading away like a phantom anyway, and I
would have remained as one who for a phantom had thrown
away her happiness as well as my own. I broke it for her sake.
That became my consolation. And when I suffered the most,
when I was completely bereft, then I cried aloud in my soul:
"Was it not good, was it not a godsend that you managed to
break the engagement? If this had continued, you would only
have become a lifelong torment for her. Even if she now
learns," so I continued, "that I have gone out like a candle,
she will see God's just punishment of me in this, she will not
grieve for me, and that is the only thing I do not want to
allow her to do." These are not overwrought feelings, and
that prattle about how she will always be glad to stay with me
because she loves me cannot be thought about. I am too old to
talk that way. I know myself, I know what I can endure; what
she can endure, I do not know. These are not overwrought
feelings, and I know this best because they are able to quell
the upheavals of my soul. Now I am calmer, and I do not anticipate such spiritual trials. Moreover I could have been exposed to humiliations in a quite different manner. Suppose that
she had had the strength to forget me, had recovered in a way
that might have surprised the world (something I had my reasons for expecting), then I would have been stuck. Those
who only considered the esthetic in the affair would have
laughed at me; those who considered the ethical would still
have called me a deceiver and a scoundrel. Is it not infuriat-
ing? I pass through this world, and I harbor healthy and powerful emotions in my breast, so many that I believe ten people
might make themselves into honest citizens with them, and
I—I am a scoundrel. But I laugh at mankind as I have always
done; I am taking a terrible revenge on them, for the worst
revenge is always to have the right on one's side. That is why

I show my hand so reluctantly. I do not want to have their insipid praises. But it is a dangerous path, as I know very well, and were it not that I had so much else to humiliate me, then I would consider continuing to follow it.

You say she is not well. Does this mean that she is provided with news about me from the Lunds? Does she get it from the children or from Miss Dencker,[3] who visits the Tiedemanns,[4] where she also visits? I hope she has not fallen into the hands of Miss Dencker. I hope she is not mired in gossip. In truth she is too good for that. And I who could not tolerate her by my side because I found it too humiliating for her, for in some way she would vanish because of my singularity, I who had worked out that plan in order really to elevate her, either so that she recovered or so that she might have the triumph that I—who even though in public opinion am nothing but the most unstable and egotistical person inside the walls of Copenhagen—that I would almost become a laughing stock by returning to her! That would be sweet-smelling to my nose, for even though I would not be a fool in her eyes, it would please me to be so in those of the world, provided that she could ascend thereby. What do I care about myself? I have myself. And now this too will disturb me, for it will after all seem as though I am returning to her out of pity. However, I refuse to be discouraged. Whenever I get to Copenhagen, I have a considerable influence on public opinion, and surely I can thumb my false nose at them once more. —For safety's sake I want you to make it generally known that as soon as Schelling has finished I am coming home. That was always my plan. My intention was to have another look at the affair then. Please say that the reason for my return is that I am extremely dissatisfied with Schelling, which by the way is only all too true. Then I shall see what is to be done. I dare not attempt anything until I am back in Copenhagen myself. There are difficulties of quite another kind that I must first straighten out. This whole affair is boundlessly complicated. But with God's help I keep up my courage. She will probably hear that I am returning in the spring. That is all I can do now; I dare do no more, although God knows that I would like to. And I do this also because I believe that I may be justified in doing it for my own sake, for I regard the relationship as broken only in a certain sense. You see how carefully I have guarded her interest. If I should return to her, then I would wish to include those few creatures whom she has learned to love through me, my four nephews and two nieces. To that end I have kept up, often at a sacrifice of time, a steady correspondence with them. Naturally, in order to divert attention, I have given this the appearance of something bizarre on my part. But like everything else, this remains between us. Therefore, you see, in returning to her I fear no danger from the same quarter that you do. Indeed, had I left her for my own sake, then everything would have been lost. But I have not done so. In my own eyes I do not return as the Prodigal Son, I am no less proud than before, her trust in me cannot be weakened by my return. But as I have said, there are other things to take into consideration.

Do you now see the difference between my relationship and yours? You have only esthetic considerations, or do you believe that on the Day of Judgment you will have to render an account because you have not become engaged to a girl to whom you would very much like to become engaged? If so, one would have to say that on the Day of Judgment you may demand an accounting for why you did not get her. There is a yawning abyss between yours and mine. Therefore I am pleased that you are thinking better of it. Anyway, when I do get to Copenhagen I shall do my humble bit to give more support.

It is absolutely imperative that I return to Copenhagen this spring. For either I shall finish Either/Or[5] by spring, or I shall never finish it. The title is approximately that which you know. I hope you will keep this between us. Anonymity is of the utmost importance to me. Only in one case would I not have come if I had thought it necessary for her sake. For her I do everything; I am profligate with myself more than with money, and that is saying a lot. In this connection I long to see you. You are used to seeing my works in the making; this time it is different. When I now take out my scrolls and read to you some fourteen to twenty sheets, what do you say to that? "Courage, Antonius!"[6] In a certain sense these are difficult times, and some of the chapters I am working on do indeed need all my sense of humor, all my wit, wherever I get it from. I have completely given up on Schelling. I merely listen to him, write nothing down either there or at home.

I suppose my stock is pretty low in Copenhagen. Even my brother Peter wrote with some reservation. All that does not worry me; I am almost more worried, if it should come about that I return to her, that people will say, "He has something decent about him after all." That contemptible rabble! Of course I might have remained with her, let her suffer all that which it was then impossible to prevent, and told her that she herself had after all wanted it—and would have been extolled and honored as a good husband. That is how most husbands are. I refuse to do that. I would rather be hated and detested.

Either/Or is indeed an excellent title. It is piquant and at the same time also has a speculative meaning. But for my own sake I will not rob you prematurely of any enjoyment.

This winter in Berlin will always have great significance for me. I have done a lot of work. When you consider that I have had three or four hours of lectures every day, have had a daily language lesson, and have still gotten so much written (and that regardless of the fact that in the beginning I had to spend a lot ot time writing down Schelling's lectures and making fair copies), and have read a lot, I cannot complain. And then all my suffering, all my monologues! I feel strongly that I cannot continue for long; I never expected to; but I can for a short while and all the more intensively. Greetings to your father and mother.

Take care of yourself, my dear Emil

Your   S. K.

[*Address:*]
An dem Herrn E. Boesen
Candidat der Theologie
Copenhagen
Philosophgangen

[*Postmarks:*]
Berlin   Hamburg
2/7   2-3   2/8   4-5

69. *S. K.—February 27, 1842—Emil Boesen.*

My dear Emil,

Schelling talks endless nonsense both in an extensive and an intensive sense. I am leaving Berlin and hastening to Copenhagen, but not, you understand, to be bound by a new tie, oh no, for I feel more strongly than ever that I need my freedom. A person with my eccentricity should have his freedom until he meets a force in life that, as such, can bind him. I am coming to Copenhagen to complete Either/Or.[1] It is my favorite idea, and in it I exist. You will see that this idea is not to be made light of. In no way can my life yet be considered finished. I feel I still have great resources within me.

I do owe Schelling something. For I have learned that I enjoy traveling, even though not for the sake of studying. As soon as I have finished Either/Or I shall fly away again like a happy bird. I must travel. Formerly I never had the inclination for it, but first I must finish Either/Or and that I can do only in Copenhagen.

What do you think of that? Probably you have missed me at times, but have a little patience and I shall soon be with you. My brain has not yet become barren and infertile, words still flow from my lips, and this eloquence of mine, which you at least appreciate, has not yet been stilled.

Really, I cannot understand how I have tolerated this servitude here in Berlin. I have taken off only Sundays, have been on no excursions, have had little entertainment. No thank you! I am Sunday's child,[2] and that means that I ought to have six days of the week off and work only one day.

I have much, very much, to tell you. I suppose that now and then you have not understood me very well. That will now be taken care of. Besides, I am not very good at writing letters. Usually I have written to you quite literally at the very moment I received yours. This makes my letters lively, but accordingly, by and large they do not say any more than a spoken conversation would. Afterwards I am often troubled by this. I may have forgotten most of it, but one thing I do remember, and now I do not think it matters. Of course, you are the only person to whom I write in this manner. I am accustomed to considering you as an absolutely silent witness to the most momentous movements of my soul. Yet I manage to keep my perspective.

I hope that it will also mean something to you that I am coming. Surely it is not presumptuous to say that there is one person to whom I mean something. Then we shall once more open our *fiscus* [treasury]. I have not been extravagant; on the contrary I have saved a lot, and on this we may have many happy days. Then, when I once more walk arm in arm with you, when the cigar is lit, or when "the Professor"[3] sits on the coachbox proud and straight and scornful of the whole world, proud that he is driving for me, who am also scornful of the whole world, and we stop, and you have friendship enough to let yourself be truly influenced by what I have to recite to you: "Cheers for me and you, say I; that day will never be forgotten."[4]

I have no more to say to you in writing. I hope you are taking strict precautions against any third party's seeing my letters or reading them, and also that your facial expression betrays nothing. This caution you do understand. You know how I am, how in conversation with you I jump about stark naked, whereas I am always enormously calculating with other people.

My dear Emil,
please take care of yourself,
Your   S.K.

[*Address on the envelope:*]
An dem Herrn Cand. th. E. Boesen
Copenhagen
Philosophgangen

[*Postmarks:*]
Berlin   Hamburg
2/27   2-3   3/1

70. *S. K.—[February 1842]—P. C. Kierkegaard.*

Dear Peter,

Schelling talks the most insufferable nonsense. If you want to get some idea of it, I must ask you—for your own punishment, even though voluntarily assumed—to submit yourself to the following experiment. Imagine Pastor R[othe]'s[1] harebrained philosophy, his whole accidental character in the scholarly world; imagine in addition the late Pastor Hornsyld's[2] persistence in the betrayal of learning; imagine these combined and then add the insolence in which no philosopher has outdone Schelling; keep all this vividly in your poor brain, and then walk out to the workhouse in Our Savior's parish or to the work halls at Ladegaarden,[3] and you will have an idea of the Schelling philosophy and of the circumstances in which it is presented. To make matters worse, he has now gotten the idea of lecturing longer than is customary, and therefore I have gotten the idea that I will not attend the lectures as long as I otherwise would have. Question: whose idea is the better? —In other words, I have nothing more to do in Berlin. My time does not allow me to ingest drop by drop what I would hardly willingly open my mouth to swallow all at once. I am too old to attend lectures, just as Schelling is too old to give them. His whole doctrine of potencies[4] betrays the highest degree of impotence.

I shall leave Berlin as soon as posible. I am coming to Copenhagen. A stay there is necessary for me so that I can bring a little order into my affairs again. You see how strange it is. I have never in my life felt like traveling as much as I do now. I owe that to Schelling. Had Schelling not lectured in Berlin, I would not have gone, and had Schelling not been so nonsensical, I would probably never have traveled again. Now I have learned that it is worthwhile to travel, but *nota bene*, not for the sake of studying. But I can talk about that with you in Copenhagen. I cannot now set out on a proper journey abroad. All things must have their particular stages with me. I shall leave Copenhagen again as soon as I have finished a little work I am engaged in.

Otherwise I am well. I am like a schoolboy on vacation, which goes to show how one may shackle oneself with ridiculous things. I think I might have become utterly stupid if I had continued to listen to Schelling.

Your brother.

71. *S. K.—[1842]—Henriette Lund.*

My dear Jette,

Although I am well aware that the enclosed flower picture by no means can stand comparison with that marvelous fruit picture with which you surprised me on my birthday, still I do not hesitate to send you my modest work as a gift, adding that you must not, as seems so probable, scorn it. It makes no claim on you to be of artistic value; it desires only to be worthy of your affection, for I can assure you that all the time I was working on this flower picture you were constantly in my thoughts. It is all the more deplorable that I began a week late, for despite my having sat up the whole night before last, I have just now finished the picture. Although the blossom itself did not take me much time, the leaf did, even though one might believe that the whole thing had been done with a single stroke. But of course I do not need to tell all this to an artist like you.

Please accept, then, my little gift, a late flower in the month of November, which thus has arrived one day late. But fair is fair: I promised to hide your picture so that nobody would see it; in turn you must promise me not to put my picture on display anywhere, nor show it to anyone, nor mention my name in connection with it—"for that is so embarrassing."

Your uncle,
S. K.
A birthday flower
respectfully
planted
by
N. N.[1]

[*Address:*]
To
Henriette Lund.

72. *S. K.—[before 1843]—[Emil Boesen?]*[1] *S. K.'s draft.*

It might seem strange that I make you a witness by reveal-
ing completely to you how my soul is torn asunder and how I
have lost hope, for on the basis of what I write one might indeed justifiably conclude either that I wanted to tell you indirectly that you, too, had been given up, or that in holding on
to you I was contradicting the very feeling described. I hope
you will draw the latter conclusion, or, to be more precise,
that is the only thing I do not doubt. To this must be added,
as you yourself have learned to some extent, that doubt, just
like feeling, never allows itself to expand steadily until it suffuses all of life, but *remains on its point* for a moment like a
spinning top for a shorter or longer period depending on the
strokes of the whip (for he who doubts is always μεμαστι-
γομενος [one who is whipped])[2]—but he cannot *remain on the
point* any more than the top can. But what it thus loses in continuity and balance it gains in momentum, and I know of
nothing, with the exception of love, about which one may so
rightly say, *loquere ut videam te* [speak that I may see you].[3] For
as its essential being consists precisely in being without essence, without being, and has nothing whatever to posit, it is
recognizable only by its own *vociferousness*, which may be imitated but which he who doubts knows very well for himself.
I say it has no essence, for doubt is the angle between that
which is to be perceived and him who perceives—smaller or

greater, but always an angle—whereas a point of view is the common denominator that resolves all the fractions of life and is that which in a good sense helps to shorten the mathematical puzzle of life.

73. *S. K.—January 18, 1843—P. C. Kierkegaard.*

Dear Peter,

You know how worried I was about taking over the management of this place.[1] Not without reason. Business matters have completely upset my beautiful sequences of thought, and I feel most uncomfortable with them. In order to avoid any precipitate step, I have persuaded Christian Lund[2] to take over the management until he succeeds in selling it as advantageously as possible. As you see, in spite of my ineptitude I shall get reasonably well out of it after all; nor am I letting you down. To that extent it was a good thing that I was not the only one in charge of the place, for I believe that I would have sold it for nothing just to get rid of it. You are the only person I can tell how seriously business has upset me, because you have an idea how preoccupied my soul is with other things that may not be important but nevertheless please and gladden my soul, just as they formerly troubled it. When Christian Lund had taken over, I became so happy—yes, so happy that I might have fallen on my knees, as Robinson did when he saw Friday, at the very thought that I could once again close my door and summon the busy servants of thought to work and could once again devote myself to the speculative reveries with which the gods have recompensed me for what I miss in life.

I want you to write to Christian Lund as soon as possible to thank him for his kindness. I do not think that you could have made a better arrangement. Then we shall share our fates again as we did of yore. I only wish I were in your place and could be in the country, for merely staying in this town is uncomfortable for me.

(Mohr[3] is the greatest *chicaneur* imaginable. The number of things he has already come up with is unbelievable.)

Well! Everything goes better now. We no longer need be afraid of acting too hastily, for Christian Lund will know how to avoid that.

You know that at times there is something premonitory in my soul. These past few days it has seemed to me as if this place, which once was the cause of my father's death, would also cause my own. On the other hand, I wanted indescribably to keep it. It would have been so fine if that place that once sustained him in a time of need might also have saved me. Therefore I take leave of it sadly, even though it is necessary.

One cannot deny that the location is very advantageous. In the right hands silk could be spun from it. It might have gone even better if Mohr's chicaneries and numerous other trivial things had not upset me.

As my thoughts so often return to the place, you can well imagine that I would have liked if possible to keep a mortgage on it. You have never cared much about getting cash or mortgages. In that respect you have always been indifferent. But we will speak about all this in greater detail at some other time.

If I do not manage to rent Mohr's apartment, as I think I shall, then I alone will sustain the loss, for it is not your fault that my soul is unsuited to this sort of thing.

I have already rented the other half of the second floor to a reliable tenant for 85 *rdl*.

Take care of yourself, my dear Peter, and please write to me soon. I shall protect your interests as well as I can.

It may seem to you that my mind is somewhat agitated, yet this is but a small tempest and I shall soon be calm again. You know that I am quite able to conceal my agitation, and when others must act, I am always afraid of disturbing them. Therefore I behave calmly with Christian Lund.

I think the whole business has now taken a turn for the better. Although this may be a bagatelle for Christian Lund, as I realize it is, it is of all the greater importance for me.

Once more my studies are rearing their head; that divining rod of thought I hold in my hand, which had withered momentarily, is in bloom once more, richly perfumed, oh, with indescribably rich perfume. Of late, my life, despite all the pain it secretly hides, has been on the whole happier, more satisfying, than I had ever imagined.

> Take care of yourself,
> Your brother.

74. *S. K.—February 5, 1843—P. C. Kierkegaard.*

Dear Peter,

After having waited for the appropriate length of time, I did receive your letter. You know that in my personal relationships with people I possess an unusually high degree of indolence. Consequently I almost never write to anybody, and if I do, I never ask for a reply. I did so in my last letter because it was a business letter, and I have very little aptitude for being a business man, unless I should make my fortune as an executioner, for when it comes to being resolute and *gewaltig* [forceful], then I am your man. I had learned earlier from Christian Lund, to whom you did write, that you had no objection to the steps I had taken.

But you are coming to town at Shrovetide, and then I shall be able to speak with you in greater detail.

I see that "in looking for another document, you happened to come upon my letter." Please do me the favor of burning it. I do the same with all the letters I receive.

Otherwise I am as well as circumstances permit. As it says in Ψ [Psalms], "my bones are vexed"[1] at times (I suspect it is a slight case of hemorrhoids), but my soul is well and I can endure infinitely more than I had thought. That is how things stand with me for the present. Once I went driving with a pair of cart horses that were in such poor condition that even the coachman was embarrassed to offer them to me—but when we had gone about a mile into the country, they began to run, and never in my life have I driven so quickly, even though it is my delight, as you know, to race with the wind. That is how I am: sometimes I have trouble standing up, but my oh my, I can really run, just like the ostrich.

You wish to find me "calm and complacent." That will be easy for you whenever you get to town, but our notions of this matter are and will remain different.

Take care of yourself,
Your brother.

[*Address*:]
To
Dr. Kierkegaard
Pedersborg
via Sorøe

[*Indistinct postmark*:]
Copenhagen
2/5   843

75. *S. K.—February 18, 1843—P. C. Kierkegaard.*

Dear Peter,   the 18th.

Although I worry less nowadays about the thin cream of news that rises slowly to the surface in these lean times, I do hear a little now and then. Thus I have also learned that you have become involved in a disagreement with the Bishop.[1] I am truly sorry about this, because it is you and because it is Bishop Mynster, who, as you know, is one of the few men in whom I take any pleasure.

It would be going too far afield to tell you how I learned of the matter, but I can assure you that so far as I can judge, it has been only very slightly distorted and in such a manner that on the basis of *criteria interna* I may accept it as true. Nor should you believe that it has become town gossip yet. So far the newspapers know nothing about it.

What do I really want to do with this letter? I want to show you, as you have surely never doubted, that whenever anything is amiss, I can certainly conquer my indolence. Thus it is to show you my sympathy that I am writing to you. To show it in any more concrete way is very difficult, for just as I myself very seldom accept advice, so I permit myself just as rarely to offer unsolicited advice.

However, here you have my opinion:

(1) It is quite possible you are right; but if it is completely at odds with your whole spiritual make-up to transform yourself occasionally into a civil servant, pure and simple, who does what he is told, then you will often feel offended. For my own part I am never more happy than when somebody wishes to command, especially if he is a genuine superior, for I always consider it easier to be he who obeys than he who commands.

(2) A faction[2] is and remains a faction. It may have good intentions towards a particular individual, it may believe it is looking out for his interests, and yet it is still more on the lookout for its own interests. Presumably the faction is pleased (by the way, I know this is the case, for when I finally begin to pay attention, I am not a bad observer) that it is reaching you. It believes that your private income assures you an independent position. Thus it might not urge somebody else to act in this way, and the faction comes to believe that this consideration about your income constitutes concern for you. Suppose your income were ample enough, does it follow from this that it would be worth it to expose oneself to all the many discomforts that will appear at once, to that enduring memory that will accompany you when the faction has forgotten everything? Certainly I am not a coward. I dissuade no one from risking everything, if that should prove necessary—one is prepared to do everything for a cause, nothing for a faction. —With respect to this I have experience.

(3) I am sure your wife consents gladly to everything you wish to do. Do not trust this. She is infirm. An event is something very enticing to somebody with a nervous condition. Momentarily the event gives strength, but this strength is rarely long lasting.

Still, you are doing what you think most right. Rest assured of my sympathy always.

Your devoted brother,
S. KIERKEGAARD.

76. *S. K.—[February 1843]—M. L. Nathanson.*

To

Mr. Nathanson,[1] Wholesaler.

Dear Sir:

A variety of rumors moves me to write the enclosed request. The very fact that I ask you to print it in your newspaper I ask you to look upon as proof that I remember what I once promised, that is to say, when I last wrote something, that I would deliver my next article to your newspaper. My only request is that the article appear in tonight's edition, and that you proofread it as carefully as possible. If the article cannot be accepted that quickly, I must ask you to give it back to Anders,[2] for in that event it must try to find space for itself in another newspaper.

Yours,   S. KIERKEGAARD.

77. *S. K.—May 6, 1843—P. C. Kierkegaard.*

Dear Peter,   Early summer, 1843.

When the accounts were closed,[1] the cash balance was found to be 335 *rdl*. When we talked about it, we arrived at 355, but we had failed to figure in the expenses. For example, taxes have been paid. Therefore I have carried over the error of including Mrs. Bakke's[2] advance payment of rent for the summer. In spite of this there is no more than 335 *rdl*., so you will see that you have amply received what might be owed you of Mrs. Due's[3] outstanding 35 *rdl*. (to wit, 17 *rdl*., 3 *sk*.), instead of which, one half of 70 has been credited to you (to wit, 35 *rdl*.).

335 divided by 2 = 167 - 3 *sk*.
          less   70 (previously advanced)
                    97 - 3 *sk*.
          less   100 (borrowed from me)
            +   2 *rdl*. 3 *sk*.

Thus you owe me 82 *rdl*., 3 *sk*. (As you know, I must have the 80 *rdl*.) But there is plenty of time for this as I leave for Germany on Monday.

I will let you know when I return, and then I wish to receive the money as soon as possible. Meanwhile, take care of yourself. I hope your wife will stay in good health.

I have destroyed your promissory note for 100 *rdl*.

Your brother
S. KIERKE[GAAR]D

May 6, 1843.

[*Address*:]
To
Dr. Kierkegaard, Pastor
Pedersborg
　　　Sorøe

[*Postmark*:]
Copenhagen
5/8　　1843

78. *S. K.—[1843]—Mr. H.*[1]

Honored Mr. H.,
　　When you receive this, I shall be on my way to Stettin.

S. K.

79. *S. K.—[May 1843]—Emil Boesen.*

Dear Emil,
　　Now I am in Berlin[1] and will stay at the Hotel Saxen for the time being. I am deeply exhausted by the journey, somewhat weak; but that will get better. Yesterday I arrived, today I am at work, and my brain is pulsating. What I told you before I left, I almost thought confirmed: I would get sick, etc. God knows what will happen, but let that be. At this moment the busy thoughts are at work again, and the pen flourishes in my hand. Now please see to it that you extricate yourself from the complications in your life. Please believe me, it can be done. I am an old swimmer, and whether or not I lose my life is another matter; it would be for far more profound reasons.

I have recommenced my old promenades up and down Unter Linden—as always when I travel—a silent letter nobody can pronounce, which does not speak to anybody, but which, as you probably know, in the absence of understanding much confines itself to understanding itself, however burdensome that may be. Forgetting is not for me; my passion is to recall every indecorous word I have spoken.

Your

S. KIERKEGAARD.

By the way, please do not burden others with news about me. I do not care to satisfy petty curiosity about myself.

[*Address*:]
An dem Herrn Cand. Boesen
Copenhagen
Philosophgangen.

80. *S. K.—May 15, [1843]—Emil Boesen*.

Dear Emil, May 15

The enclosed letter to you was written just after I arrived. My health was somewhat affected, but so be it. Now I am afloat again. In a certain sense I have already achieved what I might wish for. I did not know whether I needed one hour for it, or one minute, or half a year—an idea—a hint—*sat sapienti* [sufficient for the wise], now I am climbing. As far as that goes, I could return home at once, but I will not do so, although I shall probably not travel any farther than Berlin.

When one does not have any particular business in life, as I do not, it is necessary to have an interruption like this now and then. Once more the machinery within me is fully at work, the feelings are sound, harmonious, etc. As soon as I feel the law of motion truly within me, I shall return, for then I am working again, and my home becomes dear to me and my library a necessity for me.

As to my internal state in other respects, I will not say much, or rather nothing, for I will not tell lies.

My address is Jägerstrasse und Charlottenstrasse an der Ecke, my old address, but the owner has married and therefore I am living like a hermit in one room, where even my bed stands.

I do not want to bother speaking German, and therefore I live as isolated as possible.

[*Address*:]
An dem Herrn Cand. E. Boesen
Copenhagen
Philosophgangen.

[*Postmark*:]
Berlin 5/16   5-6.

81. *S. K.—[May 1843]—[A. F. Krieger*[1]*].*

Solon once said, "No one is happy until he is dead."[2] —This moved Croesus on an appropriate occasion to take the opportunity to remark the following, "Solon! Solon! Solon!"[3] —The same dialectic, here implicit in happiness (i.e., that it is not certain until after the event), is also present in the act of taking leave. Until one has gone, it is impossible to be certain that one is really going; and until one really goes, there is no cause to take one's leave; and when one has really gone, one cannot take one's leave.

You may remember that I asked you before I left if there would be any possible way for a passenger (traveling first class) to stop a railroad train. You may remember that you deprived me of every hope in that respect. Now I have learned that it can be done, even though the whole matter remained a mystery to me even after I had made the discovery. Thus: I take my seat in first class. The Devil take Licentiat Müller[4] for preventing our doing so last time. One is most comfortably seated. The Romans had the custom of leaving one vacant place at the table for the unexpected guest—here it is the other way around: one sits alone in the company of seven marvelous armchairs (one is oneself seated in the eighth). Honored be those armchairs! Their company puts that of many a man to shame. These seven marvelous armchairs, so dignified in appearance that the most renowned doctor, the most famous lawyer, the most sought-after confessor might sit in one of them with dignity. These seven armchairs which one might invite anybody one wishes to sit down in for a conversation—splendid!

We have left two stations behind us. Halfway to the third, the man sitting on the high seat—I mean the conductor— begins to blow his whistle. The train stops. In a loud voice he cries (and he was sitting directly above my head), *"Sie haben mit der Gardine gewinckt"* [You have signalled with the curtain]. At once this thought flies through my head: "You have been unjust to railroad journeys in thinking them too prosaic, for of course it is most poetical to stop just because someone waves a curtain—perhaps at some passerby." An easy association of ideas, and I was reminded of that stanza in which "a lady stands in a castle and signals to me with her veil." —Now he repeats his cry, *"Sie haben mit der Gardine gewinckt."* Now I realize that he wishes to speak with me and that something is up, and therefore I quickly get out my dictionary to find some possible phrase with which I might reply. But alas! Time is scarce on the railroad. In a desperate voice he cries out, *"Um Gotteswillen!"* [For God's sake!]. I do not know what else to do: I poke my head out the window (as one may do without danger when the train is standing still), look up, and meet his face with the only German I know readily, *"Bedenken Sie doch, Ihre Hochwohlgbh., dass ein Mann, der so viele Universitäten"* [Please consider, Right Honorable Sir, that a man who at so many universities] etc.—then he signals, and the train moves on.

I sit in lonely thought and attempt in vain to figure out what all this may mean. I shudder at the thought of that moment when I must leave the carriage, the solitary one who disturbed a railroad train. I arm myself with a good conscience and a few stock German phrases. We stop at Angermünde.[5] The conductor is a most courteous man, and here is the whole explanation, from which you may be able to learn something, if you travel first class. First of all, I had not in the least been the object of his address. It was the carriage in front of mine, also a first-class carriage. Somebody in it had lowered the curtain, the cord that ties the curtain down had become loose, the curtain had billowed in the wind, and the conductor had noticed this, and then—well, one may put a flag out the window, a flag that is kept for that purpose in the carriage, and the moment one does so, this signifies, contrary to all wartime practice, etc., this signifies that the train must stop.

Otherwise the trip was most comfortable. You have probably not been as comfortably seated at Prince Carl's.[6] This letter is a small courtesy in return for your visit. No reply needed.

In friendship,
S. KIERKEGAARD.

82. *S. K.—May 25, 1843—Emil Boesen.*

Dear Emil,   May
[*Deleted*: Dear *Justitsraad*]

Again a little while and you will see me.[1] I have finished a work[2] of some importance to me, am hard at work on another, and my library is indispensable to me, as is also a printer. In the beginning I was ill, but now I am well, that is to say, insofar as my spirit grows within me and probably will kill my body. I have never worked as hard as now. I go for a brief walk in the morning. Then I come home and sit in my room without interruption until about three o'clock. My eyes can barely see. Then with my walking stick in hand I sneak off to the restaurant, but am so weak that I believe that if somebody were to call out my name, I would keel over and die. Then I go home and begin again. In my indolence during the past months I had pumped up a veritable shower bath, and now I have pulled the string and the ideas are cascading down upon me:[3] healthy, happy, merry, gay, blessed children born with ease and yet all of them with the birthmark of my personality. Otherwise I am weak, as I said, my legs shake, my knees ache, etc. This is inadequate; instead I shall choose an expression used by my favorite actor, Herr Grobecker,[4] a proverb he used effectively with every fourth word, *"Ich falle um und bin hin,"* ["I fall over and am done for"], or with a slightly better variation, *"Ich falle hin und bin um"* ["I fall down and am done in"]. When I have arranged everything at home, I shall travel again. Perhaps. *Gott weiss es* [God knows].

Everything remains between us. You know I do not care for gossip.

Your S. KIERKEGAARD.

If I do not die on the way, I believe you will find me happier than ever before. It is a new crisis, and it means either that I now commence living or that I must die. There would be one more way out of it: that I would lose my mind. God knows. But wheresoever I end, I shall never forget to employ the passion of irony in justified defiance of non-human pseudo-philosophers who understand neither this nor that and whose whole skill consists in scribbling German compendia and in defiling that which has a worthier origin by talking nonsense about it.

[*Address*:]
An dem Herrn Cand. E. Boesen
Copenhagen
Philosophgangen

[*Postmark*:]
Berlin 5/25 12–1.

83. *S. K.—June 29, 1843—P. C. Kierkegaard.*

June 29, 1843.

Dear Peter,

Quite some time has already gone by since I returned from Berlin, and in all that time I have heard nothing at all from you. So it is easy to explain the fact that when the miracle of your writing to me fails to take place, then the even greater miracle takes place: the prophet goes to the mountain.

How are you doing down there? How is Jette? I have practically no contact at all with the Glahn family[1] and therefore hear nothing whatsoever. It would really make me very happy indeed if Jette were in fairly good health, for if that were so I believe you might even be able to lead a pleasant life in the country, for you like being a pastor, as far as I can judge, and besides, you have acquired some skill in dealing with life's trivialities in such a way that they do not become completely unbearable for you. This is something I understand very well; perhaps few understand it as well as I do, precisely because I am and will remain a swimmer who *nolens* and *volens* [willy-nilly] stays out in the mainstream.

If a brief visit from me would please you in any way, I would be glad to come, even though I go for drives less frequently nowadays, at least not for such long ones, and on the whole am prepared to remain in Copenhagen and put up with the heat. My room is my *Rhodus*,[2] and although I am not exactly leaping about in the heat, I will nevertheless remain there.

I really have nothing to write to you about, for you know that I am reluctant to write to anybody about my affairs; even in conversation I am rather taciturn. I have written to tell you that I am, as I have always been—even though appearances are mostly against me, as they may be *in specie* [particularly] at this very moment when it occurs to me that Jette may not be better—happy to assure you that I am

Your devoted brother.

You know that there is in town a Magister Adler,[3] who became a pastor on Bornholm, a zealous Hegelian. He has come over here to publish some sermons[4] in which he will probably advocate a movement in the direction of orthodoxy. He has a good head on him and has considerable experience in many *casibus* of life, but at the moment he is a little overwrought. Nevertheless it is always possible that this is a phenomenon worth paying attention to. —Otherwise everything is as usual, trivial, although one can get along provided one knows how to laugh—and to work. —Have you seen Martensen's book?[5] How can people go on claiming that M. is a thinker!

Let him wrestle with philosophy; that makes sense, but this kind of stuff is nothing but mindless self-aggrandizement.

[*Address*:]
To
Dr. Kierkegaard, Pastor
Pedersborg
via Sorøe.

84. *S. K.—July 3, 1843—P. C. Kierkegaard.*

Dear Peter,

You have presumably not forgotten that when I went abroad I wrote you that I would continue the loan of 80 *rdl.* and that I had destroyed your promissory note because I considered it sufficient that you yourself knew about it. Presumably you have not forgotten this, yet I almost did. I write about it now, not because I want to speed the matter, even though I could use the money, but because I want everything in order.

I hope you received my previous letter.[1]

Your brother.

[*In P.C.K.'s hand*:] ca. July 3, '43.

[*Address*:]
To
Dr. Kierkegaard, Pastor
Pedersborg
via Sorøe.

[*Postmark*:]
Copenhagen 7/3   1843

85. *S. K.—[1843]—Henriette Lund.*

My dear Jette,

Yesterday just as I was sitting happily lost in my own thoughts thinking of nothing, the following thought suddenly occurred to me, which might also have occurred to someone less thoughtful, for while it does not exactly distinguish itself by its profundity, it does on the other hand contain a significant, almost unusual degree of truth: since a birthday is something that occurs once a year, *it follows* that it must also have been Jette's birthday this year, unless it falls on one of the few days left of this year.

Allow me to take this opportunity to congratulate you on your birthday, whether this congratulation now arrives about a year late or a few days early—for one really must not take life that seriously, nor is it granted to everybody, to me in particular, always to hit on what is right, especially in these matters.

Probably I cannot—as you did, with a deft hand strew roses at my feet, which may indeed be necessary, for my path even in my living room at home is not exactly always strewn with roses—probably I cannot strew roses with such a deft hand in your path, which may not be necessary either, for I hope it is already strewn with roses and will remain so. Although in the absence of a deft hand I must resort to the hand of artifice and resort to that which others have wrought; nevertheless this, this attempt to spread fragrance in your path, still comes from my hand—if you will kindly open the bottles.

May everything go well for you in the new year which you enter upon today—ignore dates and anniversaries and all such extraneous matters as I ignore them—today is your birthday. That is how I want it, and I am in charge here. If it is not your birthday today, then an error must have crept into your baptismal certificate, in which case you will have to have a serious talk with your father, since this is a serious matter in this serious world, in which, as experience teaches, even though one otherwise knew everything and were the very model of perfection, one would still be utterly useless if one did not know one's own birthday.

Stay well, my dear Jette. Be happy, "always happy." That

is the only advice to give against whatever griefs you might have. If it pleases you, rest assured of the constant, sincere devotion with which I remain

Your completely devoted
uncle   S. K.

86. *S. K.—[October 1843]—Emil Boesen.*

Dear friend,
    You are ill. So am I, although perhaps in a different way. I do not own Blicher's short stories,[1] but I am sending you what I have, *the best I have*—my Isaac.[2]

Yours forever,
Farinelli[3]   (S. K.)

[*Address*:]
Cand. E. Boesen.

87. *S. K.—no date—Emil Boesen.*

Tuesday.

Dear friend,
    Please visit me for a little while around six o'clock this afternoon.

Your   S. K.

[*Address*:]
To
Cand. E. Boesen.

88. *S. K.—[between February and May 1844]—Emil Boesen.*

My dear Emil,
    When you called today I was just like Geert Westphaler[1] and got involved in three stories at the same time, and furthermore forgot to ask you about something or to speak with you about something on which I wanted your opinion.

Bartholin² is to be put in charge of the Borgerdyds School, and hence Stilling goes with him. But if he takes that, then he cannot want to become prison chaplain, and if that post otherwise becomes vacant on account of Visbye's promotion,³ you might apply for it. The reason I am writing to you about this now is that I want you to remind me to speak with you about it next time. Whether such an appointment is suited to your inclinations is another question, but one ought always to keep a vigilant eye on this sort of thing.

Your   S. K.

[*Address:*]
To
Cand. E. Boesen.

89. *S. K.—no date—Emil Boesen.*

Sunday.

Dear friend,
    Please visit me for a little while around seven o'clock tonight, if you can.

Your   S. K.

[*Address:*]
To
Cand. E. Boesen.

90. *S. K.—[before 1845]—Emil Boesen.*

Dear Emil,
    I will be at home Monday afternoon at half past three and completely at your service. If you are not going to Tuborg¹ tomorrow, you might also call on me tomorrow, but in that case I suppose I will see you around noon.

Your   S. K.

[*Address:*]
To
Cand. E. Boesen.

91. *S. K.—no date—Emil Boesen.*

Dear friend,

How are you? Are you alive? But I know you are! Yet I see as if darkly. Face to face I do not see you.[1] You once said to me half reproachfully, "I was sick, and you did not visit me"[2] etc., but I wanted to reply, "Just as the righteous ask with surprise, 'Lord, when saw we thee sick, when saw we thee in need,' etc., and have only the Word of Christ that this was so, now the positions must be reversed," for although you may be right in saying to me, "You did not visit me," I will reply, "Yes, I did, and I hope you believe me." I have called on you in spirit; *in body* I call on no one, but it is only with respect to you that I regret that I do not do so. Surely you are not angry, for then you have not understood me. —If you can become angry, then I have not understood you.

Your   S. K.

I cannot make myself believe that spring will follow this winter. Today I bought myself another lily of the valley in order at least to revive the thought that it is a possibility.

Yours.

I shall call soon, if you do not.

[*Address*:]
To
Cand. E. Boesen.

92. *S. K.—[1844]—Emil Boesen.*

Dear Emil,

The chaplaincy at Fredensborg is said to be vacant. This is something for you—*hic Rhodus, hic salta*.[1]

Your   S. K.

If I should not see you during the next few days, I hope to

get to see you at your parsonage[2] next Sunday—which I shall then exchange for the inn.

[*Address*:]
To
Cand. E. Boesen.

93. *S. K.—no date—Emil Boesen.*

Dear friend,
    Are you ill, or what is the reason I never see you, not even yesterday at Mynster's?[1]

                                    Your   S. KIERKEGAARD.

[*Address*:]
To
Cand. E. Boesen.

94. *S. K.—[before 1845]—Emil Boesen.*

Dear Emil,
    Yesterday I really did forget my promise to send you a message. I was ill and accordingly unable to receive you anyway, but I ought to have let you know. As I say, I had forgotten it until I sat in my carriage out on the highway and the sunbeams fell on and penetrated my pate—when I happened to ask myself, "Now why did you want to go driving?" And just as I was becoming half vexed at this, I happened to remember my promise to you. But of course it was too late. Today is not very good for me, for I have to proofread this afternoon.

                                    Your   S. KIERKEGAARD.

95. *S. K.—no date—Emil Boesen.*

Dear friend,
    Please come and have supper with me this evening. Come
at seven.
    Please reply!

                                        Your   S. KIERKEGAARD.
[*Address:*]
To
Cand. E. Boesen.

96. *S. K.—no date—Emil Boesen.*

My dear Emil,

                            A recipe

    Take an ordinary wineglass, fill it to the brim, and then
say, *"Un, deux, trois, abmarchirt"* [One, two, three, march],[1]
as does Nonpareil in *The Critic and the Beast.*

    In my own exalted person I have selected this at Capozzi's.[2]
Please drink it for your health to my health and thereby benefit both of us.

                                        Your   S. K.
[*Address:*]
To
Cand. E. Boesen.

97. *S. K.—no date—Emil Boesen.*

Dear Emil,
    Enclosed herewith is what I promised you, the latest prod-
uct I have received of this fertile season.

                                        Your   S. K.
[*Address:*]
To
Cand. E. Boesen.

98. *S. K.—no date—Emil Boesen.*

Dear Emil,
  Please call this afternoon for a little while. Come fairly soon.

Your   S. KIERKEGAARD.

[*Address:*]
To
Cand. E. Boesen.

99. *S. K.—no date—Emil Boesen.*

Dear Emil,
  Please try to keep calm. You know how much I sympathize with you and how it hurts me to see you suffering from the state of over-exertion you are in—even though in a way it is you who keep yourself in it. You gather everything together all at one time and surround yourself with it, and then you succumb beneath its weight. But existence demands to be understood bit by bit.
  Please accept these few lines as a token of my sympathy. I have a great many things to take care of, yet I do have a moment to spare to write this.

Your   S. KIERKEGAARD.

[*Address:*]
To
Cand. E. Boesen.

100. *S. K.—no date—Emil Boesen.*

Dear, dear Emil,
  Happy New Year!

  God knows how it came to be that New Year is observed in the middle of winter. I wonder if it is to comfort us, so that such a prophecy may comfort us in the cold of winter, but certainly it must, like every other prefiguration, give way when the perfect is come.[1]

Your   S. K.

Will one not soon have the pleasure of seeing you in the New Year? [*Herew*]ith [*the paper is torn*] a little festive offering for Your Honor from the outlying farm you have established in the annex, and which we strive to keep as neat and cosy as we can against the possibility of your deciding to resign and move yourself out to that which has already been moved out.—

[*Address:*]
To
Cand. E. Boesen

101. *S. K.—[1844?]—Emil Boesen*

Dear friend,
   Will you eat with me this evening? I have already ordered the food. If so, I will come at 6:00 or 6:30. Will you be in your room at that time?

Your   S. Kierkegaard

Reply requested.

[*Address:*]
To
Mr. E. Boesen, C.T.

102. *S. K.—no date—Emil Boesen.*

Dear Emil,
   About your note concerning Edvard Smidt[1]: I am very sorry I can do nothing. *Etatsraad* Holm[2] has even personally approached me on his behalf, but I had already taken an interest in a clerk in the National Bank who had been recommended by Ferdinand Lund.[3]

And now about something else. When you left me today I thought you seemed depressed. What is the matter? I am always sorry to see you downhearted. If I am mistaken, so much the better, although I should *in casu* like to consider myself something of an observer. But if there should be anything troubling you, then do tell me if I can help you in any way with advice, ideas, assistance, or the like. But please do not torment yourself. Let the whole world go hang, and above all, do not let yourself be troubled by my monologues when I speak with you.

                                        Your   S. K.

[*Address:*]
To
Cand. Theol. E. Boesen.

103. *S. K.—no date—Emil Boesen.*

My dear Emil,
    As I may not get to see you today and as you may be leaving early tomorrow, I am making sure I reach you by way of this note. It is not intended to stop you, indeed not, but on the contrary, if possible to wish you Godspeed on your journey. —Enjoy yourself, refresh yourself—regards to Carl.[1]

                                        Your   S. K.

[*Address:*]
To
Cand. E. Boesen.

104. *S. K.—no date—Emil Boesen.*

Dear friend,
    Please call for a little while this afternoon.

                                        Your   S. KIERKEGAARD.

[*Address:*]
To
Cand. E. Boesen.

105. *S. K.—[March 31, 1844]—Emil Boesen*.

Dear friend,

What monstrous sophistry that there is no difference between dining at 2 p.m. and at 4 p.m.! It might have blinded me, had I not learned just yesterday to comprehend it. The confusion of Thorvaldsen's funeral[1] was enough in itself to set me so far behind in my studies that I must catch up today.

By the way, an idea, a suspicion, a conjecture has awakened in my soul—is it your birthday?[2] If so, I congratulate; if not, I take the occasion to do so now anyway. If it is your birthday, I am sure, considering the congratulations, that you can bear my not coming to call. And if it is not your birthday, well then, how could such a surprise as my congratulations fail to make amends for my absence?

Your   S. K.

[*Address*:]
To
Cand. E. Boesen.

106. *S. K.—[1844]—Emil Boesen*.

Dear Emil,

Perhaps you intended to read something[1] aloud to me. You should have stayed for a moment, for then the man who was calling would have left, and I would have had some time. I shall not be able to do it this afternoon. Levin[2] is coming at 3:15 and will stay as long as possible, that is, as long as I can stand it. I am sorry, for really I should not like to cause you any delay or to postpone the decision that you yourself may arrive at in reading it aloud to me. But I am extremely busy and also ill. Now travel, enjoy yourself, and let the whole world, including me, go hang, and then come home again, for then we shall have time and occasion enough.

Your   S. K.

[*Address*:]
To
Cand. Boesen.

107. *S. K.*—*[May 6, 1844]*—*Michael Nielsen. S. K.'s draft.*

Dear Professor,

When you recommend somebody and when I have at my disposal that which is desired, then my wilfulness is your guarantee that your wish is my command. Unfortunately, however, I am not in the position of looking for nor can I use the person you recommend. At the moment I employ an old woman[1] with whom I am in every way as satisfied as possible. She will be with me until this fall, when I move to the family house at Nytorv, where I have arranged things differently so that I will have no need of such a person and in fact will have no room for her. Even if I did, I could hardly dismiss my old woman, since she suits me in every way, and although she has been with me for only a year, she has known how to make her dismissal almost a matter of conscience for me.

So much for the content of your letter; but now a little about something entirely unrelated that nevertheless has made your letter—which I cherish as I do everything from you—most particularly welcome in its own way. Yesterday was my birthday, a day I am very averse to celebrating and as far as possible even keep secret. But that your letter should happen to come on just that day, the only letter I have ever received from you, that the familiar handwriting should so vividly recall to me one of my most beautiful memories, that the affectionate closing should assure me of that which I certainly believed and knew, yet am always happy to hear repeated, that time, which changes so much, in this respect has changed nothing—how could I do anything but consider all this as the work of a friendly fate who sent me a birthday greeting so welcome that I myself could almost have elicited it! This is why I thank you for your note and for the impression it made on me, for it allowed me to forget completely that the last time I saw your name was in that official notice announcing your resignation as principal of the Borgerdyds School. Well, it was inevitable; but all the same, not everyone has the strength to take the step himself and the strength to resign himself to taking it. If anyone should have self-confidence, rashness, and boldness enough to want to offer you consolation, then truly it is not I. But with your permission I should prefer to be the one who is no good at consoling, understood in the same sense as Cicero understands it when he writes to Titius: *unus ex omnibus minime sum ad te consolandum accommodatus, quod tantum ex tuis molestiis cepi doloris, ut consolatione ipse egerem.* [I, of all people, am the least fit to console you, for your troubles have caused me so much grief that I myself need consolation].[2]

> With gratitude and affection
> your completely devoted
> S. KIERKEGAARD.

108. *S. K.—May 16, 1844—P. C. Kierkegaard.*

Dear Brother,

What you enclosed will be taken care of—for which you may thank me, and after which I thank you for the letter, for the invitation, and for the two-fold proposal that most likely will be an obstacle to my coming—for a two-fold proposal activates my imagination at once, and when it has been activated, deliberation begins, and with it the individual details of deliberation—and while all this is going on, I myself go (like the mill in the fairy tale, "click-clack, click-clack") for my usual walk out towards Nørre– or Vesterport[1] and beyond.

However, this is not simply because I am disinclined to visit you, far from it—the other day I was even at Roskilde[2] and had bought a ticket for the coach to Sorøe[3]—in case it might appeal to me to go there, but when I got to Roskilde, I was very tired, and hence returned home and climbed into my own bed. I consider going to bed one of the most marvelous inventions: this saying "Good day!" or "Good night!" to the whole world. I have been told of an old capitalist and bondsman who lived in Stormgade;[4] he liked to stand smoking his evening pipe before an open window or in his doorway. When the night watchman had called out ten o'clock and then came to his door, called out, and had finished calling out, then the old man summoned him and said, "Night watchman, what did you just call out?" (It is the festive ceremony of this solemn act, for he knew very well what time it was, since he had heard the night watchman call out the hour several times, and indeed right before his own door.) The night watchman replied, "That was ten, Mr. *Cancelliraad.*" —"Oh, was it," said the *Cancelliraad.* "Well, little watchman, then I shall close my door. If anybody comes and asks for me, please tell him to lick m — r —."

Seriously though, I should really like to visit you, and when one comes right down to it, it is partly my indolence, which I find hard to overcome, that detains me, and partly also that Sorøe lies so close to you that I am afraid that only with difficulty can one get an impression of being truly *vogelfrei* [free as a bird] in the countryside. Otherwise it would be very pleasant to visit you. I long especially to see Poul. I find my position in life as an uncle a gratifying employment, and usually I am also well liked by my nephews. Please greet him from me, and do not let him remain completely ignorant that he has an Uncle Søren. When I do get a chance to speak with him personally, I hope the acquaintance will make rapid progress.

My mind is working with ever greater horsepower. God knows whether the body can bear it. For I know of nothing better with which to compare myself than a steamship with too much horsepower for the structure. On the other hand, I must follow my own genius, I cannot easily bear outside contact, and in this regard I find it agreeable that you let me go my own way. I consider this a courtesy, just as when I am invited to a party with the explicit understanding that I am completely free to come or not. I consider it an expression of friendship to invite me; I consider it a human expression of one's relationship with such a non-human person as I am to phrase the invitation so amusingly, that is, if Aristotle is otherwise correct in thinking man an *animal sociale*.[5]

Here ends my letter.

Many greetings to Jette, and Poul, and yourself.

In secluded sincerity, I remain your completely devoted brother,

S. KIERKEGAARD.

109. *S. K.—[July 1844]—P. D. Ibsen. S. K.'s draft.*

Dear Pastor Ibsen,

. It would be an affront to myself were I to assure you that such a sad event[1] as that which has befallen your house, and you in particular, had impressed itself upon me in such a way that I find it mandatory somehow—not to inform you of my sympathy—but to express my sympathy, for in a certain sense I do so for my own sake. To my way of thinking there is nothing worse than that bustling sympathy that seeks in clichés and stock phrases—yes, one might best put it like that—seeks to burden him who is distraught. Generally it is rare that one person understands another completely, and this is particularly true with respect to grief, for basically every man has something, above all when he grieves, which he singles out as the object of his grief and which the undertaker or professional mourner would hardly be likely to discover. All the more so when death breaks off an already enburdened married life shared by two people [*in margin*: a tumultuous life under varied vicissitudes]. What folly it would be, then, to come forth here with stock phrases. Such a *summa summarum* of everything experienced and shared for 29 or 30 years, during which two people ate, drank, and slept together, is an empty *spatium*; such a *summa summarum* of the *residuum* of grief and the possessions of memory is an abstract, empty *factum* that the comforter has quickly done with, while he who grieves sets out only gradually on the voyage of the discovery of pain, the extent of which is known only to him who grieves; and from it he returns tired [*in margin*: one day; but sets out upon it once again the next day, filled with longing], yet also relieved by sadness, until that voyage becomes more and more precious to him.

Hence I have refrained from talking nonsense, for I know that even though I have sometimes been lucky enough to say something sensible, I would have had to talk nonsense the very moment I began to speak, because it was impossible for me to know what I ought to speak about, and thus would have been forced to grasp at thin air or at the poetic illusion that one might without further ado dream oneself into whatever some other person experiences in his most intimate relationships. And yet I know what I can speak about, for your wife is vividly in my thoughts; I did after all know her, for a short time, but I did, and knew her in your home. And in your home I have spent many pleasant hours, and in your home I have always found a kind reception, a hospitality that your wife extended to everybody, an openmindedness, a readiness to comply with my strange wishes and my strange manners. Your house has been one of the few where I have been able to count on this, and I continue to count on it.

Permit me to speak of the last event. Perhaps a dunce would say that one should not remind a grief-stricken person of his grief, just as if he might have forgotten it, and that one should take care not to mention it the following day.

[*The conclusion is missing.*]

110. S. K.—*October 31, 1844*—*The Royal Library*.

The undersigned hereby assumes liability for whatever books Henrich Sigvard Lund,[1] a student, may borrow from the Royal Library.[2]

Copenhagen, October 31, 1844.

S. KIERKEGAARD
Proprietor of no. 2, Nytorv.

111. S. K.—*[1844]*—*J. F. Giødwad. S. K.'s draft*.

Dear Giødwad,[1]

Would you please be so kind, will you, do you care to, etc.? —Danger and hard necessity knock at my door, that is: it is already several days since I delivered the manuscript. But do you not have some hours in the morning or between 4 and 6 p.m.? In any case I assume you will call on me. It is only a question of *Four Upbuilding Discourses*,[2] but whether on account of the heat or not, I feel revulsion at the thought of sitting and reading them aloud to anyone else. However, there is Levin,[3] who has just informed me that he has returned from a trip, etc. But whether you come or not, there remains something unsettled between us, not only that which I shall always be glad to leave pending because I welcome it, but something unsettled. You know what I mean. Time before last when I wanted to straighten it out, you set it aside and small-talked. The next time I forgot it, but now I remember it well.

112. *S. K.—[1844]—Henriette Kierkegaard.*

Dear Sister-in-law,

As you may remember, there is a character in one of Scribe's best plays[1] by the name of Charles (of doubtful intellect, but an infinitely comical figure) who exclaims with great pathos when his uncle has settled his debts, "That is what I told myself at once, I did: either one has an uncle or one does not have an uncle." I intend now to make these words the basis for my observations. Now, dear Jette, if I make you the observer, then you will probably think as follows: "Either one has a brother-in-law or one does not have a brother-in-law; but if one does have a brother-in-law, why does one never see him?" In this you are perfectly right, and when it comes to arriving at a conclusion, your case is, *sans comparaison*, far more difficult than that of Charles. If I were to make any observations, I would think as follows: "Either one has a sister-in-law or one does not have a sister-in-law, but what is the point of having a sister-in-law one never sees?" In this I am also perfectly right, and yet my case is far simpler than yours. For in a letter that Peter showed me, I saw greetings and an invitation to me, and it was really the sight of these that made me exclaim those remarkable words!

You see, it is very strange! When you were in Copenhagen, we did not meet very often, either, but I did receive a note from you now and then. Moreover, with these notes there was in turn an odd consistency, for they became briefer and briefer, and yet this was not an indication that you were growing colder and colder towards me, but on the contrary an indication that you had come to have increasing confidence in me. Therefore, let the fact that I have heard nothing at all from you since those days serve as an indication of the thought that having a brother-in-law, rather than seeming stranger and stranger to you, has become the more natural to you. In all honesty, that is the way it has come to be for me with respect to my having a sister-in-law. It would have been so easy to call on you when you were in Copenhagen. Whenever it then occurred to me and I did not do it, the next moment was not comfortable, and I would have to hurry away from the thought. But now the traveling distance scares me in a way, and hence it is quite fitting that I dwell on you in my thoughts occasionally, especially when I am out for my solitary walk and am most struck by the impression of rural beauty. Probably this constituted another obstacle in the end, and the motto of my life is and always was—"to Frederiksberg!"—Often in my childhood I was not permitted by my father to walk out to Frederiksberg, but I walked hand in hand with him up and down the floor[2]—to Frederiksberg.

This is more or less what has occurred to me to write to you. Although I may not display alacrity in coming, I do display consideration while I stay away. With grateful consideration I receive every piece of news from you, every greeting, every invitation. With consideration I reflect that we two are agreed that the name of *Kierkegaard* shall not soon perish, and even though our efforts are very different, I must, alas, confess that yours is a far more certain way than mine.

This letter makes no demands, least of all for a reply.

Greetings to Peter and Poul (somewhere in Europe there is a harbor called the Harbor of Peter and Poul, and so Petersborg[3] might be called), greetings to you yourself. Above all, please use the summer to gather strength. If you

yourself were happy that you were able to meet Peter at Roskilde,[4] be assured that I was very happy indeed that you were
able to do so.

Yours,   S. KIERKEGAARD.

113. *S. K.—[1844]—Hans Peter Kierkegaard.*

Dear Peter,

I am sorry that your visit to me yesterday was in vain. I
would have enjoyed spending an hour talking with you. But
please do not give up on me for that reason nor give up thinking of me or the thought of visiting me. Do believe in
repetition[1]—but no, for I have, after all, proved that there is
no repetition! But then please doubt repetition and please
come again. For of course in this case repetition would mean
that your visit would be in vain a second time. And there is no
repetition (cf. *Repetition*)—so in all human probability you
will find me at home next time.

Your devoted cousin,   S. K.

114. *S. K.—no date—Hans Peter Kierkegaard.*

Dear Cousin,

Please let these few words from me assure you that I am
thinking of you—then they will accomplish something after
all. Please think of them as a visit—and a note in my language
is the same as a visit in that of others.

Please call on me some time. I would not like you to come
in vain, so you might send your servant along to inquire if I
am at home. It is not far. If you do so, you might also find me
at home between 5 and 6 p.m.

Your cousin   S. K.

115. *S. K.—January 16, 1845—P. C. Kierkegaard.*

Dear Peter,

The librarian at the *Athenæum*[1] has a chit for a borrowed
book that has not been returned. The signature is Kierkegaard
but with some first names that I cannot decipher with any certainty. The librarian has now made inquiries of the members
with this surname, but nobody knows about it. Finally he
applied to me, because, although he knew that I never borrow
books there, he thought it might possibly have been somebody else to whom I had given permission to borrow in my
name. I have thought in vain about this, and the signature is
not mine. But if I am not mistaken, the Hahn family[2] did borrow in your name at the *Athenæum*. I wonder if that is not
what has happened. The title of the book is Grattam, *Greverne
af Mansfeldt.*[3]

The librarian has requested me to write to you. That is why
I am writing—hoping you are well—and, furthermore,
damning all such nonsense to Bloksbjerg[4] whence it comes.

Your brother.

[*Address:*]
To
Dr. Kierkegaard, Pastor
Pedersborg
V. Sorøe

[*Postmark:*]
Copenhagen
1/17
1845.

116. *S. K.—February 10, 1845—P. C. Kierkegaard.*

[*In P.C.K.'s hand*: During the crisis of '45.]
Dear Peter,

Rumors are not exactly my delight, nor are they anything I
pay particular attention to, especially when they concern myself. But this time the rumor concerns you. It is being said

that the Bishop has formally recommended that you be given a period for reconsideration and then either baptize—or in fact resign your office.[1]

It is self-evident that the matter is of concern to me. I doubt that it will come to that extreme. If you were not the party involved, I would say, "I wish it would come to that and that the Bishop would win." Now I am far from wishing this, although you know how much I agree with the Bishop. But let us suppose that the matter does come to that extreme. What then? As little as I myself like being interrupted in what I am doing by a *pro et contra*—and I am the very man to produce them in abundance—just so little do I wish to interrupt what anyone else is doing. Presumably you have thought about most of this and made your choice. Accordingly, there is only one thing I wish to remind you of, and, *ni fallor* [if I am not mistaken], I said this last time when the decision seemed imminent: Consider that here as everywhere there are of course lots of blabbermouths who, incapable of action, perfect themselves in chattering, and if you should risk going to an extreme, they would of course be able to feed on it for a long time, cite you as their warrant, and become vociferous, etc. Even though what you are doing in accordance with your honest conviction were the best you could do, the only right thing, there is in our times an abuse that one must always guard against: that cowardice and loquacity and impotent spite and drivel, etc., will always attach themselves to it, and therefore the best may produce something harmful. I do not mean to say that such a consideration should make one hold back, but such a consideration ought also to be weighed. If these were calm and easy times, it would be better, but a generation that only has the *idée fixe* that they have received the call to be reformers or imagine that they *want* to be (alas, what a contradiction!) at the very time when nobody has a call—such a generation must be handled with care.

But as I said, I do not think that the Bishop will prevail.[2] This will make me happy on your behalf, and only pains me because one of the most energetic men in the country will then become the laughing stock of dunces, for that cannot be avoided.

As you see, I speak without reserve. You would have been suspicious if my enthusiasm for Mynster had cooled completely, and really it would also have put my concern for you in a sad light, for the concern of a weathervane is not exactly to be trusted. I support both of you as always. It might be wished that you had never collided.

As you know, my life lies in decisions. Then my heart beats and then my fraternal devotion also finds opportunity and desire to express itself. Be assured of that.

Your brother
S. K.

[*Address:*]
To
Dr. P. Kierkegaard, Pastor
Pedersborg
v. Sorøe

[*Postmark:*]
Copenhagen
2/11
1845.

117. *S. K.—February 18, 1845—P. C. Kierkegaard.*

Dear Peter,

Your letter received—and burned. I knew the enclosed contents even when I wrote to you, I believe, and my source was indeed a rumor, but it became reliable information the next day. That I had so plainly stated my sympathy for Bishop M. while wanting at the very same time to assure you I felt the same for you[1] is something I assumed you would know how to appreciate. Any letter from me in which I hinted at none of it would surely have aroused your suspicion. I suppose I knew that the Bishop would have the Chancery on his side, but—what will come of that? Is the case thereby settled? Or does not the final decisive step remain? Would he not have to anticipate that you would sell your life as dearly as possible and, in other words, force the issue to the extreme? What then? Then you must be discharged. But neither the Bishop nor the Chancery can decide that; hence the case must go before the King. I hope you did not think that my opinion was that you would be let off if it remained a case between you on the one side and the Bishop, and hence the Chancery, on the other. Far from it. But that is precisely why the case has not yet gone any further, and it is still my unalterable opinion that in the end the Bishop will not prevail. If my opinion had been that the Bishop would win, I should not have spoken like that. But it is still far from being my opinion.

As you see, I write promptly, for however indolent I usually am, my failing does not lie in withdrawal or desertion when there is danger, for then my devotion is spurred on and will only increase with the danger.

Your brother   S. K.

[*In margin*:] How is Jette? Keep in mind—as you yourself must realize—that no decision will be made just now, and therefore do not depict the heights of resignation for her too soon, lest it exhaust her, should the danger fail to materialize. Regards to her and to Povel,[2] who *am Ende* will better insure the immortality of the family name than the honor that will be your lot among men or the *summa summarum* of my writings.

[*Address*:]
To
Dr. Kierkegaard, Pastor
Pedersborg
v. Sorøe

[*Postmark*:]
Copenhagen
2/19
1845.

118. *S. K.—March 10, 1845—P. C. Kierkegaard.*

Dear Peter,					March 10

Your letter of February 27 has arrived safely. This time I have not hastened to reply, for now the whole case presumably has days, a lifetime, and the highway ahead of it, etc. —Obviously I am not ignorant of what is going on in town: the continuing retreat of the Convention,[1] the continuing progress of the Bishop and the Chancery, and Emil Clausen's[2] conference with the Bishop the other day. You probably also know all about that. By the way, with respect to my initial news concerning the Bishop's appeal to the Chancery: there I was really *à jour* in the strictest sense, I learned of it the evening of the same day, but from a person who is not disinclined to exaggeration, or rather from a person who had heard it from him. But that is not the kind of thing one writes about. I spoke with him the next day, and he told me the same thing, but I do not write on the basis of that kind of information. Three days later I had my source. This was reliable. I wrote on the fourth day, I believe. It can only seem surprising in retrospect that this case has been dealt with so expeditiously, but this could not have been known in advance. I assume you have someone reporting to you, and besides I do not have a great deal of time. Meanwhile I do keep up with events. If I were to score the game, I could not deny that the Bishop has advanced slightly, for his energy has not been without influence on [*in margin*: some. But we agree that this is not the decisive point. Stay well. Greetings to Jette. Please play with Povel[3] and instill goodwill and respect in him for an uncle he has hardly ever seen.]

					Your S. K.

[*Address*:]
To
Dr. Kierkegaard, Pastor
Pedersborg
v. Sorøe

[*Postmark*:]
Copenhagen
3/12
1845.

119. *S. K.—May 10, 1845—Bianco Luno.*[1]

Dear Sir:

As I have sent Mr. Philipsen,[2] the bookseller, what remains of the edition of my *Upbuilding Discourses*, would you please be so good as to deliver to him upon request the copies that you have left.

May 10, 1845.

Respectfully,

S. KIERKEGAARD.

To

Mr. Bianco Luno, printer.

120. *S. K.—[1845]—Henriette Lund.*

My dear Jette,

No doubt I am too late to be "the first who on this first day of the year" etc., as Mr. Zierlich[1] so *ziirligt* puts it. But on the other hand, I hope I am not so very late that the door is closed.

As usual I had forgotten your birthday, in spite of every good intention. I was inconsolable. In vain I rested my head on the "comforter" I owe to your care. In vain! But no, not in vain! Suddenly I take comfort in thinking, "You must reciprocate!" The accompanying parcel is also a "comforter," although it is not to be placed under your head, as it is too hard for that. But its contents are comforting in all the various circumstances of life. And if one happens to be so fortunate as not to be in need of comforting, as I daresay you are, then it is a luxury item as well. Oh, what a comfort that the comfort is a luxury item! Please then, do not seek comfort "in the bottle" (but if you should seek it, you would not do so in vain—although it would be like writing an imitation of Homer's *Iliad* if I were to try to imitate François Marie Farina's estimate of his eau de cologne),[2] but do enjoy its superfluity when—not suffering from toothache or headache, etc.—you squander its contents healthily and gaily for fun or pleasure.

But what you must not squander, what you yourself will probably know how to treat with some economy, is something I do not squander either, regardless of how generously I would like to measure it out for you: good and well-meant wishes for you, my dear Jette. We see each other so seldom, and when we do, I usually like to tease you a little. But on your birthday I wanted to furnish your household with a little supply of my good wishes for you, with an assurance of my regard for you and your future. That is what you are always justly entitled to claim and to seek from

Your uncle.

[*Address*:]
To
Miss Henriette Lund
Accompanying parcel.

120a. *S. K.—Sept. 30, 1845—O. Kold*[1]

Sept. 30, 1845

Dear Sir:

With all my searching, as I told you, I could only come to the flattering conclusion that the broken and lost or lost and broken cup could not be matched. Fortunately, as you now know, it had the distinction in your household also of being the only one of its kind. Why fortunately? Well, usually it is assumed quite properly that to lose the only one of its kind is the heaviest loss of all, but when it comes to coffee cups an exception is made, and one finds it a consolation that the lost cup was the only one of its kind and finds lightest what is usually the heaviest loss of all—losing what is matchless.[2]

So let the accompanying pair of cups take the place of the one that is lost, and on the same condition: that if it is lost, it will not be of great consequence.

S. KIERKEGAARD.

[*Written on the back of the envelope*:] To Mr. Kold
in Fredensborg
Together with a package marked K

121. [*S. K.*] *Victor Eremita—December 25,* [*1845*]—
P. L. Møller.

Christmas Day.

Dear Sir:

Through Mr. Giødwad I received your highly esteemed and confidential note[1] today. My reply to you and to anyone who makes or has made a proposal of this sort: I never have anything completed, and I never bind myself with promises.

Yours respectfully,
VICTOR EREMITA.

122. *S. K.—*[*1845*]*—Israel Levin.*[1]

Monday.

Just as I told you: you are and continue to be the fake *literatus.* Not even able to read handwriting[2]—in the dark! This frailty in you is forgiven, but less so that you did not provide the light necessary for "reading handwriting." Do come this afternoon at 3:30.

S. Kierkegaard

[*Address:*]
To
Cand. I. Levin.

123. *S. K.—*[*1845*]*—Israel Levin.*[1]

My good Levin,

It cannot be done.[2] I am too old to copy in an exercise book for my own sake, and even though my handwriting might come to be considered a model to be imitated by the reading youth, it does not appeal to me to write a draft for the sake of the draft. That kind of draft could easily become daft.

Yours respectfully,
S. KIERKEGAARD.

It occurs to me that some time ago you wrote me a note requesting my *Upbuilding Discourses*. It is not owing to discour-

tesy or deception that I have not replied but to forgetfulness—that I have not sent a reply, for it is lying all ready
right by me and has done so since that day. I found it today
when I was looking through some papers I had tossed aside,
and I enclose it. It looks less felicitous as a companion to this
letter: I had not expected to have to say no again so soon, for
customarily I am a yes-sayer.

To
Cand. I. Levin
Farve[r]gaden
142, second floor.
Accompanying parcel.

124. *S. K.*—*[1845]*—*Israel Levin*.[1]

Sunday.

My good Levin,
   Although I am not usually much inclined to lend books, I
would have been glad to place any other book in my library at
your complete disposal and that of your love affair with linguistic studies, but I must make an exception of my *Upbuilding Discourses*.[2] If it were only true that love makes one blind,
I would have no compunctions; but what is unfortunately
also true—both seriously and facetiously—is that it makes one
see. Thus one sees the grass grow, sees beauty where none
exists, sees the guiding hand of creation (when otherwise one
could not be deceived), sees signs and wonders, sees regularity
and purpose, sees the future in a cloud of transfiguration, adds
the delusion of presentiment to that which does not exist but
which now on an added scale singles out one harmony that is
sounded only by the echo of admiration, etc., etc., for one
sees everything. But however enchanting these visions might
be for Sunday's child, the object in actuality may thus easily
come to play an ambiguous and almost comic role. You may
remember that the first time Jacob Böhme's[3] eyes were
opened to contemplation of the Heavenly Radiance of the
Trinity was when he gazed upon the reflection of the sun in a

pewter plate. Good for J. B.! Rather embarrassing for the plate! Fortunately the plate never got to know anything about it.

Please do not think that I want to make fun of your linguistic studies, as though I had no sympathy at all for microscopic observations. And do not think either that my *Upbuilding Discourses* have now suddenly become unsure of themselves, or think that what was said about my readiness to lend you books was empty politeness. But please do believe that if your note had contained nothing but the wish to borrow the *Discourses*, that if it had not, so to speak, bared its teeth or shown the linguistic machinery grinding away, I should at once have sent you—my only copy. I might also have furnished this as a reason: I have only one single copy, which I do occasionally consult myself.

Yours respectfully,   S. K.

125. *S. K.—[1844-46]—Israel Levin.* [1]

Monday.

My good Levin,

Will you please call on me this morning at 11:30 in my room? After all, you are unoccupied these days—for the fact that you find yourself squabbling[2] with all society cannot be considered any kind of activity.

Sincerely,
S. KIERKEGAARD.

[*Address:*]
To
Cand. I. Levin.

126. *S. K.—[1844-46]—Israel Levin.* [1]

Dear Sir,

Are you in town or are you going to the country? It could be that I might want to talk with you some time next week. Will you be in town then? If so, I shall let you know more

about the day and the hour. But you must in no way make the
least change in your summer plans for my sake.

Yours respectfully,   S. K.

[*Address*:]
To
Cand. I. Levin.

127. *S. K.—[1844-46]—Israel Levin.* [1]

Good Levin,
    Haste is of the essence—
    In this letter my expression of gratitude for your trouble
has also been enclosed, and enclosed in my gratitude a remu-
neration for your work and time.

Yours respectfully,
S. KIERKEGAARD.

NB. I most definitely forbid any perpetuation of the written
characters.

[*Address*:]
To
Cand. Levin
By hand.

128. *S. K.—[1844-46]—Israel Levin.* [1]

Dear Sir:
    If you call tomorrow, you will call in vain. How about not
coming? It is certainly not my fault. But may I request Saturday at 10:30?

Most respectfully,
S. KIERKEGAARD.

[*Address*:]
To
Mr. I. Levin.

129. *S. K.—[1844-46]—Israel Levin.* [1]

Dear Sir:
(Monday)   (Tuesday)
Today I have not received any proofs. Therefore: tomorrow
at 3:15.

Respectfully,   S. K.

[*Address:*]
To
Mr. I. Levin.

130. *S. K.—[1844-46]—Israel Levin.* [1]

Tuesday morning.

Dear Sir:
    They are waiting at the printer's. I am standing here in the
printer's shop—waiting. I leave the place and wait—I expect
you to make haste. Because of your stylistic precision, I do
not fear excessive haste.
    So haste is of the essence—every day is precious to me!

Yours respectfully,
S. KIERKEGAARD.

[*Address:*]
To
Cand. I. Levin.

131. *S. K.—[after January, 1846]—J. F. Giødwad.*
S. K.'s draft. [1]

Dear Giødwad,
    You may yourself have felt on more than one occasion how
difficult it is, when two men are in the public eye as much as
you and I and as such are in as much disagreement as I and
you, how difficult it is to keep up a private relationship.
    Indeed, even if I wanted to refrain from any judgment of
Fædrelandet, as I should like, I cannot, because that journal

does in fact have a relationship to my work as an author[2] as well. And with respect to this, my judgment is that *Fædrelandet* has acted irresponsibly towards it, although I do not wish to comment in further detail.

Permit me therefore to break off the connection I have had with you until now, in which it was understood that I would call on you on one particular day every week. All I want is my freedom, and then God knows that I should like to see you.

Please do not misunderstand this in any way as though my intention were to make *Fædrelandet* publish comments about my work as an author, or to influence their nature, or to let you know in advance my judgment of any possible comment. [*Deleted*: No, no! As you unconditionally have your freedom.]

But please, dear Giødwad, do not misunderstand this either, as though I had in any way forgotten the services you have rendered me, nor forgotten the faithful affection that I for my part have also felt for you, and which—I almost said with your permission, but I will not say that; no, I will say the affection which I—whether you permit it or not—will continue to feel for you.

Yours,   S. K.

132. *S. K.—[1846]—F. C. Sibbern.*

Your Magnificence:[1]

I had almost forgotten this, and now I am annoyed that I did not remember it a few days ago when I sent you a copy of the book I have published. I would have liked to address you in this way, and I am happy that my acknowledgment of the pseudonymous writings in the *Concluding Postscript* took effect in the very year[2] (indeed that was the way the Romans put it: "In the year Cicero was Consul") Sibbern was Rector.

But to the point, for I really do have a point. An elderly man named Blicher[3] is applying for the vacant job as janitor. That is the point. My request now is that you, if possible, take a strong interest in his case. If my memory is not completely wrong, it was precisely your influence that decided the issue last time in favor of the present incumbent, Valdemar Müller.[4] Now let it be Blicher's turn, that still strong, although older, man who has met adversity in life in so many ways. Please let the fact that I, who otherwise never get involved in making recommendations, am making an exception here contribute, if possible, to focusing your attention upon him.

Yours sincerely,
S. KIERKEGAARD.

[*Address:*]
To
His Magnificence
Etatsraad Sibbern.

133. *S. K.—March 19, 1846—P. C. Kierkegaard.*

3/19 '46

Dear Peter,

Thank you for your letter. It made me happy. Please ignore the big "Concluding Book."[1] Read it or not, you will regret doing either.[2] But—in any case I have a clear conscience, for I do not oblige anybody to read, least of all those to whom I send a complimentary copy as a token of friendship. As you know, I spend nearly all day doing nothing but practicing existential dialectics, from which you may readily conclude how reluctant I am to begin a serious discussion about my work with even a skillful dialectician, for I fear it will take too much time before we reach a common point of departure. That is why I have lived like this throughout the time I have been an author or have been "helpful to the pseudonyms in becoming authors."[3] I have never spoken with anyone about my aims, about the achievement. I have always listened calmly to the most dissimilar objections, which I might have refuted with a single word, had not this word been precisely opposed to my principle of silence, which always retains its significance as an epigram for the insufferable talkativeness of the theocentric nineteenth century. I know very well that

such an existence is playing for high stakes and is terribly
exhausting. I knew it in advance, and I know it from experience; I thank God all the more that I am succeeding. Just
imagine that for almost five years without interruption I have
been able to endure living every single day under the same
tension of a production that grows with every year, and that I
am still able to retain my old joy in existence, in mankind,
and in the most insignificant object in nature. So let me lose
some money; let them draw caricatures of me; let them laugh
at me who wish to, for I am so far from having anything to
complain about that I give thanks again and again for the
blessings that have been granted me. But as for talking about
what I do or intend to do: that I cannot. I am so punctilious
that recently I experienced yet another example, for I know
that in a few days I shall be misunderstood by somebody
whom I might have told something when I last saw him,
which he will not learn, and which, when I last spoke with
him, was not only something I intended to do but something
I had accomplished, even though it was not yet *publici juris*
[generally known].

But enough of this. After having made your thought dwell
for a moment on my complaisant solitude in this sun-
drenched town, I shall now make my thought dwell on your
happy domesticity out there in rural solitude. I want to thank
you for the invitation, which even has Jette and Poul joining
in to make it the perfect incantation. Please thank each one:
Jette, adding my assurance that I do indeed think of her now
and then, that I still remember with gratitude the visit she
paid me, and that I readily acknowledge myself in her debt,
and Poul, adding the admonition that he must get into the
habit of remembering his Uncle Søren. As you see, I respect
the allied powers, as it behooves the bachelor to respect marital demonstrations. Besides, as I shall have a little spare time
just now, it may be possible that my heartfelt wish to visit
you at some time, joining the already victorious inviters,
might quite literally persuade me to their side—so that I
might come. But if not, well then, the wish, the desire, the
fraternal sympathy that want to go there are after all prefera-

ble, whereas the person himself, with his indolence, his peculiarity, etc., that would have to be transported there, is the lesser good. Hence the best is sent along at once in this letter at
the suggestion of the invitation. It goes there directly, and
leaves the instant I received your letter—the rest, I myself *in
corpore* [in person], may perhaps not come.

Stay well! Rejoice in the security of your parsonage now
that all danger has passed, the only change being that you
have had a new wing added. Do enjoy your domestic felicity.
Although it may be a dubious undertaking to commence with
nothing in scholarly matters, it is proper to commence with
as little as possible in marital affairs, just as you commenced
with Jette's frail health and may now rejoice in what has been
gained and in the hope you have gained that "whosoever
hath, to him shall be given."[4] My love to her, to Poul, our
dear nephew and the mainstay of the family, and to you yourself.

From your brother.

[*Address*:]
To
Dr. Kierkegaard, Pastor
Pedersborg
v. Sorøe

[*Postmark*:]
Copenhagen
3/20
1846.

134. *S. K.—March 29, 1846—J. L. Heiberg.*

March 29, 1846

Dear Professor:

Please pardon my causing you a small inconvenience. As
you are the editor, I must turn to you concerning the author
of *A Story of Everyday Life*.[1] May I ask you to take the trouble
to send him one copy of the accompanying little book.[2]

As you will gather from the first page, the other copy is

intended for you yourself, Sir, as the immediate recipient. It is a pleasure for me to be able to send you a copy of what I write, and thus it cannot become a habit with me.

Yours respectfully,
S. KIERKEGAARD.

To Professor Heiberg

[*Address:*]
To
Professor J. L. Heiberg
Knight of *Dannebrog*.
Accompanying parcel.

135. *J. L. Heiberg—April 2, 1846—S. K.*

Dear Sir:

First of all, permit me *to testify*, as it is called, to that debt of gratitude I incurred when you so kindly sent me your two most recent works;[1] I hope that this will also be considered as testimony in an inward sense.

I have forwarded the copy of the literary review[2] intended for the author of *A Story of Everyday Life*. An evaluation so commendatory and yet so thorough, so warm and yet so penetrating, must of course be welcome and gratifying to him in the highest degree, and I will surely be able to present you with his own testimony to this before long.

I myself have also read your review with great pleasure. In our so-called critical (i.e., slashing, sneering, and scornful) times it has been utterly forgotten that criticism must be receptive at the outset before it can proceed to its productive task. This is put into practice here in a brilliant way. With generous self-denial the critic has subordinated himself to his subject. He seems to wish to be so receptive that he renounces all his own invention and work. Yet it is precisely here that he becomes genuinely constructive and productive to an eminent degree and thus avoids ending in the negative. I consider your description of the present age as contrasted with the preceding century a small masterpiece of penetrating and acute comprehension and pointed and pertinent satire.

I am especially grateful for the description of the public and its dog, but even more so for the excellent development of the concepts of "to be silent" and "to speak." Robert in *Amor's Strokes of Genius*[3] believes there is no middle way between these two, and I myself have once argued that this very polarity is an example of those in whom the *principium exclusi medii*[4] is valid. But, quite correctly, you have found that the present age has discovered the mean between the two, to wit, in chatter.

With reference to Climacus' contribution,[5] it would be too discursive in a note like this to set down the observations and objections I made while reading. I expect that at some point I shall find an occasion for a detailed explication.

Yours most respectfully,
J. L. HEIBERG

April 2, 1846.
S. T.
Magister S. Kierkegaard.

136. *S. K.—April 6, [1846]—*J. L. Heiberg.

Dear Professor, April 6

When I arrived home rather late Thursday evening I received your note[1] of April 2. On Friday morning I was to leave for a visit to my brother near Sorøe;[2] now that I have returned I immediately take the first opportunity for a brief reply.

Thank you for your welcome note. When one has written a little esthetic review and he who possesses absolute esthetic authority deems it meritorious, it is of course always nice to be the one whom that distinguished person distinguishes. There is an ingenious Oriental proverb that wisely declares that only the deaf sage can resist flattery wisely, because simple-mindedness would regard either of these elements as sufficient: deafness or sagacity. And I, who am neither deaf nor sage, how would I fare in such a dilemma! Therefore it is fortunate that it is impossible for me to be led into such temptation by your note. For when he who has authority praises or approves, then this is after all not flattery, nor would it be wise to turn a deaf ear to it, but indecorous and vain conceit not to heed it gratefully. The reverse is likewise true. If he who admiringly subordinates himself expresses, in his very utterance of admiration, a tolerably clear awareness and idea of what it is he admires, then neither is this flattery. In the former case, authority (reposing in the arbiter), and in the latter case, truth (reposing in the subordinate), are the essentials of that sincerity that precludes the emptiness of flattery.

Thank you also for the possibility you mention of a comment from the author of *A Story of Everyday Life*. What I said in my review about those stories with reference to the reading public, I may here repeat about that friendly comment with reference to my unworthy self: "I think this is a welcome present in any season; looking forward to it is in itself a pleasure; receiving what has been looked forward to is no less a pleasure."[3]

You are, indeed, the editor of these stories. But an editor has it within his power, whenever he wishes, to consider himself as dissociated from the book and the author. I had applied to you in your capacity as editor and begged pardon for causing you any small inconvenience. On the assumption that this unknown author might honor me with a note, you could have waited until the note was finished, and then you could have enclosed in a business envelope that which already constituted adequate attention to me. As I see it, you would have been fully justified in so doing. All the more, then, do I appreciate your note. The contents are indeed the judgment of him who has authority, and I have thanked you for that. But the note itself is a courtesy that in a welcome manner places me in your grateful debt.

Yours most respectfully,
S. KIERKEGAARD.

To Professor Heiberg
Knight of *Dannebrog*

[*Address*:]
To
Professor J. L. Heiberg
Knight of *Dannebrog*

137. *S. K.—April 23, 1846—Henriette Lund.*

My dear Jette,   April 23, 1846.

I had already decided on the accompanying gift for you the day before yesterday, and it was my intention to send it to you that very day. But I forgot. Then came the day of your Confirmation.[1] The solemnity of that day is of such a kind that I at least should not like to connect it with presents and gifts; and when I arrived—before the rest of you returned from church, as you know—and was walking up and down the floor in those empty rooms in serious thought, it became ever more clear to me that the congratulations that wish not merely good fortune but blessing above all, and do so on an occasion never to be repeated, so that the congratulations must thus appertain to a lifetime—then it became ever more clear to me, as I say, that only with considerable difficulty may such congratulations be made to accord with a gift. However genuine the sympathy or especially when it is so, such congratulations do not come with many words—much less with presents.

But the day after such a solemn occasion there is time and opportunity for things of lesser significance. This day has a certain festive afterglow, although it is not the day of the serious solemnity itself. Then you go calling on the minister and get written proof that you have been confirmed. But as a written proof of Confirmation is to the solemnity of the sacred act itself, so, on a lesser scale, is a little gift to the congratulations.

My dear Jette! Holy Scripture says, "Every good gift and every perfect gift is from above, coming down from the Father of lights, with whom there is no change or shadow of variation."[2] On the Holy Day of Confirmation it is God himself of course who is present to bestow the gift; he in whom there is no variation bestows the gift himself: the Confirmation of the Covenant. Then we human beings, your parents, your relatives, your friends, the participants, come forward—we congratulate. But God gives the gift. The good and the perfect gift is from God. The best that man has to offer is congratulations.

Your uncle   S. K.

138. *Thomasine Gyllembourg—April 26, 1846—S. K.*

Copy[1]
Magister S. Kierkegaard, S. T.

That I have not sent you my warmest thanks until now for the meaningful and charitable review with which you honored my novel *Two Ages* is due less to accidental circumstance than to your own book, for its rich and profound contents have given me so much substance for reflection that I have been unable to tear myself away from the many serious reflections it has prompted and which I sought in vain to find words to express. A dual feeling has filled me on this occasion: I feel myself elevated by the honor you have shown me and embarrassed because it is greater than my literary merits could hope. On the other hand, it is a great recommendation for my little work that it has been the cause of a book like yours; but on the other hand, when I compare my novel with your book, so richly equipped with such profound, such apt, and such witty observations, then my work appears to me a simple romance from which a poet has taken the subject and wrought a drama. Just as there cannot be a happier hour in life than that in which we pour out our best thoughts to a sympathetic heart from which they—transfigured, as it were—are reflected back to us, it may be that there is no greater reward for an author than being understood so well, comprehended with as much love as that with which you have examined my latest novel and all of my modest production. And just as in this life, between friends, one would like to clarify, excuse, indeed even embellish those points of view over which there may be disagreement, in the same way I ask you to permit me to explain briefly to you what I intended with a couple of particular points on which I think that we have not understood each other.

I conceived of Claudine in her first youthful passion for Lusard—if I may presume to express it like this—as a more modern version of Heloise of the Middle Ages, who so breathes and lives in her love that everything in heaven and on earth seems to her to be subordinated to it. To consider mar-

riage a Philistine denigration of love is a point of view I believe is derived less from the time of the Revolution than from
the so-called philosophical period that preceded it. But nursed
by the spirit of the times and by events, this thought strikes a
responsive chord in Claudine's soul. It is not on account of
naïveté that she does not realize the consequences of her fall
from virtue; rather, she does not have a place in her heart for
this fear as long as the beloved is still at her side and the
thought of parting from him preoccupies her above all else.
Both she and Lusard push the thought of such a possible consequence into the remote background, just as one pushes aside
the thought of the daily approach of death. Not until Lusard
is gone does that Nemesis come, which, despite the erroneous
opinions of every age, protects the laws of public decency.
Lusard is less caught up in the frivolous opinions of the age
than is Claudine herself. He would prefer to call his beloved
his wife before God and man, but in spite of all his love there
is one thing he values more highly: his military honor, the
chivalrous allegiance he owes the political and military banner
to which he is pledged. He does not leave Claudine out of
recklessness—no, with profound grief, as she says herself. On
the other hand, he might be accused of recklessness later
when, on the evidence of a not very reliable report, he believes Claudine married to somebody else, but even this cre-
dulity might perhaps also be pardoned owing to the jealous
nature of passion.

As for the Baron: with him I wanted to suggest the power
that passionate love exerted in those days even on an inferior
personality. This brings both good and evil spirits into his
surroundings. At a time when *mésalliances* were far more rare
and of greater importance than in our day, he sacrifices everything he has to bestow and believes that he has made a great
sacrifice. I have never thought of his courtship as a temptation
for Claudine. A female heart in love is surely inaccessible to
all such temptations, but his appearance provides a motive for
Claudine's expression of her feelings. In the moment of his
rage he must not be thought of as "a drunkard."[2] He is
what we have seen a hundred times, a human being who

seeks to forget his desperation with the aid of wine and thus adds fuel to the fire. In this state of excitement, which is still not what is understood as drunkenness, an ironic demon guides that creature to him who is the most bitter object of his jealousy. It is not his real intention to kill the child. It is one of those demonic impulses whereby a human being takes pleasure in the thought that it is within his power to commit a crime and that he can give voice to his daring intention, while yet feeling that his guardian angel will restrain his arm. Under such circumstances, a moment like this may readily surprise a good-natured, relatively civilized person. Nor is Claudine's influence wholly in vain, for when the boy mentions his mother, he releases him and falls crying upon the ground.

I must add yet a few words in defense of Ferdinand Bergland. It is not "out of fear of financial difficulties"[3] that he leaves his beloved, but on account of his love, owing to his pity for her unfortunate situation, which he despairs of ever altering. He believes that a man whom he honors and at whose side he regards her fate as assured is offering her a happiness to which he must not become an obstacle, and he breaks the bond that ties her to him out of a misunderstood sense of duty, which I, by the way, think is in agreement with the thought of our own day, as Lusard also accusingly remarks in their first conversation.

Having succumbed to the temptation to dare to speak of my insignificant work to one who has so kindly understood and evaluated it, I beg you not to see any other motive in this than my eagerness to win your approval. I ought not to make further demands on you to consider something to which you have already given so much attention, but I want to conclude with my assurances that your book will seem "wie des **Freundes Auge mild**" to my mind during many an hour when doubt and sadness

> "durch das Labyrinth der Brust
> wandelt in der Nacht."[4]

April 26, 1843. *The Author of "A Story of Everyday Life."*
Verbatim from the author's manuscript.

J. L. HEIBERG

139. *S. K.—[April 1846]—H. P. Kofoed-Hansen. S. K.'s draft.*[1]

Dear Sir:

For a moment you may be surprised when you see from the signature who is writing this, and when that has passed, you may perhaps be pleased that the letter is from him, and this in turn would please him from whom this letter comes.

Summa summarum and to the point. If you lived in Copenhagen,[2] I suppose I would some day put into effect a plan I have long entertained—but alas, it seems that the realization of plans long entertained is doomed, and the only thing that comforts me is that the plans I have entertained for a long time are never proportionate to my work but solely to what also ought to be performed: to pay a call, to say hello to this or that person, to accept this or that invitation, etc. In other words, if you lived in Copenhagen, I suppose that assisted by an impulse I would have come to the point and would have pitched headlong through your door and called on you. Then I might even have fallen head first through your doorway and with Eulenspiegel[3] have called out, "This haste is the devil's work!" Presumably you know that it is said of Eulenspiegel that when his foster mother sent him shopping for half a pint of wine he stayed away for four years, until one day he came tearing into her room, fell, broke the bottle, and cried, "This haste is the devil's work!"

But as you do not live in Copenhagen, I shall do something else: assisted by a letter I shall put this long-entertained plan into effect. For although (precisely in order to belong wholly and wholly consistently to the idea I have the honor to serve) I scarcely associate with anybody and indeed shun any connection, yet from this it follows in no way that I remain ignorant of what is happening around me nor that I fail, without sympathy or ready acknowledgment, to discover what is going on. In this very connection I have often thought of you and thought about the rewarding circumstances under which you work as an author and about how you still retain your enthusiasm and energy. This interests me very much indeed, for I am no friend of fawning, and just as I myself feel no need either of the warm swaddling of admiration or of the lure of favors, it is gratifying and satisfactory to me to see someone else who *"proprio Marte, propriis auspiciis,"* [independently, under his own auspices][4] realizes something similar.

Just as it is customary practice and indeed serves a purpose for soldiers at dangerous posts to call out to each other at intervals in the darkness of night, just so I wish this note to be considered my calling out, and I shall be pleased if you welcome such a call.

I hope you are well and find time and inclination to work. As for myself, I am in excellent health, God be praised. Only one thing would exhaust my soul, and that is if I were to become the object of a trivial and stale and fawning and driveling admiration. Therefore I have always *pro virili* [in manly fashion] sought to protect myself against this, and I hope to succeed. But when I succeed, then there is merry dancing in the meadows.[5] Considered from this point of view, the circumstances under which I work as an author have an advantage over yours, of course, for according to my idea of existence, work should be without any reward—for that is precisely when the dance is performed to the honor of God.

It is different for the writer who both wishes and may also reasonably insist that his work not be unrewarded toil. Thus you see why I believe your circumstances are less rewarding than mine, and that is the very reason I am pleased that you persevere, and the very reason I want to call out to you. I am also pleased that a review of your *Flesh and Spirit*[6] appeared at long last, and an extensive and favorable one at that.

That review has also meant something else to me, for it has reminded me of that which I cannot call a long-entertained plan, but nonetheless a wish, I had to review this book myself. That would in a certain sense have been to reciprocate[7]—tit for tat—but I hope that a friendship may also endure without this exact tit for tat.

With all good wishes for your efforts—that you may find both time for work and the zest happily found in work—I send you this little greeting. It is, as it were, an unusually extensive interjection, an exclamation that also serves as its own exclamation point. There can scarcely be any talk of a continuation, but I am not at work these days, and so I have had time for this and that, and I have always kept *in mente* that a call to you belonged here.

In friendship,
S. KIERKEGAARD.

140. *S. K.—November 16, [1846]—Henriette Lund.*

Monday, November 16.
My dear Jette,

Since all of *nature* is out of order these days, so that it is tempting to say with Jeronymus, "I don't think the world will last until Easter,"[1] you might [find] it quite in the *natural* order of things that I have completely forgotten your birthday.[2] But only a natural revolution would be able to erase from the slate of my memory that which was written with otherwise indelible letters upon it after last time. Now it is once again most vivid for me: it took place on a Saturday—accordingly it is quite in order that this year your birthday falls on a Sunday—I remember it very clearly, the sky was dark and overcast; it was so dark at six o'clock in the afternoon that it was already evening; the weather was—well, the weather was as it is on most days in November, and accordingly it is not so strange that I should remember *that* day. But precisely because that day otherwise had nothing remarkable about it, it made such a profound impression on me that this was your birthday. I would have considered it an impossibility that I could have forgotten it the next time around. And yet November 15 arrives, Sunday, November 15, your birthday—and I forget it. This may only be accounted for by the natural revolution that is taking place.

But joking aside, my dear Jette, let us accept that I forgot that it was your birthday last Thursday. Then, on the other hand, it is a certainty that I have not forgotten that you remembered my birthday, for now it is exactly two weeks since that cigar case was taken into use and thereby removed from oblivion once and for all, and it will also now be taken out more frequently for the sake of memory. You see, tobacco and coffee really belong with each other. You do not smoke, while I on the other hand do, and therefore your present was a considerate one. But then again, supposing that you do drink coffee, it is easy to think of returning the favor in kind. Thus, sometimes when I smoke a cigar extracted from your case, you may drink a cup of coffee from the enclosed cups. But it is true of coffee as well as of tobacco that too much is unhealthful. This you had surely taken into account, and it explains why that case was fairly small. Indeed, when I compare it with those I *really* use, then it is like and no different from a waistcoat pocket compared with your sewing bag. So I suppose I shall have to use this case in an *unreal* way. You may assure yourself of the like wisdom on my part when you inspect the accompanying cup of coffee or rather the accompanying coffee cup. Such a cup of coffee can in no way be harmful to you. And yet it is true of coffee as of friendship: a little is enough.

And so, my dear Jette, let me make up for what I neglected, my sincere congratulations on your birthday. In a certain sense it was also possible to postpone them, for my congratulations are not in so much of a hurry that they seek their sole justification in arriving on your birthday. Although I cannot forbear joking and teasing, you know very well that my regard for you and for your life is such that you may be glad to be entitled to claim it from

Your uncle.　S. K.

[*Address:*]
To
Miss Henriette Lund.

141. *S. K.—[1846]—Henriette Lund.*

My dear Jette,

A mistake! A mistake! On the outside of the letter you received a moment ago I had forgotten to write, "Accompanying parcel," and likewise I had forgotten to send the parcel.

Now that those two cannot manage to accompany each other, since you have received the letter, I shall write another letter and this I shall now send off accompanied by a small parcel.

Yes, my good Jette, I had really forgotten that it was your birthday until I was reminded of it at Uncle Christian's. But the accident is not a very serious one, after all, and it would certainly have been more serious if I had remembered your birthday but otherwise forgotten you and the regard for you and your life that you may reasonably claim from your uncle. Let my congratulations, then, be your proof of this. They come accompanied by good and sincere wishes for you, something every person may be in need of, even though, like you, he is of an age and in such circumstances that he is too happy truly to want anything. For should it not be a good and sincere wish to wish for such considerateness and its continuance in happy days? As I said, it is accompanied by good and sincere wishes for you, even though I were to withhold the wishes so that there might be something left over for next time, for the next birthday, or for the next time I forget that it is your birthday.

Your uncle   S. K.

[*Address*:]
To
Henriette Lund.
Accompanying parcel.

142. *S. K.*—[*1846*]—*Christiane Ph. Spang*.[1]

Dear Mrs. Spang,

As you see, I am hurrying—for I think as follows: "I bet that otherwise I will forget it."

Yours,   S. KIERKEGAARD.

I am almost ashamed that I cannot produce a more handsome "note," but that, of course, is the bank's affair—and when one is as interesting an author as is the National Bank in

Copenhagen (oh, that one might be that interesting oneself!),
then it is easy to be indifferent to external considerations. But
a poor author like me, whose writing has not the same inherent worth as that of the Bank, he must write his insignificant
things—on good paper.

143. *S. K.—no date—Chr. Ph. Spang.*

Dear Mrs. Spang,
   Yes, I am probably "unaccountable," and imagine! Now I
have even become unaccountable to myself, or my visit to
your home is at least unaccountable to myself. For just last
night I had counted on visiting you. But what I had not
counted on was that I would not be let in through the gate,
although I both rang—and waited. You yourself will concede
that when one is prevented from visiting you in this way, or
rather, that when one adds this to all the other obstacles, then
the unaccountability of that visit has reached its unaccountable highest.—Still, let us not despair but work with our combined powers. In spite of all obstacles I know how to get to
your gate; you know how to have it opened for me—and so
the visit may succeed another time.

                                   Yours,   S. KIERKEGAARD.

144. *S. K.—no date—Chr. Ph. Spang.*

Dear Mrs. Spang,
   Presumably you believe—well, let us not dwell on that—
everything you so believe can in no way confirm faith, everything merely strengthens your doubt as to my faithfulness. In
a certain sense this is quite a simple matter, and yet in another,
rather strange. For it frequently occurs to me: "I wonder how
Mrs. Spang is," but it always occurs at the wrong time. Almost every evening at 9:30 precisely I hear the tap of an ad-
monishing thought that says, "Do remember to call on Mrs.
Spang!" But almost every evening at 9:30 precisely I am

standing on the top of Frederiksberg-Bakke. Even though I were to hurry back to Copenhagen, it would still be too late. Meanwhile I determine on some time the next day when I shall be somewhat closer to your house so that I can make up for this neglect. But then, you see, I forget it until evening comes and the hour is 9:30—and I stand repentant on Frederiksberg Bakke. My conversion leads to nothing, although as stated, at that moment I always turn around and walk back to town. Sure enough, last night the usual phenomenon occurred. But now, having become so skeptical about myself, I write to you, for I am afraid that tonight the same story will repeat itself.

Well, joking aside, now to something serious. I should really be very sorry if you were to blame me for my negligence in any way. You will readily comprehend that I should be even sorrier than if something like this had happened to me with your husband, for he, after all, might have caught up with me in the street. But a "real widow,"[1] as the Bible says (and for this it is necessary that it really is a *husband* who has died and that the bereaved has a true conception of her real loss, for otherwise it does not follow by any means that every wife whose husband has died is a real widow), who sits at home with loss and grief in her house, she is of course entitled to make very different demands. I admit it, and certainly it would scarcely have occurred to me to write such a long letter to your husband to apologize. But from former days you ought to be familiar with my indolence, and when the weather is hot it can develop to an especially high degree.

In other words, please let this letter atone for my absence, and when you have read it, please let it be as though I had called on you today. —Perhaps the length of this letter may get me in its power so that I shall call one of these days, although I promise nothing. But to give myself credit, let me remind you that I write to practically nobody else. So one may safely conclude that you are very much on my mind, since you are now receiving this letter from

Yours,   S. KIERKEGAARD.

145. *Chr. Ph. Spang—no date—S. K.*

Monday morning.

How the mist can mystify a sound concept, dear Magister! I had not realized until today that by means of a letter I might perhaps obtain an answer to a question I pondered all last week. Every day I have studied the newspapers, but without finding your death notice. Are you ill? Or are you renouncing? I should almost prefer to believe the former—with your permission! Unfortunately, I do not have great respect for the endurance or faithfulness of people, so I am reluctant to release him in whom I think I have finally found them. —Therefore tell me: Either/Or! In any case, certainty is best, and in this I hope for the best.

Yours, C. SPANG.

146. *S. K.—no date—Chr. Ph. Spang.*

Dear Mrs. Spang,

Why an Either/Or? Would this not be a jack, with which, as is well known, it is difficult indeed to lift the most insignificant things in life, which is why it is not really a lever for everyday use? For although it is true enough that a jack is capable of lifting almost anything—one cannot lift a feather with such a jack. Please consider what it means to set such strong motives in motion. Suppose now that with the enormous impetus of your note I were to fling myself headlong across your threshold and topple everything, bringing fear and destruction along with me! As you know, it is far easier to conjure spirits forth than to conjure them away—suppose I were to remain seated far into the night: would you be served by that?

Rest assured, then, that either I shall come this evening or I shall not come; so with respect to your house I shall always remain one who is in the act of coming.

Yours, S.K.

147. *S. K.—January 20, 1847—Carl Lund.*

January 20, 1847.

My dear Carl,

If you are thinking, you may be thinking as follows: "Uncle Søren has so much to think about that it is no wonder he forgets some things, but still it is strange that he always forgets my birthday or forgets the day of my Confirmation,[1] while he can remember those of the others so precisely."

But you see, my dear Carl, this conclusion—that I forget the day of your Confirmation or your birthday on account of my many occupations—is quite incorrect; for on the contrary, I have thought more often about those days than about the birthdays of all the others combined. This is what happened: as the time for your Confirmation approached, I went looking for a little present. And then at an art dealer's I came across a writing desk that seemed so handsome that instantly it was clear to me that this must be the present. *Aber* [but], it was too expensive. Then what did I do? Then I let the bird fly away, but in no way so as to forget the matter. On the contrary, I thought, "Now, let a little time pass, then I shall just about be able—without being noticeably unfair to the others—to send Carl the present selected for him."

Here it is. As you can see, I cannot really be said to have forgotten you. Indeed, I have many times kept an eye on this writing desk lest it get away. And if the preface to *Either/Or* were not of an earlier date, I could almost believe that Victor Eremita had used this motif, for there he speaks about how he walked every day past a secondhand store in which there was a desk that had made a deep impression on him, until at last he did buy the desk that was to become so important to him.[2]

I also wanted you to learn something from this incident, for there is after all something to be learned. For you may learn, and life will one day confirm this for you, that most people behave in such a way that when they appear to have forgotten something, then they have in fact forgotten it, while there are still others who are more talkative, but who cannot for that reason alone really be said to be considerate of others. But oc-

casionally there may be a person who may look most forgetful, and yet he may be the very person who remembers carefully in his heart of hearts—as I now remember my youngest
nephew.

Therefore, my dear Carl, please accept now what has been
selected for you for some time, accept it accompanied by my
good wishes, accept it in memory of that day for which it was
really intended, accept it in memory of him who, even
though he may not appear sensitive in everyday life, may accordingly possess both sensitivity and sympathy after all.

                                    Your uncle,   S. K.

[*Address*:]
To
Carl Lund.
Accompanying parcel.

148. *S. K.—February 1847—Julie Thomsen.* [1]
                                    February, '47.
My dear Cousin,

I am very happy to know that you "would have preferred
to use the occasion" (to which I owe the receipt of your note)
for "a spoken conversation," even though this can be known
only insofar as I also hear your hidden reproach in it. But this
neglect cannot be amended now. However, I do hope that my
promptness in replying to your note will convince you that I
should not be given up completely. Alas, it is all too true (as
you say—and as I regret) that you never meet me on the
street, and worse yet, it is all too true, as you remind me reproachfully, "that I do not keep my promise to visit you."
Well then, please accept this little epistle. Let it serve, if you
please, as an encounter in the street or as a visit to your home.
After all, the streets are ruled out: the public ones (where
people meet and part), inasmuch as you do not go out, or
rather, "so rarely go there," and the official one that leads to
your house, inasmuch as I do not pay visits. But as you have
fortunately discovered the mystery street by means of your

welcome letter, I hasten not to leave it unused. Please accept my little letter now; it comes quickly, as if I knew that by turning down this or that street I would come upon you; it comes contritely as I myself would come to your house for the first time; it comes happily and merrily as I myself would come if I had finally won my liberty by defeating that indolence that tyrannizes me; it comes filled with longing from him who will probably not come himself, after all, and who therefore becomes all the more filled with longing.

My d[ear] J., all this may seem rather strange to you. Perhaps you are thinking as follows: "The time he uses to write a letter could just as well be used to pay a visit—and used far better." I concede it, I concede everything, I make every concession—in order to do something, at least, and I prefer to do it in writing, for to do it in conversation would really mean defeat. The fact is that I am actually in love with the company of my pen. It might be said that this is a poor object on which to cast one's affection. Perhaps! But it is not as though I were always content with it. Occasionally I hurl it away in anger. Alas, this very anger shows me once more that I am indeed in love with it, for the quarrel ends as lovers' quarrels do. I confide completely in my pen, whether I become angry when it sometimes seems to me that it cannot do what I can do, cannot follow the thought that I am thinking—or whether I am surprised when it seems as if it can do what I cannot. I cannot tear myself away from the company of my pen; indeed, it even prevents me from seeking the company of anybody else.

So as I sit here at home and happen to think about somebody or other who is dear to me, I think, "Now you ought to go and visit him." But what happens? I think about it for such a long time that finally the pen (yes, for it must be the pen!) tricks its way into my hand. Instead of paying a visit in town, one more letter takes shape at home. Assisted by the pen I now converse with this person, and when I have finished, the pen actually laughs at me, for it has tricked me. By then the letter is finished, and I think to myself, "Now you must be sure to seal and send it." What happens? Well, it must be the pen that makes me believe that it can inform me perfectly well as to what impression the receipt of my letter will make on the recipient: what he will say and what I will say in my turn—what he will then say, etc. In brief, instead of sending the letter, which is burned, that letter occasions a small sketch from nature. Of course that sketch cannot be sent and accordingly it must also be burned. Once again the pen has tricked me. It tricks me out of many of the pleasures of life, and the sole comfort left is that, assisted by the pen, I am able more or less to describe how easily it has tricked me—provided that this does not have to be done on one of those days when I am quarreling with it.

I do not know if I have succeeded in making myself quite clear, but in any case this time my pen shall not succeed in tricking the letter away from me, all the more so because just these days I deserve to be reproached in a stricter sense for my lack of participation in the actualities of life. I myself realize very well that it was rather strange that I did not take part in my late cousin's funeral procession, but for that very reason I doubly appreciate your sympathy and attention to me: in such circumstances to write me a letter. I am also aware of your father's kindness to me, but, really, he almost embarrassed me with his politeness, for it does seem almost too much to call on me in person to bring me his sad news and then to excuse me from attending.

The enclosure from Berlin was typical for Berlin. Brøchner's[2] notion to send it here was not a bad one, and his notion to send it to you was a happy one; but your idea of sending it to me with your letter—that was a beautiful idea. And there is (do but ask the philosophers about this, do ask Brøchner) a world of difference between a notion and an idea. So there is also a contradiction in having your letter serve as an envelope for that little slip of paper from B., for that is like wrapping a small silk scarf in a genuine Persian shawl. Of course, it would be more natural to use the silk scarf as a wrapper for the shawl. It is no less a contradiction that a letter from a lady should include a brief note from a gentleman. As a rule one is already quite struck if one is so lucky as to receive a note from a lady enclosed in a letter from a gentleman. So you see, because I have in fact often thought of visiting you and often regretted that I have not done so and because I really appreciate your welcome note—you receive this monstrously long letter in reply, which after all does correspond with the disproportion occasioned by B.

Your most devoted S. K.

149. *S. K.—May [19], 1847—P. C. Kierkegaard.*

Wednesday.
Dear Peter,

The birthday on which you congratulate me and about which you say that it "often and uncustomarily has been in your thoughts these days," that birthday has also frequently and for a long time preceding it been in my own thoughts. For I became 34 years old.[1] In a certain sense it was utterly unexpected. I was already very surprised when—yes, now I may say it without fear of upsetting you—you became 34 years old. Both Father and I had the idea that nobody in our family would live past his 34th year. However little I otherwise agreed with Father, in a few singular ideas we had an essential point of contact, and in such conversations Father was always almost impressed with me, for I could depict an idea with lively imagination and pursue it with daring consistency. In fact, a curious thing about Father was that what he had most of, what one least expected, was imagination, albeit a melancholy imagination. The 34th year was, then, to be the limit, and Father was to outlive us all. That is not the way it has turned out—I am now in my 35th year.

About the rest of my letter to you: you do not appear to have understood it quite as I intended. I did not intend to sell[2] at just this time, but I wanted to obtain your answer to my question about whether or not you wanted to increase your mortgage as proposed. This would, as I remarked, also be convenient for me whenever I might decide to sell.

It appeared to me to be quite desirable for you to be the holder of a first mortgage of 10,000 *rdl*. I shall not add any more about this, for you yourself must be able to see very well what speaks in favor of it, and better than I what might speak against it. It is only my intention that the wish should agree with what is in your best interest. If it does, you might do me the favor of granting my wish, and moreover the favor is of such a kind that I can accept it gladly because no sacrifice is involved on your part, for your property invested in such an unconditional first mortgage is just as safe as in any stock or bond, indeed, probably safer.

You yourself surely do see that a first mortgage of 7,000 *rdl.* on my house is a very small first mortgage; but on the other hand, since you do hold a first mortgage, I am unable to offer anybody else terms other than those of a second mortgage, which is not very easy to obtain, however. Thus you who hold a small first mortgage are the only one to whom I can apply, and even if you were someone else, it would still seem reasonable that that someone else would grant my wish, provided he were otherwise able to do so.

Please think about doing it. In a certain sense you do not know very much about my life, its goal and its purpose, but you do know that it is very strenuous, which in a certain sense you may not care for—perhaps because you are not familiar with it. There is a necessary silence with respect to my life, and it is precisely by silence that it gains its strength. Even if I wanted to speak, that which is most important to me and which most profoundly determines my life would be that about which I must be silent. From this arises a disparity in my relationship with anyone who has, or to whom I might wish to give, a claim to closer confidence. Therefore I have never wanted to make it appear as though I maintained a confidential relationship with anybody, precisely because I knew that even if he did not discover that disparity, I myself would realize it. In my relationship with those few people with whom I have had a little closer association (for in a discursive sense I have had association with countless numbers), I have myself on one occasion pointed out to them that there was a discrepancy in our relationship, and I have added that the relationship, such as mine was to them, was dear to me but that no real confidence was possible for me.

Thus now also in relation to you. I can well understand that
it must offend you or seem peculiar to you that in your relationship with another human being who probably has experienced a great deal internally, you are not more intimately informed *qua* brother. Leave it at that and consider if it is not a
sort of honesty on my part to have stated that this is so. I can
only say this much—that from the beginning, with sufferings
which perhaps few can imagine because I was given strength
to conceal them, I acknowledge more and more happily that
Governance has granted me infinitely more than I had ever
expected. Even now, after having worked incessantly in this
way for several years without the least bit of outside encouragement, and on top of this even having been for a long time
the object of ugly treatment by rabble vulgarity, by coarse-
ness, and by curiosity, day in and day out—even now I feel
grateful appreciation that I work more easily and am in better
health than before, indeed, that this really has worked to my
advantage and added one more string to my instrument instead of damaging the old strings. You see, if you would join
me in taking pleasure in that, I would be pleased.

Anyway, I could wish to speak with you at greater length
some time, especially now that I am 34 years old and am
gradually moving toward a change, if possible, in the outer
circumstances of my life by assuring myself of a livelihood
after all. But I do not want to be precipitate about this. So
much happiness has been granted me with respect to my
work that I must in no way at all disturb my mind by too
much haste. Therefore I will probably come down to you
sometime and stay for a few days. Greetings to Jette, Poul.

Your S. K.

[*Address*:]
To
Dr. Kierkegaard, Pastor
Pedersborg
v. Sorøe

[*Postmark*:]
Copenhagen
5/20 1847.

150. *S. K.*—*[1847]*—*Henriette Kierkegaard.*[1]

Dear Jette,

I am glad that you yourself have provided the occasion for sending the book[2] that accompanies this letter. So you yourself are responsible and will all the more carefully see to it that your reading of the book or any single part of it will not in any way conflict with my brother's idea of what is beneficial or harmful reading, for it would distress me to have that happen.

Please note, therefore, that I have arranged it so that emphasis is in no way placed on whether or not you read it, something I never oblige anyone to do, and especially not that person whom I surely would not wish to *burden* with a *complimentary* copy.

This is my own copy, originally destined for myself: thus it has a purely personal relationship to me, not in my capacity as author as with other copies, but rather as if the author had presented it to me. However, it now occurs to me that it has not fulfilled its destiny and reaches its proper destination only in being destined for you—the only copy in the whole printing suitable for that. —The bookbinder has done a beautiful job on the book (and in judging the bookbinder's craft I am after all impartial). —It has been read through by me and is to that extent a used copy. So please notice that everything is as it ought to be now. For a brief moment you may admire the bookbinder's art as you would admire any other art object; then you may—for a longer moment, if you please, take pleasure in the thought that it is a gift; and then you may put the book down (—for it has been read—), put it aside as one puts a gift aside, put it aside carefully—if it is a welcome gift.

But enough of this. I was sorry not to be able to take my leave of you. I hope this little letter in which I take my leave will find you as well as I found you when I arrived. *Above all, do not lose your desire to walk: every day I walk myself into a state of well-being and walk away from every illness; I have walked myself into my best thoughts, and I know of no thought so burdensome that one cannot walk away from it.* Even if one were to walk for one's health and it were constantly one station ahead—*I would still say: Walk!*[3] Besides, it is also apparent that in walking one constantly gets as close to well-being as possible, even if one does not quite reach it—*but by sitting still, and the more one sits still, the closer one comes to feeling ill.* Health and salvation can be found only in motion. If anyone denies that motion exists, I do as Diogenes did, I walk.[4] If anyone denies that health resides in motion, then I walk away from all morbid objections. *Thus, if one just keeps on walking, everything will be all right.* And out in the country you have all the advantages; you do not risk being stopped before you are safe and happy outside your gate, nor do you run the risk of being intercepted on your way home. I remember exactly what happened to me a while ago and what has happened frequently since then. I had been walking for an hour and a half and had done a great deal of thinking, and with the help of motion I had really become a very agreeable person to myself. What bliss, and, as you may imagine, what care did I not take to bring my bliss home as safely as possible. Thus I hurry along, with downcast eyes I steal through the streets, so to speak; confident that I am entitled to the sidewalk, I do not consider it necessary to look about at all (for thereby one is so easily intercepted, just as one is looking about—in order to avoid) and thus hasten along the sidewalk with my bliss (for the ordinance forbidding one to carry anything on the sidewalk does not extend to bliss, which makes a person lighter)—directly into a man who is always suffering from illness and who therefore with downcast eyes, defiant because of his illness, does not even think that he must look about when he is not entitled to the sidewalk. I was stopped. It was a quite exalted gentleman who now honored me with conversation. Thus all was lost. After the conversation ended, there was only one thing left for me to do: instead of going home, to go walking again.

As you see, there really is no more space in this letter, and therefore I break off this conversation—for in a sense it has been a conversation, inasmuch as I have constantly thought of you as present. Do take care of yourself!

Yours,   S. KIERKEGAARD.

[*Address:*]
To
Mrs. Henriette Kierkegaard
Pedersborg
v. Sorøe
Accompanying parcel.

151. *S. K.—[July 9, 1847]—P. D. Ibsen.*[1] *S. K.'s draft.*

Dear Sir,

   In *Fædrelandet* of yesterday I find a true and excellent comment in lucid and clear, particularly well-chosen words,
which I hereby quote: "It is to be hoped that good weather
will prevail while the Scandinavians are gathered." Superbly
put! But the great significance of what is thus stated from a
lofty and superior point of view about a splendid popular or
tri-popular undertaking[2] (a popular turning of oneself into
tri-men)*[3] contains a similar truth when applied to lesser affairs, for "it is to be hoped that good weather will prevail
when I go for a ride in the country." During the first half of
my most recent expedition I came to realize that this really
was something to hope for. I arrived at Lyngby[4] chilled to
the bone by the terrible cold (you remember how chilled I
looked, whereas your wife, to be sure, thought I had grown
fat—presumably from the trip), but oh, when I arrived at
Hirschholm . . . . . and when I then arrived at ! ! But that is
now in retrospect, and it is also in retrospect that I now remember that probably I really ought to have drunk the coffee
your wife was kind enough to provide with marvelous haste.
But when one thinks in retrospect of something that one has
left undone and that one ought to have done, then one does
regret it: accordingly I regret that I did not drink the coffee.
What happened to Herman v. Bremenfeldt,[5] who restrained

---

*[*S. K.'s note:*] I assume you are familiar with this Baggesen phrase that contains an allusion to the three men in the red-hot furnace. The phrase has the
additional peculiarity that T. C. Bruun invented a rhyme based on this "turning oneself into tri-men": "to let oneself be topsy-turvied."

himself until his wife had left but then set out after her, might
also happen to me. For had there been no obstacles, I probably would have come today to drink the coffee. But I was
punished for not having drunk it, and accordingly I hope
your wife has forgiven me. I am certain of it—on the strength
of the following syllogism: the sun has set since last
Saturday—would anyone deny that? No. Your wife never
lets the sun set on her anger. Ergo! However, my haste is easy
to explain. For if one has to return to Copenhagen by 7 p.m.,
and at 9:15 a.m. finds himself still at Lyngby on the outward
journey, then there are not many moments to waste.

Enough of this. I merely repeat "that it really is to be hoped
that good weather will prevail when I" etc.—and I hope the
weather will remain fine as long as the Scandinavians turn
themselves into tri-men here in Copenhagen. For I predict
that it will be very trying for the participants unless the pain-
fulness of these times or, and this is what I meant to say, the
happiness of these times is made briefer. Merely to be forced
on one such Sunday to be incessantly sensitive, "patriotic-
sensitive," and "tri-mennish" might well require preferential
treatment by the climate, but to have to be that way for one
whole week, not to mention two additional days for an excursion! As is well known, feeling is a delicate matter. It is the
same with feeling as it is with vegetables. Would it be possible, if one had to keep spinach boiling or on the fire for a
whole week, would it be possible to avoid scorching it a little
at the end? But why do I say "a little at the end"? No, undoubtedly the spinach would soon become very scorched. I
cannot imagine where they will find enough *turns of phrase*.
Granted that several of them have already been fashioning
turns of phrase for a long time, phrases that can hold their
own, superb phrases that although old still snap between the
teeth as ship's biscuits do, granted that somebody thus furnished with turns of phrase intended for the excursion does
go on that excursion, granted that some turn of phrase or
other goes along that can only be used on a tight turn, still I
cannot imagine how it will suffice. On the contrary, I can perfectly well imagine how painful it must be (especially in bad

weather) to twist and turn without being able to find a turn of phrase. For just as a well-turned phrase is invaluable when one can use it to get into something easily or to slip out of something adroitly, a turn of phrase is boring when it keeps recurring constantly.

In fact, not long ago I observed a literary instance of "a strange shortage of turns of phrase" (*ad modum*: "a strange shortage of vegetable dealers"). As you know, great numbers of sermons and devotional books have been published lately. As long as everything follows its natural course, so that now a work on esthetics is published, now one on philosophy, then one on natural history, etc., we pay no attention. Those gentlemen, the critics and reviewers, like vegetable dealers, have one drawer containing allspice, another raisins, etc.—but only a little in each. But look, now it all becomes clear: after one drawer has been used for such a long time, there occurs "a strange shortage of turns of phrase." This was the case with the *Berlingske Tidende*. One evening it reviewed a devotional book as follows: "It excels by its profound and clear earnestness." Good enough! But the next evening another devotional book is reviewed as follows: "It excels by its profound and earnest clarity." And on the third evening: "It excels by its earnest and clear profundity." But *Aftenbladet* had such a dearth of turns of phrase that it went so far as to review a collection of sermons with these words: "This pamphlet excels by its profundity blended with clarity." Wondrous blend! It is not quite clear what the esteemed reviewer intended with "blended with clarity." For what has been blended with clarity is *eo ipso* unclear, and clarity is above all that one quality that cannot be the product of blending.

On paper, then, things go well enough for me. I wish I had a different kind of physical strength than I do—for although my body is an excellent rag when it comes to enduring my intellectual work, it is not fit for carrying me into the presence of His Majesty.[6] If only I had physical strength of a different kind I would do it tomorrow. But unfortunately the preparations for this exceed my physical strength. I can understand all too well that the King, provided he thinks about my unworthiness for even one second, must find it exceedingly peculiar that I do not accept his favor. When a crowned head not only most graciously permits [someone to see him], but of his own volition with the most genuine kindness indicates to a poor magister that the King would be pleased to see him, repeatedly points this out (as he, I almost said "unfortunately for me," has done), then, damn it, it is no more than the damned duty of such a magister etc. And I am that person, and I am also that person who has failed to come.

The whole affair really saddens me, for I appear in an utterly wrong light, but of course I cannot require the King to take the time to comprehend the individuality of one particular subject. If I could write to the King—that would be my way. But unfortunately that is not his way, for where would he get the time to read that kind of thing? I am like the housewife who knew she could make the most exquisite pancake but had no platter to serve it on: my spirit is willing enough, but I lack the bodily platter.

And so I should like to ask one thing of you: if the King should speak to you about me again, please take quick advantage of the opportunity to make it clear to him that it is some form of physical infirmity that makes it so difficult for me. With everybody else I make use of my eccentricity. That is good enough for them. But I neither could nor would offer the like to a King, especially to a King who has treated me in this manner. Therefore do by all means remember the serving plate—lest I end up with disfavor on my plate, as they say—which I of all people probably have deserved least.

Yours, S. KIERKEGAARD.

[*Address*:]
To
The Reverend Pastor Ibsen
Knight of *Dannebrog*
Lyngby.

152. *S. K.—[July 1847]—C. A. Reitzel.*[1]

Dear Sir:

It is not possible for me to be more specific about *Concluding Postscript*, because I lack the necessary information. According to Luno's[2] letter of July 30, '47, you received 250 copies in February '46 and 244 copies on July 11. But according to your account, dated May 4, '47, you had an unsold remainder of 89 copies. In other words, since you had a remainder of 89 copies as of May 4, '47, and nonetheless obtained 244 copies on July 11, '47, from Luno, a fair number must have been sold. However, from my itemized account you will see more or less how I have calculated. I have not asked for one half of the bookstore price for any remainder, and for several I have only asked considerably less than half. With respect to *Concluding Postscript*, my claim will be 40 per cent of the bookstore price on the remainder.

Concerning my *Upbuilding Discourses in Various Styles and Spirits*, this particular book was published in '47, and therefore I can have no idea how many copies have been sold. Luno's bill of March 10, '47, was for 287 *rdl.*, 12 *mk.* Of this sum I myself have paid Luno 87 *rdl.*, because he wanted it for paper expenditures. You have very kindly allowed the transfer of 200 *rdl.* to your account with Luno. But you can see for yourself that, before I decide anything further, I must have some idea of the sales, as well as have my 87 *rdl.* returned separately. But if you want to include that sum in order to settle the matter, as I myself do also, then please make an offer that conforms with my system of calculation, which you must know by now. Undoubtedly not a few have been sold. But now that I really look into this, I see that on the whole sales have not been bad, with the exception of *Two Ages*.

It is self-evident then that throughout we are speaking only about the remainder and not about the ownership rights to a new printing.

The question of *Either/Or* may be left until some other time.

And so until Monday evening!

Yours, S. Kierkegaard.

	Bookstore retail price	*My offer*

(1) *Fear and Trembling*
    Remainder with you 13
                Luno 191
                       204 @ 1 rdl.   204 rdl.   100 rdl.

(2) *Prefaces*
    Remainder with you 195
                Luno 122
                       317 @ 3 mk.   158. rdl. 3 mk.   70 rdl.
    NB. I have since noticed that the retail price is
    3 mk, 8 sk., but I am too lazy to add it up again.

(3) *Repetition*
    Remainder with you 38
             Luno 215
                    253 @ 5 mk.   210 rdl. 5 mk.   100 rdl.

(4) *Stages on Life's Way*
             with you 108
    Remainder with Luno 172
                    280 @ 3 rdl.   840 rdl.   400 rdl.

(5) *Philosophical Fragments*
             with you 96
    Remainder with Luno 200
                    296 @ 4 mk.   246 rdl. 4 mk.   100 rdl.

(6) *Two Ages, A Literary Review*
             with you 227
    Remainder with Luno 170
                    397 @ 3 mk.   197 rdl.   70 rdl.

(7) *Three Discourses on Imagined Occasions*
             with you 93
    Remainder with Luno 226
                    319 @ 4 mk.   212 rdl. 4 mk.   90 rdl.

(8) *The Concept of Anxiety*
    Remainder with you . . . . 85 @ 1 rdl.   85 rdl.   40 rdl.
                                                     970 rdl.

[in pencil, Reitzel's figures:
(9) Climacus' *Postscript* 381 copies @ 3 mk. 14
(10) *Upbuilding Discourses* 22 ½ rdl.
                   225
                     87
                   312]

153. *P. G. Philipsen—August 23, 1847—S. K.*[1]

Copenhagen, August 23, 1847.

Mr. S. Kierkegaard, Magister!

In accordance with our verbal agreement the following is respectfully submitted in reply to your written request:

Bianco Luno has stated that the cost of a printing of 1,000 copies, including the printing and the paper, will amount to 948 *rdl.*, 3 *mk.*, 12 *sk.*

I intend to reduce the price to make it at least 1 *rdl.* cheaper than the first printing. The discount to my colleagues must be reckoned as 25 per cent, since I give a free copy with every tenth copy and in addition I still have the bookbinder and the advertisements.

Having permitted myself a summary of all expenditures, I find myself in a position to offer you 500 *rdl.* for the second printing of *Either/Or*, payable as follows: 400 *rdl.* next New Year, and 100 *rdl.* when the printing has been sold out. For these sums you will receive my note.

I admit that this is not much, but in relation to my own expenses it is not so little.

Awaiting the favor of your reply, I remain

Respectfully yours,
P. G. PHILIPSEN.

154. *S. K.—[August 1847]—P. G. Philipsen.*[1]

Dear Sir:

When I consider what it means for a merchant, and especially for a bookseller, to obtain a postponement of the payment of royalties for almost one and a half years (for a publisher normally pays in advance as a matter of course), when I consider the nature of the book, and when I consider that we are speaking of a printing of 1,000 copies, then it seems to me that 700 *rdl.*, which you yourself originally mentioned, must be considered a very reasonable demand on my part.

If we agree, I will expedite the matter as quickly as possible, which ought to be in your interest as well.

Reply requested.

Most respectfully, S. K.

155. *P. G. Philipsen—August 28, 1847—S. K.*[1]

Dear Magister:
You have good reason to smile at my vacillation. When I am with you, I forget all my calculations, I see and hear only the author of *Either/Or*, and I say yes to everything that flows from your lips.

Not until I am here in my room am I able to make my estimate. I have once more very closely calculated my expenses and all the risks, and as a result I can only refer you to my letter of the 23rd of this month and can undertake the publication of *Either/Or* only on the conditions contained in it.

As the discrepancy between what was stated in my letter and in our conversation is not very considerable, I earnestly request you to forgive my vacillation.

As soon as you have read these lines without anger and notified me in writing of your consent, I shall immediately make all the necessary arrangements.
August 28, 1847.

Yours truly,
P. G. PHILIPSEN.

156. *S. K.—August 30, 1847—P. G. Philipsen.*[1]

August 30, '47.
Dear Sir:
As you do not want what I want, then you—will not publish *Either/Or*. So, thus the matter is settled—and as you desire it, completely "without anger" on my part, for I have already quite forgotten your "vacillation."

Respectfully,
S. KIERKEGAARD.

[*No address*:]

157. *S. K.—[after August 30, 1847]—C. A. Reitzel.*[1]

Dear Reitzel:
You know how much I like to have everything settled and decided, and you also know how much I desire the other

party to be content. And whenever you are the other party, I am confident you also consider what is to my advantage. Therefore, without further ado I accept your offer for *Either/Or*, although the royalty is small enough—but this country is a small one as well. Certainly I prefer being pleased with my confidence in you and your concern for my interests, prefer to be pleased knowing that you are content, even though I mistrustfully urged you against your wishes to give me a little bit more. In other words: accepted. —I want the printing to consist of 750 copies. As for payment, I shall not ask for that until the June term, 1849. I hope this, as they say, is all you can ask for.

Please then have the kindness to give me written confirmation, as you did last time, containing these two points: (1) the royalties for the second printing are 550 *rdl.*, [*in margin*: with 300 *rdl.* payable on June 11, '49, and the balance, 250 *rdl.*, *ultimo* July, '49.], (2) the printing is to consist of 750 copies.

And so, good luck with this transaction. According to my way of thinking, you have struck an advantageous bargain, and you will find that good luck is connected with the venture. If I had not in so many ways worked against my own sales in those days when I was my own publisher, they would also have been wholly different.

As you know, I am always in a bit of a hurry with business matters. Hitherto you have indulged me in this respect; please do so now. And please reply. Such a letter is soon written.

Yours sincerely,
S. KIERKEGAARD.

158. *H. N. Clausen—September 25, 1847—S. K.*[1]

Honored Magister:

Several years ago a Scandinavian book collection was established in Rome, but owing to substantial gifts, Swedish literature has hitherto constituted by far the greater part. The books are used quite extensively, and during my stay there I conceived of the wish to assist in augmenting the Danish collection. I am still hoping to send a number of books this au-

tumn, and for this reason I take the liberty to ask if you might
not feel inclined to enrich the collection with copies of your
books—here I am, to be sure, also thinking of *Either/Or* and
its siblings, according to the relationship you are assumed to
have to them as their father.

Yours truly,
H. N. CLAUSEN

Copenhagen, September 25, 1847.
Magister Kierkegaard

[*Address:*]
S. T. Magister Kierkegaard.

159. *S. K.—[1847]—H. N. Clausen.*[1]

Dear Professor:
   You inquire if I "might not feel inclined to enrich the Scandinavian collection in Rome with copies of my books." In
truth a very difficult question to reply to! For how would it be
possible, when you, Professor, are the inquirer, for me not to
feel so inclined! But if I do feel so inclined, and to such a degree that the question becomes no question at all for me, then
it is again difficult to *reply*—as if to an inquiry.
   Unable to *reply*, yet decidedly pleased on the other hand to
feel myself so inclined, I hereby have the honor to send you,
sir, copies of my books.
   With respect to *Either/Or*, unfortunately I cannot provide a
copy, since the printing was sold out long ago,[2] but fortunately I do remember that some time ago, when I was asked
to do so by Cand. Giødwad, I sent a copy through *Justitsraad*[3]
Collin to that book collection.

With the greatest esteem,
respectfuly yours,
S. KIERKEGAARD.

[*Address:*]
To the Honorable
Professor Clausen
Knight of *Dannebrog*.
Accompanying parcel.

160. *J.L.A. Kolderup-Rosenvinge—September 30, 1847—S. K.* [1]

Magister Kierkegaard,

Please allow me to express in writing my gratitude for your book, about works of love,[2] which you so kindly sent me. Would that I might learn from it proper love and that "self-denial wherein a human being can hold firmly to his God," for then you would have performed a work of love also for me. Once again, my best thanks!
September 30, 1847.

Yours sincerely,
KOLDERUP-ROSENVINGE.

[*Address:*]
S. T. Magister S. Kierkegaard.

161. *S. K.—[September 1847]—Henriette Kierkegaard.*

Dear Jette,

As I have seen and talked with my brother a number of times in recent days, I have had you quite vividly in my thoughts. But I owe it to truth not to make myself out to be worse than I am, and it is really true that during the long period that has gone by since I last saw you or heard anything from you, I have not ceased thinking of you. But you know how it is: when one has not been present at the beginning of an event, it is hard to enter into it properly later on; one waits instead for something new to happen in order then to make use of the moment to begin. At least that is how it is with my relationship to the events of life, the sad as well as the joyous ones—if I do not get started at once, I prefer to skip my turn in order to begin at the beginning next time.

What I want to speak about now goes far back in time. You had already been sick for a long time when I was first informed of it. The very fact that I could not begin at the beginning made me not begin at all. Time passed, several times I decided to write to you, but the following scruple always got in the way to stop me: "Now that it is too late, where shall I begin?" So time passed. —"Sunday came, and Sunday went; no new boots to Hans were sent." —Finally I was so completely out of the habit, that is to say, I became accustomed to finding it impossible to overcome the difficulty of the beginning. —Alas, perhaps you went through something similar. Now and then in the beginning you probably thought: "It is strange that I do not hear from him at all; that is shameful of him, but now that it is too late, he might as well save himself the trouble."

Then my brother came to town. For me this meant a break, a breakthrough: here is a letter for you. What you get out of it will of course depend on how you read it—yet I do not believe it is in any way necessary to be practiced in the art of reading between the lines to discern the sympathy in it.

Peter told me that you are still always confined to bed. I can quite vividly imagine the burden of this in the course of time, even though I have not experienced it myself in that way. I once spoke with you about that burden, which among other things is also this: that it is almost impossible to avoid people's misunderstanding of such suffering. —"It is not fever, nor a broken arm, nor falling and hurting oneself—what is it then?" So the doctor asks impatiently, and so does ordinary human sympathy—alas, and when one suffers in this way it is precisely a question of patience, the patience not to lose courage, the patience to endure the impatience of sympathy. But we human beings and our sympathy are like that. And when one suffers as you are suffering—even though there is a person at one's side, as there surely is at yours, who faithfully shares the yoke equally with you—then one has indeed the opportunity to realize the truth that the God of Patience verily is He who can persist completely unconditionally in caring about a human being with the same eternal unchanged compassion. As the old hymn so movingly asks, "If every hour I weep and ask,"[1] that is, whence help and comfort will come—so movingly does the poet himself reply, "But God indeed still lives." And he is every day, at every hour, early in the morning, in a sleepless hour of the night, at the time of day when one feels most weak—he is unalterably the same.

Dear Jette, when I have thus taken pen in hand I could easily go on writing page upon page. I would like to do it, and perhaps you would not be displeased to read it. But I must break off this very instant, and such a letter may always be continued a day later.

Goodbye—for it seems to me as if I have been talking with you. Goodbye! Greetings to Poul; do please tell him something about me once in a while lest he grow up in complete ignorance of having an uncle. I have asked Peter to give you my heartfelt greetings. Please greet Peter once more from

Your   S. K.

162. *F. C. Petersen—October 1, 1847—S. K.* [1]

Dear Sir:

Since I have not had any luck in finding you at home, I should like to thank you very much by means of these lines for the gift, [2] which I am glad you sent me.

I am a rather slow reader and books of *this kind* ought to be read only *in guten Stunden* [at auspicious times], but if I can only succeed in finding some time for this purpose, I am certain that for your part you have provided me with something useful and pleasurable.

Your most obliged
F. C. PETERSEN

Reg[ensen], October 1
1847
S. T.
Magister Kierkegaard.

163. *Magnus Eiríksson—October 14, 1847—S. K.*

Mr. Kierkegaard:

It is true I applied to you last year for financial support I greatly needed, without succeeding in winning your sympathy, and accordingly you were probably not expecting to hear from me again. But as I am still in the same financial difficulty, if not greater—for I do not even know myself when it has been greatest during these past two years, even though I have always, often in a totally unexpected manner, been helped for the time being—I have decided to make another attempt with you, for after all, it is written, "Ask, and ye shall be given." You have recently written about works of love. I have not yet obtained that book, since lately it has embarrassed me to ask my bookseller for books, and I really do have enough books, so I do not know it, but I am convinced anyway that it is probably worth reading—but however deserving it may be to *write about* works of love, it is surely far more deserving and blessed to *perform* them, and I am certain that you will perform one by supporting me, and that you will never come to regret having tried, but might possibly do so for having failed to perform it. You may think as follows: "I myself need everything I now have if I am to live for such and such a length of time and am to continue working in the same manner as hitherto." But you do not know if you will live long enough to use up what you have, and even if that were the case, then you ought to trust in God that if your work and efforts are for the betterment of mankind he will then somehow provide you with the means to continue it, even though your own means may have been spent. I speak to you as a man of religion, although I realize perfectly well that it is quite rare nowadays in this matchless Christianity. Lieutenant Governor Lorenz Krieger,[1] whom Providence employed as an instrument to launch me in the world (cf. *Om Baptister og Barnedaab*,[2] pp. iii–v, note), had also used up most of his inheritance, for his private income and salary were not enough to meet the needs of his noble charity, yet he had sufficient until he died. By the way, as far as I am concerned, I venture to take it upon myself, even with interest if necessary, to repay whatever you might spend on me, for it will not be long before my position is changed—(for it serves the advancement of the Good)—and that in such a manner as will be unexpected by most, and awaken envy in some, but astonishment in even more. Our Lord cannot take this into consideration. He follows his own path without consulting the powers that be. It is not out of pride that I oblige myself to repay whatever I might receive in loans from you or others, but only to the extent that he who has turned anything over to me might eventually need to have it refunded.—

I have frequently speculated on what your reason might have been for not wishing to support me formerly, for you must have realized that I was one of the select few who strive in the same (or a similar) direction as you do, quite aside from the fact that several people must have found it so natural that they have spread this rumor, which I happened to hear even as recently as this summer; for it seems most natural to me to explain it in this way, since I cannot very well assume that you yourself would ever have been the cause of it. If you should be afraid it might become generally known that you had supported me against Mr. Martensen[3] and other even more powerful people, then it shall, if you so desire, remain a secret. Honorable Sir! Do now let the prophecies be fulfilled, for I had already begun to think of this rumor that has been in circulation for so many years as a *prophecy*, which, while we do not know its origin, thus has an existence that is all the more certain. The prophecy is now several years old, yet still alive, but that is exactly what is true of good prophecies that await fulfillment. If you want to do anything for me, then I need it right now. In any case, I ask you to notify me in a few words, which may either be left where I live or with the porter at Regensen,[4] *before next Sunday*.

With esteem,
M. Eiríksson
(126 Amaliegade, top floor)

[*Address:*]
S. T.
Magister S. Kierkegaard
Copenhagen.

164. *S. K.—October 14, 1847—Magnus Eiríksson.*

(Copy)

You yourself request, and I find that quite natural, that I reply "in a few words" to your very lengthy letter. That is to say, you request *without reasons pro or contra that I be brief, a* "Yes" or a "No." Here is my reply: I cannot comply with your request.

Respectfully,   S. K.

165. *S. K.—[1847]—Henriette Lund.*

It is not for me to decide if it is really true that I have more *after*thought than others. But with respect to your birthday it is a certainty that I always come after the fact, or think after the fact, or after the fact think of it, or think of it when it is after the fact, or when it is after the fact think of it, etc. I only hope in this passage, in which the style reflects my state of mind, that I may have succeeded in giving you some idea of the extent to which I feel myself in hot water, so to speak, for having forgotten that solemn day once again, until—indeed, is it not awful!—a gentleman from the country reminds me of it.

But what is to be done about it now? Nothing, and yet, no! In these troubled times, which *mir nichts und dir nichts* [without so much as asking leave] turn everything upside down much can be done. In modern fashion we might of course reverse the situation: it is not I who have forgotten that yesterday was your birthday; it is the rest of you who are mistaken in thinking yesterday your birthday. —Today is your birthday.

Granted! Accordingly I have the honor to offer my congratulations. That does seem a bit meager considering all my protestations—quite in the modern fashion. And yet I must call attention to the fact that in this case the extraordinary protestations were manifestations of the great importance I attach to this event.

But all jesting aside and on to what is just as sincerely meant as the jest was not ill meant: My dear Jette, when it comes to true and sincere regard, it is utterly immaterial if the expression of it manages to arrive on the birthday proper, or one day before or after it, or two weeks after it, or if it does not arrive at all, provided that it has a bearing on the birthday. There is one kind of regard that really comes into existence, is in existence, only during the twelve hours of the birthday, that comes calling to congratulate, drinks chocolate, stays for supper in the evening—a regard that is thus non-existent for the other 364 days of the year. Such a regard is indeed embarrassed when it mistakes the date! There is another sort of regard that is more evenly distributed over the 365 days of the year. Although far from being a conscious one every day, nonetheless it always exists most profoundly and fervently, has essentially nothing to do with chocolate, hot supper, or mulled red wine, and may easily forget to congratulate, because in the course of the year it has often silently wished that person well who is the object of this regard.

What I wanted to say is that however rarely I see you and however preoccupied I am with all kinds of thoughts, still my heart is not so forgetful nor my thought so busy that both heart and thought do not now and then unite in dwelling upon you and your life, wishing you and your life well. It was this I wanted to say to you, and on the occasion of your birthday I have occasion to say it. You are probably so happy that you really have nothing to wish for, but if you were so happy (for in another sense this might also be said and with truth) that you did have a wish—and if my wish were capable of anything, then I would certainly wish that wish for you, even though my wish could accomplish nothing. But my dear Jette will already have understood this much about life, that the good things one person may wish for another are all of dubious merit, and while somebody may certainly wish for what is truly good for somebody else, it is not obtained thereby. Everybody must earn it for himself.

So, my dear Jette, for your birthday please accept now these congratulations as well—from your forgetful uncle who

certainly does forget your birth*day*, but who does not forget
Jette, his dear niece, for whom he always sincerely preserves
all that devotion and regard by which as an uncle he gladly
feels himself bound.

Your Uncle   S. K.

You might enjoy gradually collecting a small music library.
Herewith the piano score from *Figaro*. If you should happen
to own it already, we can have it exchanged.

166. *S. K.—December 22, 1847—P. C. Kierkegaard.*

Dear Peter,   December 22.

Now I have sold the house at last.[1] I found a good buyer,
which may in a way interest you also: Madame Bützov,
widow of B., the broker.

Otherwise everything will remain unchanged. You retain
your first mortgage in the sum of 7,000 *rdl.* and half of the
bank lien. I spoke with you at one time about increasing your
first mortgage. You were not willing to do that. Now it is
unnecessary. I myself will assume a second mortgage of 5,000
rdl.

Both these are made non-cancellable for ten years on our
part. That is the way Kraft, the attorney, has drawn up the
papers. I have no objections, and it has not occurred to him
that you would be anything but satisfied with this, as I assume you are in fact. But if everything had not been settled so
quickly when at last the right buyer came along, I would of
course have written to you at once to obtain your consent, so
that I might in no way seem to have acted independently,
even where I could safely count on your consent. God knows
that these days I am so dizzy from all these financial matters
that I am all too prone to pedantry.

By the way, I do not even remember how you obtained
your first mortgage, but in any event the difference is purely a
formal one. You will still wish to retain a mortgage on the
property because it is that property and because it is an excel-

lent first mortgage. Hence it does not matter at all that it will be non-cancellable for ten years. But on the other hand, if you wish to regard it as cash, then it is just as simple, whether it is non-cancellable or not, to sell to another owner, for it is very easy to obtain a first mortgage by public financing. A second mortgage is not so easy in that respect, for public funds are as a rule supposed to be invested in first mortgages. Although my second mortgage is non-cancellable for ten years, I still consider it just as good as cash.

And now it only remains for me to ask you to come to town *as soon as you can* after New Year to sign the new mortgage papers and to collect your interest.

As I have said, I would be very sad if there should be the least difficulty on your part or if you should decide that I have acted in any manner other than you yourself would have. I am no good at practical business matters and have a fantastic anxiety about lawyers and everything about them. Please do let me know by return mail, therefore, that you are satisfied.

Besides, I am glad that this matter has been settled and that I am happily and well out of it.

I hope you are well. I have learned that Jette has been ill. Please greet her from me, greet Poul, and accept my greeting for yourself.

From your Brother

[*Address*:]
To
Dr. Kierkegaard, Pastor.
Pedersborg
v. Sorøe

[*Postmark*:]
Copenhagen
12/23
1847

167. *S. K.—[December 1847]—Henriette Kierkegaard.*

Dear Jette,

Thank you for your little letter which, in your own words, I must have before Christmas. I hasten to reply so that you may have my answer before New Year.

The period between Christmas and New Year is usually a particularly convenient time for me to receive letters, and a fortunate season for my correspondent, that is, if he thinks it fortunate to get a reply from me.

And now you are confined to bed again. Still, it was a sound and healthy—anything but sickly—decision to write to me right away as you did, even though you had not heard from me for so long. That, you see, is a favorable sign and makes me happy. "Last year at the same time you wrote a letter to me—but it was not sent." Then, you see, you were perhaps not bedridden, and yet your condition may have been more like that of a person who was.

Hence I am pleased on your behalf as well to have received this letter from you as a sign of health. Preserve it, and take care of it in the coming year, which God will surely make a happy one for you. There is something closely connected with physical illness—that quiet, deeply painful, and slowly consuming worry that now turns over in agony on one side and imagines itself forgotten by others "who probably never give one a thought" and now turns over on the other side and is afraid that whatever one has to say or write will not be good enough. Oh, do banish that worry, which is especially dangerous for you because you are so frequently bedridden and constantly live in monotonous quiet. The person who is actively engaged in life soon forgets such thoughts, but the person who only sees little change around him may easily find that worrying almost becomes a necessity. When one lives in small rooms—as you know very well—they need frequent airing out; in the same way, when one entertains but few thoughts and has little diversion, then it is extremely important that what one inhales, spiritually understood, be good and beneficent and gentle and soothing thoughts.

You also need diversion, but diversion is not easily made available in monotony. And yet it is perhaps easier than one thinks if only one is willing. It is generally believed that what determines the direction of one's thoughts lies in the external and is the greater or lesser probability of this or that. But that is not so. That which determines the direction of one's thoughts lies basically in one's own self. He who has a tendency to melancholy, for example, most probably always finds unhappiness. Why? Because melancholy lies within him. In this hypothetical case there would be as great a probability of the opposite, perhaps even greater, but he arbitrarily breaks off and immediately has enough to be able to conclude that something unhappy will happen to him.

But what is it then to "have faith"? To have faith is constantly to expect the joyous, the happy, the good. But is that not an extraordinary and blessed diversion! Oh, what more does one need then? What I am about to say next might almost seem facetious, but it is in fact very serious and very sincerely meant for you. You are in some measure always suffering— hence the task lies right here: Divert your *mind, accustom yourself by faith to changing suffering into expectation of the joyous. It is really possible.* What is required is this flexibility in the quiet of the mind, which, whenever things go wrong for one, in that very instant begins all over again and says, "Yes! Yes! Next time it will work." Oh, if one were never to see another human being again—and that is far from your case—then in this way one could *by faith conjure* up or forth a world of diversion into the loneliest room.

Ordinarily it is probably right to warn against self-love; still, I consider it *my duty to say to every sufferer* with whom I come into contact: *See to it that you love yourself.* When one is suffering and unable to do much for others, it is easy to fall prey to the melancholy thought that one is superfluous in this world, as others perhaps sometimes give one to understand. Then one must remember that *before God every person is equally important, without reservation equally important*; indeed, if there were any distinction, then one who suffers the most must be the closest object of God's care. And also in this lies infinite Godly diversion. But I will stop; I can truthfully say I have no more room. Take care of yourself, dear Jette. Happy New Year! Thank you for concluding the old one so beautifully by thinking of me. Greetings to Peter and to Poul.

Your devoted   S. K.

168. *S. K.—[1847]—Wilhelm Lund.*

Dear Wilhelm,

Today I chanced to speak with Lector Barfoed,[1] and so I happened to remember you and warmly recommended you. He took the opportunity to ask me, if I saw you, to tell you that he would begin lecturing on Monday. I am sure I far from promised to do so, for on the contrary I said "no." But as with that other brother in the gospel[2] who said "no," so it has occurred to me afterwards that I might do it anyway— and it is not yet afterwards.

Your uncle   S. K.

[*Address:*]
To
Wilhelm Lund.

169. *S. K.—[1847]—C. Molbech.*[1]

Monday.

Honorable *Etatsraad*,

That which is a pleasure to do is quickly done.[2] Accordingly I hasten to comply with your wish for one or two of my books for that German friend[3] of the Danish language. I only hope the fulfillment is in accordance with your wish. Although the accompanying copy of *Either/Or* is certainly in respectable condition, nevertheless it is not quite new. As it happens, the book has been sold out,[4] so I cannot provide a new copy, and yet it still seems to me that this might be the most suitable book to send. If you are of the same opinion, then everything is as it ought to be. But if you should desire another book in order to have a completely new copy, then just one word, please, and with the speed of an obedient genie I shall "obey the hint." It is precisely because I really do welcome the opportunity to comply with your wish that I also feel it essential as a matter of course to know how exactly what it may be.

> With respect and veneration,
> Yours sincerely,
> S. KIERKEGAARD.

[*Address:*]
To
The Honorable
Etatsraad Molbech.
Knight of *Dannebrog* and Member of *Dannebrog*
Knight of the Grand Cross of Norway a.o.
Accompanying parcel.

170. *S. K.—[1847]—N. P. Nielsen.*[1] *S. K.'s draft.*

Dear Sir:

Under ordinary circumstances an author is probably able to decide very easily and very quickly to which of two parties, whether husband or wife, he wishes to send a complimentary copy with respect, admiration, devotion, gratitude, and friendship. Or, if he decides at once to send it to both of them, ordinarily this is really because both parties are important to him by virtue of their matrimonial relationship. But in this case the matter is more difficult, more rare, the only case of its kind, whence proceeds the author's admiring bewilderment, for both of them have, each in his own right, the merit of excellence and then again the redoubled strength of their union. Under such circumstances, what is to be done? I might send you one copy, sir, and one to your wife. But in so doing I would only have expressed something quite ordinary, to wit, that there were, numerically speaking, two people for whom I entertained feelings of respect and devotion. But the rarest of the rare would not have been expressed, for in addition they constitute a pair, a married couple. Therefore, you see, I have chosen to send one copy to "the two." It is certainly not done for reasons of economy, for there are means, if need be, for several copies; no, there is another reason, that of esthetic conscientiousness. Although not very sympathetic towards my fellow man, unsociable and solitary, nevertheless in my solitude I take great pleasure in coming to terms to the best of my ability with what is unique in those individuals who occupy my thoughts, with what is unique in them and in their circumstances of life. Probably there are many very gifted persons who are far more prompt than I in repaying their social obligations, far better than I in the service of paying attention and in paying attentions. But when it comes to judiciousness, it may be possible that in its service I am, if not as bustling and clever, at any rate as alert as anyone else— although I stand "far apart by myself." To my way of thinking it would be peculiar to send you a copy of a little book that you presumably will not read and that I certainly do not wish to oblige you to read. On the other hand, if I could succeed in making the manner in which it is sent into the real object; if a certain, if I may put it like this, judicious stamp on my gift (which is quite different, however, from the gold stamping any bookbinder might apply to the book) should manage to win favor in your eyes and in those of your wife— then precisely that would constitute happiness for me, the fulfillment of my wish, the satisfaction of my heart's desire.

What I add, I am writing as though your wife were listening or as though she were reading it as I write. You have so often invited me to visit, you have persevered with rare faithfulness, and you have tolerated my stubbornness with a leniency just as rare. Now, if this stubborness of mine is strange at times, it would also be strange if I were not conscious of it myself, if I did not often regret how unjust I have been— toward myself. In your invitation there has always been something that signified to me that this was no mere politeness, but that you would truly welcome it if I were to take you at your word and visit your home at some point. I may

be wrong. Perhaps it is your superior breeding, the virtuosity
of your manners, which have enchanted a poor magister who
knows very little of the world and has deceived his vain, un-
guarded heart. In any case, please let this note serve as a visit.
It will easily substitute for my absence, while I, as a substitute
for what I lose by staying away once again, retain only the
consciousness of having done something, short of having
done what is right, towards reducing that indebtedness in
which in another sense I should more than prefer to remain.
For, as it is unlikely that I shall come calling, only when I remain indebted can I thus remain

Your   S. KIERKEGAARD.

171. S. K.—January 17, [1848]—Julia C. Werliin. [1]

January 17

"You depend on me to be silent, even if I do not come."
Indeed you can do so completely, but I, however, cannot
come. —"You have a request of me." If it can be managed, if
you could acquaint me with the gist of it in a few words, then
I could of course let you know whether the fulfillment of it
lies within the scope of my humble ability or whether it does
not.

S. KIERKEGAARD.

[*Address:*]
To
Mrs. Werliin
5 Nybrogade.

172. J. L. A. Kolderup-Rosenvinge— February 18, 1848— S. K. [1]

I am very sorry that you have called on me in vain to go
walking on two occasions, in spite of the fact that I did indeed
say that excepting Tuesdays and Saturdays I would always be
available at 2 p.m. But as accidental circumstances have now
twice upset the applecart, and as I am reluctant to give up the

pleasure of walking in your company, I propose that you call on Mondays at 2 p.m., at which time I shall always be available or in any case send you a message should unavoidable obstacles present themselves. It is of course not my intention to put any obligation on *you*.

Most sincerely,
KOLDERUP-ROSENVINGE

February 18, 1848
[*Address*:]
S. T.
Magister S. Kierkegaard.

173. *J.L.A. Kolderup-Rosenvinge—March 6, 1848—S. K.*

Dear Magister,

Inasmuch as last Monday you anticipated Shrove Monday,[1] while I unfortunately had forgotten to inform you of my absence, and I would be reluctant to have you entertain bad thoughts about me, then, if you really were intending to make a Shrovetide call on me today, I shall not omit to inform you that an extraordinary meeting of a board of directors prevents me from walking today at 2 o'clock. I hope this will not be to the detriment of future walks; I expect to be at home both Wednesday and Friday, but not until 2:15.

Most sincerely,
KOLDERUP-ROSENVINGE

March 6, 1848.
[*Address*:]
S. T.
Magister S. Kierkegaard.

174. *F.L.B. Zeuthen—May 11, 1848—S. K.*[1]

Tømmerup Parsonage
Dear Magister S. Kierkegaard: May 11, 1848

After having looked through your latest book,[2] I cannot do otherwise than send you my heartfelt thanks. I am far from having read all the way through the book, for it ought to be read slowly, with reverence and with application, like all of your recent books, but it belongs among those few writings that, precisely because they stand in opposition, are appropriate for us in our present condition. If only many of those who talk about the demands of the times would heed that most essential demand! Denmark will soon, I suppose, become a poor country[3] with neither gold nor silver, but with writings such as yours we are still rich, indeed we might even make others, make our enemies rich; at any rate they have nothing at all like this out there, and I know of no other salvation for the monstrous religious confusion in Germany and elsewhere than just such an original, profound, and rich discourse as that which you conduct.

I suppose no one can write in a more upbuilding way than you do about the cares of poverty for that day "tomorrow," but there is also a care of poverty for that day "yesterday," which is a care not about what one is going to eat, but about what one *has* eaten and—*not paid for*.[4] This care about *debt* one cannot pay, not only to those who demand, but especially to those who are silent although they are themselves in need, this care of poverty is of the most burdensome kind, and I could wish that you would at some time write something really upbuilding about that as well. There may be too much of what is true and noble in this care for it to be counted readily among the cares of the pagans, but still, a Christian can, even though not by any thought directly applied to grief (for indeed this must often increase the grief), then in prayer overcome this care as well.

Even though you do not have time to receive visitors, I do assume that you will find time to read these lines that I felt compelled to write.

Your devoted and grateful
ZEUTHEN

[*Address:*]
S. T.
Mag. art. S. Kierkegaard
in
Copenhagen
Gammel Torv, corner of Frederiksberggade.

175. *S. K.—[1848]—F.L.B. Zeuthen.*

Honored Magister:

Thank you for your little letter, which I have not only found time to read but have allowed myself plenty of time to read. I thank you for the observation about that day yesterday. Please let me thank you for it today; I shall indeed remember it tomorrow! So, you see, you have provided me with a care about that day tomorrow! When you come to town, I assume I shall also see you at my house (between 11 a.m. and 1 p.m.), as you have stipulated. Last time I had to ask you not to come, because just then I was in the midst of proofreading.

Yours most respectfully,
S. KIERKEGAARD.

176. *S. K.—[1848]—Emil Boesen.*

Dear Emil,

There was something I forgot to tell you this morning. Please remember that the summer vacation is not far off. You are in need of recreation, diversion, physical exercise, and besides, as a rule you do feel fine when you travel. So take care that you do not suffer so much these days that you cannot truly benefit from it.

There are, alas, certain things that one person cannot very well tell another. It sounds so severe when one wants to tell them to the other, as if the speaker did not need to tell himself the same things. That makes them no less true. But do by all means make it a habit to tell yourself this. When a man is thirty years old he ought to be able to act as his own physician, as Seneca remarks.[1] It is certain that in a spiritual sense a man must strive diligently to act as his own prosecution and defense.

Your S. K.

[*Address:*]
To
Cand. E. Boesen.
[*in pencil*: 1848].

177. *Rasmus Nielsen—[1848]—S. K.* [1]

Sunday.

Dear Magister,

The cowardly soldier is court-martialed and shot as "a traitor without honor." What horrible justice! The greater danger always banishes the lesser. In other words, cowardice is a crime and the coward guilty because in his very fear he forgot to be afraid. The poor devil! In order to avoid being shot, he simply ran away and—let himself be shot. How illogical forgetfulness can be! I wonder if it is not possible, since the world is always moving ahead, more and more quickly ahead, to figure out some good remedy against the unnaturalness of such natural forgetfulness.

But do you not agree, my dear magister, that one is taught this and much besides in *military training school*?

Yours,   R. N.

[*Address*:]
S. T.
Magister Kierkegaard.

178. *S. K.—June 25, [1849]—T. Algreen-Ussing. S. K.'s draft.* [1]

June 25.

Mr. *Etatsraad*:

Considered as a curiosity, a letter from me might perhaps have a special claim to your attention for a moment, and thus I might perhaps succeed in calling your special attention to the person who has prompted this note.

A widow is applying for a grant from the Kofoed Foundation. She is personally known to me as one in need and without reservation as worthy of assistance, so much so that in my view she is the only one of her kind.

I hope this will do. But alas, when one can only count on having an effect owing to curiosity value, then one can as a matter of course—if one succeeds in having any effect at all—be effective only once; a repetition is impossible in this respect, just as certainly as a curiosity is no curiosity the second time around.

Therefore, please take note of this widow's application, take, Mr. Attorney General, her case to your heart. You who daily have the enormous task of being Attorney General for all of Denmark, on this occasion please assume for curiosity's sake the droll task of being Attorney General for one single person, a poor widow.

The widow's name is Abelone Hedberg — and   I am
née Royen.

Yours very truly,
S. KIERKEGAARD

[*Address:*]
To
The Honorable
Etatsraad Ussing
Attorney General for D[enmark]
Knight of *Dannebrog.*

179. *Rasmus Nielsen—July 21, 1848—S. K.* [1]

Dear Magister,

I am sure you will agree with me that fresh air and Hebrew can have a beneficial effect on one's mind and senses.

Here at Taarbæk[2] in the fishing village between the woods and the beach, the air is as fresh and the view as beautiful as anybody could wish, but without a bit of Hebrew the refreshment tastes slightly stale. One gets annoyed so easily with the variety of the region. The highway is dusty (even though some rain does fall now and again), and the guests at the watering spa are also dusty in these pleasant surroundings. Therefore it is an additional advantage that one can take a Hebrew conveyance from "The Cliff,"[3] and without too many delays reach the desert, where solitude dwells, where fresh air breathes from the mountain, and where a solitary thornbush is the only ornament of the whole region.

Oh that I may now—*ora pro nobis*—succeed in finding the
right desert!

אַשְׁרֵי הָאִישׁ,[4] blessed is the man who finds his way to
the right desert,

אשרי האיש, blessed is the man who finds the right way
through the desert,

אשרי האיש, blessed is the man who finds the burning
bush[5] in the desert!

You, Magister, who know all things inside as well as outside Copenhagen, also know Taarbæk with its fishing village
between the woods and the beach. Here I am now living, a
little below the woods, breathing fresh air near "The Cliff,"
and studying—Hebrew.

Yours, R. N.

Taarbæk Inn, July 21, 1848.

[*Address*:]
S. T.
Magister Kierkegaard
Corner of Rosenborggaden / Copenhagen
and Tornebuskegaden.

180. *S. K.—[July 1848]—J.L.A. Kolderup-Rosenvinge.*[1]

Dear *Conferentsraad*,

I am sure you will easily remember that excellent passage in
Holberg in which Pernille says of Gert W.[2] that if one sewed
his mouth shut, he would teach himself to speak with his nostrils. How splendid! It is so descriptive, so graphic, for when
a person closes his mouth and tries to speak anyway, then his
cheeks become inflated, and one cannot help but get the impression that the words will have to escape through his nostrils. Furthermore, there is infinite *vis comica* [comic strength]
in this "to teach himself how to" with his nostrils. It is a
superb expression for the infinity of need. It may take him
ages, perhaps many years—it makes no difference, it does not
matter, provided only that he succeeds—for even though it

were the last day of his life, he would faithfully persist in "teaching himself." Only he who has an infinite goal dedicates himself in this way, and only he who strives infinitely is able to persist in this way. So also with G. W., but only with respect to that which for him is the sole goal:—to be able to speak with his nostrils, assuming that his mouth has been sewn shut. And suppose that he succeeded, succeeded beyond all expectation, and instead of speaking with only one mouth could now speak with two—since he has, after all, two nostrils. What joy! Not even the inventor of that machine with which one writes and makes copies at the same time, in other words, with which one may write *in duplo*, could be as happy as G. W. would be—although it would be horrible for the neighborhood if this infinitely garrulous person were now to have, as we speak of a double-barreled rifle, a double-barreled mouth with which to speak.

But to the point. As with G. W.'s need to talk, so also with my longing for and need to walk with you, sir. And since that is not possible, there is no other way than to teach myself to walk with you in writing.

With this my letter ends. It is brief; hence it may be taken to correspond with the manner of walking with you that occurs when I call at Kannikestræde, ring the bell, and the porter says, "The *Conferentsraad* is not at home." At some other time I may perhaps write you a letter that will deal with another manner of walking with you, as when the porter in reply to my question says, "Yes," and I hurry upstairs to the second floor where a young lady informs me that the *Conferentsraad* is not at home after all. Eventually I will finally get to walk with you. But in our present manner of walking that event will not occur, and that is the reason I now, thinking about this, beg pardon in the event that *Conferentsraad* R. should find himself sitting and waiting at some prearranged time and that scoundrel, Magister K., should fail to show up.

And so, for now—but no! After all, we did not go walking, and so I cannot thank you for the walk. And yet it seems as if I had been walking with you, and exactly as if I were standing and taking my leave of you and saying, "Please take care of yourself, my dear *Conferentsraad*; stay in good health; you have actually grown younger in the short time I have known you." And now, enjoying the rural surroundings, relaxing in the company of selected poets of several nations—why should you not grow younger every day to the unspeakable joy of that circle for whom the high noon of your health is the only determination of time that is of any real interest?

And then, when you once more return to town, when my time begins with the advent of fall, then I shall probably be so fortunate as to see you, I who in my remote solitude yet remain

Your   S. KIERKEGAARD.

N.B. In testimony whereof I hereby declare (what I cannot know is how you will take [this]—alas, perhaps as a piece of good luck) that this letter may well be the last. Once I get a pen in my hand, it says many things I must be careful to retract.

181. *J.L.A. Kolderup-Rosenvinge—July 26, 1848—S. K.*

Ordupshøj,[1] July 26, 1848

That was really a very beautiful walk,[2] dear Magister, and as usual I say, "Thank you for the walk!" I really do not think I would have gone out today, for to my mind the weather is foul and my mood likewise—if you had not come. Besides, I was rather tired because I did not get home from a journey until last night. —"What? Has *Monsieur* been on a journey?" —Why certainly, although not abroad really, but for a week I have been at Sorgenfri[3] (which otherwise ought rather to be known as Sorgensfred[4] now), and now my children desire me to be so gracious as to keep them company today. In other words, there are, as you see, many obstacles to the customary walk—nor is today Monday but Wednesday. But let that pass! Let us go walking. —Now with respect to your initial remark about my dear Gert, your commentary[5] on the two nostrils is excellent, and I only regret that I received it a week too late, for it was just a week ago that I read the part of Gert

W. aloud one evening here, and I might then have plowed
with your heifer and quite frightened the audience with the
terrible prospect that Monsieur Gert might get a double
mouth, so that he could commence with the second when the
first grew tired. Consider also what an advantage it would be
for those "Harslevian *Nobles venitiens*"[6] or those crazy fellows
in Frankfurt,[7] if every jaw were hitched to such a team; it
would become a run-away jaw, some kind of live espringal.[8]
To your query about my well-being, I must reply with Holberg: "Dost thou not know what is written back of Aurora:
Otium est pulvinar Diaboli, idleness is the Devil's headpil-
low."[9] Since I have been given my otium during the vaca-
tions and no longer tread the mill, I am in fact even worse off
than usual. Precisely because I am not *regularis*, as Canon Law
says of those clerics who are bound by rules, I drift about
ubi me vehit tempestas [wherever the wind blows me].[10] Therefore I have gotten down to work again today, but it will not
really go smoothly. I drop one thing and pick up something
else, sleep badly, and indulge in foolish notions. The weather
may also take a little of the blame—it continues to rain, and
probably we ought to call a halt to our walk. We have not
spoken about politics at all—besides, it lies in the dirt now
and is not worth touching.—"*In des Herzens stille Räume muss
Du fliehen*" [You must seek refuge in the silent room of the
heart], etc.,[11] provided it is otherwise permissible to speak
German.[12] Once more, thank you for the walk, and please
come again soon to

Yours most devotedly,
KOLDERUP-ROSENVINGE.

182. *Rasmus Nielsen—August [1848]—S. K.*

Taarbæk, August.

Dear Magister,

The sharp corner that is your stated address[1] has a marvelous effect. It is indeed a most appropriate direction (in the
right spot one sees it clearly when one turns one's back to the
Reformed Church); but, on closer inspection, it is an even

more appropriate misdirection, since no human being, however lean he might make himself, can enter directly through a
corner; one has to look down one of the sides in order to find
an entrance. What an advantage for you and what a problem
for him who enters. Now, when the latter expects to find you
in Rosengaarden, you are sitting hidden in the dark shadows
of Tornebusken,[2] and then again, when he seeks you amongst
the thorns, well, then you have moved over to the sunny side
and live among myrtles and roses. Thus always *inter et inter*
[between one thing and another] you are fairly well
protected—I do not say against worries, but still against the
vulgar and the hangers-on. As for me, I could never wish for
a more reliable address, for as direction and misdirection alternate so that the meaning (meaninglessness is of course pro-
hibited) is there *ad libitum* [in plenty], I can never mistake the
way, unless—God forbid—it should happen that some time
in foggy weather I became foggy and lost—myself.

Your   R. N.

P.S. Just as these lines were written, I received your last note,
from which I learn that I must beg your pardon for having
caused you inconvenience by skipping one week. The reason
is ridiculous enough in itself. For it has occurred to me that
my frequent writing might possibly be misunderstood. "It
might seem," so I thought, "as if in a fall from the cliff out
here you had suffered such an injury to the small of your back
that now you had to hobble on one side, and now, for lack of
other exercise, continued writing in order to have a crutch." I
dare say you will forgive this fear of being misunderstood. I
hope to see you in town, in two weeks at the latest.—

[*Address*:]
S. T.
Magister Kie[r]kegaard.

183. *S. K.—[August 1848]—Rasmus Nielsen. S. K.'s draft.*

Dear friend,

What "fear of being misunderstood by frequent writing"? After all, "Perfect love casts out fear."[1] And if it exists or ever has existed, that eminent dialectic in the form of double reflection, then there is a power that is a match for it, perfect love. I can testify to this, for I, who after all am very far from being perfect in love, in no way fear that I inconvenience you by frequent writing.

In other words, you did receive that letter. Now, either you did not read it properly, or I was mistaken in believing that about the same time you wanted to know something that would permit you to understand it differently. There was a passage in it* that you may have interpreted as applicable to your relationship to me and mine to you, whereas it was aimed at my productivity as an author in general, which was occasioned by that something that took place at the same time. Therefore, you see, in order to free your judgment completely with regard to that something, I was obliged meanwhile to move out to the sharp corner and may perhaps be forced to stay there as long as I write letters or entertain myself by corresponding with you. But as long as that is so, neither can there be any possibility of your wanting to visit me. On the contrary, the invitation was for you to visit me when you come to Copenhagen. It is really a very astute remark of yours that "however lean one might make oneself, one cannot enter directly through a corner." I would admire it, if I did not thereby come to admire myself, I who have personally realized this. But a written communication is one thing, particularly so under special circumstances; a personal visit is another and from experience you must know that the entrance is from Tornebuskegaden. Where one goes from there, you will have to decide for yourself on the basis of ex-

---

* That passage begins as follows: all communication in "the form of reduplication," a passage that otherwise would have been a ridiculous reminiscence.

perience, but I do not deceive; the entrance is not from Rosengaarden.

Oh, my dear sir, when it comes to fear and trembling, I am after all an old dialectician. I do not unconditionally fear misunderstanding; I believe that misunderstanding is a dialectical moment in understanding. Therefore I also bear it patiently when, obligated by the greatest responsibility, I know myself to have acted as carefully and, dialectically speaking, as scrupulously as possible. *Mein lieber Freund, sehen sie* [You see, my dear friend]!—and when you come to Copenhagen, then *dann hören sie* [you shall hear]!

Do let me know as soon as you come to Copenhagen so that I may send for you. I place emphasis on this invitation. With respect to written communication I even asked you in advance to forgive me if I should at some point neglect to reply. If this has offended you, then I believe that you have misunderstood me, but if you are *still* of the same opinion, all right, then I beg your pardon; that was not my intention, even though there was contained in it a teleological suspension in the direction of that frequently mentioned something that took place at the same time.

I suppose you have become stout and fat and sunburned; I have not become any fatter—and I cannot get thinner. In that respect I dare not promise you any surprise. Thus you will, when you accept the invitation, find me unalterably the same, at the corner of Tornebuskegaden and Rosengaarden, with the entrance on Tornebuskegaden.

Yours, S. K.

184. S. K.—[August 1848]—J.L.A.
Kolderup-Rosenvinge[1]

Dear *Conferentsraad*,

"We did not get around to talking about politics," you remark. No wonder! You are so polite that you forget that I was so impolite as to hold forth by myself which, however, could not be otherwise during a—solitary walk in your company, and after all you are the person who is usually informed about politics while I remain all ears.

No, politics is not for me. To follow politics, even if only domestic politics, is nowadays an impossibility, for me, at any rate. Whenever anything happens very quickly—well, then one attempts to follow it; whenever anything goes very slowly—well, then one attempts to put up with the boredom of following it. But whenever something fluctuates back and forth, up and down and down and up, and then comes to a halt, and around and up and down and back again, then I am incapable of voluntarily following. If necessary I should prefer going to war as a "coerced volunteer" to sitting at home—following it. I do not consider him who goes to war under such conditions as great a patriot as him who sits at home—following it. We have not been at war for a long time,[2] but it has never impressed me as a real war. To me the whole thing seems more like a lecture (such as Ørsted's on physics) during which experiments are conducted, or during which the presentation is illustrated with experiments. To my way of thinking this war has really always been some sort of peace making or making of peace—the most peculiar sort of war I have ever known.

That is why I keep away from politics, however much I like to hear someone talk about it who after all is so well versed in these matters that he can keep up with them. It turns sour for me, probably because I know too little, so that I become like someone who wanted to go traveling around Sjælland with the help of an ordinary little map of Denmark. Politics is too much for me. I love to focus my attention on lesser things, in which one may sometimes encounter exactly the same.

Hence I leave the world's stage, the field of battle, and return to Copenhagen, but in a manner of speaking I even leave Copenhagen. I go for a walk, and yet I shall perhaps arrive at the same thing. I shall allow myself to escort you out to one of those neighborhoods *dicht an den neuen Buden* [close to the new cottages],[3] where there is that quiet noise that emanates from the many little families there. —Act I— Two dogs have started fighting. This event causes an enormous sensation. An unbelievable number of heads appear at the windows to watch. While it lasts, all work stops. Everything is abandoned. —Act ii— From the doors of the two houses closest to the battle emerge two housewives, each from her own. These two housewives appear to be the mistresses of the dogs. One maintains that the other's dog started the fight. The women become so angry over this that they start fighting. —I observed no more than this, but it could easily be continued. —So, Act iii— Two men arrive, the husbands of the respective women. One of them maintains that the other's wife started it. The two husbands become so angry that they start fighting. Whereupon it may be assumed that other husbands and wives join in—and this is now a European war. The occasion is the question of who started it. In this you will perceive the formula for war in the second degree. War in the first degree is war; in the second degree it is a war occasioned by the question of who started the first war.

But now to something far more important. I see, to my horror, from what you write that you have stopped walking. Above all, this must not be so. For your own sake, dear *Conferentsraad*, and for mine so that I may have a clear conscience, I must emphatically request that you go on walking. Indeed, I have yet another reason for insisting so zealously on this. That little circle that is closest to you, whose sole desire is and will ever be for your well-being, may have occasionally almost thanked me silently for coming and persuading you to go out. Yes, that is how it is. I have the pleasure of walking with you and the gratitude of your family into the bargain. Accordingly I have an even greater responsibility—it may sound strange to say this—not to lead you *astray*, as I would if I were to make you *sit still* in order first to make you read—a letter from me—and then, and this would be even more irresponsible, to write to me. Oh no! You must walk. As those two lovers, Charles and Emeline,[4] promise each other in parting to look at the moon whenever it is full, wherever they may find themselves in the world, so let us two walkers promise each other whenever we receive a letter—regardless of the weather and walking conditions—to go for a walk. Next time I write I shall purposely arrange it so that inside the outer envelope there will be another one on which it will say, "from Magister Kierkegaard," so that without opening the envelope you will be able to see whom it is from. Then, provided that you consider a letter from me a burden, please read it at once—and then off with you to overcome whatever damage you may have sustained from it. But on the other hand, provided you consider such a letter a relatively good thing when compared with the rest of the boredom and mediocrity of this best of all worlds, then please go for a walk first and then read. Whichever way you choose, what I request of you will take place—for that you walk is most important. I who do not understand politics, do, on the other hand, understand all about walking. My view of life is like that of the parson: "Life is a path." That is why I go walking. As long as I am able to go walking, I fear nothing, not even death. For as long as I am able to go walking I can walk away from everything. When I am unable to go walking, I fear everything, especially life, for when I am unable to go walking, nothing goes well for me.

I shall stop here, at your gate. I take my leave. Thank you for today, thank you for the walk, thank you for the kindness I know you bear me so readily, indeed with so much friendship. Now our ways are parting. The gate is closing. Once more I look back. Then I leave, but I remain

Your   S. KIERKEGAARD.

185. *J.L.A. Kolderup-Rosenvinge—August 8, 1848— S. K.*

Ordrupshøj,[1] August 8, 1848.

It almost hurts me, dear Magister, to be forced to conclude as a result of our last conversation, or rather of your monologue (but now that you have talked yourself out, I hope that I may be permitted to get a word in), that you are a secret adherent of the movement party. Your everlasting encomium on walking, which you have elevated to a veritable system, the culmination of which is that one can *walk* away from everything, shows me clearly the state of affairs. For the other movement people also consider movement *per se* the principal point, and when all is said and done they have no other purpose than to walk away from everything. Yet in ancient times Horace taught that one cannot ride away from grief and worry (*sedet atra cura post equitem*—here I must quote from memory[2] and it is not a very good one—still, that is the sense of it), and I doubt that he believed that one could walk or run away from them. Nevertheless, you have made this discovery, and deserve—provided the cure is effective—at the very least a *testimonial*, not only from the Danish people but from all suffering humanity. For the time being you must content yourself with my addressing you as master of infantry [*magister peditum*], for in this connection the cavalry is of little use,[3] as Horace has already remarked, which is why I for my part have done away with it. Still, before you manage to persuade everybody to walk or run along with you, I must ask you to consider whether the centrifugal force would not be utterly destructive if the centripetal force did not serve as a counterbalance, and whether the consequences would not be most serious if everybody were to be on the move all the time. In the end you would not be able to find a single path for a solitary walk—everything would be crowded with people trying to run away from themselves. In this, you see, lies the hitch in the system, for you might be able to teach people to walk away from their souls by means of constant motion so that in the end, overcome with exhaustion, they would walk about in their sleep; but have you also considered that in order to walk one must be able to take one's body along, even when the latter in its frailty constantly reminds the person who is walking that he is but a sack of bones and would be far better off seated within four walls, not merely to bite his fingernails but in order to permit his soul to fly on the wings of imagination while he allows his body to rest on a sofa or in a chair, which is why the body out of gratitude—one good deed deserves another—lets the soul have peace for several hours at a time? This system recommends itself because it provides a suitable balance between body and soul, while acknowledging the claims of both parties—or in modern parlance—their equal rights, while your everlasting system of motion turns man's body into a *perpetuum mobile* that in the end gets clean way from its soul or drags the somnambulant along with it. In this, you see, lies the ultimate consequence of your system! While you may object that my system is a system of repose, I must remind you that I do not—as the Indians do, that is, the Brahmins—view absolute repose as the highest good, but that I do espouse *suitable* motion, although preferably by carriage or by ship. That I prefer the motion of a carriage to the more popular motion of walking, you may perhaps attribute to my aristocratic bent of mind, but I should add that it is precisely the peasant class that rides a lot and that there are many carriages that are not at all aristocratic, such as omnibuses (or buses), work carts, refuse carts, etc., etc., etc. The fact that I really do move you may gather from my *going* (N.B. by steamship, one of today's most brilliant *Errungenschaften*—a modern German word we have not yet conquered any more than we have *Wühler*) yesterday to Elsinore and walking from Hellebæk to Odinshøj.[4] Today I returned by steamship to Bellevue—drove here from there, and I intend to walk to the Hermitage this afternoon. What more can you ask? Three different means of locomotion in one day, and many, many miles traveled by motion into the bargain—I cannot even count them, nor do I care to. In brief, my system is in all ways preferable to the eternally peripatetic, and the formula of this system is *"ne quid nimis"* [nothing too much]!

Dinnertime at half past two. I am just returning from a walk with *Geheimeraad* Ørsted[5]—and lest I should become unfaithful to my system I have arranged it so that we *drive* to the Hermitage[6] this afternoon. —After all this boring talk of driving, walking, and sailing, which I see I have jotted down on paper, it might not be amiss if I were to adopt your system of a separate envelope so that you could avoid reading the letter when you find the initials KR—at least until you have returned from the last of your countless daily walks. You could read it at night and reflect that sufficient to the day is the evil thereof. —Thank you for the amusing account of the battle in *den neuen Buden*. I hope that the dogfight *there* has ended, even though you have depicted it in your imagination as unending, and have already set my blood astir by making me think of my big dog in Kannikestræde, who must have the rank of major at least—on account of his size he cannot be content with a lower rank. You can easily imagine the turmoil it may throw my household into if I also have to send him to the battlefield, long after my servant and his helper have departed.[7] So, by all means, do please see to it that you calm the troubled spirits, or at any rate do not put any obstacles in the way of an armistice. It is not until this point that I realize that I am writing somewhat incautiously about peace and war and similar affairs of state in these political times, and that all this discussion of the war between the two dogs at Nyboder (which you have even referred to in German) might easily make us look suspect if the letters were to fall into the right hands. If it should come to that, surely you will not deny that you began this outrage, and this could very well happen in spite of your assurance in our last conversation about leading me "astray" or out on thin ice. I should be most pleased if I could tempt you out upon the *watery* way—to use a Homeric expression—or, in other words, if I could once seduce you into walking on and aboard the steamship to Bellevue and into walking to Ordrupshøj from there. For a walker like you that is a mere shortcut—so that we might go walking in Ordrupkrat, which I shall be most willing to do, both before and after the meal. This very moment I am summoned to aforesaid table—and since I have a few guests, in particular a *philosophus*—Professor Nielsen—our written walking has to lie *sub scamno* [under the bench] for today. Thank you for the walk, dear Magister, and do please come again soon in one way or another to

> Yours most devotedly,
> KOLDERUP-ROSENVINGE.

[*Address*:]
S. T.
Magister S. Kierkegaard.

186. *S. K.—[before August 20, 1848]—J.L.A.*
Kolderup-Rosenvinge. [1]

Dear *Conferentsraad*,

As I was walking down the street the other day, it occurred
to me—not as it occurs to Sibbern[2] that people may be saying, "I wonder what Sibbern is saying?"—no, it occurred to
me to wonder what Holberg's Jeronymus,[3] if he were living
now, would say of these times, he who already in his own
time believed the world could not last until Easter. This notion was conceived as follows: In a newspaper I had read that
on railroad trains something called "a gadfly"[4] is employed in
order—yes, is this not crazy?—*to stop.*[5] Indeed, the crazier the
better. Can you imagine anything more insane? Is it not accordingly impossible for the world to last until Easter—that
is, if one can employ a gadfly in order to stop? It is true
enough that the carpenter was only partially successful—
presumably you have read the same account yourself—in
stopping the train by means of the gadfly, for he was on the
contrary run over by means of the very gadfly he wanted to
use. *Berlingske Tidende* concludes its account by saying that
further information has not yet been forthcoming. Oh, unknown to *Berlingske Tidende*, it has told more than enough to
furnish a thinker with material for a long time to come. For
inasmuch as the carpenter did not know how to use the gadfly
properly, the case remains the same: the world has advanced
so far in madness that it employs a gadfly in order to stop,
and, that being so, to return to Jeronymus, it cannot possibly
last until Easter. Because of this one actually feels less sorry
for the poor carpenter, for since the whole world will have
perished by Easter anyway, or, and this seems particularly
appropriate, will have been run over, then the carpenter is not
to be lamented that much. Indeed the world will perish before
Easter, unless one can say that it already has perished and that
the misfortune is and certainly will be the wish to stop by
means of a gadfly—either because this is impossible or because one does not know how to use the gadfly properly.

I intend, you see, to use the following sentence: "How

could a gadfly possibly be used to stop?" as the basis for my reflections. And although it may not seem so at first, it will on closer inspection become apparent that this consideration is related to and coheres with what we spoke about during our last hour of meditation.

For you are quite correct, *Conferentsraad*, in saying that I "belong to the movement party," although not secretly, no, quite openly, as I always undertake my motions out in the open. Yet, however inviting it might seem to a walker, this talk of party followers, one thing is a certainty: no one belongs less to any party than I do, precisely because I keep on walking. Just as different as I am *qua* walker from the kind of people who cannot go walking or get outside unless it is to go to some particular place, just so indifferent am I to everything that has to do with a party! —Every party follower, everything that has to do with a party, goes to a particular place, goes in order to be seated. And scarcely has the party follower been given a seat—in the ministry—before he settles himself as though he wanted and intended to stay seated for the rest of his life, so that one must believe that he has (*ad modum*: to lose one's nose, to lose one's mind, etc.) lost his legs, or that, like certain insects that have wings only for a certain period, he had legs only for a certain period. He stays seated, he does not leave the spot—indeed, to make him move, one must (here it comes again!), one must, as they say, give him legs and feet to walk on.

But now back to the gadfly and to wanting to stop by means of a gadfly, and you will see that this is related to what we spoke of last time. For is this not the law of confusion that governs recent European events? They wish to stop by means of a revolution and to stop a revolution by means of a counterrevolution. But what is a counterrevolution if it is not also a revolution? And to what can we compare a revolution if not to a gadfly? Thus they want to stop by means of a gadfly? I am sure you will agree that I am right in considering the whole development in Europe as an enormous skepticism or as a vortex. What does a vortex seek? —A fixed point where it can stop. (Therefore, you see, I seek—said *in parenthesi*—"that single individual.") We all seem to agree that a stop is necessary. But that person who, while wishing to stop, fails to find a fixed point—that person who in other words wants to stop by means of the moved or the moving only enlarges the vortex. For a long time now there has been so much discussion of the need for movement relative to what is established that the need of the established relative to movement has been completely forgotten. Yet throughout Europe nothing is really established at this moment— everything is movement. One gets tired, becomes dizzy, yearns for a foothold, a stop. One grabs at thin air and uses "a gadfly" rather like the woman who, panicking because her house was on fire, saved her fire-tongs.[6] That is what happened in France. Lamartine[7] wanted to stop curruption etc. by means of—a gadfly, alas, and so, just like the carpenter, he was run over. Citizens had been shot at—still, the Republic was also bought at that price, so probably the defense could be made that they caused the shooting. Therefore, they wanted to stop by means of a law, the first one decreed by the Republic, which abolishes capital punishment for political crimes. But alas, the Republic itself was not an established order, it was a gadfly—and so they wanted to stop by means of a gadfly. That became quite obvious, for now a stop was effectuated by shooting down citizens by the thousands. Still, once again it was a stop by means of a gadfly— — — —

And I too shall stop, for by now both of us are probably tired of pursuing this thought any further. This, you see, was a reliable stop. But no, wait! Although I suppose France tired of revolutions long ago, they have not yet stopped for that reason. Alas, it will not be so easy. There is a nemesis over Europe. And thus there may also be a nemesis over you, *Conferentsraad*, because you became acquainted with me, and now, although long tired of listening to me, you cannot make me stop.

So I proceed. All this about stopping and the mistaken belief that one can stop by means of a gadfly is related to *walking*. Only he who fundamentally understands walking (and you know I do, I who do not understand politics), understands also how it is bound up with stopping. If I have systematized walking as you remarked last time, then please permit me to essay a little theory of "motion," to which category stopping in turn belongs. Most people believe that so long as one has a fixed point *to which* one wants to get, then motion is no vortex. But this is a misunderstanding. It all depends on having a fixed point *from which to set out*. Stopping is not possible at a point *ahead*, but at a point *behind*. That is, stopping is in the motion, consolidating the motion. And this is the difference between a political and a religious movement. Any purely political movement, which accordingly lacks the religious element or is forsaken by God, is a vortex, cannot be stopped, and is a prey to the illusion of wanting a fixed point ahead, which is wanting to stop by means of a gadfly; for the fixed point, the only fixed point, lies behind. And therefore my opinion about the whole European confusion is that it cannot be stopped except by religion, and I am convinced that—as so strangely happened once with the Reformation, which appeared to be a religious movement but turned out to be a political one—in the same way, the movement of our time, which appears to be purely political, will turn out suddenly to be religious or the need for religion.[8]

And still, still, that which must agree perfectly with Jeronymus's opinion that the world cannot last until Easter, that which is the secret within the confusion of wanting to stop by means of a gadfly, is indeed, if understood at a deeper level, after all a paradox containing the truth, inasmuch as the truth is always a paradox. We know that Socrates called himself a "gadfly."[9] Admittedly he explains this in the sense of awakening (and he too was a revolutionary). But yet in another sense it is clear that he was also a person who stopped, for he stopped a Sophist vortex. He ambushed the Sophists; with his gadfly's sting he drove them forward in such a way that they really moved backward, or in such a way that Sophistry perished and the single individual came to his senses at the fixed point behind. Sophistry also sought to fix a point ahead *to which* the movement would go and reasoned that it would thereby be safe from becoming a vortex. But the

Socratic dialectic was inexhaustible in making it apparent that nothing remained fixed in this way. On the contrary, Socrates had the fixed point *behind*. His point of departure lay in himself and in the god. That is to say, he knew himself, he possessed himself. By this means he stopped Sophistry, which, like politics, always asks whither one should go instead of asking whence one should depart. Oh, that there might be such a gadfly in the confused struggle of our times who with Socratic *ataraxie* [peace of mind] would directly oppose the "whither" of modern haste, who would turn time back to this, that inasmuch as the question concerns whence one should depart, that inasmuch as all knowledge, Socratically speaking, was a recollecting, so all genuine motion is a return to or a departure from the fixed point behind. It is true that Socrates was also run over, as everyone must be who is to be used in this way. But the difference, which also determines whether this desire to stop by means of a gadfly is an insane impossibility or the profundity of truth, the difference lies in this: whether he who is going to be used for stopping accepts the fact that he must be sacrificed or deceives himself into believing that he will conquer. For both will be run over, but when he who deceived himself into thinking that he would conquer is run over, everything is lost, whereas he who accepted in advance the fact that he must be sacrificed has one more thought, his best thought, and as he is being run over, he conquers. The martyr's superiority consists in laying down his life. He conquers as the dead man who returns. The dead Socrates stopped the vortex, something the living Socrates was unable to do. But the living Socrates understood intellectually that only a dead man could conquer, as a sacrifice—and he understood ethically how to direct his whole life to becoming just that.

Dear *Conferentsraad*, I hope I have not walked you weary for now you must set out. For the agreement was that if you considered my letter a burden you would read first and then walk. —Therefore, Goodbye! I hope the walk agrees with you, and that when you have returned and assumed your favorite position, that of lying on the sofa, letting the imagina-

tion go for a walk, hastening through the giant realms of possibilities, or, if you so choose, letting it run errands in town, I
hope that then you will not regret the exertions caused by the
letter and the walk. And above all I hope that you do not impatiently damn me to hell—alas! alas! then it would become
even more insane inasmuch as I cannot do otherwise than remain

Your   S. Kierkegaard.

187. J.L.A. Kolderup-Rosenvinge—August 20, 1848—S. K.[1]

Ordrupshøj, August 20, 1848.

Dear Magister,

I could almost have forsworn going for a walk today. I am
sitting here with the doors open looking out into the rain, and
not one single sensible thought will rain down. I slept badly
last night, am in pain from a vesicant, and am more than usually testy and cross. Although I have not exactly run, I have
driven to town on a fool's errand for three days for my students, who are still pleased to remain on vacation. Basically I
ought to be very pleased by this, for I am not up to writing or
giving lectures these days—and am scarcely up to looking inside a book, or at least not without getting annoyed. Just now
I put some annoying reading matter aside, and accordingly I
must ask your forgiveness should you get splattered by my
bad humor during the walk. I was reading, or rather scan-
ning, a treatise entitled "The Five Eras of the World" in the
second issue of the sixth volume of *For Literature and Criticism*[2]
by Christensen,[3] a graduate in theology, an absolutely mad
follower of Grundtvig, who interprets Hesiod by Daniel and
Daniel by Hesiod and speaks most edifyingly about that bird,
the phoenix, and the four rivers of Paradise, about the Greeks
who represent silver and constitute the second river in
Paradise, and, to put it briefly, qualifies himself more for the
insane asylum than for the pulpit. He has nonetheless had his
nonsense accepted by a journal that has a shingle on its door

saying, "For Criticism"! Indeed, when the mad and the blind thus continue to act as guides for the people so that they may go mad in the most popular manner, I become almost ready to join you and Jeronymus[4] in thinking that the world probably will not last until Easter, regardless of the number of brakes they attach to the steam engine of madness. It is really going full speed ahead! I had depended somewhat on Cavaignac[5] as a brake, but look! Now he has gone off and gotten himself married—and it is well known that we are "unfortunately without our senses when we get married or get hanged!"[6] How much I relied on Cavaignac you will best understand from a little poem written in German by a count who died in 1847. When it fell into my hands some weeks ago, I got the idea of translating it, and here you have my somewhat free translation, which of course I prefer to communicate rather than the original, because one does prefer one's own.

> The Gordian Knot[7]
> With furies' frenzy, cannibals' gall,
> You wreck what once was castle wall.
> You build in haste, cement with blood
> Your modish hut in ancient mud.
> And when you complete that wondrous hall,
> A Bonaparte destroys it all;
> The crushed and scattered rubble shows
> Where spirit's work once proudly rose.
>
> With silent might and head unbowed
> The hero preens before the crowd.
> With abject hunch you scrape and bow;
> Your necks, though yoked, extol him now.
> Be slaughtered then, with great good cheer,
> 'Tis written in your faces clear:
> "At Waterloo much sooner die,
> Than with the Guillotine comply."
>
> O, thus it goes, ye men of Nay,
> Whose bright bold pens would tyrants slay!

You pave the way for despots cruel,
While writers drivel, 'tis they who rule.
Do strive in vain with all that's clever
To stack the cards with sly endeavor.
Not till the Gordian Knot is tied
Will God send Alexander to our side.

By the way, I do not know if you are a lover of poetry, especially the political kind, and I really ought to have inquired before saddling you with this poetical freight, but it is in any case up to you to throw it overboard, i.e., to leave it unread, for from the waistline and overall appearance of the words you will see at once that they have legs or feet, even though they may only be bandylegs or clubfeet.

As I can see from the space left on the paper that we still have a good way to go before we reach Nørreport[8] and, as I cannot very well keep my mouth shut "like the dumb dog that has neither means nor mouth,"[9] I shall add to my apropos about Cavaignac an apropos about the French, which Livius (V, 37)[10] gives in the following apt characterization, which I happened to come upon in the course of some work I am doing at present on the *oldest* French system of justice (I cannot be bothered with the most recent justice or injustice). He calls the French *"nata in vanos tumultus gens"* ["a people born for futile tumult"]. Is that not marvelous? One has to believe that regardless of all their commotion the French have not progressed much beyond those days, with this exception: they have managed to get other people to run along with them or after them. By going on with my apropos about the French I can even demonstrate that they have regressed instead of progressed. For Pomponius Mela[11] says of them, the ancient Gauls, *scilic,*[12] that they were so persuaded of the immortality of the soul that they often negotiated loans of money on condition that it be made repayable in the next world. This might be credit in the next world—but where can that be found in France today? That, you see, was "the fixed point—behind" to which they ought to have held fast,[13] but they have been kicking up their heels for so long that the fixed point has become just as [*a hole in the paper*; loose?] as all the rest. —Now I can see Kannikestræde, and I thank you very much [*covered by the writer's seal*; for?] the walk—but one more thing: Have you seen the double of [*a hole in the paper*: *The Tinker*?] Turned Politician?[14] He is a political foundry worker by the name of Lunde;[15] cf. *Witchcraft or False Alarm*,[16] Act IV, scene 4.

On our next walk I would like to have an answer to the following question: "What is the relation of iron to copper and [especially] in politics?" Good morning!

Yours most devotedly,
KOLDERUP-ROSENVINGE

[*Address*:]
S. T.
Magister S. Kierkegaard
Tornebuskegaden N.

188. *S. K.—[August 1848]—J. L. A. Kolderup-Rosenvinge.*

Dear *Conferentsraad*,

First, a little story by way of introduction. It is said that great comic actors often occupied themselves, for their own private amusement, with seeing to what extent one could make the other laugh during a performance. Thus it is also told of Frydendahl[1] that he made a bet with another older actor, whose name I cannot determine, as to which of them could make the other laugh first during a particular performance. I cannot remember what play it was, and besides it does not matter. Frydendahl acted the part of Zoroaster or someone like him, some sort of oriental high priest with a long beard, a turban on his head, and dressed in some kind of robe. Even though I did not see it, Frydendahl stands vividly before me, a figure who must irresistibly make every spectator laugh, even though he did not succeed in making the other comedian laugh. Two acts had already been performed and still Frydendahl had not succeeded. But in the third act he had the following line, which he had to address to the other comedian who accordingly must also have been some sort of Zoroaster: "You fancy yourself a saint, but you worship false gods!" Having said this, Frydendahl was supposed to walk off stage, expressing the greatest contempt for the other. And so he did. But just as he reached the wings, he turned around once more and, summoning all his *vis comica* [comic strength], he said, "Phooey!" This was not in the script, and combined with the high pathos of his line ("You worship false gods") and with Frydendahl's mastery, it brought about the desired effect: the other burst out laughing.

Oh, dear *Conferentsraad*, I would do the same if I were to meet you in person in the bad mood you complained about last time. I would try everything to chase away this bad mood. If I did not succeed, I would finally say "Phooey!" Somehow I have gotten the *idée fixe* that you are becoming and must continue to become younger—but when you thus (pardon me for speaking this way, but it is connected with my *idée fixe*) yield in any way to that bad mood, then you do not become younger. But it is over now, is it not? It was a little cat's paw—and now you are once more in the process of getting younger, and I look forward with longing to the moment when I shall assure myself of it in person, when I walk by your side as an "audience."

But now on to something else. You who heed the events of the day and who still keep up, surely it cannot have escaped your attention how appropriate it is that the newest public assemblies here in town take place in a hippodrome. To him who knows how to interpret the signs of the times (if not as profoundly as Cand. Christensen,[2] who, said *in parenthesi*, for me has the distinction of having first been my secretary who copied *Either/Or* and later of attacking me bluntly in *Kirketidenden*, strangely enough "in order to show me that he dared write against me"), to him it must be remarkable that more recent times are gradually doing away with the designation "man" in order to substitute the designation "horse." Thus nowadays one does not speak of manpower as in former times, of the strength of Holger the Dane,[3] or the like; no, one always speaks of horsepower, of so and so much horse-power. But a group of people who will function only as a crowd, as *numerus*,[4] also really function only as a machine. Accordingly I propose that a new linguistic usage be intro-duced. Assuming that fifty men = one horsepower, then, if this is so, rather than saying, "Last night in the hippodrome[5] there was a meeting of one thousand men," one would say instead, "Last night in the hippodrome there was a meeting of twenty horsepower—Balthasar Christensen presiding." And further, it would be very much in keeping with the times if someone could work out a table, or a kind of *regula Petri*,[6] which one would consult in order to see how much horse-power would be necessary relative to the various purposes. Here is just one example of a *regula Petri* sum in this manner: If ten to fifteen thousand people in the streets—that is, be-tween 200 and 300 horsepower—are sufficient for a change of ministry, how much horsepower is required to bring about a change of councilor of chancery [*Cancelliraad*], i.e., to have one *Cancelliraad* dismissed and another installed? Yes, indeed! Horsepower, this horsepower, is a splendid invention and the pride of modern times. The question is not so much one of the power of spirit and brain at these big meetings, for it is really just as Lichtenberg[7] so excellently puts it, "Ohne Hände (that is, for the purpose of balloting) ist nichts an-zufangen, aber der Kopf ist nur eine Art von Hut, den man zwar zuweilen trägt, der aber bei den eigentlichen Galla-Begebenheiten unsers Lebens abgelegt werden muss."

But before we proceed, or maybe more correctly, as we proceed, for we are of course on a walk: it is true that when we spoke together last time there was something you asked me to clarify the next time: "What is the difference between a foundry worker and a tinker?" —You will remember Rahbeck's[8] reply to Lars Mathiesen when he had to answer the question about the difference between him (L. M.) and an ass. L. M. answered, "I don't know," and then R. said, "Neither do I!" —The difference does not consist in educa-tion, for they have both studied, and basically they have both been educated by means of that political stockfish, that strange pamphlet that keeps being published as "printed in this year." Nor does the difference consist in the fact that one casts iron stoves and the other tankards, for that is only an accidental difference, whereas the similarity is the essential factor, inasmuch as they both mold states, and again the similarity is the essential factor, that in doing so they may both forget how to mold iron stoves or tankards, thus completely cancelling out the erstwhile difference. Still, there is a small difference after all. Insofar as one can judge, the tinker is an autodidact who has studied the political stockfish on his own, while the foundry worker on the other hand certainly has a tutor who goes over the assignment with him and then rehearses until he has memorized the stockfish and can spew it out again. To that extent the foundry worker almost seems to resemble the tinker's future son-in-law, whom the tinker wants to rehearse every night. Accordingly the foundry worker is the tinker's son-in-law. Furthermore, there is this difference, that with a certain grandeur the tinker utterly forgets the tinker and everything that brings the tinker and tinkers to mind, whereas the foundry worker can by no means forget about the foundry worker and wants to mold the state to favor foundry workers.

But apropos of foundry workers, it is in other words your opinion that if not a foundry worker, then surely an iron fist or a tyrant with an iron fist, a military despot with an iron fist, is needed to bring order into European affairs.[9] However, you yourself are dubious about Cavaignac,[10] and indeed with good reason. As we know, he has only one arm, but that might suffice, provided he had an iron fist on that one arm. For one needs only one arm in order to have an iron fist; what is the point of having so many arms? That might easily become a contradiction, just as it once seemed a contradiction to me that everyone was so busy knitting stockings for the army, while *Berlingske Tidende* every day assured us, and *Fædrelandet* as well, that we were all determined to die united as one man—so that accordingly only one pair of stockings would be required. But to return to Cavaignac's one arm. You have indeed discovered the trouble: he has married, and so he does not even have the freedom of that one arm—while at the same time he has been relieved of the other arm. The man who has to rule with an iron fist should never be married, but if it does come to that, then he should never contract more than a marriage to his left hand. But he has no left hand, and accordingly, by marrying he has given away his right hand—unless he let his beloved marry his stump. If that is the case, then this is such an "offhand marriage vow" and such a stumpy relationship that there might still be hope for Cavaignac, for whom I, by the way, have no hope at all, because I only think of him as Thiers' new tool.[11]

But all jesting aside. For where could I have learned that you are expecting a tyrant while I am expecting a martyr? I have learned this from a little poem, the significance of which and the significance to me I genuinely appreciate in more than one way. You say that you do not know if I am a friend of political poetry, but I do not know how you can think of calling this little poem political poetry. For it is so clearly marked with the essence of a serene spirit that although it perceives the political in an idea, it is still as far removed from all political uproar and noise—as far removed from them as your country house is, indeed even farther removed—as far removed as that remoteness in which *you* reside is from the bustle of politics. Rather, one designates as political poems those that do not seek the remoteness of the idea, but want to roar into the midst of the uproar. As to your poem: it is a mood born in secret and communicated in secret. And therefore I again see in this one more proof of the kindness you bear me, for you send me your poem in all confidence.

Thank you, then! Thank you for every so very welcome communication from you. Thank you for letting it signify to me that I may remain.

Your   S. KIERKEGAARD.

189. *S. K.—[1848]—J.L.A. Kolderup-Rosenvinge.*

Dear *Conferentsraad*,

I am sure you remember that place in *Don Ranudo*[1] where—in reply to Gusman, who has pointed out to him that he, who is about to receive the distinguished visitor, has holes in his boots—he declares that it is of no importance, for it may be explained by his having corns and hence is a mark of distinction. You probably remember that Gusman then asks him if the fact that he has only one tail on his coat may also be explained by his having corns. The same would be true of me if I tried to explain or make excuses for not having been out walking with you for such a long time, for I would surely get lost in contradictions. Accordingly I prefer to leave it as one of those inexplicable things. Furthermore, the time will soon be here now, indeed in only a few more days, when you return to town—the time when I shall have the pleasure, in a more literal sense, of walking with you. Therefore, please think of this letter as a little jaunt out to you, as a farewell visit to the countryside, by means of which I thank you for the summer and for the summer walks. It was I, appropriately enough, who started this, who inquired whether you might feel like going walking, so please let me be the one who ends it now, who thanks you for every time you felt like it.

I happened to think of you most vividly yesterday, because yesterday I went walking with His Excellency Ørsted.[2] Strange about that man! It appears to me that our national catastrophe[3] has had the effect on him of a reviving and invigorating shower. You will see how invaluable he will become in the National Assembly.[4] In this topsy-turvy world where candidates become ministers, he is still the man who can perform the feat (for the other is after all far from being a feat) of turning Ørsted, the minister, into A. S. Ørsted, *candidatus juris*.[5] I am so convinced that he will dumbfound the Assembly that I really am taking pains to tell everybody about it in advance. Just let them live with the delusion that he has grown old and, now that he has been pushed out of the ministry on Shrove Monday, that he has become a senile discard. But let them watch out, for Ørsted, the candidate, will be far more dangerous to them than the minister could ever be. Probably it took this kind, and precisely this kind, of catastrophe to force His Excellency, modest and respectable as he is, into becoming conscious, just this once out of pride, of what he seemed so charmingly to have forgotten: his importance, his superiority. But you will see that it will be incomparably becoming in him. I suppose his mood is not without indignation, but otherwise he retains his former seriousness—with one new, small addition: a certain kind of playfulness or sense of humor. The change of ministry became, by virtue of what replaced him, so much of a stark raving mad and devil-may-care farce that it had to make him smile. In this mood, faithful as ever to his native country and its cause (and in this lies the pathetic), he now wants to find his satisfaction, almost his entertainment, in spending the remainder of his life treating his *politica* quite *con amore*, in one sense untroubled, almost like a young man, as Mr. Ørsted— no more nor less. He has been relieved, albeit in such an ungrateful and ridiculous manner, relieved of the burden he has borne, the weight of which he himself knows best, relieved of the responsibility (and I dare say it is possible that the responsibility he took upon himself, in other words, the responsibility under which he has labored throughout his life, has meant something different from that of those gentlemen, the responsible ministers); he has been relieved of having to live day in and day out in that awful crossfire of considerations and of having to steer through their midst. His intrinsic nobility is satisfied because he will still be serving his nation, but how beautiful this spiritedness is, this hilarity, that will finally envelop the situation. He is presenting himself as a candidate in the election. That, after all, is a kind of examination. Now, he really could (as a conscientious candidate usually does in order to promote himself) offer a little something extra, this or that little thing with which he is familiar from his time as Attorney General, Commissioner, Minister. But he refrains and is, quite simply, a candidate. The mystification is superb, and even if he were ten years older, I believe he would almost have to be playful.

[*In margin*: For you see, at the time that unfortunate currency change[6] occurred, many a man who *really* had owned an enormous fortune *really* became impoverished—and why? Because money is not a reality. But in the spiritual world there is, God be praised, an eternal security for property. So even though a change, a currency change, may also occur in the external world, turning concepts, language, merit, etc. upside down, he who possesses spiritual wealth does not lose one whit of what he possessed—no, not even in all eternity. This is the humor of it, for with such a change a spiritual person only finds occasion for heightened self-awareness.]

So he will be elected in the third precinct,[7] and one thing is a certainty (yes, the ridiculous does recur here, but these days it is really impossible to poke one's nose out the window without falling over the comical or to say two words without having one of them touch on the ridiculous): he will always be able to take on the candidate who is opposing him, Melbye, the greengrocer, and he will always know more than the latter about current events. I do not know if you have noticed that [Melbye] declares in his platform that among other things he intends to work especially for the abolition of negro slavery[8]—superb! It is as though someone were to state in his platform that he intends to work especially for the building of a railroad between Copenhagen and Roskilde[9] or to have Vesterbroe[10] repaired.

But I shall stop. Still, in a little while, I shall hurry eagerly to Kannikestræde and impatiently ring the bell. "The *Conferentsraad* is at home"—and then we shall go walking!

Yours,   S. KIERKEGAARD.

190. *S. K.—[1848]—J.L.A. Kolderup-Rosenvinge.*

Dear *Conferentsraad*,

Enclosed is the little essay,[1] which, among other things, was also so illegibly written while on a trip into the country at Hirschholm that it presents itself only upon explicit request and, per agreement, as a private communication.

In looking through my most recent papers, I also came across a letter for you in an envelope addressed to Ordrupshøj. Accordingly it must have been written while you were still in the country. Now I have partly forgotten what it says, and I cannot make up my mind to open it, for then the *summa summarum* would probably be that I would find it so trivial and boring that I would decide not to send it. But after all, since it has been written, let it be enclosed as well. Whatever you may find it it, I am certain of one thing without having reread it: you will find in it, as in everything from me, unmistakable testimony to the devotion with which I was and am and remain

Your devoted
S. KIERKEGAARD.

191. *S. K.—October 30, [1848]—J. P. Mynster.*

October 30.

Right Reverend Bishop,

However welcome a gift[1] may be to the recipient and however strongly he may feel himself prompted to express his thanks, surely the act of giving or having given does not entail any subsequent obligation to accept the gratitude of the recipient, for after all, that would be yet another kindness on the part of the giver, or in other words, the same thing once more. Accordingly I hereby request your permission to thank you, or, because I cannot of course hear your reply, I ask your indulgence, for in thanking you for the gift I have received, I almost reward you with ingratitude, insofar as this note inconveniences you by wasting a moment of your time.

With profound reverence,
S. KIERKEGAARD.

[*Address:*]
To
His Excellency
The Right Reverend
Bishop, Dr. Mynster
Grand Cross of *Dannebrog*, Member of *Dannebrog*, a.o.

192. *S. K.—[1848]—S. M. Trier. S. K.'s draft.*

Dear Professor,

Please permit me to thank you once again for my carpenter.[1] Once more he is what he had the honor to be for twenty-five years, a worker with heart and soul, a worker who, although he thinks while he works, does not make the mistake of wanting to make thinking his work. For this reason I hope that I in turn am not making a mistake in thinking him essentially cured. I have allowed him to go on living with me, because I felt it would distress him very much to have to move now.

Thus everything is in order. But indeed—as you yourself said when I last had the pleasure of speaking with you, which I appreciated and appreciate as added proof of your kindness to me—indeed, you will please remember, if that time ever comes and he has a relapse: then I am to inform you at once, and then he will be admitted to the hospital as quickly as possible.

In conclusion, please allow me to add special emphasis here to that "Your" with which I would sign every letter to you,

Your gratefully obliged
S. KIERKEGAARD.

193. *S. K.—[1848]—J. L. Phister. S. K.'s draft.*

Dear Sir,

I daresay you will be able to determine with ease who is the author of this little piece; yet he wishes to remain unknown.

In several respects, the time spent working on this constituted a pleasant vacation for me. In the first place, it is a pleasure in and of itself to be occupied with an interesting and worthwhile subject, a genuine artistic achievement.[1] Secondly, I enjoyed working on it, because somehow I have conceived the idea that I owe some kind of debt of gratitude to the artist. Finally, it was no less enjoyable to me because I—as

I continue to hope—and not in vain—flattered myself with the hope that I might possibly please you with it.

Please, then, do not disdain the gift of this little manuscript, which is, after all, intended for one reader only. For if I had the essay printed, and if in that case it were read by everybody, still it would not have found its reader if you had not read it. But on the other hand, if you read it, even though nobody else did so, it would have reached its destination and found "the reader," the only one, indeed the only one, for not even I, the author, dare compare myself with this reader—as though I were as competent as he.

To end where I began: in many ways it was a pleasure for me to write this little essay—so now I hope that in some way or other you will take pleasure in receiving it, and with it a greeting from an—unknown—admirer.

To
Mr. Phister, the actor.

194. S. K.—[1848-49]—P. C. Kierkegaard.

Dear Peter,

I was glad to read the statement you made at the most recent Convention[1] on the subject of nationalism. Of course it would give me even greater pleasure some time to read that you had made a statement at the Convention cancelling your membership, for in a certain sense you do the most harm precisely when you speak the truth most forcefully, for thereby you contribute indirectly to strengthening the Convention, which—like the countless other attempts in our time to be effective by means of sheer number—is evil. There are of course certain things that I could never imagine saying to some people, for despite their best intentions they would be unable to understand, but in the case of one who is so dialectically advanced, and who has as much strength of character as you have, and who is, moreover, my brother, it would be unwise and repugnant to give up hope of being understood.

                                         Your brother.

This letter, better considered a note, I would like you to destroy when you have read it.
[*In P. C. Kierkegaard's hand*: Must be from 1848 or '49.
P. Chr. Kkgd.]

195. *S. K.—[1848]—Julie Thomsen.*

Dear Julie,
    It is obvious that we wronged your little son today, for we walked too fast, and we, or I, am to blame for his beginning to cry, which from a child's point of view he was completely justified in doing. It is for this reason that I am writing and sending the accompanying parcel.
    You see, with respect to the world—by which, according to Balle's Catechism,[1] is understood heaven and earth and all therein contained, but by which I more or less understand all the human multitudes therein contained—my advice to everybody is to let the world "be blown," each to the best of his ability. Perhaps you remember one of Grimm's fairy tales.[2] As usual, someone is setting out into the world. He walks and walks and keeps getting farther and farther away until he stops by a mill. Said *in parenthesi*, one sees in this how easy, but in another sense how difficult, nay impossible, it is to go out in search of adventure when one lives in Copenhagen, for in order to set out on an adventure one would first of all have to set out through the city gates, and yet it is of course impossible to walk through those gates without having come to a mill. In other words, the mill lies too close for it to be the occasion of any adventure. And herein lies the difference between actuality and the fairy tale, in proximity and distance. Given distance, infinite distance, then you have a fairy tale, for then any object—be it a mill, a horse, a sheep, a moo-cow, yes, be it even that which at times may

cause most sadness in the real world, a human being—takes
on a fairy tale aspect, as does the mill in this fairy tale. So the
wanderer stops by the mill. He is surprised to discover that
the mill is turning under full sail—although there is no wind
at all. (Here one must agree with the wanderer, for I almost
do believe that one would be surprised oneself if this happened with the mill on the city wall directly across from
where one lives.) Now the wanderer proceeds. Nine miles
farther on he encounters a man who is closing one nostril
with his finger while blowing through the other—on that
mill! And that is how it came to pass that it was turning under
full sail. Thus, not even using both nostrils, but with a finger
phlegmatically closing one nostril, one should, while blowing
through the other, say, "The whole world be blown!"

However, a little child—indeed, be it ever so tiny, the least
offense against this little child—indeed, be it ever so tiny—
when I have offended against this little one, that is a very serious matter to me, something about which I cannot say "be
blown!" I am very reluctant to have the sun set before I have
made up for it, but at this time of year when the days are so
short, the sun could easily set before I could possibly have
made amends. But since our civic lives are so wisely arranged
that the night watchman does not sing out the passing of the
day until it is 8 o'clock, I may after all manage to do it before
the sun sets. The town council and the police, and hence also
the night watchman, constitute authority, and although it is
not astronomical, it is still authority, and to children something very close to astronomical authority; whereas their elders, who have hardened themselves against all authority, no
longer arrange their going to bed according to the night
watchman's bidding, yet the children probably still do so.

Please, then, give my love to the little fellow and present
him with this box of toys from the strange man who walked
too fast for him today. And you, my dear Julie, you who—
yes, that certainly suffices as punishment for your having
walked so *fast* today—you who have now been forced to go
all the more *slowly* as you have had to spell your way slowly

through my illegible handwriting, receive in conclusion an
assurance of the devotion with which I remain your wholly
devoted

                                        Cousin   S. K.

[*Address:*]
To
Mrs. Julie Thomsen.
Accompanying small parcel.

196. *S. K.*—*[1848]*—*Hans Peter Kierkegaard.*[1]

Dear Peter,

   Happy New Year! I never go calling to offer my New Year
greetings and send them in writing only rarely and as an
exception—but you are among the exceptions. In recent years
I have often thought of you, and I intend to do likewise in this
one. Among the other thoughts or considerations I often have
had and intend to go on having about you is this: that recon-
ciled to your fate, with patience and quiet devotion, you carry
out as important a task as the rest of us who perform on a
larger or smaller stage, engage in important business, build
houses, write copious books, and God knows what. Undeniably your stage is the smallest, that of solitude, and inwardness—but *summa summarum*, as it says in Ecclesiastes,[2] when
all is said and done, what matters most is inwardness—and
when everything has been forgotten, it is still inwardness that
is most important.

   I wrote this some days ago, was interrupted, and did not
manage to conclude it. Today your father visited me, and that
circumstance once more reminded me to complete or at least
put an end to what I had begun. For there was something
more I wanted to add. If I were to give you any advice about
life, or taking into consideration your special circumstances,
were to commend to you a rule for your life, then I would
say: Above all do not forget your duty to love yourself; do
not permit the fact that you have been set apart from life in a
way, been prevented from participating actively in it, and that

you are superfluous in the obtuse eyes of a busy world, above all do not permit this to deprive you of your idea of yourself, as if your life, if lived in inwardness, did not have just as much meaning and worth as that of any other human being in the loving eyes of an all-wise Governance, and considerably more than the busy, busier, busiest haste of busy-ness—busy with wasting life and losing oneself.

Take care of yourself in the new year. If you would enjoy visiting me once in a while, please do come. You are welcome.

Your cousin   S. K.

Perhaps you yourself will notice that many days have now gone by since your father visited me; so once more some time has passed before you finally get this letter.

[*Address:*]
To
Mr. Peter Kierkegaard.

197. *S. K.—January 1849—Julie Thomsen.*

January 1849.

Dear Julie,

That you were a resolute woman with courage in your breast is something I have really always believed, but that you should have lumps in your breast—what kind of lumps are they?

Well, all jesting aside—but no, certainly not! Jesting to the fore, if possible! I suppose this has been a serious matter, but I hope that it is so happily concluded now that the physician, working on this assumption—provided he knows his business—has nothing more to do than to prescribe encouragement, the fortifying remedy of jesting, that strangely volatile thing, a sublimate that is sometimes more potent and of greater density than the most concentrated earnestness, and yet, just like naphtha, quickly, quickly evaporating, but not, mark you, until it has produced its effect.

All in all there are two things, two remedies—both for
internal use—which, regrettably enough, physicians nowadays forget or neglect to prescribe. —Alas, it is all the more
regrettable that neither one nor the other is particularly easy
to manage, even though the physician did remember to prescribe it. One of these, used when everything is safely
over—a small dose, a drop is sufficient; too much is detrimental and may even elicit the opposite effect—is jesting, a timely
jest, a felicitous fancy, a priceless, surprising something, a
droll, jesting incident, a turn of phrase that all of a sudden
turns everything upside down. This medicine may be taken at
any time of day, whether on an empty stomach or just
after a meal is immaterial. There is just one unconditional re-
quirement: one must absolutely be in the mood for it. When
that is the case—and provided the medicine is the genuine
article—then the effect is priceless. It is true enough that when
everything is safely over, one is, to be sure, on the mend
anyway, but one must not forget that the spiritual aspect, if a
genuine human being is at issue, is like a coiled spring, and
that this is precisely why—with respect to recovery so complete that one becomes one's old self again—it is so important
with this mysterious tension, which is released when the medicine prescribed is the right one and is taken at the right moment.

In other words, jesting is one; the other, which physicians
nowadays do not prescribe either, is the pastor. In bygone
days it was the custom, and I praise both that custom and
those bygone days, but will refrain from further information
about the use of this medicine, for, God be praised, your case
is not one that calls for the "prescription" of a pastor; rather,
your case is just the opposite.

My dear Julie, if I were to say that now I had no more to
add, then, in the words of the poet, it would be "all sorts
of—lying in my throat."[1] All the more so because it seems as
though the pen, if I may put it like this, were begging for
permission to continue now that it has been given leave to begin. Nor is it because I wish to show the pen that I am master
of my own house and that what I want and where I want it
determine how the matter must stand, or, to keep the expres-

sion more in character, where the period must stand. That is not the reason for my stopping. No, the reason is a quite different one, and furthermore of a sort which I could imagine setting down only when I am addressing someone dear to me, so that I know I will be understood in this respect: quite literally I have no more time.

Just one more thing. Permit me to thank you for that which I know how to appreciate and therefore to admire: the tact you will display by not replying to such a letter from me. Such epistles are sent with the "Flying Post" and in a certain sense it is as if they were written by the postilion, and to send a return message with him is an impossibility, and a reply by mail would upset everything. That is why I have been so very pleased that you have understood this instantly, for being understood, though it may be only a little bit, is a great pleasure and a pleasure very rarely accorded me.

Stay well, dear Julie! You have courage in your heart. Do keep that, but rid yourself of the lumps. Right now I would enjoy seeing you and talking with you. From this it does not follow that I would be just as glad to do so tomorrow at the same time. This kind of thing is a mood that comes and goes, but however easily such a mood changes, still, concerned as I became for you on the occasion of this danger, I remain with particular devotion

> Your completely devoted cousin.

198. *Henrik Lund—May 3, 1849—S. K.*

Dear Uncle,

Hørup,[1] May 3, 1849.

Although separated from you in space, I do not forget you but remember you daily, these days especially. A number of moonlit evening walks with conversation here in this lovely region have contributed much to this. On such a walk I remembered that your birthday is on May 5—and that is why I sat down to write a couple of words, which I hope will arrive on the very day of the occasion itself.

My dear Uncle, please accept my sincerest congratulations

and all good wishes for—well, "for what" I shall leave to you
to decide—from

> Your nephew who never forgets you,
> HENRIK.

199. *Michael Lund—May 5, 1849—S. K.*

Dear Uncle,   Sønder-Vilstrup,[1] May 5, 1849.

It gives me pleasure to take pen in hand in order, as I promised, to write you a few lines from my distant abode, and I
take all the more pleasure in doing so because I am then able at
the same time to send you my sincere congratulations on the
occasion of May 5. This is probably the first time I have spent
that day outside Copenhagen, but we are also living in unique
times, and instead of coming to congratulate you in person, I
must today, i.e., May 5, go on an advance patrol towards
Kolding.[2] It is a very different life I lead over here, but I must
say that I am fairly content by and large, even though our military exploits promise to be less lucky than last year. —What
contributes greatly towards making life interesting is the constant moving around to different places, always to new quar-
ters, so that one quickly changes from quite exclusive quar-
ters to a lowly peasant's room, then quickly out to the fields
in straw bivouacs, etc. During the whole campaign I have
been in good health, and I certainly feel as well as in
Copenhagen.

I imagine that so far you have kept up fairly well with my
journey, so you know that I am getting to see a good deal of
the country. I had a letter from Henrik a couple of days ago.
He is now on the island of Als, where he is very comfortable.
I suppose you know that I was in the battle at Kolding, so that
now I have smelled gunpowder, as they say.—

It is not easy to know how long we shall continue to be at
war,[3] but here it is said that peace will soon be established,
although that has been said so often that one cannot rely on it.
Last year the campaign began very luckily for us, but the con-

clusion was nothing but bad. This year it began unfortunately, and maybe it will end better, and all's well that ends
well.

Stay in good health, dear Uncle, and accept warm greetings
from

Your devoted nephew,
MICHAEL.

[*Address*:]
S. T.
Mag. art. S. Kjerkegaard.
Copenhagen.
Rosenborggade 156 A
[*On edge of envelope*:] From M. Lund, subordinate physician
with the 5th Reserve Battalion.

200. *A. T. Schmidt—May 7, 1849—S. K.*

Most Honored Sir:
Presumably you will have read in the newspapers of the
horrible fate that befell Nøddebo[1] on the Great Day of
Prayer[2] and also that the awful fire reduced the school to
ashes, whereby I lost almost everything I owned and must
now with my wife and five little children live with strangers.

In my great plight I have appealed to former friends and acquaintances, and since I know you have both the capacity and
the heart to go with it, I venture to appeal to you for a helping
hand so that with assistance I will be enabled to supply myself
and my family with the barest necessities.

Respectfully,
SCHMIDT

Nøddebo, May 7, 1849.
My address is:
Teacher Schmidt, Nøddebo
v. Hillerød.

S. T.
Mag. Art. S. Kjerkegaard

[*Address:*]
S. T.
Mag. Artium S. Kjerkegaard
1 Gammel Torv
in
Copenhagen

201. *Frederika Bremer—[May 1849]—S. K.* [1]

To *Victor Eremita*:

A recluse, like you (even though she lives in the midst of society), sincerely wishes to meet you before she leaves this country—partly to thank you for the heavenly manna in your writings and partly to speak with you about *Stages of Life*, the metamorphoses of life, a subject that at present is more profoundly interesting than ever to her. She cannot call on you. You will easily understand why. Would you be willing to call on her? I know it is a lot to ask. But the excellent men of Denmark have made me reckless. They have given me grounds to believe that one cannot desire too much of them nor hope for more than they can give.—

I shall be at home on Thursday, Ascension Day, after church and again in the afternoon from 4 p.m. until evening *if* I may hope to expect you. If I may do so, if you would come for a while, how kind you would be to the most sincerely grateful

FREDERIKA BREMER.

Amaliengade 121, 2 floor.

[*Address:*]
To
Victor Eremita.

202. *Hans Peter Kierkegaard—May 14, 1849—S. K.*

May 14, 1849.

My sincere thanks, dear esteemed friend, for the book you sent me. —Fortunately I do not need to seek recourse in the common worn-out cliché, "You don't know how pleased I was!" etc. for I can and prefer to say, "You know that such a token of your esteem gives me great pleasure, which is why you favor me with it." —Thank you for this and for every pleasure that you have sent my way, whether directly or indirectly—they have all helped to refresh, strengthen, and cheer me on!—

I would certainly have preferred to thank you in person to-day. But as I do not have the carriage at my disposal for the next few days, and as I did not want to postpone thanking you, I hope you will permit me to inquire if you will be at home in a few days, and if so, I shall call on you for about an hour.—

> Your devoted,
> PETER KIERKEGAARD.

[*Address:*]
To
Magister Kierkegaard
Of this city.

203. *Frederika Bremer*[1]—*[May 15, 1849]—S. K.*

You will, I am sure, have the kindness to give my messenger a word as to whether I may expect you to call on Thursday or some other day, or, if you are not at home when this arrives, to send a message to my home!— —

> FR. B.
> Tuesday evening.

[*Address:*]
Bachelor of Divinity
Mr. Søren Kierkegaard.
Gammel Torv.

204. *S. K.—May 1849—Frederika Bremer.*[1] *S. K.'s draft.*

It is my hope that I shall not be misunderstood, for it would grieve me deeply were I to be misunderstood, but even if that were so, I still cannot accept this invitation. Unaccustomed as I am to being understood, I am all the more accustomed to having to endure being misunderstood. The sole difference consists in this, that sometimes it is easy for me to endure being misunderstood, and sometimes I find it a heavy burden—as I would in this case, if I were misunderstood.

[*Deleted*: Permit me a straightforward and forthright word: I really feel it to be a punishment for my singular way of life that through my fault a lady is brought so unjustly into an awkward situation.]

From Sweden's authoress, famous throughout Europe, as though I did not know how to value and appreciate such a distinguished lady's benevolent attention.

Just one more word: you refer to your invitation almost as if it had been ventured recklessly. Indeed that is almost to mock me. No, I am better versed with respect to recklessness—and I appeal most recklessly to your own judgment. I venture the utmost in recklessness, I who decline the invitation, I the unworthy; I venture to ask you to accept, as completely and fully as it is intended, my most sincere thanks for the invitation. Indeed, I venture the very utmost in recklessness, I venture to believe that you will do so, as I now most sincerely beg you to do; and this I do—I who will not come, I remain sincerely in a debt of gratitude.

[*In margin*: And yet, yet this is after all not so reckless, because I do have some idea of your exalted character.—]

205. *Frederik Paludan-Müller*[1]*—May 15, 1849—S. K.*

May 15, '49.

With this I send you my heartfelt thanks for your welcome gift (*Either/Or*).[2] I shall strive to demonstrate my gratitude by studying this book carefully, so far as my ability and knowledge permit, which is not always the case when it comes to the reading of philosophical writings and probably will not be so in this case either.

From what I have learned so far from the work, it seems to me that with your *Either/Or* you set the reader the task of seeking a *tertium*, in which the difference between the two opposite points of view about life is cancelled, or in which the reconciliation is brought about. Whether this is really so, or whether the book is to be understood as the perfect solution of either by means of or—that knotty problem I shall, as I said, seek to answer for myself, insofar as I am able by a more careful study of the work. —Once more, thank you for your gift and please continue to remember me with friendship.

> Your most respectfully devoted
> Fr. PALUDAN MÜLLER.

S. T.
Mag. art. S. Kjerkegaard.

206. *Hans Christian Andersen—May 15, 1849—S. K.*

Copenhagen
Dear Mr. Kierkegaard,   May 15, 1849.

You have given me really great pleasure by sending me your *Either/Or*. I was, as you can well understand, quite surprised;[1] I had no idea at all that you entertained friendly thoughts of me, and yet I now find it to be so. God bless you for it! Thank you, thank you!

> Yours with heartfelt sincerity,
> H. C. ANDERSEN

207. *Carsten Hauch*[1]—*May 17, 1849—S. K.*

May 17, 1849.

To
The Author of Either/Or.

I take the liberty of entrusting these few lines to your publisher because I know of no other way to put them into your hands. I beg you not to take it as the usual compliment but as the simple truth when I tell you that not only have I followed your literary career with interest, but that I have truly found many hints and suggestions in your writings that have furthered my own spiritual development. Therefore I was all the more pleased to receive a work from you personally, and if I were put in a lonely prison and permitted to choose just one single book as my companion in solitude (as is told of an old learned man with reference to another book), I might well decide to choose it, because in it I would find so much substance for reflection that my time would scarcely waste away without spiritual progress.

　　With true gratitude and veneration,

Your most respectfully devoted,
C. HAUCH.

208. *Rasmus Nielsen—May 25, 1849—S. K.*

Dear Magister,

　　You are right, which is to say: I am wrong, and I hereby beg your pardon.[1] Last Thursday it was not yet clear to me what I ought to do.

Yours,　R. N.

May 25, 1849.
S. T.
Magister Kierkegaard.

[*Address:*]
S. T.
Magister Kierkegaard.

209. *Rasmus Nielsen—May 25, 1849—S. K.*

Tuesday, May 25, 1849.

Dear Magister,

　　You will still remember the moment when you "called upon me" for the first time. What you said then was surely too serious to be imparted during a walk.

In accordance with that impression, what is on my mind at present is now also of such a nature that I would not at any cost have it dealt with during a walk.

The solution of completely ignoring my personal concern while casually strolling about with you, discussing something utterly different, is too artificial and repugnant to me.

Accordingly you may conclude that it is unlikely that we shall meet again until you find the time at some point and the opportunity "to call upon me" once more.[1]

Whether this will ever happen, whether it happens this year or in future years, must of course depend on you: I have the time to wait.

Yours,   R. N.

P.S. Your *Devotional Discourses*[2] has arrived safely, and I hereby express my grateful thanks for the beautiful gift.
S. T.
Magister Kierkegaard.

[*Address:*]
S. T.
Magister Kierkegaard.

210. *S. K.—[1849]—Rasmus Nielsen. S. K.'s draft.*[1]

Wednesday noon.

Dear friend,

Having just come home from a little trip to the country, rather exhausted, the first thing I find is a letter from you, which not insignificantly displays a lamb as a vignette or emblem. And the first thing I do is also to reply at once—and even though this does not dare claim that it manifests the sweetness of the lamb, it is still something after all.

We had agreed to meet Thursday noon for a walk. I—like a humble servant—was on the spot. From your note I must conclude what I otherwise had found no cause to conclude, that you were officially absent. Now if "that which is on your mind at present is of such a nature that you would not at any cost have it dealt with during a walk," what would have been more natural than meeting me *per agreement* and telling me this, or *informing me in advance* with a note so as to prevent my going *per agreement* in vain in a certain sense? "In a certain sense," because after all I did then go for a walk in my own company.

I can well imagine that at present you might wish to talk with me in a manner different from what is feasible during a walk, but it seemed to me that a walk was the very thing suited to momentary concerns—and an agreement is after all an agreement. The natural thing would have been for you to come; your staying away deliberately and intentionally does seem somewhat artificial to me, which, however, does not change anything essential in what I had intended to do anyway.

211. S. K.—[July 1849]—J.L.A. Kolderup-Rosenvinge.

Dear *Conferentsraad*,

It might almost be tempting to make you a proposition: for about two weeks please try, as I am doing, to keep abreast of the times, assisted solely by the *Adresse-Avis*. It has the negative benefit of sparing one a good deal of annoyance and the positive benefit [undecipherable deletion] of developing one's sense of the emblematic. An immediate example: thus I see today in another advertisement from the horse butcher at Christianshavn that he has obtained some "unusually succulent meat."[1] But that is not what I wanted to talk about; I wanted to talk about his illustration. The office of the *Adresse-Avis* presumably owns only one illustration of a horse. Presumably it was designed as an illustration for an advertisement stating that some place or other one or more thoroughbred horses were for sale. Such a horse has been depicted, a genuine thoroughbred, a tall, long, lean fellow, mere skin and bone, a veritable bone-rack. Under this illustration the butcher announces that "the meat of *two very fat horses*, which were slaughtered today, is for sale" etc. This, you see, might be called illuminating the text with the help of illustrations. But now for the emblematic! Well, it lies close to hand. Wherever one looks these days, does one not discover the same thing, except in reverse: an advertising illustration and then the actuality, which is something else entirely? But it is even worse when reversed, for the butcher is an honest man, and under the illustration of a lean horse he is selling "unusually succulent meat." To that extent the horsebutcher with his illustrated advertisement is not so much an emblem as an epigram on our times, although one must first discern the emblematic before one can discover the epigrammatic. The emblematic consists in this, that the illustration says something other than what the actuality contains, as when for example it states under an illustration of a free Constitution: "More tyranny than ever under the most absolute monarchy"— or when it says under an illustration: "The responsible minister is conceded not to have been responsible"— something rarely conceded to any irresponsible minister, etc., etc. The epigrammatical consists in this, that the butcher, like the true satirist, cunningly makes this apparent by means of the reversed disparity.

So Denmark got a free Constitution[2] at last—and finally a more serious concern for this cause seems to have been awakened. Once more I cite the *Adresse-Avis*. The National Assembly had already long ago become bored with sitting together; those who read the *Rigsdagstidende*[3] had long ago become fed up with reading it; it seemed as if concern for the whole cause had vanished! The Constitution is adopted, but everything takes place as quietly as possible, unless one wants to cite the thunderstorm that occurred later the same night after the guests at Skydebanen[4] had quietly gone home. "Alas, sad sign of the times" is what a politician would have to exclaim, I suppose. Then concern for the cause suddenly awakens again—petty commercial mentality! I cite the *Adresse-Avis*. What a lot of different editions of the Constitution! Some to be framed behind glass to hang on the wall, some to be glued on cardboards, some to be carried in the pocket, in the hat, on the back, under the arm! And oh, what a difference in price—even greater than that (oh, that there may not be something emblematic in this as well) of hearses, where the most expensive hearse is the simplest. Let anyone try to tell me that there is no concern for the cause! Philipsen,[5] the bookseller, is selling an edition for 8 *sk.*, and if you take one hundred copies you get them for 4 *sk.* each. What concern for the cause and what concern for the cause [*two lines deleted*] is not presupposed by his assumption that there are people who out of genuine interest would buy 100 copies? I intend to buy the 3 *mk.* edition—which, noted *in parenthesi*, presumably can be bought by the score for 2 *mk.* I intend to buy this edition so that I can spend all the more on the binding. There is really something to Trop's idea of wanting to have his *Destruction of the Human Species* bound in Morocco with gold edging.[6] And so I shall also have my copy bound. On one side of the cover will be printed in gold letters, "Forever" and on the other side, "Medicine" for—no, not really for an ecstasy of love but for an ecstasy of liberty.

But what about you yourself, dear *Conferentsraad*? *Wie gehts Ihnen*? [How are you?] Are you going for walks? By all means see to that. Please take walks, but take care also not to come to a standstill, which can happen by not going walking, to be sure, but also by going too far in both the literal and figurative senses. I, who go walking a great deal in both senses, know of nothing more horrible than coming to a standstill. *Est quadam prodire tenus, si non datur ultra* [It is worthwhile to go forward, even if there is no advance][7]—and certainly there is no *ultra* in walking after one has come to a standstill. Therefore I never go very far—*est quadam prodire tenus*. I go no farther, I sense the boundary, I shiver—and then go on, which is to say that I go back, yet I do go on in the sense that I continue to keep myself moving. To come to a standstill! In a certain sense there is something inviting and tempting about this thought, especially when one dwells on it: to come to a standstill, and what that means. Herculanum, Pompeii, Stabia came to a standstill, as did several others. That is what is characteristic of the whole East Asiatic development (as opposed to the European, where something perishes and something new develops from its ruins): coming to a standstill. China, for example, has come to a standstill. What a vast world-historical consideration is contained in this alone! To come to a standstill! How many a man must there be, of whom it may be said that there was one particular, usually painful, event, the impact of which brought him to a standstill and in which he got stuck, so to speak! Alas! And nothing is more dangerous.

So you see why I praise going for walks, and once more, walking (the physical activity) is to me an emblem of spiritual activity. And this spiritual activity is most especially necessary in relation to grief. For there is nothing, nothing so insinuating as grief. Nothing, no other passion, no other impression, not even that of joy, is as insinuating as that of grief; not even the most insinuating female creature is as insinuating as grief, provided it finds its *sinus*, an inwardness into which it may insinuate itself. Most people believe that grief has something repellent about it, something that makes one strive to avoid it, something that makes one close oneself off to it. Oh, those people have no idea what grief is, no idea of the enchantment it exercises, moving a man to open himself completely to it, completely as to nothing else and to nobody else. And then, when one has opened oneself completely to it, and when this, of all insinuations the most insinuating, has found its proper home, in other words, when one has opened oneself completely to it and, enchanted by its insinuations, done even more for it and quite concealed from others how one opened oneself to it—when that has happened, oh, then not even the woman married to the most faithful of men can be as certain that he will remain faithful to her for life as grief can be that "he will remain faithful to me." When grief has now found a home or been given a home and knows itself provided for, then it establishes itself. Not even the most domestic of women has so much that is captivating at her disposal as does grief. And so grief becomes "the company," because that which is most insinuating understands the insinuating from the ground up. It knows very well that even the most cherished company may become boring at times, but that the company that endures the longest is the company of solitude—where grief is the company.

Oh, how often have I not thought about this myself! I would be able, provided the ink continued to flow in my pen by itself, I would be able—without even the interruption of dipping my pen—to go on uninterruptedly writing whole books on the subject.

But instead I will break off here. Just one more observation. The more resonance there is in grief, the more captivating it is, and the more profound its insinuation. That is what I think. Echo probably exists almost everywhere in nature. So then, one hears it but retains control of it oneself. Still, there are in fact places where the echo repeats itself several times. This is where the captivating commences, for hearing this repetition captivates again and again; this repetition—and repetition is after all like a description of insinuation or of the motion that insinuation possesses. So it is with grief. When a loss causes grief, for example—however profound that grief may be, there is really no resonance in it yet. But when another loss occurs and, mark you, is of such a kind that it unequivocally repeats the first loss, then resonance accrues to grief. I can imagine that there must be—yes, for "the grief"—that there must be something indescribably captivating in finally becoming all attention, hearing only the resonance, the echo, the resounding of one loss in another. Thus it must be with grief, and if it were allowed to hold sway, it would of course also be like that for the one who grieves.

St. James the Apostle says that one should be slow to speak.[8] That is what I strive to do. I have almost not spoken with you at all about that which I realized very well must have pained you profoundly, the loss of your little grand-daughter.[9] Alas, the difference in years also deepens that grief. The loss of a grandchild is always heavier for the grand-parents to bear than is the loss of a child for the parents. That is on account of the intensifying effect. And although it would seem that the grandfather and his daughter, the young mother, that those two must understand each other in their common grief, this is by no means the case, at least not in or-dinary psychological terms. The grandfather grieves in a manner quite different from that of the young mother. And then, when she has been helped by youth and life's hope to bear the loss more easily, indeed, often by degrees to forget it—that which was inherently easier for her than for the grandfather—he has meanwhile forgotten nothing, because for him the loss at once gained resonance by serving as a reminder, by repeating a former loss. So rather than being understood by the young mother, it is more likely that in the course of time he would almost become slightly introverted in this respect. However gently approached, it might still come to sound like the mildest of reproaches whenever he wanted to speak to her of this loss he continued to mourn, while she had more or less conquered her pain. It might almost sound like a reproach of her, the mother, for not mourning as profoundly—as the grandfather. But this would be unavoidable, and therefore he must be silent. Indeed, far from being fully understood by her, he must take pains to make her forget if possible—in order to reserve grief to himself. For the reverse is impossible. It is at odds with nature's order that the young mother should make the grandfather forget and she remain the one who grieves.

Dear *Conferentsraad*, if I were to compare this letter with a conversation on a walk, I would have to say that today we chose a different route from the usual one, or that after having put a small section of the usual route behind us, we had turned off and gone another way. Pardon me if walking with me has been disagreeable in any way, but if walking along this path has agreed with you in any way, I ask no more, but thank you for the walk. Now we are parting. I hope and I wish—and whatever one wishes, one usually hopes for; and whatever one hopes and wishes for, one prays for—therefore I pray that you may keep for me that goodwill, that friendship, which, although I certainly cannot be said to have deserved them, I have nonetheless appreciated all the more with a devotion that makes me wholly

Yours   S. KIERKEGAARD.

[*Written on the inside of the envelope:*]
Usually I am the one to say, "Let us leave at once." This

time I have to say it to myself, for only I know how much I am to blame for our not being able to leave. The enclosed had already been written some time ago. I longed to go walking with you. But then, then the letter remained in my desk, I remained waiting for the result, and thus in the most unreal sense possible it became a walk, a walk during which both parties stayed at home. But now I do come at last, and if it is agreeable with you, then "let us leave at once."

Your   S. K.

[*Address:*]
To
The Honorable
Conferentsraad, Dr. Rosenvinge
Knight of *Dannebrog*, Member of *Dannebrog*

212. *Rasmus Nielsen—July 20, 1849—S. K.*

Friday, July 20, 1849.

Dear Magister,
  "The System"[1] has arrived. It got here day before yesterday with "the Omnibus."[2]

Yours,   R. N.

S. T.
Magister Kierkegaard.

[*Address:*]
S. T.
Magister Kierkegaard.
A black attempt to improve on a bad job of sealing.[3]

213. *S. K.—July 1849—Rasmus Nielsen. S. K.'s draft*

Dear friend,
  Your note of Friday of last week duly received. It may perhaps have escaped you that the association of ideas from omnibus to omnibus[1] is evoked in the maxim: *de omnibus dubitandum* [all things are to be doubted]. Hence, when Johannes

de Silentio[2] calls the system "an omnibus," it must be understood as having a double meaning.

I am sending along a new book.[3] Presumably you will have no difficulty in discovering why this pseudonym is called *Anti*-Climacus, in which respect he is quite different from Johannes Climacus, with whom he certainly does have something in common (as they do also share parts of a name), but from whom he differs very essentially in that J. Cl. humorously denies that he himself is Christian and, in consequence, can only make indirect attacks, and, in consequence, must retract everything in humor—while Anti-Climacus is very far from denying that he himself is Christian, which is evident in the direct attack. There is no more space here, except for this:

Yours,   S. K.

214. *S. K.—July 28, 1849—J.L.A. Kolderup-Rosenvinge.*

July 28, '49.

Dear *Conferentsraad*,

It was indeed a remarkable year, that year of 1848.[1] In this I agree completely with Professor Lamartine,[2] who is already, I notice, busily engaged in cutting it up and preparing it for history. Marvelous! Ultimately, I suppose, the same thing will happen to history as to New Year's gift books and the like, which usually make their appearance the preceding year—so in the end we shall see the history of '51 appearing in the guise of a New Year's gift for '50. Who knows, perhaps Lamartine will take this next step and do so. And perhaps it is not impossible either, for since '48 everything has in a certain sad sense become possible. And it is not surprising that Professor Lamartine should become so excited. Just imagine a history professor who in the year of '48 almost becomes historical subject matter himself for a couple of months. He probably thinks, "Let other historians choose their own subject matter—I shall choose my own, something I know quite *extra ordinem* and which, well prepared, I must therefore hand over to history at once."

As I say, it was a remarkable year, that year of '48. It has, as we have often noted, in all respects turned everything upside down or "topsy-turvied"[3] everything. Also in a way that has just occurred to me. Suppose a writer were to recreate *The Catastrophe* of '48 in dramatic form and had to make his drama conform in some way to actuality, he would then have to create a wholly new kind of drama, a monstrosity, a drama that makes a mockery of all the rules, a drama in five and a half acts. This half act is just what is most characteristic about it, this half act, which is not to say that there is half an act left and then it is over, not at all, but that there is always half an act left. The catastrophe cannot be said to have lacked a head or a tail, for although it had no head—in a manner of speaking—it definitely had a tail. What is most characteristic about it is—that there is always some tail left. One imagines that now it is over—but behold, there is the tail!—and so it continues all the time. In a way there is both something inhuman and something exhausting about it. It seems to me rather like eating some dish (*Gemüse* [vegetables], for example) in which there are long, long stringy bits. One takes a forkful, but look out! Just as one is about to put it in one's mouth, a whole lot remains dangling outside so that one must resort to the fork again to gather up the loose ends; but that is not enough, one also has to resort to the knife, one has to use both hands; but that is not enough, and in the end a waiter has to hold a plate or bowl underneath—*Ich möchte rasend werden*[4] [It is enough to drive one mad]. Do you call this eating! And so it is with the events of our time. Lucky the man who like me declined at once the invitation to keep up with the times. Do you think the war is over yet?

But enough of this. What is going to become of our walks? Ye friendly powers, ye benevolent spirits who protect those who walk and who help them to get together! Can you not take pity on me and help me arrange a walk with the *Conferentsraad*? But to tell the truth, unless something extraordinary occurs, I can see no possibility of it, all the worse for me. One would think that it would certainly be easy enough for two walkers—to get together. One might say that surely it is a different matter altogether for someone who is in prison or for someone who is prevented by some external force, but for two walkers nothing should be easier for them than to get together first (the coinciding) in order then to go walking in each other's company. However, this does not apply to me *qua* walker. It is a very simple matter. That which wise and learned men have enjoined and recommended to all, nature has benevolently placed very close to me: that is, not to exceed my limit. It has placed it very close—alas, in setting my limit so close it has practically left me no *spatium* at all—for going astray and the like. So one day while I am sitting at home, the desire awakens and beckons. I say to myself: "Today I would really enjoy going for a walk with the *Conferentsraad*. But how? Well, I might walk out to his place," I think to myself, and so the walk begins. Still, that limit, that limit I cannot exceed! It cannot be done, for after having gone all the way out there, I will not feel fresh enough to begin going for a walk. Whereupon I sit pondering this and become quite exhausted from pondering. "Well," I think, "You might drive out there—marvelous, that can be managed. But then what? That limit, that limit, *respice finem* [consider the goal]! Either I shall have to drive home again or I shall have to walk home. If I drive home after having walked, I am afraid of catching cold. If I walk home, I will arrive home so tired that I forfeit the pleasure of the walk." Then I sit pondering this until I become quite tired from pondering.

At last I reach a decision. On the assumption that you live several miles from town—I give up hope of a real walk; I pick up the pen and now it *currente calamo* [proceeds on the run]— and so long as you do not tire, I will surely not tire either.

How are you feeling? Is the water cure helping you? If not, then I have another cure to propose, a miracle cure. At first glance it looks like pure gibberish and nonsense, and yet there is some truth in it. Let me describe it, for even though you do not intend to use it, perhaps merely thinking of it will have some effect. One morning you wake up very early and say to yourself, "Today I feel extraordinarily well; I have never felt so well in my whole life." If this is not the case, something almost the opposite may be so. [*In the margin*: That does not matter; if just the opposite is the case, so much the better]— herein lies the secret of this cure, which truly is a miracle cure and for that reason one that no physician would be likely to think of or have the courage to recommend. While I myself am not the inventor of this cure, neither have I found it described by any physician, but by an emperor, *Antoninus philosophus*, in his work *ad se ipsum*.[5] He says: "You have it within your power to revive to a new life (αναβιωναι σοι εξεστιν); everything depends on the manner of representation. Consider everything in a new way; that is what is meant by reviving (εν τουτω γαρ το αναβιωναι)." Accordingly you say to yourself, "Today I feel extraordinarily well; as far as I can remember, I have never felt better." Then you get up. You get dressed, and throughout all this you continue to repeat the formula. In certain cases I have also noted a beneficial effect from pronouncing one's full name in a loud clear voice and afterwards adding the formula: "Today you feel better than you ever have before." Then you join your family. Even before anyone manages to bid you good morning, you anticipate him by saying in a firm voice and with the most trustworthy countenance in the world: "Today I feel better than I have ever felt in my whole life. I myself have no idea where this sudden sense of well-being has come from, but *eh bien*, now it is here." Everything now changes to pure joy. Your daughter becomes so happy that even though you are feeling unwell, the mere sight of her joy contributes significantly to a genuine sense of well-being. Her joy suffuses everything. Now the step has been taken, and as always it is only the first step that is costly. Your entire surroundings will now force you into the untruth with which you began. The secret, you see, consists in giving a completely new direction to the reflection of the surroundings. Such a reversal of what is a certainty is as refreshing as a shower. The mere thought of it brings a pleasurable shudder that does no harm to one's sense of well-being. But in particular I think that such a daring reversal can be useful as a means of refreshing the relationship with one's physician. It is easy to get fed up with a physician without its meaning that one therefore wants a different physician. One gets fed up with the fact that he can, in the end, do nothing. So just once, for the sake of mischief, one takes pleasure in feeling better than one ever has before in one's entire life.

Is this not a miracle cure? Assuredly so. But even if you do not intend to use it, the mere fact that one can think of proposing it to you proves my old saying that you are growing younger. For a cure,

[*The conclusion of the letter is missing.*]

215. *Rasmus Nielsen—July 28, 1849—S. K.* [1]

Dear Magister,   Lyngby, July 28, 1849.

Thank you for the note, many thanks for the book, a thousand thanks for the contents of the book. Yes, there is no doubt that this Christian psychological argument may build up a seminarian who believes and bring a professor who teaches—to despair. Among the many points where Climacus and Anti-Climacus make contact, I would particularly single out the one concerning offense (cf. *Unscientif. Postscript*, pp. 308-09[2] with the psychol. argum., pp. 84-88).[3] Is this not the threshold where both meet and, as if in a single breath, inspire each other?

                                        Yours,   R. N.
S. T.
Magister Kierkegaard.

P.S. By the way, it is rather curious about that omnibus.[4] Struck by the well-known "double meaning," it must throughout the ride continue to lurch from side to side so that with each lurch the passengers (*omnes in omnibus*)[5] and even the driver are forced to say, "*De omnibus dubitandum est.*—"

[*Address:*]
S. T.
Magister Kierkegaard.

216. *J. L. A. Kolderup-Rosenvinge—August 1, 1849—* S.K.[1]

Bakkehuset[2]

Dear Magister (*vivendi!*),[3]   August 1, 1849.

This title must of necessity be yours for discovering that new miracle cure you so kindly sent me in the letter I have just received and to which I proceed to reply at once, as I am otherwise afraid on the basis of past experience that nothing will come of it—(he who puts off until tomorrow etc.).[4] But in replying I must make this general remark that may have special application to every line: I am *taking the waters at a spa.* I beg you to reflect carefully on the meaning of that, and inasmuch as I was already thinking of writing to you some mornings ago (N.B. *morning*—nowadays I am able to do a little thinking only during the morning—I spend the rest of the day struggling against sleep and pain) about the privileges[5] granted guests at the spa, I shall now—as a perfectly appropriate introduction to my reply and as a commentary upon my general remark—discuss *the privileges of the spa guests* a little more extensively, which are all the more important because I suppose it will not be long before they remain the sole privileges left by the tooth of time, for even the so-called *privilegia pauperum* [privileges of the poor] (the right to free trial, help in sickness, etc.) will be abolished as a matter of course when everybody becomes rich or everybody becomes equally poor. To proceed: the most important privilege granted a spa guest is that he may demand that everybody heed him while he has only to observe the prescriptions of the cure. When one takes the waters at the spa, one is entitled, for example, to be rude, to abandon people in the midst of a walk without offering excuses, to neglect to tip one's hat, to break off a conversation whenever anybody annoys one, to be argumentative, etc., merely prefaced by these words: "Excuse me, please; I am taking the waters; it is against the rules to annoy me," etc.—or whenever somebody is talking nonsense (N.B. one is permitted to talk unending nonsense oneself—as *figura* shows—the pen continues to run on by itself on the paper)—and as far as I can see, presumably as a consequence of all that water I enjoy daily, the nonsense is becoming more and more diluted, but that is not much of a help on account of the aforementioned privilege, the meaning of which you will now begin to realize from experience. —Perhaps you are already asleep? To rouse you a little, I shall now, provided it can be done without exertion, come to grips with your letter. You begin with precisely the right man! Yes—that Mr. Lamartine[6] is a wonderful fellow! In fact I have just read that he says that the *greatest immorality* of which the government of Louis Philippe was guilty was to announce that the Duchesse de Berry had disgraced herself![7] That is what I call really sound moral judgment! Elsewhere he says that in 1848 the French were in need of fresh air—of a revolution, in other words. That is exactly as though a man, well-nigh suffocating in his room on a stifling summer day, instead of opening the window, were to smash all the panes. True enough, the glaziers would make money, but it might be a while before the windows are repaired—and that is just what has happened to the French and to all who mirror their example. —But I might feel inclined to argue against your comment on the drama of 1848[8] with its five-and-a-half acts and the *tail*, provided I were able to *absque præsidio* [dispute without assistance].[9] I might say, for example, that everything has a tail—the Devil himself has one, and the so-called King of Rats[10] has an infinite number—and that the whole business is little more than a bunch of tails—tail-thrashings, often so entangled in such a mess that it is hard to get hold of the main tail and finally of the body to which it is attached, unless, as many do, one boldly takes hold of the whole tangled ball of knots and says, "Look, this is where it really begins." It all depends on descending from what is known and certain to what is unknown and uncertain, unless one wishes to experiment with the unknown X and seek to make everything fit some hypothesis or other. Even sticking to what one knows can be a little embarrassing, for on closer inspection it often turns out that what one thought one knew well is in fact something one does not know at all, and so one ends up with a new tail. Inasmuch as it is possible to do injustice even to a scoundrel, I shall not blame that year of 1848 for having a tail, so long as it does not beget too many rat tails! In all this tail-tattle I have completely forgotten to thank you for your new book—and after all, that was really the original reason for my wanting to write to you before I got your letter, but memory seems to evaporate along with the taking of Kissingen water[11]—yet another *privilegium*, but in many cases a *privilegium flebile* [privilege of the miserable]. With respect to the book,[12] I must once more invoke the spa privilege here, and not only the privilege,[13] but the regimen that at present prescribes my duties. According to this, any book entitled *The Sickness unto Death* should not be read any more than Professor Sommer's[14] gruesome lectures on cholera should be heard. Therefore I must postpone my reasoned thanks until this campaign is over and I have the peace to read and am able to take stronger sustenance than Chateaubriand,[15] Lamartine, and Spanish tragedies. In the meantime, the motto has given me inexpressible pleasure. Who wrote it?[16] Speaking of finished campaigns, I must remember to say that my doctor has given me a reprieve of three weeks on bread and water instead of four (when all is said and done, physicians are now really the only absolute sovereigns after Our Lord) on the condition that I promise to take a journey—just as in days of old a pilgrimage to Jerusalem or a crusade—and the destination of that journey is Stockholm, no less, with departure on Sunday or Monday, and will be for three weeks. People may think I am being sent to fetch the auxiliary troops that we are still waiting for,[17] but to you I shall confide that I am traveling—to follow my nose. If I ever dared hope for a little health, I would say I was traveling for the sake of it, but true enough, that is not necessary, for today I have received the Kierkegaardian *arcanum* [secret], the cabalistic formula: "Feel well, and you will feel well; *aude sapere* [dare to know]," etc. In fact I did begin to use that prescription the day before yesterday when I seemed to feel a little better for the first time in many days, but yesterday I was a rag once again, and today I am ragged (*sit venia verbo!*) [pardon the expression!] as well, and I suppose that is the way it will continue despite spa cures and prescriptions. But I do not care to talk about that. As I have now delivered myself into the hands of my doctor for four weeks, I shall be receptive and obedient to him during that period—and if the cure does not help by then, I shall emancipate myself, which is to say that I shall wrap myself in my cloak of resignation,which after all suits me best. Here you have now been given, in addition to a fair amount of babbling, some sort of description of my status, which is sad enough. I have not looked at a solid book for three weeks, much less one on law. My escape has primarily been Calderon, with whom I have made excursions into the realm of the imagination—but even he has not always been able to protect me against sleep, which, on account of my early rising and frequent walks, pursues me incessantly whenever I sit still, and during the day I am strictly forbidden to give in to its temptations (I sleep badly enough at night)—but I have found another means to keep me awake—which is to translate Calderon while I am reading *Gran Zenobia.*[18] —It would be quite entertaining, whenever [*paper damaged*: I] do get it finished (I have already translated two of the three acts of the play), if the reader were to fall asleep over the work I have used to keep me awake. Perhaps that is the way it has been with this letter. If you are already asleep over it, then "Have a peaceful night!" and please let me hear from you when you wake up, and do continue your friendship for

Yours most sincerely,
KOLDERUP ROSENVINGE.

[*Address*:]
S. T.
Magister S. Kierkegaard.

217. S. K.—[*August 1849*]—*J.L.A. Kolderup-Rosenvinge.*

1849 [*in another hand.*]

Dear *Conferentsraad*,

Well, since you *are* traveling to Sweden, that perfectly justifies my assumption that you live several miles away,[1] so that it really is an impossibility to go walking in your company.

In that way all problems are resolved, for when something is impossible, then it is manifestly no longer problematical. If this had not happened, in some way or other I would still have gotten stuck with the problems without being able to get away from them, because the fiction that you were living several miles away might not have been strong enough to suppress the thought of the possibility of getting away to see you. Have you read Bille's book?[2] Somewhere he relates, and it might well be true, how a sailor who has been to sea for several months fervently longs for firm land so that he can go walking. He arrives at one of the Nicobar Islands. At once he joins a small, select company of officers and natural scientists going ashore for a sociable walk. What happens? Barely have they taken a few steps before all of them, every single one of them, sink almost waist deep into vines.[3] Imagine a group of walkers who go walking—waist deep into vines. They walk—yes, either that or they get stuck. Yet one cannot call this trip of theirs a wholly futile walk, for the reader can always laugh at it, and, as is told some place of a man who died in a ridiculous accident that at least one could now say of him that he did not die utterly in vain, so neither can these walkers be said to have gone walking utterly in vain.

But there really is something comic about going for a walk in that way—and probably there also would have been about my walking out to the Bakkehus, for I would have ended up getting stuck with the problems.

And now only a parting farewell.

Your idea of taking a trip, particularly to Sweden, was certainly a happy inspiration, and I do not doubt for a moment that the trip will be a pleasant one.

Meanwhile I remain in the same place, quietly devoting myself to the disquiet of longing until I can see you again and we begin walking again. A devout man has devoutly distinguished between having *die Worte der Wahrheit* and *die Wahrheit der Worte* [the word of truth and the truth of the word].[4] And with respect to longing, which is my subject matter, this is certainly so: *die Worte der Wahrheit* is in

Your   S. K.

218. *S. K.—August 4, 1849—C. E. Kiellerup.*[1]

August 4, '49.
Dear sir,

Did not that bottle of Madeira you sent me cross the Equator six times? Please rest assured that at least seven times I—I almost said, "have remembered"—and obviously I could say that, but then I would also have to say that at least seven times I have forgotten that I really ought to thank you for the gift.

But in order to avoid becoming immersed in difficulties and details about remembering and forgetting, [*in margin*: but oddly and remarkably enough, while it is impolite to have forgotten something one ought to have remembered, it is on the other hand polite to have forgotten it seven times, which at first glance one might be tempted to consider seven times as impolite] details that might result in my forgetting to thank you for the eighth time, I break off—by breaking out in thanks for your gift, my dividend from that great scientific expedition during which, as I gather from Bille's book,[2] you almost became a victim of error on account of your zeal. It is not easy to calculate what the result of this might have been for yourself, for the expedition, for Denmark, for Europe; but on the other hand it is very easy to see what the consequence would have been for me, i.e., I would not have received that bottle of Madeira. In other words, I was so close to missing out on what you sent me that I have all the more reason to thank you for it.

Yours respectfully,
S. KIERKEGAARD.

To
Mr. Kiellerup, M. Sc.
Adjunct.

219. *S. K.—August 4, 1849—Rasmus Nielsen. S. K.'s draft.*

N.B. This is the letter of August 4 that was sent to R. N. in a fair copy, but which *was lost.*[1]

Dear friend,

What an anti-climax! Is that proper for a logical professor?[2] You thank me a "thousand times"[3] for the contents of the book, less for the book, least for the note—but surely you are forgetting that I am only the editor so that the climax ought to be reversed when you write to me.

But this is only to trap you, too, in the fallacy that I consider characteristic of all that is modern: to confuse climax with anti-climax, to consider what is an anti-climax as a climax, and, as is appropriate with a climax, to raise one's voice most when the climax is at its height—but alas, it is concealed from those eyes that this is an anti-climax. With respect to everything that "goes further"—and everything modern does "go further"—it is true that one rises with an anti-climax and thus arrives with a triumphant expression and the most boastful clichés, *rising*—to that which is *lower.* One "goes further" than faith—one rises to the system! One goes further than [*deleted*: the congregation] "the single individual"—one rises to the congregation! One goes further than subjectivity, one rises to objectivity! etc., etc.

With the help of the new pseudonym, Anti-Climacus,[4] my own pseudonym, Climacus, has scored a point. I consider "Climacus = Anti-Climacus" a felicitous epigram. Even though one were completely to forget the contents of their writings, these two clues would still retain the illumination inherent in the epigrammatic, provided one had the requisite ability to take a hint.

And, how about you, how are you? Are you working, and to what end? "Everything depends on what comes next," you once said to me in speaking of your writing. In a sense I am in complete agreement with you about that, as you must know from my statements about your earlier work. Surely you are willing to grant me that I am some sort of "connoisseur," but I am no less willing to assure you that it would give me great pleasure if your next work were to exceed even my expectations with respect to certainty and clarity of point of view. In the eyes of the "professors" I dare say you have now been degraded to a "college student"[5] [*deleted*: Accordingly you then belong under my department, I who consider myself quite *con amore* a sort of master apprentice over the students who, before one notices what is happening, might become the terrors of the professors.] Console yourself. There is a book entitled *The Torture of the Clergy*[6] that contains many capricious questions suitable for embarrassing a clergyman. If a *Torture of Professors* were to be written, it would have to be by a college student. N.B. This was an allusion to [*in margin*: the then just-published Preface to *The Sickness unto Death* in which Anti-Climacus calls himself a college student.][7]

220. *S. K.—[August 1849]—Rasmus Nielsen. S. K.'s draft.*[1]

But why hesitate so long before replying to a letter—that demanded a reply? And next, why this fear of "becoming a nuisance by writing too much"—if you yourself feel like writing more often? That was not what I feared. I explained the absence of a reply by thinking the letter lost. That was not what I feared; I did not fear that I would be guilty of discourtesy (which one would not even show a stranger) by asking forgiveness in advance in the event I failed at some point to reply. I did not nor do I now fear misunderstanding. On the contrary, I believed and believe that misunderstanding powerfully assists understanding of whatever kind. He who is truly self-possessed has no fear, for whatever he can lose he can lose only by accident; nor does perfect love fear, for perfect love casts out fear[2]—; nor does the true dialectician fear, for he fears only one thing, to be in error, and to prevent that he does not fear to venture everything in order to bring forth the truth, for he does not fear to perceive the truth, but he fears that he will not perceive the truth. Anyone in whom one of these is found does not know fear in the sense of being unsure of himself. But, on the other hand, he certainly is very well acquainted with that which is more terrifying: fear and trembling, dejection in tribulation.

So, in two weeks at the latest, you will be writing to Copenhagen, and then I shall get to see you, or, if you prefer, let me know when you arrive so that I may invite you by means of a note as usual.

Yours

221. *Rasmus Nielsen—August 10, 1849—S. K.*

Dear Magister,

I have seen the light; I have made a new discovery. In my last note[1] I remarked that Climacus and Anti-Climacus met in offense from opposite sides. That was a hasty remark occasioned by the fact that the example of the emperor and the laborer[2] amused me so very much. No, now I certainly know better. The point lies in despair. The Appendix to the *Postscript* (p. 475) begins as follows, "The undersigned, Johannes Climacus, who has written this book, does not claim to be a Christian, for he is, to be sure, completely preoccupied with how difficult it must be to become one."[3] When Anti-Climacus reads these lines, surely he will have to exclaim, "My dear Johannes Climacus, you also are a person in despair."

I hasten to inform you of this, partly so that you can see how diligently I study the writings, partly so that you may know that when it comes to making a discovery, I am not exactly a dunce either.

Lyngby,[4] August 10, 1849.

Yours,　R. N.

S. T.
Magister Kierkegaard.

[*Address*:]
S. T.
Magister Kierkegaard
in
Copenhagen.

222. *S. K.—[August 1849]—Rasmus Nielsen. S. K.'s draft.*

Dear friend,

As far as the "discovery"[1] goes, or more precisely, as far as the "new discovery" goes, I must be brief, or more precisely, I must refrain completely from getting into a subject that would lead too far afield for a letter. Some time when there is an opportunity for verbal communication, I shall be glad to be more explicit concerning the dubious relationship of this new discovery to the earlier discovery and to my first note that accompanied the copy of *The Sickness unto Death*.

[*Deleted*: I must indeed thank you for "diligently studying the writings," and I must indeed thank you as well for "hastening to inform me about it." But if I may venture to ask it, then please make haste also to let me know (this I cannot perceive from your last note—) whether you have received a slightly more explicit note from me, sent on August 4.]

Please do let me know when you are coming to town. And since I cannot tell from your note whether or not you have received a somewhat more explicit note from me, my second, which was sent on August 4, please let me know about that as well.

223. *Rasmus Nielsen—August 28, 1849—S. K.*

Dear Magister,

It is certainly annoying that your note of August 4 has not arrived. I have made inquiries both at the inn and at the other baker's, but there was nothing.

With respect to my two remarkable discoveries, I am still of the opinion that I shall be able to bring them into harmony with a third, which I hope to do when I have the pleasure of listening to your own verbal communication. Therefore, please permit me in anticipation thereof to consider myself until further notice,

The Knight of the Three Discoveries.
Lyngby (c/o Wiedemann, the baker)
August 28

                                        Yours,   R. Nielsen.

P.S. It goes without saying that you will hear something from me when I get to town; perhaps you will in addition see something from me very soon.

[*Address*:]
S. T.
Magister Kierkegaard.

224. *S. K.—[August 1849]—Rasmus Nielsen. S. K.'s draft.*

Dear friend,
    Please do me the favor, if you will, of inquiring about that note at the post office in Lyngby. It may, after all, be there. My servant had forgotten to put a stamp on it. If you do get it, please be so kind as to send it back to me unopened. There is a certain order to my letters, and I would not like to have them read out of sequence.
    Now, to move from my in all respects lost note—yes, even though I may get it back again—to your latest safely delivered note.
    This might indeed almost be called a *furor uterinus* [imaginary pregnancy] with respect to wanting to make discoveries! Now you will not even content yourself with two discoveries but want a third, which presumably has to be that—of mediation.[1] For you do say that you hope to bring your two into

harmony with mine—and in such a way that you become the Knight of the Three Discoveries. Can I believe my eyes? Do you now want to become the mediation? Or is this perhaps a new pattern so that the third discovery is merely number three, but not a third? If so, where is the "harmony"? [*Deleted*: Incidentally, in that way it is easy enough. You hang on to your two discoveries, and when I present mine, "you can include that as well." That makes three in all, for two and one do make three—and you become the Pasha of the Three Horsetails of Discovery or Discoveries.]

But all jesting aside. Not that something serious is about to follow, no, but when you come to town and we have an opportunity to talk, I shall, as I said, deal very seriously with the matter. [*Deleted*: In one respect you are right, for you will probably succeed in bringing your two discoveries into harmony with the third—for the third is that very harmony.]

225. *Rasmus Nielsen—August 28, 1849—S. K.* [1]

Dear Magister,

Once more you are right and once more doubly right. I have really come quite close to burning myself on the mediation.[2] Here, briefly told, is the story:

Last Sunday there was a grand dinner party out here. His Excellency[3] and retinue were present, including "the Mediation."[4] I saw "the Mediation," and behold, it was very good; I saw His Excellency, and behold, I was in disgrace. But it was, as you may well imagine, a handsome disgrace. To display a certain condescension toward a person of humble station is nothing; but to allow someone to be in disgrace in such a handsome manner, to overlook a poor man so completely and yet without giving insult—to do that requires a self-assurance that only native talent and many years of practice can bestow. His Excellency possesses this self-assurance in the highest degree and to that extent I derived some pleasure from it in my distress. On the other hand, I cannot deny that I was put in a somewhat awkward position when M.[5] wanted

to visit me after the coffee. God knows the man is still heartily welcome to me, but—"the Mediation!" You know how weak I am when it comes to resisting the mediation; you know what a powerful effect the mediation has on a weak constitution, especially right after coffee. However, I managed quite well, if I do say so myself, a piece of luck I attribute not so much to that paternal *quid pro quo* as to those words spoken by Anti-Climacus[6] (p. 61, 1. 10 from the bottom— p. 62, 1. 3), a passage I often read for my edification!
August 28

Yours,   R. N.

No one at the post office knows anything about your note.

[*Address:*]
S. T.
Magister Kierkegaard.

226. *S. K.—1849—Rasmus Nielsen. S. K.'s draft.*

Dear friend,

Your note of August 28 duly received.

I cannot say, "I hasten to reply," but on the other hand I can say, "I have waited before replying," or, more correctly, "I had not expected to reply in writing as I thought your vacation was over at the end of August." But in the meantime, as I have heard nothing from you about your arrival in town, I know that you must still be in the country.

And now, now I am in haste. But I suppose that is all it will amount to; I shall not "go further" to the point of hastily instigating something that would probably have to remain half finished or half done [*deleted*: because it would be going too far in a letter] for several intrinsic and extrinsic reasons, including the fact that I have also firmly gotten it into my head that the vacation is now over.

Please forgive me if I make it too boring for you to correspond with me—as boring as it would be to play opposite the dummy. I have always been somewhat superstitious, and from the moment my explicit note of August 4[1] was lost, I have in fact despaired of the correspondence. But I repeat, as soon as there is an opportunity for discussion, there are a great many things I would like to talk about with you.

Yours,   S. K.

227. *Rasmus Nielsen—September 1849—S. K.*

Dear Magister,

Thank you for the note. You may well wonder that I am still staying here and wasting time, but the fact is that I became quite ill last week. My physician, Professor Stein,[1] found me so weak that he has ordered me to stay here for another two weeks. For a convalescent, I am tolerably well. When I have been working for an hour or so, I break off and look at nature and the baker's hens. I really look forward to coming to town, where I can see you again and listen to you talk.

Yours,   R. N.

[*Address:*]
S. T.
Magister Kierkegaard.

228. *S. K.—September 1849—Rasmus Nielsen. S. K.'s draft.*

Dear friend,

But what is this? *Quid hoc sibi vult* [What does this mean]! *Ihr Götter* [Ye gods]! etc. I almost said, to recall a saying by Frederik VI[1] of blessed memory, "A philosopher can die, but he cannot get sick." At any rate, I have not been far from believing that to be my own case upon occasion, I who *qua* philosopher can say quite literally that my weakness is my strength and that my genius is my suffering. I am also sure that more genuinely concrete thinking about the existential must be exceedingly painful, if not impossible, if one has a very healthy body. In order to deal with this thinking, one must—from one's earliest days, be tortured and broken, with as cavalier a commitment to one's physical body as possible—a ghost, an apparition, or the like.

But how did you happen to become ill? You have not over-exerted yourself or allowed yourself to become annoyed, have you? One ought not to do either of these things. One owes it to oneself not to do the former and to the world at large not to do the latter. As you know, one ought not to love the world; one ought to hate the world. But if one truly wishes to express one's hatred of the world, one needs only to avoid getting annoyed. Then the world becomes furious—with annoyance. How profound—how subtle the Christian element always is. When one loves the world, one becomes annoyed with the world, and then the world rejoices. When one hates the world, in a Christian sense, one is not annoyed—and then the world is annoyed. *Glück zu*! [Good luck!] [*Deleted*: I, who patiently strive to bear the thorn or stake in my flesh, I also comfort myself at times with the up-building thought that this very thorn in my flesh[2] has changed me spiritually as well, and in such a way that my life has become and will continue to be a thorn in the world's eye.]

Finally, as to the "baker's hens,"[3] I quite agree with you that when the opportunity is available, one ought not to miss making that sort of thing the object of one's meditation. Such a "devotional hour" is surely far, far more beneficial than many of those much praised "devotional hours" that go to make a mockery of what is Christian.

As you can see, however superstitiously I had gotten it into my head that your vacation was over at the end of August and that obviously I would not have to write any more notes to Lyngby, as you can see, I, like everybody else, yield in the face of sickness. But I do hope that you are already so completely recovered by now so that this may really be the last note to Lyngby from

Yours   S. K.

229. *Rasmus Nielsen—[September 1849]—S. K.*

Dear Magister,

In expressing my thanks for your note this time around, surely I ought not to confine myself to a simple thank you but to treat the matter quite seriously and thank you systematically on three grounds.[1]

In the first place I must thank you for having proved so clearly that a philosopher prefers to die rather than get sick, for that was exactly, that is to say, that was almost what happened to me. My case began, before I knew what was happening, with my awareness of the world being reduced to zero. Now, when a man's awareness of the world is close to the zero point of his self-awareness, I conclude that death cannot be closer, N.B., if that same man is to rise again without a miracle. Now, since this was the case with me, I further conclude from this (systematically) that although I am not yet a complete philosopher, I must certainly be pretty close to becoming one.

In the second place, I must thank you for the telling dialogue in your note about hate and love—of the world, a dialectic from which my family and I can both benefit. As to whether I, too, know myself to be innocent, whether I have loved too intensely, oh, what can one say? "C'est an Uebergang, Monsieur" ["That is transitory, sir!"][2] as Pernille says in the comedy. Even though I were to be pushed about and oppressed a bit by this world, I would not like to become too thick-skinned and would far prefer to make my *resistentia passiva* as a small porcupine does than to let myself be turned into an elephant.

In the third place, I thank you for the arrival of the note, for it was indeed like a physician's visit for me, which also fits systematically, inasmuch as it brought such a good prescription with it. Accordingly, if I must thank my physician for driving out here in his own conveyance to care for me, I must thank you even more for entrusting your note to the mail service, even though you have, in a manner of speaking, a case against the postal service.

Yet, as I write this, it occurs to me that I really ought to thank you for a fourth reason, for inasmuch as the note, as you say, is the last I shall receive from you this time here in Lyngby, I cannot look at it without also seeing all the preceding notes from one and the same perspectivist-speculative point of view, and thus I hereby send you my perspectivist-speculative statement of gratitude as well.

But apropos, now that I have gotten started with babbling speculatively and prattling perspectivistically (for—do you not agree?—it is surely God's own misery with this nonsensical perspectivist-speculative system), I might just as well say goodbye to the system and in the fifth place thank you for the friendly greeting you sent me day before yesterday through my brother.

                                               Yours,   R. N.

230. *Rasmus Nielsen—September 20, 1849—S.K.*

Have arrived here.

                                               Yours,   R. N.
Thursday, September 20.
S. T.
Magister Kierkegaard.

[*Address:*]
S. T.
Magister Kierkegaard.

231. *S. K.—[1849-50]—Rasmus Nielsen. S. K.'s draft.*

[*Fragment:*]

. . . . . It would probably be best if you undertook some modest opposition to "the System."[1] The enclosed is something I have jotted down with reference to a statement in the "Preface" to the System. Please read it through. I myself cannot very well take *partes* in any way. In the conclusion it might perhaps be best to include a couple of remarks to the following effect. (1) A dogmatic system is, in Christian terms, a luxury item; in fair weather, when one can assume that the average person, at any rate, is a Christian, there may be time for such things, but when was that ever the case? And when it storms—then the systematic is evil, for then everything theological must be upbuilding. The systematic contains an implicit falsification, as if it were all right to say that indeed we are all Christians—since there is time to systematize. (2) A dogmatic system should not be erected on the basis of comprehending faith, but on the basis of comprehending that one cannot comprehend faith. The fact is that in Christian terms, "the pastor" and "the professor" ought to say one and the same thing, only the professor ought to quadruple the intensity with which he says it. If there are rebel spirits who will not be contented with the pastor, then they must proceed to the more rigorous by going to the professor. In Christian terms everything is discipline; ascending means submitting to the more rigorous discipline. By running away from "the pastor," we ought not to escape into speculative mawkishness but ought to come to an even more rigorous discipline. . . .

232. *S. K.—[October 1849]—Emil Boesen.* [1]

Dear friend,
   This is not feasible.

                        Your   S. K.

[*Address:*]
To
Pastor E. Boesen.

233. *S. K.—[October 1849]—Emil Boesen.*

Dear friend,
   How are you? I hope you are not ill.
   Someone told me today that you were not feeling well, so

from that I concluded something different from what I concluded from your note.

Your   S. K.

[*Address:*]
To
Pastor E. Boesen.

234. *F. C. Petersen—November 19, 1849—S. K.*[1]

Dear Sir:
   Inasmuch as *that* good old custom of meeting you has also
fallen into disuse, I must for the time being express my considered thanks with these lines for your having remembered
me so kindly with your most recent work.[2]
Rengentsen, 11/19 '49

Yours,   F. C. PETERSEN.

Magister S. Kierkegaard.

[*Address:*]
S. T.
Magister S. Kierkegaard.

235. *S. K.—September 10, [1849]—Regine Schlegel.*
S. K.'s draft.[1]

Under the date of the Preface[2] should be added
September 10.

To
Mrs. Regine Schlegel with sincere
   affection from
   the author.

"There is a time to be silent
and there is a time to speak."[3]

   That I was cruel is true; that I, committed to a higher relationship, not simply for the sake of my virtue, had to be so
because of love is a certainty; that you have suffered indescribably I realize; but that I was to suffer more, I believe and

know. —Nevertheless, I am ready to ask your forgiveness—provided you understand it as follows, provided you harbor no other explanation of our relationship than the fabrication, provided and forced upon you by my solicitude, that I was a black-hearted villain who broke a sacred obligation out of self-love, cruelly deceiving a lovely young girl who with all the righteousness of innocence on her side, with almost worshipful admiration and almost childlike devotion, entrusted herself to him. Provided you understand the matter in that way, then let me remain in the character of that pious deception: I am a villain, but now I come as a suffering penitent and beg forgiveness.

But if you understand it in another way, then the question of forgiveness presumably becomes irrelevant [*in margin*: even though it will always be my fault that "I dragged you out with me into the mainstream."] The relationship becomes a different one; I become the one who thanks; I thank you with all my heart (whatever your intention may have been) for having fulfilled my only wish, that at which all my cruelty was aimed: to marry and to marry Schlegel in particular. Thank you, oh, thank you! *Thank you for everything I owe to you; thank you for the time you were mine*; thank you for being childlike [*deleted*: which taught me so much] [*in margin*: you, my enchanting teacher, you my lovely teacher. You lovely lily, you, my teacher, you airy bird, you, my teacher.]

[*In margin*: Thank you for being childlike, which was to become my ennoblement and education. Thank you for being childlike, which was to become my instruction; thank you for being childlike, by which with God's help I was to become in the loftiest sense ennobled and educated.] Thank you for everything I have learned, if not from your wisdom, then from your lovely character; thank you also for your tears that have matured me so immensely, thank you—but why so many words for what my life has expressed: she was the only beloved; and when she married she then became the human being among those still living to whom I owe the greatest gratitude.

How much I have wanted to express my devotion on a different scale and in a different manner is something I do not yet think it will serve you to know, but what you [*in margin*: who in your suffering did not hesitate to obligate me in a religious sense, and even went so far as to charge my conscience with murder without considering or having an inkling of what has since proved true, that you had both the strength to go on living and to marry Schlegel—what you] asked me when we parted—"to remember you now and then," I have honestly observed. Oh, in the hour of suffering, I suppose you have sometimes thought—but without rebelling against God, I hope—: "It is really terrible 'that such a horrible trick has to be played on a poor young girl,' that she has to be sacrificed to somebody's whim as if she were nothing at all." —Be assured that in Denmark there breathes not one girl, without reservation, not one, of whom it will be said as it will of you, "Her life had *extraordinary* significance." I have not been tempted by the honor and esteem of the world; I have [*in margin*: not just for the sake of my virtue] belonged to something higher, gladly made sacrifices, gladly sought out dangers in order to have the honor of serving the oft-despised cause of truth; yet all my fame—that is our will—shall be owing to, shall belong to you, "our own dear little Regine," you whose grace once enchanted and whose grief forever moved him whom neither the world's flattery nor its opposition has moved. There are only two people who affect me thus, my dead father and our own dear little Regine, who in a manner of speaking is dead [*deleted*: for me].

And then just one more word—it might seem strange that I should be the one to bring it up, but dear God, at the time we were engaged I was already practically ancient in comparison with you, and I have not grown any younger—so please permit me this word of admonition. No doubt you yourself have profoundly, clearly, and reverently understood your duty; after having suffered what you have suffered with me, the worthy and admirable Schlegel is the very man whom you can make happy and with whom you can become happy, and so you must; there must not be so much as a fleeting moment's hesitation. I am convinced that the time has now come when you may benefit from reading these cold mute characters; my voice you will not hear. You are in an awkward position with respect to me, but honest willingness is capable of much, particularly when such favorable conditions exist as they do for you through a happy marriage to Schlegel. Oh, my girl, when all is said and done, it is really easy to be a young girl who, by understanding what matters in the most profound sense, simply employs [*deleted*: (—shall I say selfishly, or cruelly, or merely inconsiderately—)] all her power against "the cruel one." It is a heavy burden to be that cruel one who is forced to be cruel out of solicitude and love; but beware, for if it should become necessary—God forbid— if it should become necessary, I shall the second time with God's help become crueller and colder than the first time. But that will not become necessary; I am convinced of that. Take care of yourself. For your own good, let yourself take pleasure from hearing it repeated once more; so hear it now: "Yes, you were the beloved, the only beloved. You were most beloved when I had to leave you, even though you rather saddened me with your vehemence, which could not and would not understand anything so that cruelty became necessary; (and if in the future you wish to show me affection, then concentrate on this: never, for your own sake, force me to have to be cruel to you, for that is indescribable torment to him who has always wished and wishes you as well as I do)."

With this comes, from me, S. K., a small gift intended for your wife. Now decide for yourself [*in margin*: whether you will present the gift to her or not,] whether you believe it will please her and whether it will be beneficial to her—and if so, please be kind enough to give her the present. I cannot, after all, very well [*in margin*: unless she herself demands it] defend my approaching her [*in margin*: least of all now when she is yours, which is why I have never availed myself of the opportunity that has constantly presented itself or perhaps has been presented over the years], and yet I have an idea that a few words from me and about me from a proper distance might be beneficial to her. But if you do not think so, may I then ask you to return the parcel unopened.

This step, to which I felt myself religiously committed, is one I have wanted to take, and in writing, because I feared that my distinctive personality, which at one time probably made too strong an impression, might once again make too strong an impression and thus be disturbing in one way or another.

On the title page of her copy it should state: "This little book[4] is·dedicated to Mrs. R. Schlegel."

Your marriage with Schlegel has now presumably become so firmly established that without any danger [*in margin*: —God be praised!—] I have the courage to dare—that which I so much wanted to do in the moment of parting, and of course also would have done, had not your somewhat inconsiderate despair forced me [*deleted*: the most melancholy and most kindhearted of men] [*in margin*: out of love] to use cruelty—have the courage to dare that which I have always wanted, merely awaiting the moment because I have always felt that I owed you a debt of gratitude and have honestly observed what you asked in the hour of our parting, "to think of you now and then."

Thank you [*in margin*: my enchanting teacher] etc.—the whole passage.

[*In margin*: Thank you for your lovable simplicity that was to become my education; thank you also for the injustice done me by your passionate despair: it was to become the decisive moment of my life.] Of what follows, only one sentence is to be used: Oh, in the hour of suffering, I suppose you—but without rebelling against God, I hope—etc. That is my will, and that is what you have deserved, you, our own dear little Regine, you who once with your grace enchanted and with your grief forever moved him whom neither the world's flattery nor its opposition has yet moved. Only two people affect me thus, my dead father and then—someone else who is dead, our own dear little R.

Take care of yourself, do take care of yourself. Forget me or remember me, do as you like in that respect, whatever you think will best serve you and your marriage, but neither I nor history will forget you. There will always be something inexplicable for you in this whole affair. Resign yourself to that;

do not trouble yourself about it, for you will not be able to figure it out anyway. It seems to me that a girl can demand no more than a happy marriage—and then to be of such great significance to someone else.

If you would like it, if you would really enjoy talking with me sometime, I too would like it, provided you have first sincerely tested yourself before God so that you dare do it, and provided of course you are in the most perfect agreement with Schlegel about it. This is what I have to say. However innocent I may be, and however conscious I am of the purity of my intentions, it is after all possible that I overwhelmed you with my personality the first time I approached you.[5] I shall guard carefully against that another time. There is—yes, why not admit it?—there is a satisfaction to be found in having this powerful personality, but the responsibility becomes all the greater. Now, however, tranquility surrounds you, so, with reverence for God, weigh everything carefully. Then choose—but remember that you have your share of the responsibility as well.

This opens immediately with the passage, "Thank you" etc. *Then*, but in the same passage, this sentence, "Oh, in the initial hour of suffering" etc. *Then*, but in the same passage, this sentence, "That is my will, and that is what you have deserved, you, our own dear l. R., you who once with your grace" etc. *Then*, but in the same passage, this sentence, "Only two people affect me thus, my dead father" etc.

Now take care of yourself; be happy. Forget me or remember me, do as you like in that respect, whatever you think will best serve you; but neither I nor history will forget you. I have honestly observed what I promised when you asked at our parting, "that I would think of you now and then."

236. *S. K.—[1849]—Frederik Schlegel. S. K.'s draft.*[1]

In a sense, it is remarkable what I experience in a certain way with this girl. At the time we parted, I was, after all, as I continue to be, the only one who held and holds the explanation of my relationship; I was the only one who knew how to appreciate the girl's worth, the only one who had the relationship in perspective, the only one who sensed that it would turn out as it has turned out, something I intimated often enough. And yet at the time I was "a villain, a black-hearted villain," etc. —"Our parting would be the death of her!" And now, now she has long been happily married—and I remain completely unchanged.

Nevertheless, the girl's worth was quite extraordinary. In one sense I am completely in the wrong and guilty toward her: perfectly innocent, she has suffered a great deal, a very great deal on my account, so I in turn would now like—only with your consent of course—to do something for her, the final, the only thing—and provided of course she herself desires it. I am able, only all too easily, unfortunately, to give her an explanation of her relationship with me, an explanation that will enhance for her the relationship she has with you; I can give her some idea of the significance that is hers and that will endure and be remembered after her death [*deleted*: of the immortality of the name she bears.]

For that matter, a young girl may be lovableness personified and highly gifted as well—and still lose her foothold when she is led into such terrible decisions as those, alas, into which she had to be guided by my hand. Her relationship with me in the latter days of the engagement constituted just such an ill-judged step, although in essence she lost none of her lovableness—despite the fact that almost without understanding it she strove to do so. —Then after some time has passed and the same girl has had time to collect herself, she may, by what she then does (by becoming engaged and then married, and to one person in particular), demonstrate that not only is she lovable and gifted, but an extremely sensible girl as well, and then she may by that very step assure herself of the lasting gratitude of the other party. This is the case with "her" in relation to me through her marriage to you. —Then when such a marraige has had time to consolidate itself properly, when some external difficulty or other has also been removed, then the moment may be at hand when it is one's duty—a most welcome one—to let the girl realize her significance, a wealth of a different sort that has been honestly saved up—by the "villain"—for her. [*In margin*: For the full force of my entire activity as an author must be brought to bear and absolutely brought to bear upon her: out of grief that I had to make her unhappy I became an author; out of grief that I had to make her unhappy, I have as an author embraced almost inhuman exertions and, in the service of truth, sought out dangers that all others shun.] In the ordinary course of events, a wife is in such a position that only in her marriage can a distinction be made between her everyday dress worn for everyday use and her festive gown worn on those few festive occasions; but this extraordinary girl differs from the ordinary in that, in addition to the everyday dress of her marriage, she owns a far more precious ornament, the festive gown of fame and historical significance, which I have already prepared for her after her death, unless the girl's heart, perhaps as modest compensation for so many offenses, desires to be robed in it at once. —Then when the communication that explains my relationship with her and her significance has been imparted, I shall ask her to do her best to forget me so that she may belong completely to you, enhancing your life. That which I once promised her and have hitherto honestly observed, although in ways that differed depending on the demands made by concern for her future well being, I shall continue to keep: "to think of her." With that, from then on, she will for all practical purposes be denied the opportunity of seeing me. God bless her! In this life she belongs to you; in history she will stand by my side; in eternity it cannot distress you that she also loves me who already on the day I became engaged to her was ancient and a thousand years too old to be able truly to love any girl, as I ought to have realized beforehand and as I now realize all too superbly well, now that the matter has long ago aged me another couple of thousand years.

Reply at once as to whether you consent to this; reply at once as to whether she desires it. If so, I suppose it would be best if it took place in writing.

And the reason I suggest that it be in writing is that I wish to leave you both in complete peace, without being subject to undue influence. The presence of my unfortunately all-too-distinctive personality might possibly disturb you both in some way or other, persuading you of something undesirable, or causing you to refrain from something that might, after all, be desirable. That is the reason why I have not personally availed myself of the opportunity that frequently has presented itself or perhaps has been presented.

Therefore, if it is your opinion that it might please her, if it is your opinion that it may be of service to her [*deleted*: if it is your opinion that it might enhance your marital life] to have a milder, that is, [*in margin*: *in another sense*, a harsher] explanation of her relationship with me, then I am not unwilling now to do that which I can all too easily do.

If your reply to this should be "no," then the matter is thereby settled.

If your reply is "yes," then I must stipulate a few conditions in advance, should you yourself not feel prompted to do so. If the exchange between us is to take place in *writing*, then my condition is that no letter from me is to reach her without having been read by you; likewise I shall not read any letter from her unless it bears your written approval and has been read by you. If the exchange is to be a *verbal* one, then my condition is that you be present during every conversation.

Perhaps—who knows?—this will be the first and the last time I shall have the pleasure of your company. Therefore I take this opportunity to apprise you of my special regard; [*in margin*: I would not at any cost let the opportunity be wasted, because in a sense I consider myself indebted to you]. [*Deleted*: I should be sorry to die without having found the opportunity for it.] That good fortune that united you with a girl who *poetice* deserves to be named Regina,[2] that good fortune of yours was a true act of kindness to me. [*In margin*: How beautiful for her as well! And besides, what] more can a girl ask? You make her happy in this life—I shall see to her immortality.

She may not at any cost be allowed to read this letter. If she should insist on it, then tell her that if she reads it she will for the first time in her life truly sadden me who am

> With special regard
> Yours sincerely,
> S. K.

[*In margin*: I am in a sense indebted to you; the good fortune that united you with her, that good fortune was a true act of kindness to me—so I have all the more reason to sign myself

> With special regard
> Yours sincerely,

P.S. As it is possible that I shall go abroad for a little while, I should like to have a quick reply.]

237. *S. K.—[1849]—Frederik Schlegel. S. K.'s draft.*[1]

[*Deleted*: Dear Sir,]
   The enclosed letter is from me (S. Kierkegaard) to you.
   It concerns the girl to whom I once had the honor to be engaged and with whom I have never, from the day the engagement was broken, exchanged nor ever wanted to exchange a single word.
   It is now up to you to decide whether or not you will open this letter; but above all do not consult her about it [*in margin*: and weigh the matter yourself before you speak with her about it and also bear in mind that I am not urging you to open the letter].
   In case you should decide not to open it, just one more thing. I believe that with this step [*in margin*: to which I have become committed on religious grounds] I have taken the only and final one I can be obliged to take with respect to her, and, in other words, that I have thereby discharged my [*in margin*: subsequent] responsibility [*deleted*: in both this world and the next with respect to everyone in even the most distant future in this life]. [*In margin*: "That one ought to make peace

with one's adversary while one still shares the path with him."]²

However, the reason I suggest that it take place in writing is that I wanted to leave both of you in complete peace and not subject to undue influence. My personal presence, which may, as I have later come to realize, from the first time I approached her have been too strong, and which may, without my having used any persuasion, have swayed her to take a step that she might not have taken, had I addressed her in writing—and it might possibly once more disturb both you and her in some way or other, set something in motion that may after all not be desirable or keep you from doing something that may after all be desirable. That is why I have not availed myself of the opportunity for a personal approach that has frequently presented itself or perhaps has been presented.

It would have pained [*deleted*: and distressed] me, it would have saddened my spirit if I were to die without having found the opportunity for this step, [*deleted*: the consequence of which is really a matter of indifference to me, whereas on the other hand, I am wholeheartedly committed to having taken it] [*in margin*: which is also why I am wholeheartedly committed to having taken this step I have now taken, a step to which I have always acknowledged myself obligated, while at the same time, from the moment she became your wife, obviously I have realized that, if anything should be done, you ought, by me as well, to be considered the arbiter to whom she, when she became your wife, personally submitted herself and thereby also my case with regard to her.]

I have the honor, etc.,
Yours respectfully,

238. *S. K.—[1849]—Regine Schlegel. S. K.'s draft.*¹

If you would like it, if you would enjoy talking with me [*deleted*: now and then], I too would like it, provided you have sincerely tested yourself before God so that you dare do it, and provided of course you are in complete agreement with Schlegel about it.

I have not wanted to talk with you, because, however innocent I am, I may perhaps have overwhelmed you at one
time. I shall guard carefully against that a second time. That is
why I write. Now in all tranquility you may weigh this matter with God, yourself, and Schlegel. Consider it carefully.

My guilt is expressed in a saying I often used, "that I
dragged you out with me into the mainstream," for which I
have asked your forgiveness often enough. Your guilt is that
[*in margin*: in the last period after I had broken the engagement and asked your forgiveness] in passionate desperation
you could not and would not understand anything and forced
me to use cruelty, which was perhaps really most cruel to me.
However, my guilt is so great that yours is nothing by comparison.

When you could not become mine, my sole wish was that
you would marry and marry Schlegel. That you have done.
Thank you, oh thank you for that! That which you asked at
the moment of parting, "that I would think of you now and
then," I have honestly observed, surely on a much greater
scale than you ever dreamed.

When I became engaged to you, I was already ancient, and I
have not grown any younger. Perhaps nobody understands
this as well as you do. It now depends on whether you can
make Schlegel understand it.

But I will not speak with you, as I said, until I have written,
for you must have peace and quiet.

If you would prefer to communicate with me in writing, I
am also willing to do that. If there is anything you might
wish, anything you think might enhance your life—provided
that I think you would benefit from it—oh, please pardon my
speaking in this way; I am after all the elder—and provided it
is in my power to do it, then rest assured that I should be
happy to do it.

Your father's death[2] has made a strong impression on me;
something else I have in mind as well has had a determing influence, and I have decided to do that which I [*in margin*: have
so much wanted to do, but which I have not dared to do out
of concern for you, that which I] really had not thought
would take place until the hour of my death. However, there

might also have been something deplorably cruel in withholding from you for so long something that might possibly gladden you.

In any case, remember for the sake of a better world that I have now taken this step as well, while you—presumably with no knowledge at all of what you did,—by making use of a religious adjura [*in margin*: tion against me (without obligating yourself), have complicated existence on such a gigantic scale that superhuman powers would really be required to introduce a little understanding on that point. For that reason I intend, if you wish to talk with me, to reprimand you severely, for after all you did once go beyond a certain limit in your passion.]

239. *S. K.—1849—Regine Schlegel*. [1]

> There is a time to be silent, and
> there is a time to be silent. [2]

That I was cruel is true; that I, thinking myself committed to a higher relationship, not simply for the sake of my virtue, had to be so because of love is a certainty; that you have suffered indescribably I realize; but that I nevertheless have suffered more, I believe and know. Enough of this.

Your marriage with Schlegel[3] has now presumably become so firmly established that finally, God be praised, I have the courage to dare that which I now dare. In the hour of our parting, oh, how much would I not have liked to do it—would indeed also have done it—had not your somewhat inconsiderate despair forced me to use cruelty. Awaiting only the moment from that time on, I have always wished for the courage to dare it, for I have always felt that I owed you a debt of gratitude and have honestly observed what you asked me when we parted, "to think of you now and then." For a long time I believed that I ought to remain silent until I died, but I have once again come to realize that perhaps it would be cruel in another way to withhold from you what might possibly give you happiness. —May God only grant that it is of use to you.

Now I dare it.
Thank. . . .

This move was occasioned by the impression made upon me by the death of *Etatsraad* Olsen. The letter was dated November 19, '49.

The letter to Schlegel read as follows:
"Dear Sir,

The enclosed letter is from me (S. Kierkegaard) to—your wife. You yourself must now decide whether or not to give it to her. I cannot, after all, very well defend approaching her, least of all now when she is yours and for that reason I have never availed myself of the opportunity that has presented itself or perhaps has been presented for a number of years.

It is my belief that a small item of information about her relationship with me [*in the draft*: concerning my relationship with her] might now be of use to her. If you disagree, may I ask you to return the letter to me unopened [*in the draft*: but also inform her of this].

[*In the draft*:] I have wanted to take this step, to which I felt myself religiously obligated, and in writing, because I fear that my pronounced personality, which probably had too strong an effect at one time, might once again have too strong an effect and thus in either one way or another be disturbing.

I have the honor to remain etc.,
S. K."

I then received a moralizing and indignant epistle from the esteemed gentleman and the letter to her unopened.[4]

Your father's death has changed and made up my mind for me. I had thought otherwise.

Cruel I was, that is true. Why? Indeed, *you* do not know that.

Silent I have been, that is certain. Only God knows what I have suffered—may God grant that I do not, even now, speak too soon after all!

Marry I could not. Even if you were still free, I could not.

However, you have loved me, as I have you. I owe you much—and now you are married. All right, I offer you for the second time what I can and dare and ought to offer you: reconciliation [*in earlier drafts, first*: my love, that is to say my friendship; *later*: friendship; *and finally*: reconciliation. *One draft contains the following*: P.S. I had really expected you to have taken this step. When one is so absolutely in the right as was your late father, for example, with respect to me, then I know very well who ought to take the first step. It never occurred to me to doubt, and I took it once. With you the matter is somewhat different.].

I do this in writing in order not to surprise or overwhelm you. Perhaps my personality did once have too strong an effect; that must not happen again. But for the sake of God in Heaven, please give serious consideration to whether you dare become involved in this, and if so, whether you prefer to speak with me at once or would rather exchange some letters first.

If your answer is "No"—would you then please remember for the sake of a better world that I took this step as well.

> In any case, as in the beginning
> so until now, sincerely and completely
> devoted, your   S.K.

[*Address*:]
To
Mrs. Regine Schlegel.

I do not know the date on which I broke the engagement, but on this sheet of paper, which dates from November, '49, I have written down the facts immediately surrounding it that I do remember; I have found these dates by reading through *Fædrelandet* for the period in question.   October 11 or 18[5]
10/31[6]

> They performed *The White Lady*[7] at the theater on the evening of the day it took place, and I was there to find somebody I had to meet.

> Sunday, October 17,
> Mynster preached. On
> Thursday the 21st, *Kean*[8]
> was performed, and
> Printzlau was the guest
> actor. I was at the theater.

My first letter from Berlin is dated October 31.

One last step concerning "Her."
November '49.

> cf. Journal
> NB[14] p. 65[9]

It is my unalterable will that my writings, after my death, be dedicated to her and to my late father. She must belong to history.

240. *S. K.—[December 1849]—P. C. Kierkegaard.*

Dear Peter,

I have now read your article in *Kirketidenden*.[1] To be honest, it has affected me painfully in more ways than one. But it would lead too far afield to go into detail here. However, let me thank you for your article, inasmuch that it was well intended on your part.

Incidentally, if I am to be compared as an author with Martensen, I do think in any case that it would be reasonable to say that only one aspect of me was considered, that I am really an author in a different way and by criteria by which Martensen is not. This, however, is of minor importance. But if I am to be compared with Martensen *qua* author, it does seem to me that the essential difference ought to have been indicated, namely this, that I have sacrificed to an extraordinary extent and that he has profited to an extraordinary extent. And perhaps it ought also to be remembered that Martensen really has no primitivity but permits himself to appropriate outright all of German scholarship as his own.

Finally, it seems to me that both for your own sake and for mine you should modify your statements about me. If what you have said is to fit reasonably well, then it must have been said about a few of my pseudonyms. For it really does not apply to me as the author of *Upbuilding Discourses* (my only acknowledged work, which is thereby already sufficiently voluminous). I myself have asked in print that this distinction be observed.[2] It is important to me, and the last thing I would have wished is that you of all people should in any way have joined in lending credence to a carelessness from which I must suffer often enough as it is.

241. S. K.—[December 1849]—P. M. Stilling.[1] S. K.'s draft.

Do let me thank you for the copy of your little book[2] that I have received. We see each other so seldom that it is almost as if we were not living in the same town. The next time an accident, Governance, or whatever it may be, happily permits our paths to cross, I shall, if you like, give myself the pleasure of expressing my opinion about what has been achieved in this book.

I trust you are well. Be strong when pain would make you weak; fight back when rebellion rages within; be silent when it is at its height, and then, when there is a moment of silence, talk to yourself so that you may store up memory for the next time; build yourself up by means of the beautifully paradoxical in language, which will put your mind at rest; remember that the chief prerequisite for metamorphosis is being spun into a cocoon, that the chief prerequisite for really getting started is stopping.

"This Merry Christmas Season" will undoubtedly be a time of grief[3] for you. I understand that. That is precisely why I thought that you might welcome a little note from me. For [*in margin*: is it not true that] if I were to thank anyone [*in margin*: besides you] for my having obtained in you an attentive reader, [*in margin*: whom reading liberates as it captivates,] it would most probably have to be your late wife. So, as you refer everything to her, I in turn refer you to her, and thus I, a complete stranger to her, have found occasion to think of her.

Yours sincerely,   S. K.

242. *O. L. Bang—December 28, 1849—S. K.*[1]

Dear friend,

Would you care to meet one of the female admirers—of whom you have such countless numbers—of your pen, your words, your thoughts? That was the introduction! The text is as follows:

Will you dine at my place tomorrow at 4:30 p.m.? In addition to Mrs. Bang and our daughter, whom you do not know, you will also meet a female cousin,[2] whom you are sure to like, and her cousin,[3] whom you will also like.

Speaking as a physician, I can assure you that my invitation is utterly harmless.

Yours,   O. L. BANG

R.S.V.P.

[*Address:*]
S. T.
Magister S. Kierkegaard
Rosenborggade in the new building next to Tornebuskegade.

243. *S. K.—[1849]—J. P. Mynster.*

Right Reverend Bishop:

When it comes to receiving a gift[1] from you I hope never to grow older, but I also hope that you will not take amiss the juvenile, almost childish way in which I thank you again and again. I dare not be profuse, as gratitude loves to be, or rather, not *here*. For in the quiet of my mind where "recollection"[2] completely hides all the particulars that "memory" now and then piece by piece has transmitted to it, there indeed is the proper place for the profusion of grateful recollection and faithful memory. *Here*, however, the greatest possible brevity, and therefore I beg you to forget it at once if I have been too profuse after all.

With deep veneration,
S. KIERKEGAARD.

[*Address:*]
To
His Excellency
The Right Reverend Bishop, Dr. Mynster
Grand Cross of *Dannebrog*, Member of *Dannebrog*, a.o.
The Bishop's Residence.

244. *S. K.—[1849]—Henrik Lund.*

My dear Henrich,

As you see, this old man is at your beck and call. Barely have you favored me with a word before I instantly take my pen in hand and dispatch something at once. Postponement is a dangerous thing.

Yes, postponement is a dangerous thing, as I myself all too unfortunately realize these days with respect to a matter that cannot bear postponement. The fact is, I am suffering from a stubborn obstruction, and just as one can speak of suffering from lockjaw, similarly and no differently, I inform you respectfully that I am suffering from locka[ss].

Quid tibi videtur domine frater? ["How does that strike you, master brother?"][1]

I am not writing this in order to consult you *qua* physician,[2] for as you know, for one thing I have my own physician and for another I do not usually consult any physician, and so I am in that respect as well supplied as one can be, but I am writing this in order to illustrate my thesis that postponement is an extremely dangerous thing.

With this, period. To be sure, this matter ought not to be postponed, but it must also come to an end. Again, this is something I have to be especially on guard against, for once I get a pen in my hand and some blank paper, then there is a risk that I will go on and on and on, however disinclined I otherwise am to write letters and the like.

Come to an end it must, but not without my expressing how pleased and happy I am, this time once again, as always, when you give me occasion to think about you, my dear Henrich!

Take care of yourself now. Write—do not write. *Either* you write *or* you do not write, but you may be sure that you are equally dear to me and always regarded with the same true affection with which I remain

Your most affectionate Uncle.

245. *S. K.—January 7, [1850]—Emil Boesen.*

Dear friend,

Well, Happy New Year! I suppose the rush[1] is over now, and happily and well, I trust. If so, then you are truly to be congratulated, for it is not simply a question of its being "just as well to jump in as creep in." No, for it is far, far better to jump in than to creep in! You have always had a tendency to [*paper damaged*] petty reflection that both delays and slowly devours powers of a nobler sort. Rejoice therefore that you were taken with a trump. Otherwise you would have discovered difficulties which in this case you have not had time to perceive or have already learned to overcome.

As for me, everything is as usual, but you do know that when it comes to writing about myself, *item*, how I *qua* author participate in public affairs, then I am a very taciturn correspondent. But I suppose that you will learn what is important in that respect from others or from what appears in print.

Do let me hear from you. If you should encounter any difficulties at all that you think I might be able to resolve, just write. Since I am willing, I can surely also find the time to reply.

Take care of yourself. I have only seen your fiancée² once, the first or second day after you left.

Your S. K.

[*Address:*]
To
Pastor E. Boesen
Horsens

246. *Henrik Lund—January 14, 1850—S. K.*

Odense,¹ January 14, 1850.
Dear Uncle,

How can I adequately express my gratitude for your extraordinary kindness in coming to say goodbye the last time I left Copenhagen, a kindness which is all the more appreciated inasmuch as it is not an everyday occurrence shown to simply anybody? Perhaps best by letting you know through these few words that, undeserving of it as I am, I have understood what it means and appreciate it, and thereupon recording it in my grateful memory among the many other proofs of your goodness towards me?

Your nephew, HENRIK.

[*Address:*]
S. T.
Magister S. Kierkegaard
Corner of Rosenborggade and Tornebuskegade, 2 floor
Copenhagen.

247. *Rasmus Nielsen—January 17, 1850—S. K.*

Thursday, January 17, 1850.
Dear Magister,

Today I must unfortunately renounce the pleasure of going for a walk with you, inasmuch as and because it has pleased an honorable cold to confine me to house arrest for some days.

Yours, R. NIELSEN.

S. T.
Magister Kierkegaard.

[*Address:*]
S. T.
Magister Kierkegaard.

248. *Henrik Lund—February 18, 1850—S. K.*

Dear Uncle,

Odense,[1] February 18, 1850.

Thank you for your letter and everything it contained. It has always been and always remains a joy to hear from you, even though my own words and feelings do become the butt of your facetious criticism. I can take a joke. But here is the rub. What can I write to you about? Over here on this frontier duty that we perform, as did those Athenian youths of yore, nothing happens that could interest you. Here one day passes like the next for me, for I rarely go out in company and thus am reduced to my own company and—true enough—to that of those men whose writings I am lucky enough to obtain. But that can really be quite entertaining, and so I find it. Time passes easily in studying myself and others, well and usefully too, I hope. But however much I study, and wherever I go, affection for you remains equally sincere and devotion to you equally great in

Your nephew, HENRIK.

P.S. As you have always taken an interest in the Agerskov family, I can send you greetings from Niels Agerskov,[2] at present a lieutenant with the Reserve Batallion of the Second Corps of Chasseurs stationed here.

The same.

[*Address:*]
S. T.
Magister Kierkegaard
Corner of Rosenborg– and Tornebuskegade, 2 floor
Copenhagen.
[*On edge of envelope:*] H. Lund. Subordinate physician at Odense Field Hospital.

249. *Rasmus Nielsen—February 22, 1850—S. K.*

February 22, 1850.
Dear Magister,
   Today I regret that I am unable to have the pleasure of
going for a walk.

Yours,   R. N.

S. T.
Magister Kierkegaard.

[*Address:*]
S. T.
Magister Kierkegaard.

250. *Emil Boesen—March 7, 1850—S. K.*

Horsens,[1] March 7, 1850.
Dear friend,
   You have probably been wondering why I have not written
you before now, but I have often thought of you and wished
that I could visit you or meet you as I was walking along the
highway on my way out of town. In the same way, the fact
that I miss you has now moved me to take out the writing
paper. I long to know how everything is going with you over
there, whether anything remarkable has happened since I left,
and how you yourself are. I have read a little of what has
come out, Stilling's pamphlet,[2] for instance, which is more
decisive and shows greater strength than I had expected; over
here nobody cares about such things. What little is known
about you here is mostly based on what has been said in
Kirketidende[3] recently and then *Either/Or*. That little man
Helveg should stick to his church history.
   I myself am tolerably well, and there is a great deal I must
familiarize myself with, but I cannot get away from myself
and am in need of a vacation soon and of getting over to you.
Here I live alone and must keep to myself, and, as you can
well imagine, this has been a pretty difficult time for me. On
Sundays I am usually in my vestments from 9 a.m. until 7:30
p.m. First, Confession, then Holy Communion after the

Pastor has preached, then I have to preach at the hospital, then vespers in the parish church; when I have to work out the sermon I am usually quite impoverished, and when I have to speak loudly enough so that people can hear what I am saying, in the parish church especially, then I find it hard to make my words suit the thoughts, or some feeling gets too strong a hold on me, but to all appearances I believe things are going all right. In the hospital chapel I have a strange audience consisting of a couple of decent old women, a few who are half crazy and drunk, usually a couple of members of the count's family at Boller, and finally a few townspeople. The confessional homilies have more of an effect on me than on anyone else. The Pastor[4] is an odd, unapproachable fellow, and the church administration is divided between him and me in a boring way. So far I have gotten along well with him, but now the town council wants to remove him as chairman of the school committee and from the committee altogether and have me replace him, which could easily lead to friction. I do not particularly feel like becoming chairman of the school committee, for the school system here is in a terrible mess and there are no prospects of getting enough money to straighten it out, and besides I may not be very good at it. Here there is a peculiar mixture of respect for the traditional aspects of the Church and indifference to it.

I am glad and grateful that I became a pastor, but I often feel myself to be impoverished and bereft, and then I miss you, which may very well be good for me. Mother's death has grieved me deeply; it came too soon for me. Being weaned is not an easy thing; yet I do believe Mother is happy. Unfortunately Father fell and hurt himself so badly that he has to stay in bed; with all my heart I want to talk with him one more time, and I think that this must of necessity happen.

You write that if I should encounter difficulties you might resolve, then I ought to write. Thank you! They may well occur. There was one occasion when I found it hard to make up my mind, but it turned out all right. Now there are three things I should like to ask of you, and all three are very easy to do: visit Father, who would be very happy if you were to do so and who needs a friendly word; visit Louise Holtermann,[5] who would be very happy if you were to do so, because she also needs to talk with you a little, and you can, after all, easily do this—I only hope she will not suffer too much from homesickness when she comes over here; and then write to me.[6] When I used to visit you, you were usually the one who did most of the talking, and therefore you ought to do most of the talking to me now when I cannot visit you. Father, Louise H., and I are, all three, very receptive.—

After I have officiated at Confirmation, it has been decided that I am to go over and fetch L. immediately, which I am very much looking forward to. I am happy about her and proud of her every day, and happier with every letter she writes to me. Too bad for you that you did not meet her before I did.—

There is a lot of disturbance where I live. Today a big horsemarket is in progress just outside my windows, and there is steady traffic through the house from early morning to late at night.—

The 8th. Can you not teach me the secret of formulating good sermon topics? Take care of yourself! Dear friend, thank you for everything good! Please fulfil the three wishes soon!

Your EMIL BOESEN.

[*Address:*]
To
Magister S. Kierkegaard.
Rosenborggade in
Copenhagen.
postage paid

251. *Henrik Lund—March 8, 1850—S. K.*

Odense,[1] March 8, '50.
Dear Uncle,

It is entirely possible that Cicero once said that "the most interesting letters deal with nothing," but that does not make every letter that deals with nothing—interesting. Therefore, if this letter, which deals with something that is as good as nothing, should fail to interest you, then please relegate it to the latter category and forgive me for having bored you!

You wish to learn something about the bird life over here! I shall try to satisfy you.

In town one sees the crows—as in Egyptian and Syrian towns, the vultures, or in South American towns, the condor—assuming the task of public sanitation. After market day the square is a special gathering place for many of these birds, who in almost no time at all completely clean the square of the refuse from the butchers' and bakers' stalls. Then there are no sparrows to be seen in the square, just as these birds generally seem to be in much smaller number here than in Copenhagen. —Circling constantly around the spire of St. Canute's with hoarse drawn-out cries are many jackdaws who have their nests in the church walls. It is well known that there are no magpies on Fyn,[2] where the martins have taken their place, while the opposite is the case on Sjælland.[3] —In the course of some wonderful moonlit evenings last month, I strolled about on the outskirts of the town and enjoyed hearing a rare concert, that is, of owls. They were flying about, but it was impossible to see them or to hear their flight; only their long, penetrating, plaintive hooting was heard now here now there.

In contrast to this melancholy cry, the merry, rising, twittering warble of the lark delighted me a few days later in the flat fields that surround the town. —Goodbye for now. I hope that the singing of the Sjælland birds may please you as much as that on Fyn has me in this idle period.

Your devoted nephew,
HENRIK.

[*Address:*]
S. T.
Mag. art. S. Kierkegaard
Corner of Rosenborg– and Tornebuskegaden
Copenhagen.

252. *Rasmus Nielsen—March 19,*[1] *1850—S.K.*

Dear Magister,   Thursday, March 19, 1850.

Under the circumstances I must now for the time being renounce going for walks with you on Thursdays, and accordingly I must ask you not to expect me today.

Whenever it transpires that I am able to have that pleasure
once again, I shall permit myself to inquire if it might possibly be convenient for you as well.

                                            Yours,   R. N.

S. T.
Magister Kierkegaard.

[*Address:*]
S. T.
Magister Kierkegaard.

253. *S. K.—[March 1850]—Rasmus Nielsen. S. K.'s draft.*[1]

Dear friend,

How very remarkable! The day before yesterday and yesterday I was really afraid that under the circumstances (for I
had caught a cold during the moving so that daily I expected
to be ill) I might have to cancel today—and then today I receive your note, from which I gather that you "under the circumstances" etc.

It is not for me to ask what these circumstances may be, but
inasmuch as your note (in which you say, "under the circumstances I must *now*," etc.) seems to imply that I know and understand what these circumstances are, I am forced to reply: I
do not understand; I do not understand why, whenever I prod
a little, you leap aside at once as if you wanted to provoke me,
whereas this is just the sort of occasion when you ought to
show me your power of understanding.

Then, strong and healthy as you are, in the conclusion of
your note you anticipate some future possibility, but surely

you realize that I rarely turn in that direction. I turn to what is in the past: therefore permit me to thank you for whatever good intentions there may have been in your efforts on my behalf and that of my cause. If a relationship exists between us, I consider it my duty just this one time to apply my own standard; furthermore, in my opinion (provided a relationship does exist between us) I do not have very much to thank you for anyway. If there is a break, then I will always have a good deal for which to thank you. If the former is the case, then you shall privately receive the more severe judgment in accordance with my own standard, and in my opinion this would also be something for which to thank me. If the latter is the case, the judgment, my public judgment is: Although Professor N., with respect to the idea (but I suppose virtually no one will understand that), has lost a number of points for the cause, he has nonetheless in another sense furthered the cause, drawn attention to it, and while working for it has also exposed himself to some danger and has sacrificed something, even though I cannot definitely make up by mind what persuaded him to do so. Nevertheless, this constitutes a debit in my account. And such a debit may be settled by saying thank you—which I am most willing to do.

254. *S. K.—[March 1850]—Rasmus Nielsen. S. K.'s draft.*

Dear friend,

How very remarkable! The day before yesterday and yesterday I was really afraid that under the circumstances (for I had caught a cold during the moving so that daily I expected to be ill) I might have to cancel today, something I would have been most reluctant to do, and then today I receive your note, from which I gather that you "under the circumstances" etc.

"The circumstances!" As you know, one speaks of "not dragging in circumstances": but I am almost forced to assume that in this case you yourself are responsible for "the circumstances." But inasmuch as your note (in which you say, "under the circumstances I must now," etc.) seems to imply that I know and understand what these circumstances are, I can only reply

However, there is nothing I can do about this since it is a matter of the circumstances; I can only strive to comply with the old Socratic advice: "modestly to conclude from the little I do understand of something the great deal I do not understand."

> Dear friend,
> Your note has been duly received.
> Yours,   S. K.

255. *S. K.—[March 1850]—Rasmus Nielsen. S. K.'s draft.*

Dear friend,

Your note has been duly received.—How very remarkable! Until yesterday I was really afraid for a few days that under the circumstances (for I had caught a cold during the moving so that I expected to be ill) I might have to cancel yesterday, something I would have been most reluctant to do—and then yesterday I received a note from you, from which I gather that you "under the circumstances" etc.

> Yours,   S. K.

256. *S. K.—March 1850—Rasmus Nielsen. S. K.'s draft.*

Dear friend,

Your note has been duly received. I caught a cold during the moving and was indisposed for a couple of days, and therefore I really was afraid that I would have to be the one to cancel yesterday on account of sickness, something I would have been reluctant to do. Things have turned out differently, and probably they have turned out for the best, but it is still possible that the outcome will be quite different from that which you or I expect, yet nonetheless the best one for you and me and the cause.

Yours, S. K.

[*Address:*]
To
Prof. R. Nielsen
Knight of *Dannebrog*.

257. *S. K.—[March 1850]—Rasmus Nielsen. S. K.'s draft.*

Dear friend,

During the years I have conversed with you, our relationship has been approximately this: with regard to every single one of your public performances (your writings),[1] I have most firmly told you that from my point of view I could not approve of them. Furthermore, I have explained why not, and you yourself have also spoken in such a manner that I must consider myself as having been understood. Moreover, in private you have always expressed yourself very differently from the way you have in public. But you always said that I would find that your next book would be different. Therefore I have continued to wait.

But now this will have to come to an end. I must hereby—completely without anger—break off a relationship that was indeed begun with a certain hope and that I do not give up as hopeless at this moment either.

That is to say, I am no longer able to go walking with you according to a set agreement. It is another matter if our paths meet by fate or by chance; then it would be a pleasure for me to speak with you as with so many others.

Please do not misunderstand this, as if it were my intention to prompt you to make a public statement or in any other way to influence its nature [*in margin*: or hereby to let you understand what my judgment would be of such a possible statement]. Not at all! As you have your unconditional free-dom, so I reserve my unconditional freedom to myself. I can-not do otherwise.

But do not make the mistake, either, of interpreting this as a complaint about something, as though I were reproaching you. No, I am unalterably the same as in the beginning, but I dare not let any more time pass in this manner.

Yours, S. K.

258. *S. K.*—*[March 1850]*—*Rasmus Nielsen. S. K.'s draft.*

Dear friend,

Had I known [*deleted*: had the least inkling] last Thursday when I talked with you that "for the time being" it would be the last Thursday I would be talking with you, then I am not the man to forget what ought not be forgotten: a response, and moreover a response dealing with the considerateness you have shown me by humoring my eccentricities. Accord-ingly, I must deplore your last note, for you have deprived me of the opportunity to be that which I am and burdened me with seeming to be something I am not.

Further, in the last conversation I introduced a theme, perhaps deliberately somewhat awkward, perhaps disagree-able, but in any case on the assumption that of course I would be talking with you the following Thursday [*deleted*: and sev-eral subsequent ones]. Therefore I must deplore your last note, which transforms a beginning into an ending and by this abrupt breaking off turns what was said into something different, thereby doing injustice to us both.

To my way of thinking there is something bizarre in this last note. Allow me to state how I think the same thing could have been accomplished more felicitously. Despite "the cir-cumstances" you might have found the opportunity to meet me the following Thursday and thus have informed me in ad-vance, or you might have told me the moment we met that this Thursday would be the last and that "under the circumstances you must now, for the time being, decline going for these Thursday walks."

You say that it is "under the circumstances." How desirable it would have been, at the moment you decided to absent yourself the following Thursday and to write the note, if a good fairy had stood by your side and said, "Don't drag circumstances into it." —You have often told me that you— something I do not consider completely true, by the way— are the only man who has dared to believe me. Well, now, I myself have also spoken quite openly to you. There have only been three occasions when I have raised some small objection, and in that same second Professor Nielsen has indeed made such a gigantic leap to the side that one might think he wanted to knock over the poor Magister.

Yours, S. K.

259. *S. K.—[March 1850]—Rasmus Nielsen*

This note was sent
See Journal N.B.[14] p.154.[1]
Tuesday.

Dear friend,

Last Thursday when I spoke with you, I expected—and that was certainly quite natural—that of course I would meet you again the following Thursday. That did not happen; a note from you informed me of your absence in the future.

I fear that a misunderstanding has now arisen. What was said dialectically directed towards a next, and teleologically directed towards a next, has now perhaps become a something else—but that is not really my fault.

One should confront misunderstandings at the right time—at least that is my opinion. A little patience and meekness are required to be able to do so, and of these I may possibly have a bit more, while you in turn have greater strength, are far stronger than I—almost as if one of us were a living person and one of us a dying.

And by the way, it is also my wish that in the future there should be no definite day for our possible meetings. Let it depend on accident and inclination. Indeed, I am not very difficult to find, and it will be no less a pleasure for me to see you when I know, as I now do, that both you and I have our complete freedom. [*Deleted*: But when I am tied to a definite day, the standards easily become distorted partly because of my perhaps too great conscientiousness. On this point I could wish to explain myself further, verbally.]

My proposal, well meant as ever—even when I, zealous about an idea, possibly am misunderstood for the moment by you who believe that you have understood best and believed me most—is that we meet tomorrow at the usual time and place and see where we stand. Please reply.

Your   S. K.

260. *Rasmus Nielsen—[1850]—S. K.*

Thursday.

Dear Magister,

Let me thank you, oh, let me thank you for being willing to call to me. I am coming soon—in silence, for I feel that one must be very silent with you in order to be able truly to hear what you say.

Yours,   R. NIELSEN.

S. T.
Magister Kierkegaard.

[*Address*:]
S. T.
Magister Kierkegaard.

261. *Rasmus Nielsen—April 4, 1850—S. K.*[1]

Dear Magister,

I am—awkwardly enough!—prevented from going walking today.

Yours,   R. N.

Thursday, April 4, 1850.

[*Address*:]
S. T.
Magister Kierkegaard.

262. *Henrik Lund—April 12, 1850—S. K.*

Odense, April 12, 1850.

Dear Uncle,

You will, I hope, forgive me for not having written to you for such a long time when you take into consideration the extensive task you assigned me in your last letter: to provide you with an outline of the time of arrival of the most important migratory birds.[1] In order to answer it fairly completely, I have both explored the local woods myself and gathered information from several farmers and zoologists about their experiences. Here are the results of my investigations to date:

The *lark* and the *yellow bunting* stay when the winters are very mild. Otherwise they go South and usually return in late January or early February.

The *starling* arrived in February this year. The *lapwing* and the *kite* likewise in February 1850.

The *waxwing*, February 4, 1850.

The *heron* has been seen near Hvidkilde at Svendborg in late February or early March 1850.

Several kinds of *ducks* at the same place at the same time, especially *mallards*; likewise the *swan*.

The *songthrush* in March, likewise other *turdidae*.

The *pipit* in March 1850; that is, *motacilla alba*.

The *stork* arrived in late March, but I have not yet seen it.

The *ringed plover* in early March 1850; the other marsh birds arrive in late March or, usually, in early April.

The *doves* throughout March.

The *wheatears* (*saxicola*) in April. *S. oenanthe*, April 5, 1850. *S. rubetra* in late April.

The *swallow* usually in late April.

The *swift* in early May.

Various songbirds (*sylvia*, etc.) in late April or early May; likewise the *yellow pipit*.

The *reed bunting* in early April.

Snipes arrived in early April 1850; otherwise, late March; sometimes during all of April.

The *laughing gull* in early April 1850.

The *night hawk* (*caprimulgus*) in late April and early May.

Shrikes (*lanius colluris*) in April; the other shrikes are non-migratory.

Hawks and *falcons* in early April.

The *nightingale* usually between the tenth and twelfth of May.

The *wryneck* in late May.

Some of the *chaffinches*, *brown creepers*, *woodpeckers*, and *goldcrested wrens* do not migrate; others do.

There is indeed a bird called the wood jay (*corvus glandarius*). It is light ash-brown, has a crest on its head, which it can erect, and a speculum with white, black, and skyblue checks, which makes it a very beautiful bird. I believe that in the shopwindow of a furrier on Østergade[2] there is a stuffed specimen of this bird. As it is non-migratory it is very likely that you may have seen it in the woods this winter. It is not particularly rare. I have spotted some in the woods near Vedbæk.

As for me, I live over here without having very much to do and without getting much done, but am otherwise well. In the hope that the latter is also true of you, please accept sincere greetings from

Your devoted nephew,
HENRIK.

[*Address:*]
S. T.
Magister S. Kierkegaard
Corner of Rosenborg– and Tornebuskegade, 2nd floor
Copenhagen.

[*On edge of envelope:*]
H. S. Lund
Subordinate physician
in Odense.

263. *S. K.—April 12, 1850—Emil Boesen.*[1]

Dear Emil,

First a reminder: if you want to write to me, will you then please write so that I can read it? This is not handwriting at all, but such tiny pinpricks on such infinitely thin paper that I could use a microscope for reading it.

Iam ad alia [Now to something else]. So I finally got a letter[2] from you. And then what do I read in it? I read "that when you used to visit me, I was usually the one who did most of the talking and therefore I ought to do most of the writing as well." Superb! That is gratitude for you! But enough of that.

You have three wishes. The first two concern your father and your fiancée, both of whom I am supposed to visit. Answer: Not feasible. That you could have forgotten me so completely in such a short time! I happened to run into your fiancée in the street and told her that you had asked me to visit her, and I took the opportunity then and there also to tell her what I had decided to reply to you on that subject. With respect to your father, you know how fond I am of him, not to mention how much I treasure those memories that are recalled when I see him, but I have been away from it all for so long that it would take an accident to get me started again.

Finally, you wish to learn the art of formulating *themata*.[3] Now that, you see, is to give me a theme. It is my opinion, however, that nothing is more foolish than to sit down and try to work out a theme. To that end, you must arrange your life in a sensible way. Every day you must see to it that you take at least half an hour for incidental reading of the N. T. or some religious discourse. When you go walking, you must let your thoughts fly about aimlessly, sniffing here and there, now trying out this, now that. That is the way to set up housekeeping. *Themata* are the accidents that your week ought to furnish in abundance, but of course the more you see to it that they are unexpected dividends, the freer, better, richer they will become and the more striking, surprising, penetrating.

Incidentally, I am also happy to note that you are pleased

with your new position. I had expected as much. In a sense
you have a lot coming to you, but also much to catch up
with, for, as I have always said, far too much time elapsed
before you took orders.[4] But that will soon pass, of course.
Lately your relationship with me had ceased to be truly beneficial for you, precisely because you yourself were not quite
sure what you wanted to do. As soon as you have consoli-
dated yourself a little as a clergyman, *item* as a married man,[5]
you will see that you will be able from this more substantial
basis to view me with a different equanimity and derive more
pleasure and satisfaction as a result.

As for me, everything is as usual. As you know, I am reluctant to discuss this further in a letter.

Take care of yourself, be healthy and merry, happy and
cheerful. Before you stretches, I hope, a smiling summer,
which you are looking forward to, I suppose, and which will
also bring you both encouragement and smiles. So be happy,
and let me have the happiness of being happy with someone
who is happy, and let that happy someone be you.

Your   S. K.

[*Address*:]
To
the Reverend
Pastor E. Boesen
Chaplain in Residence
Horsens.

[*Postmark*:]
Copenhagen
4/12   1850.

264. *J.L.A. Kolderup-Rosenvinge—April 28, 1850—S. K.*

April 28, 1850.

Dear Kierkegaard,

It seems as though an evil fate has frustrated our Monday
walks. Last Monday I could not resist my daughter's wish
and the invitation of the weather to enjoy a ride, and tomorrow and throughout the rest of the week I shall, if possible,

persevere at the examination table[1] roughly from 12 p.m. to 4 p.m. In other words, you must not inconvenience yourself tomorrow, and I take this opportunity to offer an apology more solemn than the usual one by word of the porter and his wife. Besides, I have been so sure that I would see you at some point that I have not even sent you the enclosed pamphlet,[2] which, however, can no longer bear to wait until we meet again in person.

By the way, I am suffering more than usual,[3] to which the east wind no doubt also contributes. I am making use of all kinds of spiritual vesicants, such as issues of *Rigsdagstidende*, newspapers, etc., and Spanish *incitantia* as well, but I certainly miss my good Magister's calming sense of humor. My big Valdemar[4] has also been ill for some days—which comes very inconveniently—but he is better now, and on Tuesday his examination begins, for which *patientia* is indeed required but which cannot be satisfied by patients. —Finally, I hope that in the enclosed little pamphlet you may find at least something or other that will please you, even though it is historical—and partly legal.

Your devoted,
KOLDERUP-ROSENVINGE.

265. *Emil Boesen—April 29, 1850—S. K.*

Dear friend,

You are hereby invited to my wedding on Wednesday afternoon (May 1) at 6 p.m. (or 7) at Frue Kirke.[1] I cannot call on you myself, because I have caught a bad cold and must try to get rid of it quickly again.

R.S.V.P. It would give us great pleasure if you would come.

Yours   EMIL BOESEN.

Copenhagen, April 29, 1850.

[*Address:*]
To
Magister Kjerkegaard
45 Nørregade.

266. *Henrik Lund—May 5, 1850—S. K.*

Odense, May 5, 1850.

Dear Uncle,

This year I must once again confine myself to sending my sincere congratulations on your birthday in writing and not, as I would have preferred, deliver them verbally. But I suppose the means and the manner are immaterial here, as long as they result in congratulations, just as the road, in the words of that Byzantine Christian, is immaterial, so long as it finally leads to Hagia Sofia. So I wish you many happy returns and hope you will accept my sincere congratulations and best wishes! Similarly, I also take this opportunity to say that I hope you will accept my thanks for your kindness and affectionate interest in me. I offer my congratulations—and so as not to mix talk of other matters into this letter—I conclude with many greetings and congratulations.

Your affectionate nephew,
HENRIK.

[*Address:*]
S. T.
Mag. art. S. A. Kierkegaard
Corner of Rosenborg– and Tornebuskegade, 2nd floor.
Copenhagen
Nørregade 43, 2 floor [*in pencil*].

H. Lund, subordinate physician, Odense Field Hospital.

267. *O. L. Bang—September 25, 1850—S. K.*

Copenhagen
September 25, 1850.

Magister Søren Kierkegaard![1]
　　A book[2] for me! from whom?—in haste
　　The seal beneath my nimble fingers broke;
　　From Anticlimacus? indeed, or from
　　The editor, the celebrated Søren!
　　Scarcely had I read it before
　　I felt I must take up my pen

That I might on paper pour
The thanks that from my heart arose.
Now flushed, now pale, I asked myself
What might this signify?
I, the physician,[3] who was not free
Of a little innocent meddling
With all kinds of philosophy—
To send me such a book, of which
It is not possible to think anything
But that—so Christian a name
It has imprinted on its bow—
It often sailed to that distant realm
Where only "Profound Thought" casts anchor.
And mine, the all too lightweight, stands still
At the frontier, looks on with yearning,
But dares not push the door on its hinges;
And now—I see a man near it
Who seems to be coming toward me
Saying with a smile, "My friend!
There were indeed many empty-headed men
Who went ashore and for whom
This realm at last did become a home,
Which they would not exchange for anything;
For it is there that thoughts, once hidden
In the million tubes of the brain,
Are bred to—be useful in some way.
So do come in! Take my word for it!
The valves—surely not rusty in you—
Must soon be opened, and when
First the dams in earnest are burst,
You cannot slake your own thirst,
You will not, as I cannot, prevent the stream
From pouring forth against your will."

Without bothering my brain about this speech,
Without long hesitation, without hemming and hawing,
I simply reply, "Maybe and maybe not!"
I shall remark, as you must surely know,
That him you spoke to—me, that is—that I

Who often tried to ride Pegasus,
Even though I never attended the school itself,
That I, who attained no small station
Among the priests at Mrs. Hygeia's temple,
That I, who bear the seal of Minerva[4]
On my finger ring and before my name,[5]
Steered my bow toward the philosophic realm
And sailed round those shores that touch the clouds,
Yes, I even ventured to go ashore
When the stores, which were needed
For the above-mentioned couple,
Demanded that I should multiply them;
But no deeper into that country
Much less to the capital, did my path go,
Nor did I dare to be so reckless
As to venture into the Holy of Holies,
And hence I halted my step in time.
I am so old and yet so young
That when I come to be alone, I will surely know
To choose the philosophic purse.—

"But," you cry, "Why all this talk?
Read in that book for which you thank me!
To find the philosopher's name on the title page
Is not enough for believing that here
Is the place for that which is hard to grasp;
My book is only the passport
To that which is the sole benefit of the world,
And which can open, but only if honestly used,
The many locks and the strong shutters
With which the Lord hath closed his heaven
To all, who boastful of the name of Christian,
With lipservice under a mask of piety,
Do not stop the wheels of sin on the chariots of their lives,
Yet have never embraced that Christ,
Who by his deed, by his example
Has placed his seal eternal upon his teaching"—
If that is so—well, then, you may believe
That when the cholera grants me respite,

That black book trimmed with gold[6]
Shall I take out and soon find
Those diamonds which you affixed therein,
And other passages that often beckoned me;
Although—even among the friends of truth
You are the foremost, so do not be angry if
I follow here the inner call of truth—
Although I recognize in the binding
The ultra-artistic hand of philosophy,
Which often requires a genius to understand it,
Difficult to find among the brains of the multitude,
My thanks meanwhile—accept again!
Your treasure shall not be placed
Among the profane books
That crowd a physician's shelves.
I shall seek out a better place for it,
Where it will be used again and again,
In my wife's bookcase; there it will
No less frequently be found by the young miss,
Who long has listened to the *Works of Love*,[7]
That product of your fertile thought.

A verbal greeting have I sometimes brought
To you from Julie,[8] from that cousin,
Who according to yours and also to my
Views—but this is only between us—
Of all the women in the family,
Has been given the most intellectual weight.
Recently I saw her toward the end of the week,
And as my eye happened to light on
A book by you that lay open there,
She said, "I shall not refrain from
Showing you a few of these pages."
Towering, foaming, and undammed,
The waves of your thought crashed therein,
I could not see their limits,
They almost put me in that mood
As when—well, that you must guess yourself,
For now—now my pen runs dry.

If it wrote too much, ran along too fast,
It was not my fault—No, into my cloak
And thence into myself it stole,
Put there perhaps by a mere demon,
A certain I know not what, quicksilver perhaps,
Which can be heard and can be seen
In everything I undertake
And from which I benefit least.
And now advice, so honestly meant
That it can hardly arrive too late:
Although habit has put you in chains,
You who forged them yourself will understand
Very well and how you can break them—
I am sure you guess my intention with this!
Let not mere lucky chance provide
In street encounters the companionship
Which you yourself think wise and useful;
Strive bravely to conquer your habit
And—your principle! Seek out what now you only
     chance upon!
Visit the many who esteem you so highly!
And believe me, everywhere people will
Mount the image of your presence
In memory's frame behind the glass of joy.
But should you be pleased with my advice
And should you intend to follow it,
Then do not let only a thought-wave
But yourself as well in bodily form
Find the road to your

OLUF BANG.

[*Address:*]
S. T.
Magister Søren Kierkegaard
146 A Rosenborggade.
postage paid

[*Postmark:*]
F: 10 9/26   50 P.

268. *Anonymous—October 15, 1850—S. K.*

A True Dream

A few nights ago I dreamed that we met or ran into each other somewhere. Of what took place between us, I remember only that you gave me an envelope full of silver coins. It was remarkably large and so full that some coins fell out of one end and into your hand. You gave me that money as well. It seemed to me that in all it must be at least 50 *rdl.* As you gave me the money, I was touched and said with sincerity, *"May God reward you for this; I was in great need of it,"* and instantly I awoke.

I tend to attach great importance to dreams on account of personal experience in that field, but at the same time I realize that many dreams have no significance or in any case no *rational* significance, and that others that do have significance are difficult to interpret. The latter is precisely the case with respect to this dream—regardless of the fact that I believe that this is one of the dreams that does have significance—I cannot interpret it. Whether you are able or willing to do so is something I know just as little about, for I do not know to what extent or in what ways you personally practice Christianity towards your neighbor *in real life.* When I give a penny or two to a pauper and he prays with reasonable sincerity for God's blessing on me or that something good will happen to me, then I become genuinely happy and consider it a great treasure. Whether or not it is the same with you is something else I cannot know nor have any opinion about. Yet, as I really did dream that dream without knowing of any cause or occasion for it from my point of view, I decided at once to tell you of it, since it might possibly contain a suggestion either for me or for you or for us both.

> Your neighbor and brother
> (James 2:14 etc.)

Copenhagen, October 15, 1850.

[*Address:*]
S. T.

Magister S. Kjerkegaard
Copenhagen
Rosenborggade 156—a

[*Postmark*:]
F: 10 10/16   50 P.

269. *A. G. Rudelbach*[1]*—November 18, 1850—S. K.*

In thanking you for *Practice*,[2] which, in that it practices, justly strikes and strikes down all that Christianity that is slapped together by the state and by habit and exists in name only, I send my dear friend the enclosed book[3] with the wish that in it you may find the identical battle spirit.

Your old friend,
A. G. RUDELBACH.

Slagelse, November 18, 1850.

270. *Lodovica de Bretteville—December 10, 1850—S. K.*[1]

Copenhagen
December 10, 1850.

To Kierkegaard, the philosopher, from a confessant:

Please forgive a little creature for disturbing your studies! But the world often lies heavy on my shoulders, and no matter where I turn there is no one to whom I can bring my troubles. If you do not have unlimited patience for a stranger or the time to listen to a little nonsense, then please throw these confessions into the fireplace and let them be devoured by smoke and flames. Were I Catholic, I might perhaps kneel with burning devotion before the image of my saint and pour forth all that is in me in the hope of an answer; were my father alive and could he understand me, then I would sit at his feet, rest my head on his knee, and tell him everything that pains and distresses me and read the answer in his eyes; had I my friend, I would rest my head on his shoulder and confide everything in him, and ask for his counsel and advice. But I can do none of those things; I have no one to talk with. Were I to ask about something, I would be laughed at, meet a shake of the head, and be told, "That sort of thing is unsuitable for ladies," or at best be given an incredulous reply, some comfortless Byronic remark or other—and therefore I come confidently to you, for although I know you only from your works I have always recognized you as one who is on the path and on the path to truth and light.

Yet perhaps you too will laugh at me, ridicule me, but you will give me an answer I can trust, will you not?—one that will enlighten my thoughts so that there will be some order in things. You could probably turn my head completely, but you will not do that because you know how one can brood over the enigma of life and how infinitely much one wants to resolve it. I come to you openly, hoping for your indulgence; judge me leniently—or judge me harshly, I shall thank you anyway.

There have been times when I have met you when many, many questions were on the tip of my tongue; you were so close to me, and yet I had to be silent, for convention is the dragon that guards the golden apples of the Hesperides. But I ought not to waste any more of your time than necessary, and therefore I shall come to the point.

There is a total revolution in my mind and thought, which I think I can best tell you about by sending you the following little comments. Last summer I was out in the country, and there I read *The Spirit in Nature*.[2] It appealed to me very much; here expression was given to many theories that I had only felt obscurely, even though there was too much physics and too little philosophy, too much religious restraint and too little dialectics in it to satisfy a searching soul; it is as if it were cloaked in a veil behind which one is supposed to divine the godhead. But then Mynster's reply appeared in *Videnskabsskriftet*, which was lent to me for a few hours—and I was told that it contained a statement of the popular objections, that this was what people found fault with in *The Spirit in Nature*. I read it through and was so absolutely amazed

—for it was like hearing my own opinion affirmed—that I had to cry aloud, "No! This is impossible! Can he be right?" In order to clarify my thinking a bit, I then wrote down what I could remember and added my differences of opinion. I realize very well that this is carelessly jotted down, that many important points are probably passed over. Now that I have come this far, perhaps I ought to get hold of the work again, study it thoroughly, and correct and improve my opinions. But in the first place, it is not, after all, a critical essay I want to send you, for it is matchless effrontery on my part anyway to dare to raise objections—it is like the dog barking at the moon. In the second place, I found it so terribly alien and contrary to me that I shrank from doing so. I was reminded of Goethe who in his *Die Wahlverwandtschaften* [*Elective Affinities*] compares our sympathies and antipathies with the process of elective affinity and repulsion in chemical substances—my being was separate from his. In the third place, what happens to me is really similar to what happens to someone who has walked a long way in the dark and then discovers that he has lost something; he dreaded that long walk in the dark but still he went forward, hoping to reach the light—only to have to turn back now, to turn away from the light and the hope, and make the road even longer. No! That is more than one can bear. Therefore, I have hope in you as in the light, and that is why I longed to write to you, to reach the end of the road.

> Zwei Eimer sieht man ab und auf
> In einem Brunnen steigen,
> Und schwebt der eine voll herauf,
> Muss sich der and're neigen.
> Sie wandern rastlos hin und her,
> Abwechselnd voll und wieder leer,
> Und bringst Du diesen an den Mund,
> Hängt jener in dem tiefsten Grund;
> Nie können sie mit ihren Gaben
> In gleichem Augenblick Dich laben.[3]
>   SCHILLER

Is this not the battle of faith? The conflict between religion or feeling and awareness? That battle is most difficult, and yet we must all experience it, we must strive and seek until we have found the point of affinity, for otherwise we slay our best selves. This is a battle of despair, because feeling is nourished with our hearts' blood, so to speak; it has its roots in our earliest thoughts and is closely tied to our most sacred memories. We are accustomed to considering ourselves the children of God; we believe that He guides our every path invisibly; we pray to Him in His mercy to protect us and our loved ones. If we encounter grief, then this is a trial with which Our Lord afflicts us; if our loved ones die, then it seems to us as if they are watching over us invisibly, we speak to them, we seek them in Heaven. A beautiful image for this is:

> Doch in deiner Ueberwinderkrone
> Senkst du noch den Vaterblick auf mich;
> Betest für mich an Jehovas Throne,
> Und Jehova höret dich.
>
> Schwebe, wann der Tropfen Zeit verrinnet,
> Den mir Gott aus seiner Urne gab,
> Schwebe, wann mein Todeskampf beginnet
> Auf mein Sterbebett herab.[4]

> HÖLTY.

This pious devotion is our comfort; it is the invisible thread that binds us to Heaven; thereby it is as though we had not completely lost them. If our awareness now begins to wander along its own path, then it is as if we were tearing ourselves away from our ties to God and were caught up in the infinite responsibility of having to wander alone; then we come to think of our departed loved ones as independent spirits who have a more exalted relationship than the simple relationship they had with us when we lost sight of them; then our old faith reproaches us—we fear for ourselves—we fear being disobedient to God's Commandments, we seem to ourselves to be willful and ungrateful. In our fear we then cast ourselves into the arms of faith, but soon we sense that the former trust has been shaken. In order not to see the manifold shapes of doubt, we must then close our eyes; in order not to hear its thousand voices, we must close our ears—a dumb stupor has replaced the former devotion.

But this condition is unbearable. One must free oneself from it lest one succumb; and once more the battle begins, and it is truly desperate, this gradual annihilation of everything we were nursed on, of everything we have learned to love and revere. The temple crashes down on our heads; our past fails us and the present is alien to us. The old world has been lost to us, and we have no roots in the new one. —But in a way I have now regained my foothold, and essentially my religious faith satisfies me, although I do not feel truly at home in it and dare not really believe in it, and that is why I feel in infinite need of hearing a human being in whom I have confidence say to me, "Here you are wrong, and here you are right." From my point of view I feel as if I had worked my way up to the top of a cliff and were sitting up there in the pure clear air with the world spread out before my feet. There it lies in all its beauty, but I cannot get down to it; everything lives and breathes, stirs and moves, but I can only look and not perceive—I cannot reach up to Heaven and I cannot get down to earth; I cannot truly be myself and make life external a revelation of life internal, for everything that surrounds me, almost everything I hear and see and read, stands in unending contradiction to everything that is sacred, profound, and true to me; I dare not truly believe in myself, for if life is to be lived, then it seems to me that one must become like the Yggdrasill tree[5] with its roots in the earth and its crown in heaven.

Now my confession is over. Perhaps you will say that in despair I have willed to be myself and am now too weak to sustain myself. Now the judgment is up to you. Oh, if it is possible, please restore my faith in myself. If you are now angry with me, distressed with me, surprised at my presumptuousness, then I beg you to remember how difficult it is to find anybody to whom one can turn for refuge. The Church confines us in chains and shackles that kill our moral consciousness. It takes the bread away from us and gives us a stone instead. People talk about the freedom of the Protestant Church. The chain is a little longer, *voilà tout* [that's all], so for a moment one imagines that one is set free; yet do but try a gigantic assault on heaven, and the chain grows taut, constricts itself around us—and with wings clipped—we let fall our arms and we desist.

If you would indulge me with a reply, dare I then send for it on Wednesday the 18th or Saturday the 21st between 1 and 2 p.m.? Perhaps it could be addressed to "Miss F. L."

Once more, pardon a confessant.

271. S. K.—[1850]—Lodovica de Bretteville. S. K.'s draft.

In your letter you call yourself a "confessant"; but indeed, what you enclosed is in a way the work of an author, a small scholarly essay. This is a self-contradiction that indicates that it is either not quite clear to you what it means to confess or what it means to think.

Not having any particular inclination toward what must at times surely be the exceedingly difficult task of trying to understand others, I strive all the more to understand myself.

And long ago I understood that I am no confessor, so much so that I even scrupulously refrain from explaining why I am not.

But suppose that I were or could be: it would still be impossible for me to be one for you. For you have put what is wholly disparate into one envelope and turned everything into self-contradiction. In your letter you call yourself a "confessant," whereas what you enclose [*deleted*: the confession, that is,] is in a way the work of an author, a small scholarly essay of emancipated thought, a philosophical sample, or the like. [*Deleted*: but in other words to be brief, no confession, which] This indicates that it is either not quite clear to you what it means to confess or what it means to think, something I *qua* thinker can tell you.

Just one more thing. It is typically feminine, whenever one has ventured too far in self-reflection, then to cry out suddenly to another person, "Restore me to myself!" But that cannot be done, and to demand it is self-contradictory. Yet, it is also typically feminine in a more momentary mood to consider the danger far greater than it really is. Should this in any way be the case with you, then you yourself will surely come to realize in time that it was fortunate that I am not a confessor.

What you have written is being returned to you. I would not dream of burning it, let alone for the reason that occurs to you, that I do not have the time to read that sort of thing. Oh, no, I am not all that busy. But I do not see what good could come of it when that which needs doing is something you will have to do yourself. And besides, such an act on my part might seem akin to being a confessor, which I am not.

You write that you are turning to me with confidence. That I do not doubt; your letter does indeed seem to bear the mark of it. But do ask yourself if you have not been expecting or if you ought not to have been expecting that to happen which now has happened. [*Deleted*: In any case, I am unable to act.] That I—as you believe—should burn what you have written because I do not have the time to read that sort of thing: no, I am not all that busy. But I do not see what good could come of it; if this is what needs doing, you will have to do it yourself. Besides, any other act on my part might also seem akin to being a confessor, which I am not.

The papers were merely put in an envelope, and on it was written,

I cannot become involved in this.

272. *Emil Boesen—December 20, 1850—S. K.*

Dear friend,

Thanks, many thanks for sending me your latest book, *Practice in Christianity*.[1] I hope you are not angry over my not having thanked you for it until now. I probably ought to have done so long ago, but I felt that the letter I wanted to write to you would require a long time; an hour or so would not be enough, and therefore it was postponed. But now the letter cannot be allowed to take a long time, and I do want to have thanked you for the book before Christmas. Of course one might also thank you for it several years after its publication, if need be. It is possible that I have been more pleased with it than with the similar ones that preceded it, as likely as not because I am over here now and have often missed you, especially of late; but when I received your book and read it, it was like going up to your place and talking with you. I have, however, really felt and continue to feel that the book is aimed more at me than is out and out comfortable.[2] Thank you for it. It seems as though it will create as little stir as its predecessors, which I had not expected, judging by the last part (for example, section VI about "judging"). Meanwhile Mynster has probably aimed some of his *Remarks*[3] at you on account of that, although so infelicitously, it seems to me, that I must doubt that he really intended to hit you. I cannot imagine that he was pleased with it, but how is it possible that it can pass by so quietly, or is it supposed to work all the more in secret?

Spandet's proposal[4] has set Jutland on end. Because of it Brammer[5] has written to the Diocesan clergy urging them to encourage the local community councils to issue declarations as to whether they consider the marriage service in the church as prejudicial or superstitious, or whether they would not prefer to consider those parishioners who only want to live together in a civil marriage as not truly wedded before God and man, and their children as illegitimate. Most likely all the townships have sent in protests against Spandet's proposal, and in some places the farmers have established committees to keep watch on the National Assembly lest it get out of hand. If the proposal truly offends people, then the danger is probably not too great, but I do think it unreasonable and ill considered; still, people are in fact speaking about it in an unreasonable way. Most people here are very conservative with respect to the Church, whether or not they care about Christianity.

Have you seen anybody from my old home recently? I

suppose you know that my sister Louise died. She was the one who most resembled Mother, and her death has been sad for all of us. The dispute continues about whether one can comprehend things divine, and yet God's thoughts in their particular manifestations are as often as not incomprehensible. My brother Peter has become a pastor near Holstebro,[6] which is out on the heath but in a fairly good district, and the people there are said to be a decent sort. It is a very fine thing that he was transferred, if only they can get Father comfortably settled now; as long as my brother Frederik stays in Copenhagen, it will probably be all right.

Soon I shall once again have to deliver many sermons in a short time. I preach as well as I can, but that is often rather poor! I must often sit biding my time and waiting until late Saturday afternoon before I can get started. By then I am forced to ignore all my misgivings and endeavor to surrender myself to God. I have to preach three times on Christmas day, the first time at 6 a.m.—

Greetings from Louise. She is in fairly good health and is busy preparing for Christmas these days. It is cramped and unusually noisy where we are, but it is very difficult to find a good place to live; however, we are doing our best so that we can receive you when you come to visit. We often speak of you.

Please think of me now and then, and do write to me once in a while. I hope you stay in good health. Merry Christmas and Happy New Year! Once again, thank you for the book and thank you for so much else besides.

Affectionately yours,
EMIL BOESEN.

Horsens, December 20, 1850.

[*Address:*]
S. T.
Magister S. Kierkegaard
Nørregade in
Copenhagen.
Postage paid.

273. *Henrik Lund—December 24, 1850—S. K.*

Dear Uncle,   Hørup,[1] 12/24 1850.

But I must write to you as well.

Several times I have started to do so and even more often wanted to start when I opened my briefcase and saw an unanswered letter from you, but for some unknown reason I have always torn up the letter again, and your letter has remained unanswered because I thought my reply was so stupid, so empty, and so embarrasing. Perhaps this one does not concede anything to its predecessors in that respect, but it will have to be allowed to survive.

Please pardon my long silence; it is not as though you have been absent from my thoughts at any time—but, to tell the truth, I would rather talk with you than write. Writing is not my forte.

I have nothing to write about the birds here; they have all flown away with the exception of a single little yellow bunting whose color resembles that of a faded leaf left on the otherwise naked branches.

There is very little I can write about myself. One day passes like the next with surprising speed in spite of the fact that I am doing nothing and for a long time now have neither seen nor studied a medical textbook; so, I suppose I have regressed in knowledge, inasmuch as I have not progressed. Believe me, I am longing to be able to get home so I can get to work again, but there is no prospect of that in the immediate future. Yet it is the same way with my friends, *commune naufragium dulce* [to be shipwrecked together is sweet].

Goodbye, dear Uncle. Do be lenient and forgive my long silence, for you are constantly in the thoughts and on the mind of

Your devoted nephew
HENRIK.

Merry Christmas!

[*Address*:]
S. T.
Mag. art. S. A. Kierkegaard
Copenhagen.

[*On edge of envelope*:]
H. Lund, subordinate physician with the siege troops.

274. *S. K.—December 31, 1850—J. L. Phister.* [1] *S. K.'s draft.*

New Year's Eve, 1850.

That this book[2] does not reach *you* until now is the result of a quite accidental circumstance, which I should like to confide in you if it can remain a secret between us, because, *unter uns gesagt* [confidentially speaking], it concerns a certain Magister with whom we pseudonyms do, after all, have a relationship from which we cannot liberate ourselves [*deleted*: although, God knows there have been times when we wished he had gone to the Devil long ago or had departed this life so that we could get to act the part of the eccentric man].

When the second edition of this book appeared, in which your famous name, as you may know, has also found a place,[3] a copy was reserved for you at once. But at the time, the above-mentioned Magister chanced to be living in the same building[4] with you, and he took it into his head then that I should not be allowed to send it as long as you were both living in the same building.

At first I was annoyed by this eccentricity, impatient, perhaps all the more so as I knew very well that any attempt on my part to alter his decision would be in vain. A moment later, I told myself, "*Bien*, you will have to put up with it." But in the third moment, after I had reflected a little, I said to myself, "But my God! The Magister has actually hit on what is right; [*deleted*: has once again pretended to be eccentric] under the guise of 'eccentricity' perhaps he has concealed something very different, or in any case [*deleted*: by means of a seeming discourtesy that was in fact a courtesy] helped me to find what is right, to reach a decision based on reflection that quite accords with my way of thinking." And, after all, I do have some skill in reflection, something I do not mind mentioning here since I am speaking to an artist whose strength is that of reflection.

For if you had received this copy at that time and supposing it had occurred to you for a single moment that "this is just because I live in the same building as the Magister"—and that might have occurred to you—then this would have interfered with all the pleasure I felt in sending it to you. No, with respect to what we pseudonyms do, the Magister ought to be kept completely out of things, as if he did not exist.

Please accept it now. Throughout all this time I have been pleased with the thought that the right moment would surely come, and now I am pleased to send it, free from any element of the accidental, secure from what I might call the very unpleasant possibility of being misunderstood, yet not as a sudden impulse—no, too much time has been spent dwelling on this thought for that to be so—and yet as easily as a sudden impulse.

[*Deleted*: As you may know, you will also find your famous name mentioned in this book. Well, let people say what they will about *Either/Or*; let them say "either/or." But one thing cannot be said: that your name by being inscribed in it was written in the Book of Oblivion.]

VICTOR EREMITA.

275. *Henrik Lund—January 1, 1851—S. K.*

Hørup, January 1, 1851.
Dear Uncle,

"As you speak, so speaks no one else," is what I should like to say, but it is also a certainty that I have not been so displeased with myself about anything for a long time as I have been for letting so much time go by without writing to you. But I have been punished for that, of course, for neither have I heard anything from you. Yet I have heard something from you, or rather read something, for your books also get over here, and it has been a pleasure and a comfort for me to read them, for as you speak, so speaks no one else.

I received your letter on New Year's Eve, and I am happy that before the old year completely passed I did receive, albeit in the eleventh hour, a few such friendly and affectionate words from you. So in order to begin the new year right, I shall write to you at once.

You think I am "bored,"[1] but I do not think that I could have written that, and if I did write it, then I should not have written it, for it is not the correct, the appropriate word. It may well be that I am not exactly overjoyed with this futile job as subordinate physician in a field hospital where there are only a few patients to care for, none of whom are suffering from anything important so that it is impossible to learn much from them—but things have not yet gone so far that I am bored. The days pass quietly and monotonously, as does life over here, but as I have always had enough within myself to keep me occupied, I have it here as well, and I hope it will not be wholly without profit for me.

Goodbye. Once more thank you for your gentle and indulgent words to

Your ever-devoted nephew,
HENRIK.

[*Address:*]
S. T.
Mag. art. S. A. Kierkegaard.
Copenhagen.

[*On the edge of the envelope:*]
H. Lund, subordinate physician with the siege troops.

276. *S. K.—[1851-52]—Henrik Lund.*

Dear Henrich,

Can you meet me this evening at the usual time and place? If not, then please call on me tomorrow morning between 11 and 12 a.m.

Your Uncle,   S. K.

[*Address*:]
Mr. H. Lund, M.D.
Fredrik's Hospital.[1]

277. *"e——e"—May 21, 1851—S.K.*

Copenhagen

e——e [*in a different hand*] May 21, 1851.

Dear Magister,

May a grateful reader and listener venture to ask for a few moments of your precious time? I have been told that you are gracious and kind to the young and lenient to those who have gone astray, and therefore I address myself confidently to you. In the frivolous, or perhaps, as you remark somewhere,[1] the melancholy spirit of the times, I long ignored God and my relation to him, but this was an unhappy state of affairs, as I soon realized. I sought comfort in prayer, but I felt that God would not hear me; I went to church, but my scattered thoughts would not follow those of the preacher; I tried, in the philosophy books that I could understand, to find rest for my lost soul, and I found some. I had read *Either/Or* with profound admiration, and I tried to obtain some of your works by borrowing since I could not afford to buy them. I received the *Christian Discourses* of 1848, which were not what I had wanted, but I read them—and how can I ever thank you enough? In them I found the source of life that has not failed me since. When I was troubled, I sought refuge there and found comfort; when need or chance brought me to church and I walked away downcast, conscious of one more sin for having been in the House of the Lord without reverence and humility, then I would read your discourses and find comfort. In everything that happened to me, in sorrow or in joy, this small portion of the riches you have bequeathed to the world became the constant source from which I drew comfort and sustenance.

Last Sunday you were listed as the preacher[2] in the Citadel. What could I do but walk out there, and I was not disappointed. This was not one of those sermons I have heard so often and forgotten before it was concluded. No, from the rich, warm heart the speech poured forth, terrifying, yet upbuilding and soothing at the same time; it penetrated the heart so as never to be forgotten but to bear the eternal fruits of blessing in rich measure. Forgive me for having detained you so long; I come now to my intention with these lines. I have heard that you often preach in various churches but always have yourself announced as "a graduate." If I were a man I would apply to you directly and, with confidence in the humanity for which you are well known, appeal to you, so that I, who in my spiritual need would consider it a gift of love from him on whom God has bestowed all spiritual wealth, might at least be told when you are going to speak in public. But I am a woman and dare only approach you under an assumed name. I have no other means than to beg you, in the name of that Lord Whose Glory you have been called to spread, to put aside that anonymity by which you do injustice to your faithful audience. Why leave it to chance to bring you a few listeners who may not understand you or appreciate you, while the many, who would not be detained by distance or weather if they only knew where to find you, languish in vain? They can not find you, and they will not listen to anyone else, for he who knows the best is not easily satisfied with the good. Do not close your ears to the supplicant, and remember that Christ says, "As you did it to one of the least of these, you did it to me."[3]

> With the deepest respect and gratitude,
> e——e.

[*Address:*]
S. T.
Magister S. Kierkegaard
43 Nørregade
Østerbroe[4]

[*Postmark:*]
F. 9 5/23 51 P.

278. *S. F.—May 21, 1851—S. K.*

May 21, 1851.

A cup runneth over when it is too full, but what can a poor heart now do when it is too full? Either it must burst or, like the cup—run over. This is what mine is doing now [*deleted*: but indeed it is not without fear and trembling that I approach the extraordinary] as I dare, in spite of your strict injunction against it, to set pen to paper to thank you, oh you remarkable man! for that infinitude of wealth I owe to you. Please do not think that I shall be guilty of the gross misunderstanding of becoming mired in personal adulation, that which of all things you truly have least deserved, inasmuch as time after time you efface yourself solely in order to further the cause, but you *must* allow a frail being a moment's pause. I shall neither delay you nor myself for long with what I know you consider a waste of time and completely superfluous, yet I will not be able to die until I have managed to tell you that you are absolutely matchless. —I know very well that in a way you do nothing but *put one in the right spot, focus the eye, expand the circle of vision, enchant the soul* with your mastery of language and thought—and that what you proclaim is not really a new discovery you have made but something that has endured as have eternal truths since—since eternity, of course. But in spite of this, inasmuch as nobody has proclaimed those truths to *me* before you did so in such a way that I could hear them, that is, with the ears of my soul so that they dwelt with me and became my eternal possessions, then surely I am entitled to feel grateful to you who inspire and enrich my thought!

"Yes, but not to thank me personally," you may say, and to this I really have no answer but stand ashamed. For am I to suppose that you would accept as valid the fact that I am a woman who knows no other way out? Were I a man and therefore someone who could think and write coherently, surely it would then be a different matter, for I could publish something about you and would have no need to trouble you privately. Yet it seems to me that my personal gratitude to you is nobody else's business, which is why it no longer suffices for me to go around talking about it to everybody else but yourself. I concede that it must be hard on *you* to be subject to such human conditions as having an address, which, it is to be hoped, can be ascertained, thus exposing you to written pursuit, but I promise you that as far as I am concerned this will be the last as it is the first time, and then, as you burn this the moment you have read it—you will scarcely feel it at all.

From the very outset when you began to publish your pseudonymous works, I mean, from the time when you began that work of love of sharing your divine inspiration with mankind, *I* have pricked up my ears and listened lest I should miss any sound, even the faintest, of these magnificent harmonies, for everything resounded in my heart. This was what needed to be said—here I found answers to all my questions; nothing was omitted of that which interested me most profoundly—I was happy, reposing in blessed communion with this spirit which knew so well how to express everything I hardly knew I felt, much less thought, yet which had indeed been inside, though vague and confused. And then this enchanting irony that renders you so indescribably superior and has an almost intoxicating effect on me—oh, please do not become angry at my speaking my mind, but it is really remarkable how talented you are—that is *the* marvel! For I doubt that there is a single string in the human heart that you do not know how to pluck, any recess that you have not penetrated. I thought I knew what it meant to laugh, before 1843 as well, but no, it was not until I read *Either/Or* that I had any idea what it meant to laugh from the depths of my heart; and it is with my heart that I have come to an overall understanding of everything you have said. Many a time I have been almost embarrassed to hear clever people say that they did not understand S. Kierkegaard, for I always thought that I understood him; I had to make myself appear stupider than I was so as not to appear conceited. I am never lonely, even when I am by myself for long periods of time, provided only that I have the company of these books, for they are, of all books, those

that most closely resemble the company of a living person.
But please do not think that these books have only taught me
to laugh; oh no, please believe that again and again I have
been roused by them to see myself more clearly and to understand my duty, to feel myself ever more closely tied to "the
truth, the way, and the life"; I have become infinitely liber-
ated just by musing on them—but—also infinitely tempted to
give up all that gregarious society in which one lives, which is
so far from knowing what it really means to live that, if anything, it mostly resembles a parody on it. Yet it is not by
fleeing that one shows one's strength.

Please believe as well that I have been struck with terror by
those supreme demands of the ideal which you know how to
throw into such sharp relief—and my distance from them!
—Indeed, if one were as concerned about the salvation of
one's soul as one should *always* be, then you could truly
frighten to death a poor person who can still only approxi-
mate the ideal. But you are perfectly aware that you speak to a
lethargic generation, one that knows how to recuperate after
such a battle and that has almost completely recovered from
the repercussion when it has had a night to sleep on it. Much
of this untamed irresponsibility is in me as well, but I swear to
you that I never sleep off awareness of my sins, thanks to that
"gadfly of the times"[1] who has understood so thoroughly
how to awaken it. But it is no easy task to remake one's
whole congenital nature—as I hope you will concede—
indeed, it would be impossible without grace and if God did
not grant growth where we but sow and plant.

Oh, what am I thinking of, pestering you so long with the
feelings and plight of a stranger! Please pardon my taking the
liberty of comforting my own heart. You! you who constantly desire to be considered someone who is absent—but
one can still write occasionally to someone who is absent,
especially if one is somewhat acquainted with him—. However, it is not really to you personally that I have dared to write,
[*deleted*: when I have mailed this I will not be able to understand where I got the courage] it is merely to the author of
your works and to the man who delivered your sermon[2] last

Sunday in the Citadel, for when all is said and done, it is he who made the cup run over for me. If only you would preach more often, but please, always with your name posted, for you cannot know how many souls you may save from perdition by so doing. It is your clear duty. For me that day was a festival day of upbuilding, and I think many came to feel as I did. Now, if you believe that I have managed to say one twentieth of what I wanted to say to you, you are wrong, but now I shall, as a matter of form, stop as I sign myself with gladness and gratitude

> One of your most devoted female readers,
> S. F.

[*Address:*]
Magister S. Kierkegaard.
108 Østerbro, by the lake.

[*Postmark:*]
F: 62 3/5   51 P.

279. *H. P. Kofoed-Hansen—July 11, 1851—S. K.*

You are probably not expecting a letter from me, although I would be pleased if you were, for then I would know that my letter had reached its true destination. After all, I am entitled to consider myself obliged to write to you anyway. This is the consequence you will have to put up with for taking people under your wing, this time at least insofar as it applies to me.

For although I have not—as you predicted I would—thought more about you here than I did in Copenhagen—nor would it have been easy for me to fulfill that prediction—I have in any case thought about you just as much, and this thinking has increased as I have gradually become accustomed to the new surroundings[1] and arranged things so that they have become more and more familiar to me. And now everything around me will soon seem familiar once again. I have accustomed myself—in a manner of speaking—to being neither fish nor fowl, that is, neither a Danish nor a German clergyman but both at the same time, and moreover I have accustomed myself to being a married man. With respect to the latter, there is a host of possibilities, and with respect to the former, it will have to remain that way until the Germans again get the notion of muddying the waters for us. So in my opinion it may very well be that the latter will get worse than the former.

On alternate Sundays and Holy Days I preach alternately in German and in Danish. This is an unhappy state of affairs, although one might say, as I to my own unspeakable surprise could say from the very beginning, that it is easier for me to compose a German than a Danish sermon. Can you solve that riddle? In the beginning it was difficult for me to *deliver* a sermon in German because I dared not deviate from my manuscipt. In desperation I came close to relying on the manuscript once again, in Danish as well, until I turned the desperation in another direction and put it, as well as the German one, aside. Since then it has been a matter of indifference to me which language I use. What pains and troubles me most is the alternation itself and my fear that my Danish will come to suffer from it.

By custom and preference it is expected here that a pastor ought to be able to eat and drink well and chat gaily and jovially with people, especially at baptisms, weddings, and funerals. Whatever else he is able to offer is considered less important. Very few attend the services. The church is one of the most beautiful I have seen, built in true, pure Gothic.

From the above you may gather that I am as a rule more pleased with my German than with my Danish sermons, which is a fact that has often saddened me. I have frequently thought that I delivered a really good sermon in German; I have almost never had that feeling about the Danish ones. However—I believe I can venture to say or assume about myself that I have truly made progress as a preacher with respect to the clarity of my exposition—albeit unfortunately mostly in German—and the liveliness of my delivery. I trust that I can say that this has been so until now; I also trust that I shall be able to maintain it, although that is difficult when one cannot manage to arouse any interest or response. You may safely conclude that political circumstances contribute *some-thing* to this. Still, I do know that those who sympathize with the Germans have nothing against me, and I have been told that I made a favorable impression on them when I was in-stalled here. You realize that I do not participate in any sort of politics whatsoever.

The most unfortunate place for a preacher to find himself is, I do believe, a provincial town, for there is almost no audi-ence to be had. In a capital it is possible, after all, even though it is mainly on account of the large population.

Strangely enough, one thing you said to me the last time we talked together has often cropped up in my mind. It was occasioned by the remarks with which I took leave of the congregation—or rather of my audience—at Christianshavn. "There you see," you said, "how dangerous it is to be a speaker." At that moment your words touched a rather sensi-tive spot, and I was unable to produce the question, "Why?" It has often resounded in my soul, but I suppose that now I shall never have a reply, probably not even if I were to talk with you.

I have begun reading a treatise[2] about you in *Tidsskrift för Literatur*, ed. Bergstedt (Stockholm). No doubt you have read it with only moderate edification. So far I have only read the beginning and that without any edification.

It is only recently that my duties have begun to leave me any time to myself. I have plans for two pamphlets in my head, but I do not know if they will get any further than that, because for me preaching and speaking are still, strictly speak-ing, like producing, and therefore I have very little energy left for anything else.

It would probably be superfluous to observe that my letter is not one of those that require the methodical consequence of a reply, just as it is superfluous to observe that were it to do so, it would be appreciated. I have written to you because I have often missed you and longed to talk with you. Goodbye! God be with you!

Yours sincerely,
H. P. KOFOED-HANSEN.

Haderslev, July 11, 1851.

280. *Petronella Ross—July 12, 1851—S. K.*

Østerbro, July 12, 1851.

Doctor S. Kierkegaard:

May I, a complete stranger, be so bold as to ask you to do me a favor? Would you lend me your most recently published book, *Christian Discourses*, for a while? If you have only one copy and are reluctant to part with it, you might perhaps lend me one of your other works that you will not need to have returned in too much hurry. If I could talk with you, I would call on you in person. I know your brother on Sjælland,[1] and in my youth I was a friend of his first wife, Marie B.;[2] for many years I lived in the late Bishop Møller's[3] house (you knew Poul Martin,[4] his dear son). Bishop Boisen's wife placed me there. I lost my hearing after the Bishop's death, and I am now living in a small home for ladies on Falster.[5] I enliven my solitude by testing my writing talents. A couple of little tales set in a village have been published with the assistance of *Etatsraad* Sibbern;[6] he has entitled them *Tales for Unsophisticated Readers by Fr. Godtkjær*.[7] I am not particularly happy with that pseudonym, but let it be. —There are a number of misprints in the last brief installment published by Steen's. If I dared to think you would read these little pieces, I should be pleased to send them to you. —At present I am visiting my mother, Mrs. Ross, at Suhms-minde at Søllerød;[8] she is ill and has been so for a long time. I am staying with my brother, Captain Ross, 107 Østerbro,[9] for a few days. If you would be willing to lend me a book, it could be left here. Recently I read a few pages of "The Cares of Lowliness."[10] Thank you, good doctor, for every shaft of light with which you enlighten the dark lives of your fellow man, "dark," I suppose, because the eyes are not truly open.—

Your sincerely obliged,
PETRONELLA ROSS.

P.S. I would be very grateful if you would occasionally be so kind as to find the opportunity to lend me some good book or other that you think would be truly beneficial to me.

All of this may be, or appear to be, a somewhat peculiar whim on my part, but in a manner of speaking my hands are tied, or I should go to the bookseller and choose among your works. I cannot hear your homilies, and you do say something that fortifies me.—

If my mother were not ill I would have preferred to apply to you through her.

[*Address*:]
Dr. S. Kierkegaard
Østerbro.

281. *S. K.—1851—J. L. Heiberg. S. K.'s draft.*

Dear Sir:

Although I almost have reason to fear that receiving this little pamphlet[1] may once again cause you some discomfort by letting you sink deeper into a debt that you have repeatedly assured me that you hoped soon to rid yourself of by returning the favor, surely you will easily be able to understand that I, who know best how insignificant my gifts are and how insignificant the giver is in comparison with the recipient, cannot in this case give in to such an unreal fear; I must instead reverse the relationship and consider this a new debt I owe to you or as an old debt to you into which I am sinking more deeply because once more you have the kindness to be willing to accept such an insignificant little gift from the insignificant author of all these insignificant gifts.

Yours respectfully,   S. K.

282. *S. K.—[August 1851]—J. L. Heiberg. S. K.'s draft.*

Honorable *Etatsraad*:

Please pardon my inconveniencing you. Would you be so kind as to give your wife the accompanying little parcel intended for her?

Just as that resolute number three, of which Socrates speaks, would rather put up with anything except becoming

number four,[1] with just such persistence have I, probably
making a nuisance of myself to you, clung to my original decision that you must have a copy of everything that comes
from me. I realize fully the truth of what you once told me in
a conversation, that I shower you with books; I realize it so
well that I understand that it is you, Mr. E.,[2] who, while I
persistently followed my inclination, have shown resolute-
ness or patience by being willing to withstand these steady
showers.

Permit me then to make a small change for once. You
hereby receive a copy of a little book.[3] But at the same time
another one[4] has been published, and I have been so bold as to
designate it for your wife. This is certainly not done for reasons of economy or because I have changed, indeed not, but
as I had decided to send a copy to your wife in any case, I was
afraid that it would be altogether too much with these showers, since there would then be two copies.

Yours respectfully,

283. *S. K.*—[*August 7, 1851*]—*Johanne Luise Heiberg*.[1]

To

That happy artist
whose perception and determination were nonetheless
—happily once again!—exactly equal
to her happiness,

Mrs. Heiberg
with admiration
from

the author.

It is not, not even remotely, my intention with this to persuade you in any way to read a little book that in the final
analysis, and perhaps long before then, would probably be
boring and exhausting.

No! But somewhere in the book[2] mention is made of a
small essay on esthetics by a pseudonymous *Inter et Inter*,

"The Crisis and a Crisis in the Life of an Actress,"[3] *Fædrelandet* (1848), no. 188-91. If by any chance you happened to notice this article at the time, it would please me if I might tell myself that you, Mrs. Heiberg, were aware that this article belongs among my works, as will be evident from this book. If you did not notice this article at the time, then it is the author's wish that you might find some idle hour that could be filled by reading it. For if you—I request this only for a moment and on behalf of this subject—if you will permit me to say this in all sincerity, that little article has special reference to you. Whether it was read at that time by many or only by a few—if you did not read it, then it is the author's opinion that it has not reached its destination. But on the other hand, if you have read it—if it was then found to be, if not in perfect, yet in happy accord with your thoughts on that subject, then it is the author's opinion that it has indeed reached its destination.

[*Address:*]
To
Mrs. Heiberg.

[*Added in pencil by J. L. Heiberg:*] 1851.

284. *O. L. Bang—August 17, 1851—S. K.*

Copenhagen, August 17, 1851.

The other day, upon returning home, I found[1]
On my desk two beautiful vessels[2]
Of raven-black marble edged with gold.
"Who," thought I "can have given me these?"
I raised the lid and saw in each a dish
With the stamp of "Kirkegaard,"[3] but did not fear
That the meaning was that at which
A superstitious person might easily arrive.

There was no death between the lid and base,
But there was life, both in Friday's fare
And in the other, which not without reason

May be assumed to be the butter and the cheese
That is served as the last course at so many tables;
I sampled both, and I can still taste
That Søren-sauce, which most certainly
Will please, with a few exceptions, every gourmet.

Just let that common man who loves gruel
And pork stew and cabbage and peas and
Everything similar offered his fine palate
Not find that he likes this. To feed his body
And fill his belly is his own affair;
The alcohol that he prefers is of the light kind,
Which evaporates quickly and intoxicates for but one day;
It would be a waste to offer him liqueur.

So I did accept the dishes, but
I only sampled them a bit,
For with Flora I fled at once my home
To hide myself in a castle[4] on Lolland.
It was of course the patients whom
I did not want to discover me,
And I was lucky enough to reach those coasts
Where the glittering waves of the Baltic roll.

Here the Sophie[5] whom you know
From *Eva Homo*[6] and from Blancogade[7]
Had just finished five weeks' residence
But would not yet leave the castle.
That castle is Aalholm, of great renown,
Whose yard-thick, strong red walls
Have not yet been sentenced to destruction
But stand unshaken, albeit with the furrows of old age.

Now my wife and children dwelt there,
And thither I hastened with the dishes sent to me.
And over them, indeed like a hungry eagle,
The mother and the daughter swooped, and I assume
That they were sated, both of them.
I do not know for sure, for the next day I myself
Returned home in order with my claw again
To plunge into errant blood and wasted strength.

In other words, to be with my sick patients,
To be what I would always want to be:
Nature's servant and her truthful spokesman
Who politely leaves art quietly alone.
That is possible for the physician who merely
Cares for bodies; but that is not so, unfortunately!
For him who has the care of souls, as long as
Nature is unruly lord in that abode.

I am ashamed when now I look
On what you gave me and on what I sent,
The stew that left my kitchen,
In which you surely recognized the cooking skill
That often in the field turns into cooks
The lad with fife, the Captain's groom.
You must have found it inedible with the first spoonful
And been unable to stand the martyrdom of eating more.

Yes, stew, thin soup with a few
Raisins in it, served in a clay bowl—
I see it clearly now, that *Eva* was a trifle,
Which I so recklessly sent to you,
While you brought wholesome game
Well roasted in Søren's oven and with plum relish
And other fruits conserved in spirits
Of which your cellar is never empty.

I honestly confess that I quickly repented
That Eva had been called to life by my song
And no less that I had offered her
The surname I never should have used.
Surely no one realizes as well as I
How poor this Eva looks by Adam's side,[8]
But it is useless to be wise after the fact,
For I have *sinned* and must suffer now.

But what is this? —I see that page three
Has already been filled by my busy pen,
And now, if I, like everyone, might know
That at home you have one resembling it,

I would let apologies pour forth from it.
I know in advance that you will forgive
And that you will judge my sin with mercy;
My warrant for that is—your love.

That love that fills all the pages
On which you set down your rich thought
Is so beautiful, so holy, and does no harm
Like that upon which my poor Eva foundered.
Yes, it is that I rely upon, when confidently
I send this letter to that churchyard[9] [*Kirkegaard*].
Which is not Death's but Life's abode,
Where this daily arises from each grave.

For now, farewell! Until possibly in a lane,
In a square or street or doorway
We have pleasure in an accidental meeting,
As I at any rate have often had,
Farewell, and do not turn up your nose too much
At what I wrote; but enough for now!
Now Hygeia calls me to her work
And tears Oluf Bang away from his muse.

Magister
Søren Kierkegaard.

285. *Emil Boesen—September 25, 1851—S. K.*

Dear friend,

Many thanks for sending me your three most recent
books.[1] I have not even thanked you yet for the first of these,
The Woman Who Was a Sinner, but you know how happy it
makes me whenever I see your handwriting on an envelope.
It came at a time when there was a great deal of fuss and
bother here over Spandet's proposal,[2] which has been rather
confusing for the people in this region, and I was longing to
hear something from you. Perhaps you did not have that affair in mind at all when you published it,[3] but I read it to my

upbuilding with reference to that and enjoyed it very much. Your article in *Fædrelandet*[4] appeared soon after, and by means of it you have quite succeeded in winning over the Jutlanders. Of the *Communion Discourses* I have given particular attention to the last one. The other book, on your activity as an author, surprised me a little when I first read it; I did not think you would express yourself so explicitly at this time, and it also seemed as if you were saying goodbye;[5] but later I read it again without any mental reservations. Now I see that you have published a major work,[6] but as yet it has not arrived over here; I do hope it will come one of these days.

How are you otherwise? Are you in good health? You could, after all, write me a few words once in a while so that I might know where you live. Last summer Steenstrup[7] told me that you were living out at Østerbro. Are you still living there? Louise asks me to send greetings. A little boy named Johannes[8] is lying in his cradle in her room, and it is strange to look at him. Soon after the stork brought him, it returned and bit her breast so badly that she was bedridden for a long time, but now she is well again and is decorating the house with flowers.

My sermons are going as well as might be expected. At least I take great pains to make them as good as possible. On Saturday I often sit quietly for several hours without writing a thing. The pen does not begin to move more quickly until evening, and I am not finished until 10 p.m., which bothers Louise, who must postpone supper for me until then. Sunday is far too taxing, but that is partly because there is something wrong with all that studying. I would like to go to Copenhagen when the Confirmations are over in the middle of October, but I do not yet know if I am going, especially since I would also like to go next spring.

Please write to me once in a while!

Your   EMIL BOESEN.

Horsens, September 25, 1851.

This letter has now been lying here for a few days, and I have read your last book.[9] What a good thing it is that you published it. We are all in great need of having it constantly impressed on us where we stand.

[*Address:*]
S. T.
Magister S. Kierkegaard
Østerbroe near Copenhagen

[*Postmark:*]
10/3

286. *S. K.—[after October 1851]—J. P. Mynster.*
S. K.'s draft.[1]

To His Excellency, the Right Reverend Bishop, Dr. Mynster:

In a recently published little pamphlet, *On Mag. K.'s Activity as an Author; Observations by a Village Pastor,*[2] there is, in spite of the arrogant tone, a good deal of dishonesty, a good deal of pure gibberish, a good deal of dialectical obscurity—I have nothing to say. In the postscript my most recent book (*For Self-Examination*) is dealt with in an almost indecent way. I have nothing to say. Even though the village pastor were not anonymous, I would probably still have nothing to say.

But toward the end of the postscript there is a remark that in a way concerns you, Right Reverend Bishop, or rather my relationship to you,[3] or the manner in which I have permitted myself in my latest publication, *For Self-Examination,*[4] to describe my, the younger person's, relationship to "the venerable old man." This concerns me very much indeed. That it does so, that it concerns me very much indeed, will, I hope, serve as my excuse for inconveniencing you in print.

And now to the quotation from my book and then to what the village pastor says.

Now I will not discuss the fact that in my opinion it is an impertinence on the part of the anonymous village pastor almost to want to appropriate your *partes* to himself in that way, to speak in a manner that only one person is entitled to affect with respect to that affair, you yourself, Right Reverend

Bishop, who, in any case, even though you might have
wanted to say something similar, surely would not have said
it in the same manner.

But to my point! Occasioned by this published remark by
the village pastor, I should like—pardon this!—to refer the
question to you, whether you are of a similar opinion,
whether you disapprove of my having in some way attempted to define my relationship with you.

Whenever Bishop Mynster is involved, I am, as everybody
knows, immediately ready to serve. I try immediately to obtain reliable information—as I have done by addressing you
yourself, Right Reverend Bishop. Only one word from you
and I shall be available immediately with every additional bit
of information; *item*, if there is anything erroneous in what I
have said, anything untrue, I shall immediately retract it.
That which I suppose most younger people have received
transmitted to them by their elders, but which I have received
to a very special degree from my late father, reverence and
devotion for—him whom I should so much like to call—"the
venerable old man," κατεξοχην—that I have honestly maintained to the best of my ability. I shall, I hope, follow Your
Excellency with the same devotion until the very end—and
even though some anonymous village pastor may think that I
am pursuing you with that devotion, I do not intend to let
that upset me. Indeed, even though you yourself were of the
same opinion—My God! what could I do? Anything as in-
grained in my being as my devotion to you cannot be altered.

287. *H. N. Clausen—November 8, 1851—S. K.*

Magister Kierkegaard:

Though I hardly dare expect any particular interest on your
part, dear sir, in the accompanying historical-dogmatic
study,[1] this thought cannot make me refrain from wanting to
put it into your hands nevertheless, as I hope that in any case
you will find proof in it of my desire to demonstrate in more

than mere words my appreciation for those beautiful gifts[2] I have received from your hand.

> With high esteem and gratitude,
> Yours respectfully,
> H. N. CLAUSEN.

Copenhagen
November 8, 1851.

288. *S. K.—[1851]—H. N. Clausen.*[1]

Reverend Professor:

That the same hand may both wound and heal I have come to realize from the brief note that accompanied your latest work sent to me as a gift from the author's hand. For how wounding it is when you say "that you hardly dare expect any particular interest on my part in the accompanying historic-dogmatic study"; how wounding! Good Lord, I did after all graduate with highest honors in theology—and then to have *summus Theologus* at my own university tell me that sort of thing, how wounding! But then again, how healing that in spite of this the reverend author "cannot make himself refrain from wanting to put the work into my hands," will indeed even do so himself, will send me a copy, thus lending the gift twice as much weight; or rather, how more than healing, inasmuch as there is twice as much healing as wounding. So do permit me to thank you for it.

But my thanks arrive somewhat late, or so at least it seems to me. Yet why? The instant I received the gift I instantly wanted to thank you for it in a few words. "But," thought I, "to do so instantly would be inconsiderate, for it would imply that you have not read the book." Accordingly, I have waited considerately until I finished the book, and on account of this waiting my considered thanks arrive—inconsiderately?—somewhat late.

> With respect and veneration,
> Yours sincerely,
> S. KIERKEGAARD.

[*Address*:]
To
The Very Reverend Professor
Dr. H. N. Clausen
Commander of *Dannebrog*.

289. *"S.S.M. No. 54"* [*Ilia Marie Fibiger*][1]—*November 21, 1851—S. K.*

If it is not possible for the blind trust with which I approach you for a favor to provide me with an excuse, then I do not know where I shall find an excuse. I do not know you, either personally or as an author, for my brain has always been far too feeble to follow you; yet this much I did feel whenever I put the book aside once more without having read it, that you must find it just as easy to understand others as others might find it difficult to understand you. It is understanding that I am in need of, and I appeal to you with no other justification than my knowledge that you can and my hope that you will grant me what I need.

This does, to be sure, make some demand on your time. I would like to ask you to read through the accompanying plays and to give me your opinion of them. The first play, *M. S.*,[2] was submitted anonymously about a year ago, and last summer I received a reply[3] I believe I may call fairly favorable, even though the play was returned because the subject had been dealt with so recently. There was also some talk of a few minor modifications, although not as any specific condition. Then the next one, *Fairy Tale*,[4] was submitted but rejected. To be truthful, this surprised me, considering what has been accepted this year. But I know very well how ignorant I am in practical matters, and I have such good reasons for doubting my own talents that I would have relied on Heiberg's decision, had he not stated his reasons for it. But his principal objection happened to concern a particular point where I am sure I know more than he does. *H. and S.*[5] has not been submitted.

The world is, as you know, so peculiar that I suppose I

must assure you that I have no intention of taking advantage of your opinion, even if it were to be more favorable than the *Etatsraad*'s.[6] I am not looking for an authority to lean on but for the inner assurance implicit in an impartial and thoughtful evaluation. My becoming a writer was unintentional. In my youth I had poetical friends,[7] but I could not understand why they had such a great desire to write; I felt like living. All of a sudden, just at the time when the last trace of the poetic light usually fades for others, it dawned for me—or so it seemed to me—and I was writing as a matter of course. And how strange it is: when something has been written, it is as if it must then reach others. Since I could not have my plays performed, I considered having them printed. Yet I am but ill suited for battle; I have not yet made any attempt but am already tired. My faith in my calling has been blind, precisely because it has never been my wish to pursue this path, so that even now when it seems to be frustrated, I cannot view it as a misfortune—it is merely that I should really like to know. Now I am tired. Perhaps this is something passing, perhaps it is because I have finished my work. I do not know whether I can get it published, indeed I hardly know whether I even desire it at the moment. But I do feel that I need to hear the opinion of someone in whose judgment I dare place my blind trust. I know of no one better than you, and just as I freely invoke the rights of the weaker, I hope that you will be willing to assume the responsibilities of the stronger, to read these three plays, the major and most important part of what I have written, and then to tell me what you think.

Early next month I shall send someone to inquire at the postal delivery office, where I would request you to leave your reply marked "S.S.M. No. 54." I am ashamed to add that I would like to ask you not to speak of this matter to anybody, but I am afraid that, owing to custom, not to ask for silence might in fact seem to stamp this as a wish to publicize the matter.

November 21, 1851.
To
Magister S. Kierkegaard.

290. *C. R.* [1]—*[1851-52]—S. K.*

A complete stranger takes the liberty of appealing to your generosity with a request, the immodesty of which he fully appreciates, while at the same time he also hopes that you, familiar as you are with our literary affairs, will not think the worse of him on this account. One of our booksellers[2] has offered to publish the enclosed manuscript, without any royalties in any event, provided that upon publication it is furnished with a commendatory preface by one of our literary notables. As it is important to me to hear a public opinion of it, I take this opportunity to appeal to your generosity with the request that you read it when you have a free moment in order to see whether it merits a recommendation from your hand and whether you dare and are willing to take it upon yourself to furnish one when it is published. For several reasons I desire that the strictest anonymity be observed upon publication, which is why I also ask you not to investigate my identity but to leave the manuscript with your much-appreciated reply in a sealed parcel as soon as possible at *219 Nørrevold, 2 floor, by the door directly opposite the stairway* at noontime between 12 and 1 p.m.

I consider any assurance of my gratitude superfluous.

Yours respectfully,   C. R.

291. *Rasmus Nielsen—February 4, 1852—S. K.*

Thursday, February 4, 1852.
Dear Magister,

As I am feeling unwell, I am prevented from going walking today.

Yours,   R. NIELSEN.

S. T. Mag. Kierkegaard.

[*Address:*]
S. T.
Magist. Kierkegaard.

292. *L. H.—March 19, 1852—S. K.*

March 19, 1852.

L. H.

Perhaps you will think it strange to receive a letter from someone completely unknown to you. —Yet, if I have understood you even a little, I do not believe that you will dismiss me as a woman with a desire to do something strange (that would, to tell the truth, if anything be repellent to me) or consider this "writing to you in such a light, but in my soul dwells such profound gratitude that I feel compelled to express it to you." I have read your *For Self-Examination*, your *Practice in Christianity*;[1] indeed I *have read them* as best I could with all my soul, and I *believe at least* that I have understood the *spirit* in them. Through you I have learned to understand myself better; you have, as it were, relieved me of one of my most profound afflictions, that of being misunderstood by those whom one loves and, while understanding one's own feelings, of not being able to make oneself understood by others, and finally, the most unbearable thing of all, of being *uncertain* at times whether this inability to go along with the others in many of their views might not be due to the extreme selfishness of *not sufficiently* agreeing with the others because it is so difficult to let go of that which in one's own view has become the truth—and yet I fully recognize that for *them* this is the truth. I have prayed with all my heart that the Holy Spirit would make it clear to me whether I might be allowed to keep for *my own* that which I understood, that in which I found rest, which I could bring into harmony with the simple, true fundamentals of Christianity, whether I would then have to forego being understood by the others and leave it up to them whether they could find Christianity in my life with them. I was not brought up as a Christian, but the deepest love prevailed in my blessed home; I knew no fear; but my mother, who herself possessed the most tender conscience, enjoined us always to let that be the judge of our actions; yet, subsequently, when the world and the things that are in the world did not offer anything in which my soul could find rest and after God had taken *that* away from me in which I had believed I might find happiness here on earth (for I had made earthly love my false god), then I prayed and prayed again until I saw clearly where that consolation was to be found that could help one to endure this life with confidence and joy and to attain the goal with faith, hope, and charity. —Now I live among good Christian people whom one can love whole-heartedly, but they belong to a so-called faction (that of Grundtvig). I am opposed to everything that is factional, for in my view it disrupts the life of charity, places concise, conspicuous limitations upon it, as in the drastic assertion that "this person is a Christian, and this one is not." Who but God dares to say this? I recognize most clearly the life of faith here, but it seems to me as though the life of charity lacks true fervor and does not go hand in hand with the former (and so pride comes to rear its head); but let me not, narrow-mindedly and unjustly, merely to prove to myself that I am right, condemn the beliefs of a man about whom I myself know very little, just because I happen to observe that they are well accepted [*may be read as*: grossly misunderstood] by the others and because it seems to me that the spirit assumes such a peculiar, obstinately predetermined form that in my view it imparts a prejudiced quality to *"that man"* whose very *language* they employ when they speak of Christian matters. —How is it possible for me to express that which truly fills me and which has been truly accepted by my soul, which has become *my own*, when I have to express it in an alien form? If the *spirit* is present, will not the form follow as a matter of course? Or am I now the one who lacks clarity? —With *all* those whom they call "the enlightened" they speak freely whenever they meet. —I *cannot* do so; for me it would be false to talk *exclusively* about Christendom—in order, as they put it, to feel the joy of congregational life. To my way of thinking, Christianity thereby loses fervor. With all my heart I would like to approach the afflicted and the sufferer willing to understand me with charity and show him or her where I *myself* find peace and comfort (for example, how often have I not found them in "The High Priest"[2]), but I am never allowed to introduce such Christian talk, for they do not believe that the life of faith can exist in someone who is unable or unwilling to express himself in their manner. This, you see, *troubled me* at first, for I felt that Christianity could never manifest itself in me in that way—and yet these people must be acknowledged as true Christians (as indeed they are), but—in *your* works I have found that which suffices for me in this respect, for that which most profoundly and sincerely captivates my soul will always fill me with *silent* bliss, which I do indeed feel a need to communicate to those I love through my life and behavior toward them, even though I am unable to put my bliss into words for them. Still, it is possible that they find it hard to understand such a contradiction in my nature, for there are many other things I can talk about in a quite lively manner. I can readily imagine that my Christian joy would be enhanced by talking about it with one individual—even though he has different views—who might feel and recognize the identical spirit. They have a profound, general awareness of sin, yet it seems to me that they do not—as *you*, Dr. Kjerkegaard, did in your writings in which you have singled out the component parts of sin—in their own hearts acknowledge what *you* proclaim; they do not say: "*You are the man.*"[3] But if I am now becoming uncharitable and perhaps unjust, it is not because I want to blame those whom I love but because I must explain to myself why I so frequently cannot share their views. —This, you see, may appear to be a childish and insignificant affliction to *you*, but it is not insignificant when love for those people is great, yet love of truth is greater still, and the mind does not possess sufficient clarity to defend that which one feels has the ring of truth. I have now tried to explain why my soul is filled with gratitude for your having led me to self-understanding, thus bringing more peace and less sadness to my heart. It is not to the clever, brilliant, and satirical Dr. Kjerkegaard that I am writing this, for he might smile pityingly at the muddle-headedness that lies in my thinking that I can understand him. —Certainly I am far from being able to do so with my reason, but I believe that I am able to do so with my feelings (something at which the modern, intellectually enlightened woman would probably scoff, but which I must believe in, for whenever I have prayed to the Holy Spirit to give me purity of feeling, that has always brought me farther on the path to awareness than reason has). No, it is not to the clever Dr. Kjerkegaard that this is written, but to him who seems to me to comprehend all the inwardness of Christianity and who because of this inwardness will understand the feeling and need that made me, *contrary to my custom*, go so much outside myself that I *had to say thank you*; but here I shall remain silent about all this, for I cannot argue about feelings, yet the heart still feels compelled just this once to express its thanks, even though I now see that I have been egotistic enough to bore you with such a long letter, and I become terribly ashamed, but my consolation will have to be that I have only expressed myself to *one soul* and that only two eyes will light on this, eyes that look deeply enough into the human heart to be indulgent. This is not the enthusiastic thanks of an eighteen-year-old girl, but the abundant, profound thanks of a thirty-four-year-old unmarried woman who stands alone among strangers but who has gained clearer awareness of her innermost being through you—and thereby more peace and more courage not to let herself be overwhelmed by feelings which cannot be the truth for her, more strength to fight the good fight with constancy.

Yours gratefully,   L. H.—

[*Address*:]
Doctor Søren Kjerkegaard
108 A Østerbro
Copenhagen.

[*Postmark*:]
F. 9 3/31 P. 3
[*Sealed with black wax and stamped with the signet*:] H. H.

293. *H. P. Kofoed-Hansen—March 30, 1852—S. K.*

So you will in fact hear from me once in a while. As you see, I do not treat that remark lightly, although less so than I

might have wished, for it seems to me that I must have received your letter a very long time ago, even though I do not
know exactly when, for it contains nothing that could indicate a date or the like. However, this much is apparent: it
must have been written during the summer months since you
speak of going swimming and of a benefit to be derived from
it, one that ordinary swimmers have probably never even
thought of, not even *die Helden des jungen Deutschlands* [the
heroes of the New Germany], whose swimming excursions
are conscientiously recorded in the German newspapers regardless of the fact that there is nothing to indicate that
they—*badenden Helden* [the swimming heroes], that is—profit
in the least from these swimming trips, not psychologically at
any rate, since what is said in II Peter 2:22 fits them much better.[1]

By the way, I believe that you have found the correct solution to the riddle[2] I posed, although I might want to add
something or other; for example, that it is undeniable that the
German language has a rhetorical forcefulness that often almost by itself tears the thought out of the soul—perhaps not
always for the best, for it also easily leads to *"Viel Geschrey
und wenig Wolle"* ["a lot of noise and little wool"].[3] The other
day I felt strongly in need of hearing a sermon, so I took some
time off and drove out into the country where I did indeed
hear a sermon that really was *lautere Wolle und gar kein
Geschrey* [pure wool and no noise at all] delivered by Pastor
Boisen[4] at Vilstrup.[5] That is how I would prefer to preach,
but I do believe that there is something German in me, for
when I most desire to hold myself in check, there is often
most *Geschrey*, whether in Danish or in German. In the sermon[6] I am sending you with this I am not sure whether there
is more *Geschrey* than the subject warrants or at any rate permits. When you have a moment, you might perhaps be kind
enough to tell me if there is. Although I have no particular
desire to publish a collection of sermons, I do occasionally
want to send one out into the world, but as it is likely that I
shall have to pay my fine even for this one—since I have not
been able to find a publisher—my treasurer will probably not

find it advisable. And perhaps you will not find it advisable, either, after you have read it. If so, then I shall in any case persist until I have scrambled up one more rung of the ladder. For I am aware of and thank God for my having already ascended one rung since I left Copenhagen.[7]

Had I not realized that you know how to evaluate human life in all its shadings, I would have marveled at the striking way in which you have been able to fathom all the reasons why I now have fewer opportunities for writing than before. Formerly I did not believe it could turn out this way; I believed, for example, that when one got married one would have more time to spare, and now I find that the opposite is the case, and how will it be when I—not too long from now, I hope—enter upon a new stage of human life and reap the consequences of my marriage in a living, tangible presence. It is a very special thing to be anticipating this, yet if that is so for the male, what must it be for the female?

And I also have all kinds of duties, and in general many more of them than any clergyman could possibly have in Copenhagen, for it would not fall to the lot of anyone there to have to preach five times in two weeks, alternating in two languages.[8] I suppose I could say that the weddings are the most burdensome for me, and then once in a while there are strange requests, such as the one yesterday from a skipper who asked me to celebrate Holy Communion tomorrow for himself and his wife, with the additional request that at an appropriate point in the confessional homily I say something comforting to her concerning his imminent departure. It is not yet quite clear to me how I can reconcile that with the one thing that is needful, although there is something inside me that whispers that one really could not wish for anything better for oneself.

Please consider yourself herewith thanked for the two pieces[9] you sent me last summer, the two discourses on judgment, which I have read with great benefit, one of them not without a certain—how shall I put it?—*horreur*, and this of course precisely because I was forced to recognize in it the truth that if one does not feel forgiveness it is because one is deficient in love. Otherwise I am happy in the feeling that I seem to myself to be growing in Christian insight, and I consider this a reward from Our Lord for my cumbersome task of teaching the Confirmation class, for that is the most troublesome of all and the job is a cumbersome one, almost more cumbersome than at Christianshavn, and "the certain reward is a small one."

Then I also thank you for *For Self-Examination*,[10] which you have not, to be sure, sent to me, but that will not help you, for somehow I get hold of everything you produce anyway. Whether the present day will heed what it recommends—well, I almost have to doubt that even though the second printing presumably has appeared, but in any case there will come a day when it will be heeded. The same Pastor Boisen mentioned above gave a lecture at the town club a while back on the Danish proverb, "Many a battle has been fought in the Øresund after which nothing is known,"[11] and among other things he said that there were two kinds of Øresund, the great one through which the ships sail to Copenhagen, and the little Øresund through which one sails into the harbor of the human heart. But it sometimes happens that one cannot reach the harbor by way of that sound, and this might be due to several reasons, among others, that there is no harbor to be found but merely a desolate empty space. Ever since then I often tell myself that many a battle has been fought in the Øresund after which nothing is known, but all the same, one cannot help striking the blow in the hope that it might after all hit some part of the target.

You are waiting to see what I am capable of when I put my mind to it. I do want to accomplish a lot, but I do not know whether I am capable of it. Sometimes it seems to me that I am capable of a good deal; at other times I have other views. But indeed I do not have much time. In any case I shall bide my time, for I do know that somehow it will come and that I cannot escape it then, and I also hope that I will be of good courage no matter what is demanded of me. As it happens, I did not feel courageous when I went to Christianshavn as a clergyman.[12] That was the most daring moment of my life, and it was not until I had declined it that I clearly saw that I ought to have accepted it, and there was one minute left to change my mind, which I took; and, thank God, I have not had any reason to regret it. —I notice that the reverse has been the case with Martensen in regard to the Superintendent's position[13] over here: after he had accepted, it became clear to him that he ought to decline it and he had time enough to change his mind. I almost believe that he will come to regret it at some point. I would have liked having him over here, for I do believe it would have been the best thing for us, although what I have learned since then has caused me to waver slightly in my opinion. One thing is certain: it will be a lofty undertaking rich in blessings for whoever comes here as Superintendent or Bishop if he has the abilities and the will. I hope we get a man who has both. Where to find him? Come over here yourself! There is a lot to be done here. If only I knew C. Moltke[14] as well as my wife does, then I would propose that he kidnap you by force and install you in the Bishop's throne at Slesvig, for I do not suppose that you would come willingly.

I was very surprised to receive a letter from you and so quickly too, for I almost believed that you had a *horror naturalis* of letter writing, and needless to say, the surprise I felt belongs under the heading of "happiness." Now I have sent you another letter, but the fact that I received such a speedy reply to my last one would not prevent my happiness from being just as substantial as the last time, were the same thing to happen once again. I assume that you are not inclined to engage in a regular correspondence, but if you were, then there would be quite a number of things I should like to ask. So I prefer to write the kind of letter to you that may have consequences or may not have consequences, depending on whether it annoys you or does not annoy you. I do not really know where my letter ought to seek you out, and therefore I am giving it an indeterminate address[15] and trust you do not have so much trouble with the name of S. Kierkegaard that my letter will fail to reach you. To do what I did last time and write 43 Nørregade on the envelope would probably be no help, especially since I clearly remember that during that summer when I was in Copenhagen you were irritated by the sun's reflection from the cobblestone pavement[16] at that very number in Nørregade. I cannot really understand why you moved from Rosenborggade, unless perhaps it was because you had everything to lose and nothing to gain.

I live very comfortably on the outskirts of town, privately in a big house with a *small* garden that stretches down to a large lake on the edge of town and which I can see from many of the rooms. Perhaps I told you all this in my last letter, in which case I say what Pietro in *Pretiosa*[17] says—cribbed, as far as I remember from Shakespeare[18]—it will be singularly good for you to hear it one more time. It daily grieves my wife and me that they have separated the downstairs rooms by placing the kitchen in the middle, so that we are prevented from having our bedroom in line with our other rooms, for which reason our bedroom is now in one part of the house and then in another, just as with Cromwell,[19] and consequently we frequently hold family councils about how we might afford the necessary change. *Die ärgsten Nüsse des Lebens* [The most annoying nuisances in life]—as I once heard the late composer Weyse[20] remark—*sind die Kümmernüsse* [are the puny ones]. We do have other *Kümmernüsse* as well, but otherwise we live very happily, now in German and now in Danish, for she is German born, although she does speak excellent Danish by now and with an accent that has a certain sweet sound to my ear, although I cannot vouch for others.

If I should happen to remember something I wanted to tell you—which is not at all unlikely—then I shall soon remedy that by writing a new letter. Goodbye!

Yours sincerely,
H. P. KOFOED-HANSEN.

Haderslev, March 30, 1852.

294. *S. K.*—*[April 1852]*—*Jonas Collin, the Elder. S. K.'s draft.* [1]

Your Excellency[2] did, I believe, receive a copy of the accompanying book some time ago, so I shall not venture to trouble you with yet another copy simply because a second edition has been published.[3]

Yet . . . . . well, you have probably seen too much already. For the address on the outside does give everything away. But please humor me—let us play a game! —Please humor me by pretending that you have not read the address; do it in order to please me, the child, and then perhaps you will see that what I have thought of is also intended to please the child, that dear child whose name is on the parcel.

You have a granddaughter, and let us simply put it like this: she is the apple of your eye. This is something I might have learned from many different sources, very remote ones. Were this the case, it would never have occurred to me to think of what I am doing here. But I have learned about this from the closest source, the very closest—from the grandfather himself, and in such a touching way that I am thoroughly persuaded that my idea is not a bad one.

Oh, Your Excellency, single as I am and living in solitude as I do, I have nonetheless made the acquaintance of what may be an extraordinarily large number of people and have had the opportunity to form some idea of the emotional relationship between one human being and another, of the love, the devotion, the care, etc., with which one person is bound to another, another person with yet another, etc. Alas, I am not the object of that love, that care, that devotion, etc. —I merely become a witness to that precious state, for, alas, it passes me by. Yet I venture to testify on my own behalf that I have rarely been envious of the fortunate person who was the object or impatient with my melancholy circumstances.

But at some point there comes to me an old man, a handsome old man, indeed, a very old man, a most lovable old man, indeed, that rare being who in every sense belongs to the first rank. He spoke of his granddaughter. This was not a discursive speech, nor was it delivered in solemn phrases; no, it was more a matter of the feeling, the manner, and the expression. —This, you see, became too much, was more than I could bear, and at first I became envious of this granddaughter: to be so deeply loved and by such a person! How beautiful; to my mind the relationship itself was that which was most beautiful: a very old man and his granddaughter! But what is most important in order for the relationship to be perfect is the very old man, the kind of person he is, for the granddaughter is, after all, the object, and thus it is unnecessary to know anything else about her, provided that the very old man is a given entity, for one may conclude that when the very old man is such-and-such a person and he loves his granddaughter so deeply, then she also deserves it, insofar as one may be said to deserve love. And imagine now, Your Excellency—but oh, perhaps there is something that makes it difficult to understand me completely in my happiness, something that prevents you from grasping as well as I do how very fitting it is that the very old man about whom I am speaking was precisely the right person! —Imagine; this very old man was *Geheimeraad* Collin!

And the very old man also told me that in this granddaughter I had a reader, a reader who thought she owed my work so much that nobody—yet, I have not forgotten what was said, but it ought not to be repeated.

Now my thought was as follows: "How would it be if we two old people (I am referring to the very old man and myself, whom I really consider the elder, regardless of the fact that in the preceding I have acted the part of the child and therefore cannot have grown much older since that time) were to join in pleasing this granddaughter"; more precisely, my thought was as follows: "What if you were to contribute your little bit to enable the very old man to give some small pleasure to his beloved granddaughter?" And I told myself, "You ought to do that," for—let us not forget it!—the very old man did once ask me if I did not feel like meeting his granddaughter, to which I replied with a most emphatic "no."

Therefore you are receiving the accompanying copy of *Works of Love*. In her turn, your granddaughter will receive it

from you; in other words, you are receiving it from me for
your granddaughter from you.

Does this please you? God knows that it pleases me, provided that it pleases you to whom I feel myself indebted for
the affection and good will you display towards me.

295. *S. K.—[April 1852]—Caroline Amalie, Queen of
Denmark. S. K.'s draft.*

It so happened that one day at Sorgenfri,[1] as I was presenting a copy of this book to the late Monarch,[2] a door opened to
a side chamber and was closed again at once. Bowing, I re-
treated a few steps as if to ask whether this signified that I
should leave. Then the Monarch said, "No, you may stay,
Mag. K.; I think that was the Queen; she has been wanting to
meet you. I shall go and get her now."

Thus I was left alone for a moment. If of all people I had
been the one least accustomed to filling a solitary moment, I
would still have managed to do so here. "How beautifully," I
thought—this was my immediate thought and I have often
subsequently thought so—"how beautifully and with what
admirable finesse Christian VIII always knows how to lend
the proper emphasis to things! He, the Monarch—and I, if I
were in any way the object of his royal favor—the Monarch
had within his power countless ways, thousands of ways, in
which to express his royal favor." But still, with respect to
every other way I might in solitude—but indeed I am alone at
this very moment, alone in the hall at Sorgenfri, left in utter
solitude to my own thoughts—I might perhaps have told myself, "However gratefully appreciative I am of that which I
dearly welcome as testimony of his favor, in some sense I do
not recognize Christian VIII in this." Solitary thoughts!

At that moment, by the King's side, entered the Queen.

I might now—my memory faithfully preserves it in grateful recollection! —I might now with epic precision continue
to detail what the King went on to say and what the Queen
then said; I might omit what I said myself—and thus to a rare
degree be assured of relating something interesting, some-

thing that, insofar as it would mean quoting the words of the departed, would be of particular interest to the exalted reader of these lines. What an enviable situation to be so certain of being interesting! Do pardon my going nonetheless to the opposite extreme of what is interesting and becoming boring, extremely boring, in venturing to bother you with the memory of one of my remarks, something I shall strive to remedy as best I can by quoting a remark by the late Monarch as well.

For when his Majesty the King had told the Queen in a few words that I was presenting a new book and had shown it to her, I was so bold as to address the following to the King: "Your Majesty puts me in an awkward position; had I known in advance that I would be so fortunate as to be presented to the Queen, I would have brought a copy with me especially for her." Christian VIII replied, "No, Mag. K., that is not necessary. The Queen and I will make do with one copy." How beautifully put by the King, how consistently in character with the beginning, how clearly I recognized once more in Christian VIII his incomparable flair for the one thing that was fitting. For surely this was the way to look at it all; the point of the royal favor being shown me was this: for one moment, as though with a magic wand, to transform the castle into a rural residence, the King and the Queen into a commoner's family where the husband goes out to get his wife, and where it is obvious that the husband and wife (and this is precisely what is most beautiful about the royal reply) can easily make do with one copy—of *Works of Love*. Indeed, among the crowned heads Christian VIII may have been the only one with a sufficiently liberal mind to think of something like that, and it is certain that he was absolutely the only one who was able to carry it out to perfection. For in order to bring about this transformation, a perfect invention of a liberal mind, radically opposite qualities were required: a King who in the ordinary course of events was so possessed of royal dignity that he would even lend to it his augustness and majesty, just as Christian VIII in fact did. In any other way it could easily become bad taste for a king to attempt to behave with a commoner's forthrightness.

But even though the late Monarch was correct in the enchantment he conjured up at that moment, I am also correct in my idea that—had I but known it in advance—I ought to have brought a copy with me especially for the Queen. Therefore I have decided that this is now the moment, now that the second edition has been published, now I must send a copy to the Queen.

Therefore, please be so kind, most gracious Majesty, to accept this copy, and permit me, in seeking to make amends for my former negligence, to do it in such a manner that I also strive to express the gratitude with which I preserve the memory of the late Monarch and the favor with which he smiled also upon me!

296. *Rasmus Nielsen—June 2, 1852—S. K.*

Magister!

As I am about to leave for the country, I must for the time being do without the pleasure of walking with you.

> With friendly regards,
> R. NIELSEN.

June 2, 1852.
S. T.
Magister Kierkegaard.

[*Address:*]
S. T.
Magist. Kierkegaard.

297. *H. P. Kofoed-Hansen—July 13, 1852—S. K.*

Lately it has not infrequently happened that I have found myself in conversation with you, insofar as this is possible when the person one is addressing lives many miles away so that one must provide the replies oneself on the basis of the premises one has from former times. I shall not burden you now with what we have been discussing. Yet there is one thing that has prompted such conversations, which really ought to have been dealt with in my last letter to you; however, because that which was to have been dealt with had already long ago become a thing of the past, I forgot it at the time and only remembered it a few days later. For I know that you sometimes reveal a familiarity with what is in the newspapers that borders on the amazing, and thus you might also have noticed a brief skirmish last fall—I no longer remember if it ran for more than two issues—in that laudable journal, *Dannevirke*,[1] which mainly concerned you. Even then I decided to inform you at some point that I have not written anything at all about you nor had anything printed anywhere at all since I was ordained, and that a newspaper is the last place I would do so. Just as I became a clergyman in spite of my great reluctance to speak in public, so I have also developed a great reluctance now to have anything printed. I have had to overcome the former reluctance, and perhaps it will also some day be my lot to overcome the latter.

And why should I not tell you that due to me the number of human beings has been increased inasmuch as my wife bore me a daughter[2] about a month ago?

And then you may as well be notified that apart from several other struggles in my inner man there is also this, that I have an extraordinarily strong desire to conduct Bible studies with my congregation, but I cannot overcome a fear that restrains me, a truly Protean fear. Now it disguises itself as my inability, now as the impossibility of getting anybody to attend, and now as the impossibility of finding an hour that will be convenient for people.

If you were ever to write to me—but perhaps you have given that up—then I should like to ask you about that strange society that according to *Berlingeren*[3] has been founded in Copenhagen and that is searching for the truth in religion after having become drunk on negation. I almost think that reading that announcement was the first time I felt the stirring of a quite vivid desire to have remained in Copenhagen. For then one would have something to fight against and would have no need of first identifying the opponent oneself. When one has gone along this way, having to speak and work in the very face of such indifference that it does not even bother to express itself, it would be a relief just for once to see the enemy come charging forth with armor and sword. But perhaps this is a mere Bajazzo[4] who masquerades in order to carry out some pretense at fencing. This, you see, is what I might enjoy knowing, but I suppose I shall get information about it in some way or other.

We have had a fight here about hymnals in which I did not participate, although I was in fact involved in the affair to the extent that I would like to introduce the Convention's[5] here. We are using the old Pontoppidan hymnal, and as I believe that the latter constitutes indigestible food for my congregation and I would prefer to give it milk, I attempted to make a change, said attempt foundering not on the opposition of the congregation but on the interference of outsiders. By the way, I confess that I, too, find the Pontoppidan hymnal fairly indigestible food. Oh, if only it had been the cause itself that had aroused a few of them on this occasion rather than selfishness, conceit, prejudice, and pride, for then I would not have had to eat so much indigestible food—in another sense—as I then got.

How I long to talk with you again, but unfortunately this is not likely to happen in the near future, for there is no prospect of my having to go to Copenhagen soon. One is reluctant to leave wife and child, and besides, travel money is not abundant.

Have you ever spoken with His old Excellency at Espe— Otto Moltke?[6] He is a splendid man of the old school, and as recently as last year he was still very lively and interested in everything in spite of his 83 years. Now he has unfortunately become afflicted with hypochondria and is depressed in body and soul. It occurred to me to ask you about this simply because you are, after all, acquainted with everybody, so much so that one ran the risk of meeting anybody on the stairs of the Athenæum[7] when one was with you. Said Count Moltke is my wife's grandfather.

Commended to God!

Yours sincerely,
H. P. KOFOED-HANSEN.

Haderslev, July 13, 1852.

298. *S. K.—[1852]*[1]*—A.C.D.F.G. Iversen.*

The enclosed copy that arrived in the mail was, as you see, intended for Dr. Rudelbach. On the assumption that as his publisher you keep in regular touch with him, may I ask you to do me the kind favor of forwarding it to him.

Yours respectfully,
S. KIERKEGAARD.

[*No address, but added in pencil*:]
Mr. Iversen, bookseller.
S. Kierkegaard.

299. *S. K.—[1854]—F. J. Mynster.*

Thank you, dear Pastor Mynster,[1] for remembering me with such affection! I found it, in all sincerity, most touching, and that is also why I shall keep your little note that accompanied the book you sent me.

But I cannot accept the book itself. My relationship with your late father[2] was of a very special kind. From the first time I spoke with him I told him privately and in as solemn terms as possible how much I disagreed with him. Privately I have told him again and again—and I shall not forget that he had so much good will that he listened to me with sympathy—that my principal concern was the memory of my late father.

Now that he has died, I must stop. Now I must and intend to have the freedom, whether or not I want to use it, to be able to speak out without having to take any such thing into consideration. And to that end I ought to deflect everything that might lead to any sort of misunderstanding that might be binding on me, such as accepting this book now, for example. For, as you in sending it to me declare (and that was noble of you!) that everything is as it used to be, so, in accepting it, I would declare that everything is as it used to be—but that is not the way it is.

Dear Pastor M., if this should have such an unpleasant and

disturbing effect that you do not believe that you will be able to maintain your affection for me, please be assured of one thing: I remain

Yours affectionately,   S. K.

[*Address*:]
To
Pastor Mynster.
Accompanying parcel.

299a. *S. K.—May 4, 1855—M. A. Kierkegaard*[1]

Great Day of Prayer

Dear Uncle,

Today the undertaker[2] came, did not find me, but left word that a carriage would come at a specified time to pick me up.

It is in this connection that I write you these few lines to tell you what I otherwise would have let you know through the undertaker: that you must excuse me. For many years, I have not attended the funeral service for anyone, not even the service for a close relative, which you, Uncle, know, for I did not attend the service for our Aunt in Gothersgade[3] nor for Nephew Andreas.[4] Therefore I probably would offend others who will be present if I were to make an exception in this case.

For this reason, dear Uncle, please excuse me. And perhaps you will also inform the undertaker, lest there be any misunderstanding and he sends a carriage to pick me up.

Greet Peter[5] from me.
Yours,   S. KIERKEGAARD.

[*Address*:]
To
Mr. Wholesaler M. A. Kierkegaard
Store Kjøbmagergade

300. *S. K.—July 19, 1855—C. A. Reitzel.*

All right, then, print only five hundred copies of *The Moment, No. 2*.[1] And then, if there is to be a second printing, as I promised you there would be, we will increase that to make it correspond with the originally proposed one thousand copies.

I shall remember the other matter.

Yours respectfully,
S. KIERKEGAARD.

To
Mr. Reitzel, bookseller.

[*Address*:]
To
Mr. Reitzel, bookseller.

ADDITIONAL LETTERS

The following letters cannot be placed chronologically or cannot be adequately identified.

301. *Chr. Ph. Spang—[1850-51]—S. K.*

Tuesday.

May I, dear Magister, ask you outright if you have Øehlenschlæger's memoirs?[1] If so, may I borrow them? But only if you will do so willingly and if there is no hurry about returning them.

I will not tell you that I, that we, miss you, for you are well aware of that. —I merely send you friendly greetings.

Sincerely yours,
C. SPANG.

[*Address*:]
Magister Kierkegaard.

302. *S. K.—no date—perhaps H. F. Lund's children.*
S. K.'s draft.

Dear friends,

Thank you for wanting to strew roses in my path this way! But meanwhile, that which is characteristic for my whole life will now undoubtedly recur: I never go where the path is strewn with roses—and so this carpet will probably have to be laid away [*in margin*: not as you have lovingly laid it beneath my feet, no, laid away and kept].

Nevertheless, thank you and thank you again. It was beautiful, and the color harmonies were nicely chosen, not without persuasive power, and gave me an un. . . .
[*The draft is incomplete.*]

303. *S. K.—no date—Carl Lund.*

My dear Carl,
  These books have been sent to me by Mr. Møller,[1] the bookbinder. Have you charged them to my account? Please let me know about it so that we do not end up paying for them twice.

Your uncle,   S. K.

[*Address:*]
To
Carl Lund
7 Store Kjøbmagergade

304. *S. K.—[July 2?, no year]—Carl Lund.*

My dear Carl,
  With this I am sending you a book for your birthday. You may have thought I had forgotten it and you, but you are wrong about that.

Your uncle,   S. K.

[*Address:*]
To
Carl Lund
7 Store Kjøbmagergade, 2 floor.

305. *S. K.—[1843-49]—Henrik Lund.*

Dear Henrich,
  A field is a field and a man is a man.

Your uncle.

[*Address:*]
Mr. H. Lund, student
7 Store Kjøbmagergade.

306. *S. K.—no date—Henriette Lund.*

As I have been unable to obtain that edition of *Figaro* that I had in mind for you, I am sending along *The Apothecary and the Physician*[1] with this.

S. K.

[*Address:*]
To
Miss Henriette Lund.

307. *S. K.—[no date]—Henriette Lund.*

It has subsequently occurred to me that I cannot very well lend you my copy of *Aus meinem Leben.*[1] But that is a book you will easily be able to obtain.

Your uncle.

[*Address:*]
To
Miss Henriette Lund

308. *S. K.—no date—Henriette Lund.*

My dear Jette,
The enclosed letter to Sophie did not reach her because she is in the country, so I am sending it to you with the request that you open it and read it, for it concerns you as much as it does her. Thus it is accidental that the letter to you becomes the envelope for a letter to Sophie; but only an accident could also establish this difference which does not otherwise exist between the letters, [*deleted:* for the letter to Sophie might just as well have served as an envelope for the letter to you in which I am asking you to] for one letter is *basically* no more of an envelope than the other—just as with reference to "the bellrope"[1] it is impossible to say which strand wraps itself around the other strand—it simply depends upon which one of them one *accidentally* begins with. And so it is with these

two envelopes of these two letters; the letter to Sophie might just as well have served as the envelope for a letter to you in which I asked you to greet Sophie from her or from

Your uncle.

[*Address*:]
To
Miss Henriette Lund.

309. *S. K.—no date—Henriette Lund.*

My dear Jette,

You will remember that the notebook with which you surprised me at the time arrived after the birthday..I assume that the bookbinder was at fault. Oh, those bookbinders, those bookbinders! Now a bookbinder has been at it again, for the piano anthology with which I hereby *surprise* you *after* the birthday would have reached you long ago, had not the bookbinder let time drag on in a most irresponsible manner—regardless of the fact that I told him that the book was intended for you.

Now, one thing is a jest, and another is something serious. Please accept the scores and enjoy the music, if you have the time or the opportunity or the inclination or the ability to familiarize yourself with it. If not, then put it aside for a more opportune time, and do believe me, although my good wishes may be wrapped in a bit of teasing at times, they are always basically well meant.

Your uncle, S. K.

[*Address*:]
To
Jette Lund.

310. *S. K.—no date—unknown diocesan dean. S. K.'s draft.*

Very Reverend Dean,

"Tea" is something I never drink. —"My brother" I have spoken with for two hours today. —For "the other sensible men" I entertain all conceivable respect and reverence. From you, Mr. Dean, I am hoping that as a "reasonable man" you will forgive me for not coming, and nevertheless—I beg of you—that you will permit me to remain

Yours,

311. *Anonymous—no date—S. K.*[1]

From one who is insignificant, as these lines testify, and in education as well, but who has nevertheless been granted the gift of being able to comprehend and receive your works, which are equally valuable to somebody who has not received any of those things that the world considers valuable, I feel powerfully within myself something that I cannot leave unsaid. I am far from daring to consider myself as that single individual—but I do consider myself as one who is eternally grateful for every word that proceeds from your hand.

S. T.

Magister Kierkegaard.

312. *S. K.—no date—anonymous.*

Dear Sir:

This is a peculiar affair. Why is your note anonymous? Since it is your son who delivers it, I might of course ask him for the name. But as you yourself do not give any name, I am of course not entitled to ask your son for it.

So it would be better if you were to come in person to me. Certainly it is laudable that a man wants to read, and surely it is an honest thing if a man cannot afford to buy a book.

Respectfully,
S. KIERKEGAARD.

DEDICATIONS BY
SØREN KIERKEGAARD

1. *The Concept of Irony, 1841*

(a)
To
    S. T., the Very Reverend Professor Martensen, Doctor of Theology.[1]

(b)
To my friend H. P. Holst[2]

from the author—

2. *Three Upbuilding Discourses, 1843*

(a)
To
    Professor J. L. Heiberg, Knight of *Dannebrog*[3]

most respectfully from the author.

(b)
To
    Professor M. Nielsen,[4] Knight of *Dannebrog* and Member of *Dannebrog*
    The excellent headmaster of the Borgerdyds School, the unforgettable teacher in my youth, the admired *paradigma* of my later years

most gratefully and affectionately from the author.

3. *Four Upbuilding Discourses, 1843*

To
    Professor J. L. Heiberg, Knight of *Dannebrog*[5]

most respectfully from the author.

4. *Three Upbuilding Discourses, 1845*

To
> Professor Madvig, Knight of *Dannebrog*[6]
>> with respectful regards from the author.

5. *Concluding Unscientific Postscript, 1846*

To
> His Excellency the *Geheime*-Prime Minister,
> A. S. Ørsted, Grand Cross of *Dannebrog* a.o.[7]
>> with the deepest respect from the editor.

6. *Upbuilding Discourses, 1847*

(a)
To
> The Honorable *Etatsraad* Hansen,
> Knight of *Dannebrog* and Member of *Dannebrog*[8]
>> with deep respect from the author.

(b)
To
> Professor Madvig, Knight of *Dannebrog*[9]
>> with respectful regards from the author.

7. *The Works of Love, 1847*

(a)
To
> Professor Heiberg, Knight of *Dannebrog*[10]
>> respectfully from the author.

(b)
To
> His Excellency the *Geheime*-Prime Minister A. S. Ørsted,

Knight of the Elephant, Grand Cross of *Dannebrog*,
Member of *Dannebrog*, a.o.

> with deepest respect from the author.

(c)
To

His Excellency the Right Reverend Bishop Mynster,[11]
Knight of *Dannebrog* and Member of *Dannebrog* a.o.

> with profound reverence from the author.

8. *Christian Discourses, 1848*

To

Professor Heiberg, Knight of *Dannebrog*[12]

> respectfully from the author.

9. *The Lily of the Field and the Bird of the Air, 1849*

(a)
To

The Honorable *Conferentsraad* Hansen,[13]
Knight of *Dannebrog* and Member of *Dannebrog* a.o.

> with profound respect from the author.

(b)
To

His Excellency the Right Reverend Bishop Dr. Mynster,
Grand Cross of *Dannebrog* and Member of *Dannebrog* a.o.[14]

> with profound reverence from the author.

10. *Either/Or*, Second Edition, *1849*

(a)
To

Christian Winther, the poet[15]

> with grateful respect and admiration.

(b)
To

the Danish poet Henrik Hertz[16]

with grateful devotion from Victor Eremita.

11. *The Sickness unto Death, 1849*

(a)
To

Professor Heiberg, Knight of *Dannebrog*[17]

Respectfully from the editor.

(b)
To

His Excellency The Right Reverend Bishop Dr. Mynster[18]
Grand Cross of *Dannebrog* and Member of *Dannebrog* a.o.

with profound reverence from the editor.

(c)
To

The Very Reverend Dr. Rudelbach[19]

with friendly regards from the author.

(d)
To

His Excellency *Geheimeraad* A. S. Ørsted, Doctor of Law,[20]
Knight of the Elephant, Grand Cross of St. Olaf, a.o.

with deepest respect most sincerely from the editor.

12. *"The High Priest"—"The Publican"—"The Woman Who Was a Sinner"; Three Discourses at the Communion on Fridays, 1849*

(a)
To

H. N. Clausen, Cabinet Minister and Knight of *Dannebrog*
with profound respect from the author.

(b)
To

Professor Heiberg, Knight of *Dannebrog*[21]
respectfully from the author.

13. *Practice in Christianity, 1850*

(a)
To

The Very Reverend H. N. Clausen, Cabinet Minister[22]
Knight of *Dannebrog* a.o.
with profound respect from the editor.

(b)
To

Mrs. Rothe[23]
from the editor.

It is in no way my intention with this to induce you to read—far from it; no, just let it pass.

But do please accept this book as a small token of how, as I reminisce, I dwell upon the memory of him in relation to whom I could truly call myself his "wholly devoted," while I derived pleasure from the safe assumption that he was not displeased that I so described myself.

I, too, have lost the pleasure of knowing that there was one who truly cared for me, the pleasure of seeing him happy, and the pleasure of conversation—the pleasure, when he was downcast at times, of contributing, if I could, to making him happy.

S. K.

[Omitted from draft:]

I confess that he is the one I am thinking about at this moment; it really is not you; [*deleted*: but] I believe that he would have been pleased that I am sending you this book. [*Deleted*: I am] If I could speak with him and then wanted to say: "I have thought of sending your daughter a copy," then I believe he would reply: "Oh, please do that. That would be kind of you." That is why I am now doing it. [*Deleted*: And is it not true, then it is welcome to you?] Thus I am thinking of him, not really of you. And is it not true, do we not agree about this: you do welcome the receipt of this book—and why? Well, strangely, precisely because—what a rudeness, especially towards a lady!—I am not thinking of you; in other words, because I am so rude—as to be thinking of him. And is it not true, then you would welcome the receipt of it, and—strangely enough, precisely because I am not thinking of you?

(c)
To

The Very Reverend Dr. Rudelbach, pastor[24]

with friendly regards from the editor.

14. *An Upbuilding Discourse, 1850*

(a)
To

The Very Reverend Dr. H. N. Clausen,[25] Cabinet Minister,
Knight of *Dannebrog* and Member of *Dannebrog*

with profound respect from the author.

(b)
To

Miss Rosenvinge[26]

from the author.
It would not displease me if you would read this little book; but that is not why it is being sent.

No, please accept this little gift, and as you accept it, please think—yet surely I need not ask you to do that, for of course it goes without saying that you are thinking of him all the time; but let it then signify to you that I too think of him in whom I did in fact lose a great deal, as I realize more and more whenever I consider how precious that memory is to me which I acquired when I lost him.

S. K.

(c)
To

The Very Reverend Dr. Rudelbach, Superintendent,[27] Knight of *Dannebrog*

with friendly regards from the author.

(d)
To

His Excellency
Privy Councilor-Councilor of Conference Collin,[28] Grand Cross of *Dannebrog* and Member of *Dannebrog* a.o.

with deepest respect from the author.

15. *On My Work as an Author, 1851*

(a)
To

Johanne Luise Heiberg[29]
that happy artist whose perception and determination were nonetheless—happily once again!—exactly equal to her happiness, Mrs. Heiberg

with admiration from the author.

(b)
To those two who only by their union could accomplish the rarer than rare, Mr. and Mrs. Nielsen[30]
with that devotion which comes from admiration

from the author.

16. *Practice in Christianity, 1850*

(a)
To

Prof. R. Nielsen,[31] Knight of *Dannebrog*

with friendly regards from the editor.

(b)
To

Your Excellency the Right Reverend Bishop Dr. Myns-ter,[32] Grand Cross of *Dannebrog* a.o.

with profound reverence from the editor.

17. *To J. F. Giødwad. S. K.'s draft.*[33]

Dear friend,

Permit me by means of this dedication to give expression to my appreciation for services that would always lay claim to gratitude, but doubly lay claim to mine owing to the special nature of the relationship. What is special is that a person who is decidedly a politician, who in the purity of his heart desires only one thing, who, without seeking and without finding any reward, womanlike in everyday faithfulness and modest frugality, is a man devoted in his work to but a single cause, that he cheerfully, kindly, with the greatest possible accessibility, finds the time in his limited leisure, with the greatest possible readiness and repeated kindness, to help him who may only be said not to have the opposite political persuasion insofar as he has none whatsoever—him who, preoccupied exclusively with his own affairs, has been completely unable to return any favor at all, not even with respect to the literary aspect that is immaterial in political differences.

S. KIERKEGAARD.

18. *To J. L. Phister. S. K.'s draft.*[34]

To
the great comic actor of reflection and thoughtfulness,
Denmark's greatest, Mr. Phister

> from the author.

19. *To C. N. Rosenkilde. S. K.'s draft.*[35]

To
Humor's inestimable, not to say priceless, comic actor,
Denmark's greatest, Mr. Rosenkilde

> from the author.

20. *To Thomasine Gyllembourg. S. K.'s draft.*[36]

To
the author of *A Story of Everyday Life*, this work, which
thereby at any rate is not such a story of everyday life that
it is quickly forgotten, for indeed it is unforgettable,
with the devotion of one who does not forget

> from the author.

EDITORIAL APPENDIX

Acknowledgments
441

Key to References
443

Notes
445

Appendices

I. Kierkegaard Family
501

II. Maps
503

Bibliographical Note
507

Index
511

ACKNOWLEDGMENTS

The present volume is included in a translation grant from the Danish Ministry of Cultural Affairs as part of a general grant from the National Endowment for the Humanities for work on *Kierkegaard's Writings* during 1978-81.

I should like to express my thanks to Ejnar Munksgaards Forlag, Copenhagen, the publishers of *Breve og Aktstykker vedrørende Søren Kierkegaard*, for permission to use their text. More particularly, I am deeply indebted to Niels Thulstrup for his generous permission to translate the text he edited and to draw freely upon his extensive notes.

This volume would not have been completed without the experienced guidance of Howard V. Hong and the innumerable and sensitive emendations and suggestions of Edna H. Hong. With unfailing patience they put up with my inexperience and assisted me when I went astray. Perhaps the scope of their help may be surmised when I say that at the outset the Hongs kindly placed at my disposal their own English versions of almost fifteen per cent of the letters, so as to insure uniformity of translation of those letters appearing both in *Letters* and in *Journals and Papers*, V-VI, published by Indiana University Press.

Thanks are also due to Carol Orr of the Princeton University Press. She has been helpful at crucial times. John Hendricks aided by checking the entire typescript. In Denmark I received generous assistance from Jørgen Schultz, a most perceptive and wise reader of Kierkegaard.

My greatest debt is to Judith Hsiang Rosenmeier. I suspect that in most ways this has been as much a husband-wife effort as the collaborations of the Swensons and the Hongs. Her contribution is everywhere.

KEY TO REFERENCES

References to Kierkegaard's works in English are to this edition, *Kierkegaard's Writings* [*KW*], I-XXV (Princeton: Princeton University Press, 1977–). Specific references to the *Writings* are given by English title and *Søren Kierkegaards Samlede·Værker*, edited by A. B. Drachman, J. L. Heiberg, and H. O. Lange (1 ed., Copenhagen: Gyldendal, 1901-06) [*Either/Or*, I, *KW* III (*SV* I 100)].

References to the *Papirer* [for example, *Pap.* I A 100; note the differentiating letter A, B, or C, used only in references to the *Papirer*] are to *Søren Kierkegaard's Papirer*, I-XI³, edited by P. A. Heiberg and V. Kuhr (1 ed. Copenhagen: Gyldendal, 1909-48), and 2 ed., photo-offset with two supplemental volumes, I-XIII, edited by Niels Thulstrup (Copenhagen: Gyldendal, 1968-70). References to the *Papirer* in English [*JP* II 1500] are to the volume and serial entry number in *Søren Kierkegaard's Journals and Papers*, I-VII, edited and translated by Howard V. Hong and Edna H. Hong (Bloomington: Indiana University Press, 1967-78).

References to books in Kierkegaard's own library [*ASKB* 100] are based on the serial numbering system of *Auktionsprotokol over Søren Kierkegaards Bogsamling* (Auction-catalog of Søren Kierkegaard's Book-collection), edited by H. P. Rohde (Copenhagen: Royal Library, 1967).

In the notes, internal references to the present work are given as: see Letter 100; see Appendix I (II or III).

Three periods indicate an omission by the translator-editor; five periods indicate a hiatus or fragmentariness in the text. A terminal unspaced period or other punctuation mark is additional.

NOTES

DOCUMENTS

DOCUMENT I

1. I.e., daughter of Søren [Lund].

2. Søren Aabÿe (usually written later without the umlaut) was the name of a deceased relative.

DOCUMENT II

1. For information about the sponsors, see Sejer Kühle, *Søren Kierkegaard, Barndom og Ungdom* (Copenhagen: Aschehoug, 1950) and Appendix I.

DOCUMENT III

1. The monogram of King Frederik VI (1768-1839).

DOCUMENT IV

1. Jakob Peter Mynster (1775-1854), Bishop of Copenhagen and Primate of the Danish Church from 1834 until his death. As leader of the Church, he was a powerful and influential figure in Danish life and drew large congregations by his preaching. Among his listeners were S. K. and his father. At the time of S. K.'s confirmation Mynster was a close family friend. S. K. retained a lifelong respect for Mynster despite radical differences between them that were to become apparent in S. K.'s attack on the institutional church following Mynster's death.

2. Preceding the Confirmation, instruction was given and at the Confirmation service the children were examined by the officiating clergyman. S. K.'s grade, *m*[*eget*] *g*[*odt*], would correspond to the American "B."

DOCUMENT V

1. This document dates from 1830. It is a companion piece to Document VI, the formal address to the rector and professors of the University. Document V represents the general evaluation of S. K. with a summary of the texts S. K. had studied at the Borgerdyds School, a normal secondary school curriculum.

2. Peter Christian Kierkegaard (1805-88). P.C.K. had graduated from the Borgerdyds School in 1822.

3. Edvard Julius Anger (1813-95), who graduated with distinction from the Borgerdyds School.

4. Søren Michael Kierkegaard (1807-19) died from an injury sustained while playing at the school.

5. Standard textbooks.

DOCUMENT VI

1. Michael Nielsen (1776-1846), titular professor and headmaster of Borgedydskolen ("School of Civic Virtue"), where S. K. received his secondary education.

DOCUMENT VII

1. Documents V and VI (in Latin) were submitted to the University, which then conducted a series of entrance examinations. Upon completion, the *artium* degree was awarded, and the candidate became an accepted member of the academic community (see Document VIII). The possible grades were *illaudabilis* or *haud*, failure; *haud laudabilis*, barely acceptable; *laudabilis*, praiseworthy; and *laudabilis prae ceteris*, praiseworthy before others, i.e., distinction.

2. Jens Wilken Hornemann (1770-1841), a professor of botany and in 1830-31 Dean of the Faculty of Philosophy and Rector of the University.

DOCUMENT VIII

1. This letter of admission (in Latin) to the academic community approximates a B. A. diploma.

DOCUMENT X

1. After one year at the University all students were required to pass a series of tests in the disciplines listed below.

2. For the grades achieved, see Document VII, note 1.

DOCUMENT XI

1. Written in Latin.

DOCUMENT XII

1. This record of S. K.'s theological examination falls into five general areas: (1) dogmatic history, (2) the Old Testament, (3) ethics, (4) the New Testament, and (5) the history of the Ancient Church. S. K. was examined in Danish in dogmatic history, ethics, and the history of the Ancient Church, and in Latin in the Old and New Testaments. The written record of this oral examination contains a Latin evaluation of each of S. K.'s replies, couched in standard contractions as follows:

rsp. or *r.* (*respondit*): replied
mod. (*moderavit*): modified
em. (*emendavit*): declined
non accurate: inaccurately
adj. (*adjuvit*): assisted

corr. (*correxit*): corrected

add. (*addidit*): added

non accuratissime: not quite correctly

aliq. (*aliqua*): partial reply

exp. (*explicavit*): explained

Ex. (*examinator*): the examiner.

2. The Very Reverend Professor Dr. Scharling conducted this examination (C. E. Scharling, 1803-77).

3. I.e., a recitation of the Augsburg Confession.

4. C. T. Engelstoft (1805-89).

5. The reference is to eudaemonism in ethics.

6. M. H. Hohlenberg (1797-1845).

DOCUMENT XIII

1. Doubtlessly this recommendation by the Principal of Borgerdyds School was intended as supporting evidence for S. K.'s petition to the King for permission to write his dissertation in Danish. The recommendation is repeated verbatim in the petition with the omission of one sentence. See Document XV.

DOCUMENT XIV

1. The Pastoral Seminary was a postgraduate course, in which the theological graduates received training and instruction in the conduct of the ministry. S. K. was enrolled for two semesters. *Pap*. III C 1-25 contains his own record of his participation.

2. Johan Georg Wittrock (1812-88), a fellow student at the seminary.

3. I.e., to the end of the chapter.

4. Gollich Frederik Peter Strøm (1819-98), a fellow student at the seminary.

5. See Romans 13:12.

6. Apparently the critics, S. K. and Gollich Strøm, were given a copy of Wittrock's sermon.

7. Literally, in the shell, i.e., too sketchy.

8. Mattias Wad (1816-97), a fellow student at the seminary.

9. Rasmus Theodor Fenger (1816-89), a fellow student at the seminary. See also Letter 1, note 3.

10. Ingvard Henrik Linnemann (1818-92), a fellow student at the seminary.

11. Jacob Nicolai Theodor Thomsen (1815-85), a fellow student at the seminary.

12. Balthasar Münter (1794-1867), the principal of the pastoral seminary.

13. Joachim Christian Chievitz (1815-93), a fellow student at the seminary.

14. Hans Henrik Licht (1814-86), a fellow student at the seminary.

DOCUMENT XV

1. This petition follows the formal chancery requirements in all respects. The first page of the petition was folded down the middle, and in the upper left corner was written the summary of the contents and on the right appeared the slightly more personal address to the King.

2. The Magister degree was the highest postgraduate degree in the philosophical faculty and corresponded to the Doctor's degree in other faculties of the University of Copenhagen. In 1854, those with the M. A. degree were declared to be Doctors of Philosophy. On July 16, 1841, the faculty of philosophy resolved to accept S. K.'s dissertation as worthy to be defended in public, and the defense took place on September 29.

3. Martin Hammerich (1811-81) was granted permission to write his dissertation in Danish in 1836, and Adolph Peter Adler (1812-69) was similarly favored in 1840.

4. S. K. was fully aware that his dissertation deviated from the standard academic product. In *Pap.* III B 3, he writes: "If something should be found, especially in the first part of the dissertation, that one does not otherwise encounter in scholarly writings, the reader is asked to forgive my cheerfulness and also this, that in order to lessen my troubles I sometimes sing while I work."

5. Cf. Document XIII.

DOCUMENT XVI

1. A standard contraction of *Magister Artium*. Another contraction is *Mag. Art.* See Document XV, note 2.

2. See Document XIV, note 12.

DOCUMENT XVII

1. See Document XV, note 2. The diploma was written in capitalized Latin.

2. Until 1972 this was the full and formal title of the King of Denmark.

3. Hans Christian Ørsted (1777-1851), Danish scientist and professor of physics at the University of Copenhagen, primarily known for his discovery of electro-magnetism (1820), which introduced a new epoch in the science of electricity and magnetism. Keenly interested from youth in philosophy and literature, he was also a significant cultural-intellectual figure in S. K.'s time.

4. An honorific title. The literal meaning is privy councilor.

5. *Dannebrog* is the name of the Danish flag and of an order of knights founded in 1219. The members of the order are appointed by the King. There are three classes in the order: (1) Grand Commanders of D. and Wearers of the Grand Cross of D.; (2) Commanders of the First Rank of D. and Commanders of the Second Rank; and (3) Knights of the First Rank of D. and Knights of D. Ørsted was, in other words, a higher ranking knight than the dean of the faculty, Sibbern. See note 6 below.

6. Frederik Christian Sibbern (1785-1872), versatile Danish philosopher,

who wrote a number of treatises on psychology, ethics, metaphysics, philosophy of religion, civics, and other areas. He became professor of philosophy at the University of Copenhagen in 1813 and later S. K.'s teacher, adviser, and walking companion.

DOCUMENT XVIII

1. Before ordination, theological graduates were required to deliver a trial sermon in public. The sermon would be delivered in the presence of two university censors whose task was to evaluate the sermon. Their grade would be entered in the records of the theological faculty, and the candidate would receive a certificate. For S. K.'s sermon, see *JP* IV 3916 (*Pap*. IV C 1), *Pap*. IV C 1 A in XIII.

2. See Document VII, note 1.

3. See Document XII, note 2.

4. J. H. Paulli (1809-65), the Royal Chaplain.

DOCUMENT XIX

1. This series of instructions about the family burial plot is probably from 1846 (Thulstrup).

2. Michael Pedersen Kierkegaard married Kirstine Nielsdatter Røyen (ca. 1758-1796) in 1794. In 1797 he married Ane Sørensdatter Lund (1768-1834).

3. Maren Kirstine Kierkegaard (1797-1822) and Michael Kierkegaard (1807-19).

4. Hans Adolph Brorson (1694-1764).

DOCUMENT XX

1. On October 2, 1855, S. K. fainted in the street. He was brought to Frederiks Hospital, where he died on November 11, 1855, at 9 p.m. This record describes the day-by-day deterioration in his condition. The diagnosis, "paralysis—tubercul?" seems in agreement with modern medical estimates. During his last days, S. K. received visits from friends and family, but he refused to see his brother, Peter Christian Kierkegaard. Emil Boesen called on S. K. almost daily, and from him we have the report of the following exchange between the two old friends: Emil Boesen: " 'Have you been angry and bitter?' "—S. K.: " 'No, but dismayed and worried by and indignant to a high degree, for example, with my brother, Peter. I refused to see him when he called on me last, after his speech at Roskilde [see Letter 240 and notes]. He believes he is my elder so that he ought to take precedence.' " *Søren Kierkegaards Efterladte Papirer*, VIII (1854-55), p. 593.

2. Most likely the incident recorded by Israel Levin: "He was sitting on the sofa and had been so gay, amusing, and charming, and then he slid to the floor; we helped him up, but, exhausted, he murmured: 'Oh, leave it - let - the maid - sweep it up - in the morning.' " *Udtalelser*, Søren Kierkegaard Archives, D, *PK*. 5, Læg 31, Royal Library, Copenhagen.

DOCUMENT XXI

1. This will is presumed to have been written in 1849 and to be contemporary with the drafts and letters to Frederik and Regine Schlegel (Letters 235-39). Peter Christian Kierkegaard found it sealed and locked up in S. K.'s desk. In the desk was another sealed document, dated August, 1851. On the cover it said, "To be opened after my death." It contained S. K.'s literary will and testament: "The unidentified one whose name shall one day be identified—to whom all my activity as an author is dedicated—is my erstwhile fiancée, Mrs. Regine Schlegel." Mrs. Schlegel refused the inheritance and only requested the return of a few personal items and of her letters (Thulstrup).

LETTERS

LETTER 1

1. S. K. was in his eighth year at the Borgerdyds School when he wrote this letter to his brother, Peter Christian Kierkegaard (1805-88), who was studying in Berlin. The Borgerdyds School, a private day school in Copenhagen, prepared students for admission to the University of Copenhagen. For an idea of the curriculum, see Document V.

2. Theodor Vilhelm Oldenburg (1805-42), a former classmate of P.C.K. at the Borgerdyds School.

3. Carl Emil Fenger (1814-84), Rasmus Theodor Fenger (1816-89), and Peter Andreas Fenger (1799-1878).

4. Johannes Ferdinand Fenger (1805-61), P.C.K.'s companion and fellow student in Berlin.

5. Henrichsen *et al*. Teachers at the Borgerdyds School.

6. An honorific title awarded Michael Nielsen (1776-1846), the headmaster of the Borgerdyds School. See also Documents VI and XIII and Letter 107.

7. I.e., the Efterslægts School, a school comparable with the Borgerdyds School.

8. I.e., the *rigsbankdaler*. The *daler* of the National Bank was the basic monetary unit until 1875, when it was replaced by the *krone*. The *daler* was divided into six *marks*, and each *mark* was divided into sixteen *skillings*.

9. S. K.'s relatives. See Appendix I.

LETTER 2

1. This Latin word denotes the curriculum requirements for graduation from the secondary school, which in turn must serve as the basis for a student's application for admission to the University of Copenhagen. See Document V.

2. I.e., a graduate of the faculties of theology and law.

3. One of the inseparable consequences of Denmark's disastrous interven-

tion in the Napoleonic wars, as well as a consequence of the brutal bombardment of Copenhagen by the British in 1807, was Denmark's cultural and commercial focus on Germany and France.

4. Barbers of the day still performed various surgical and related medical tasks that had not yet become the exclusive domain of dentists and physicians.

5. Frederik Olaus Lange (1798-1862), a former Greek instructor at the Borgerdyds School.

6. Mother of F. J. Fenger. See Letter 1, note 4.

7. S. K.'s relatives. See Appendix I.

8. S. K.'s father, Michael Pedersen Kierkegaard (1756-1838), kept a copybook of his letters and expenditures. In this he obliged S. K. to write the following: "I do not know what is the matter with Søren. I cannot make him write to you. I wonder whether it is intellectual poverty that prevents him from thinking of something to write about or childish vanity that keeps him from writing anything except that for which he will be praised, and inasmuch as he is unsure about it in this case, whether this is why he will write nothing." Thulstrup, II, p. 24.

LETTER 3

1. Reprinted from the draft in *JP* V 5192 (*Pap*. I A 72). In *JP* V 5160 (*Pap*. I A 75), written at Gilleleje (see Letter 4, note 3) two months later, August 1, 1835, S. K. elaborates on the ideas in this letter. Peter Wilhelm Lund (1801-80), natural scientist, was a brother of Henrik Ferdinand Lund. See Appendix I.

2. See, for example, *JP* II 1178 (*Pap*. I A 104).

3. In *Les Âmes du Purgatoire* by Prosper Mérimée (1803-70), Don Juan repents and chooses the monastic life.

4. See Luke 12:16-21.

5. Hans Christian Ørsted published some studies on sound vibrations (Chladni-figures) in 1807-08. See Document XVII and note 3.

6. Joakim Frederik Schouw (1789-1852), a botanist.

7. J. W. Hornemann (1770-1841), a botanist.

8. In 1835 Denmark was still an absolute monarchy. The National Assembly was then an advisory body composed of appointed members representing the several classes and professions. (A free constitution was not adopted until 1849. Cf. Letter 211.)

9. G. H. von Schubert, a German natural philosopher, discusses certain mysterious and frightening nocturnal noises that can be heard in Ceylon in his *Die Symbolik des Traumes* (2 ed., Bamberg: 1821; *ASKB* 776), p. 38. The idea appealed to S. K., who considers the sounds illusive mockers of man's enterprise in *The Concept of Irony*, *KW* II (*SV* XIII 331) and in *Philosophical Fragments*, *KW* VII (*SV* IV 270).

10. Johan Ludvig Heiberg (1791-1860), poet and esthetician, introduced Hegel's philosophy to Denmark. A leading cultural figure in S. K.'s time, he was influential through his activities as playwright, critic, translator, and di-

rector of the Royal Theatre and through his marriage to Johanne Luise Heiberg, the most celebrated actress in Denmark at that time.

11. The coastal road from Copenhagen to Elsinore. About ten miles north of Copenhagen it skirts *Dyrehaven* [Deer Park], a popular goal for excursions and picnics. *Bakken* [the Hill] is an amusement park with sideshows, restaurants, beer halls, etc., situated in the southeast corner of the park, just off the Strandvej. See Map II.

LETTER 4

1. This is the only preserved letter from Michael Pedersen Kierkegaard to his son, Søren. He was seventy-nine years old when he wrote it. For information about their relationship at this time, see especially Gregor Malantschuk, *Kierkegaard's Thought*, ed. and tr. Howard and Edna Hong (Princeton: Princeton University Press, 1971), pp. 26-30.

2. The innkeeper at Gilleleje where S. K. was staying.

3. A fishing village at the northernmost point of Sjælland. See Map II.

LETTER 5

1. Peter Engel Lind (1814-1903), founder of a student debating society to which Kierkegaard belonged.

2. S. K. had gone to Gilleleje. See Letter 4; Foreword, pp. xviii-xix.

3. Possibly notes on the lectures by H. N. Clausen on the hermeneutics of the New Testament.

4. H. Steffens (1773-1845), Danish-German philosopher. The allusion is to his *Caricaturen des Heiligsten*, I-II (Leipzig: 1819-21; *ASKB* 793-94).

5. See Matthew 21:28-31.

6. Tage Algreen-Ussing (1797-1872), Danish politician.

7. On May 28, 1835, Algreen-Ussing had characterized certain political opponents as eau de Cologne and then had gone on to compare them unfavorably with Brøndum's well-known aquavit.

LETTER 6

1. *Kjøbenhavns flyvende Post*, ed. Johan Ludvig Heiberg (1791-1860). In this journal Kierkegaard published an article, signed B., "On the Polemics of *Fædrelandet*" (no. 82, col. 1-8, and no. 83, col. 1-4; March 12 and March 15, 1836), *Early Polemical Writings*, *KW* I (*SV* XIII 16-27). Besides being an editor, Heiberg was the leading literary critic, writer, and Danish Hegelian of the time.

2. The bookseller who had *Flyveposten* in commission.

LETTER 7

1. Christian Agerskov (1809-92), a student contemporary. See also Letter 13, note 4.

2. The sum of 50 *rdl.* was given Kierkegaard by his father to repay the loan.

LETTER 8

1. On the wrapping of a parcel of letters to Emil Boesen, S. K. wrote: "This parcel is to be burned unopened after my death. Survivors please note. The contents are not worth four *sk*." Emil Boesen (1812-79), pastor, S. K.'s lifelong friend and confidant, as stated in Letter 60. He was a repeated visitor to Frederiks Hospital in S. K.'s last days. See Map I. This letter was written a few weeks before the death of S. K.'s father on August 8, 1838. Thulstrup believes it was never sent.

2. See Letter 72 and note 3.

3. See *Pap*. II A 801.

4. A garbled quote from a Danish version (ed. P. W. Tribler) of a German popular ballad, "General Bertrand's Farewell Song to Napoleon" in *Die Volkslieder der Deutschen*, I-V, ed. F. K. von Erlach (Mannheim: 1834-36; *ASKB* 1489-93).

5. See Corinthians 6:14.

6. Presumably a reference to King John of England, John Lackland.

7. E.T.A. Hoffman, *Auserwählte Schriften*, I-X (Berlin: 1827-28; *ASKB* 1712-16).

8. A peak in the Harz mountain range in Germany. In folklore, the home of witches and trolls, hence the common Danish expression "to wish something to Bloksbjerg," i.e., "to hell with it."

9. The passage is repeated almost verbatim in *Either/Or*, I, *KW* III (*SV* I 8).

10. From Adam Oehlenschläger's *Sanct Hansaftens-Spil*, *Poetiske Skrifter*, I-II (Copenhagen: 1805; *ASKB* 1597-98).

11. See Exodus 6:12.

LETTER 9

1. A reference to *From the Papers of One Still Living*, *Early Polemical Writings*, *KW* I (*SV* XIII), published September 7, 1838. This was originally intended for J. L. Heiberg's journal *Perseus*, but became too extensive. Apparently this letter is S. K.'s reply to Heiberg's criticism of his style. In a letter to Martin Hammerich of July 20, 1838, Emil Boesen wrote: "He has recently written a piece about Andersen intended for Heiberg's *Perseus*; its style is a little heavy but is otherwise ably done."

LETTER 10

1. The ponderous style of this letter suggests that S. K.'s aunt received assistance from someone else, perhaps the village teacher at Sedding [Sæding]. See Map III.

2. Michael Pedersen Kierkegaard died August 8, 1838. See *JP* V 5335 (*Pap*. II A 243).

3. See Matthew 25:40.

4. The parish farm at Sedding [Sæding]. Such a farm was known as a *Kirkegaard*, a word more commonly used to denote a cemetery, and is the origin of the family name.

LETTER 11

1. On internal evidence, the recipient is assumed to be M. H. Hohlenberg, a professor of theology who examined S. K. See Document XII and *JP* 5435 (*Pap.* II C 10). It may, however, be one of the series of "Faustian letters" Kierkegaard considered writing. See *JP* V, note 245.

2. A traditional dogmatic-historic phrase. S. K. would have been familiar with it from Karl Hase, *Hutterus redivivus* (4 ed., Leipzig: 1839; *ASKB* 581), p. 56. See also *Philosophical Fragments*, *KW* VII (*SV* IV 212) and *Pap.* II C 22.

3. See *Stages*, *KW* XI (*SV* VI 92).

4. The spider image is employed in a similar manner in *Either/Or*. I, *KW* III (*SV* I 8).

5. From *umkeeren*: to turn around.

6. Carl Daub (1752-1836), German theologian.

LETTER 12

1. *From the Papers of One Still Living*, Kierkegaard's first book, was printed by C. A. Reitzel on September 7, 1838. Carl Andreas Reitzel (1789-1853), printer and bookseller. The note and enclosure are of special interest because of the distinction between the author and the publisher or editor (Kierkegaard), a distinction maintained in the Climacus and Anti-Climacus works. The number 48 [shillings], or 8 marks, or ½ *rigsdaler*, is a clue in reckoning comparative money values. At 1 rd. = $5.00 (1973), the paperback cost about $2.50.

2. A college residence of the University of Copenhagen, where Frederik Fabricius, secretary of the Royal Library, was a resident vice-provost.

LETTER 13

1. Michael Andersen Kierkegaard (February 6, 1776-March 12, 1867), son of Anders Christensen Kierkegaard (1715-83) and a cousin of Kierkegaard's father.

2. See Letter 10, note 2.

3. Michael Pedersen Kierkegaard's sister-in-law.

4. The widow of C. Agerskov. C. Agerskov's sister was Michael Pedersen Kierkegaard's first wife.

LETTER 14

1. While Letter 10 appears to have been written with outside assistance, this one was not. The Danish orthography and grammar are those of an untutored person.

2. Peter Christian Kierkegaard had visited Sedding [Sæding] the previous summer.

3. See Matthew 28:20.

4. See Acts 14:22.

5. The author of Letter 13.

LETTERS 15-46

1. The letters to Regine Olsen follow Thulstrup's sequence proposed by Emanuel Hirsch in *Teologisk Tidsskrift*, Series 5, Vol. II (1931), pp. 198-212, and based on Kierkegaard's account of the engagement. See especially *JP* VI 6482 (*Pap.* X¹ A 667). Because the letters were delivered by hand, bear no postmarks, and are undated from S. K.'s hand, any sequence must be conjectural. Henning Fenger in *"Kierkegaards onsdagskorrespondance—et forsøg paa datering of Kierkegaards breve til Regine Olsen"* ["Kierkegaard's Wednesday Correspondence—An Attempt to Date K.'s Letters to R. O."], *Kierkegaard Studiet*, published by the Søren Kierkegaard Society in Japan (Osaka), no. 6 (June 1969), proposes a somewhat different sequence. Starting with the assumption that nos. 37 and 43-46 are irrelevant and immaterial notes, and hence apparently ignoring the possible relationship between no. 46 and S. K.'s last note appended to no. 239, he attempts to date the remaining twenty-six letters according to a fixed schedule. All the letters are supposed to have been written on Wednesdays as commemorations of a Wednesday in July 1839, when the couple are thought to have met in the Ibsen parsonage in Lyngby.

LETTER 16

1. Not preserved.

LETTER 17

1. Regine Olsen lived next to the Knippelsbro (see Map I). In the Kierkegaard drawing, her house is supposed to be behind the man with the telescope.
2. Probably Jonas Olsen (1816-1902). See *JP* I 888 (*Pap.* III A 185).
3. Poul Martin Møller (1794-1838), Danish poet and philosopher, served as professor of philosophy first in Oslo and, from 1830 to his death, in Copenhagen, where he became S. K.'s favorite teacher and close friend. His death was deeply felt by S. K., who referred to him as "confidant of my early days" and dedicated *The Concept of Anxiety* to him. S. K. gave Regine Volume I of Møller's *Efterladte Skrifter* (Copenhagen: 1839; *ASKB* 1574).

LETTER 18

1. Grief ceases / As does jesting / As does the night / Before one expected it to do so. Ludwig Achim von Arnim, *Halle und Jerusalem* (Heidelberg: 1811; *ASKB* 1623).
2. From Poul Martin Møller's "Den gamle Elsker," *Efterladte Skrifter*, I-III (Copenhagen: 1839; *ASKB* 1574-76), I, pp. 11-12. In this dramatic monologue the old lover laments the difference in age between a young girl and himself. See also Letters 235-239; *JP* II 1804 (*Pap.* III A 95); *Repetition, KW* VI (*SV* III 177).

LETTER 19

1. Christian Winther, "Violinspilleren ved Kilden" *Sang og Sagn* (Copenhagen: 1840).
2. Plato, *Symposium*, 197 c, quoted from *Udvalgte Dialoger of Platon*, tr. C. J. Heise, I–III (Copenhagen: 1830–38; *ASKB* 1164–66), II, p. 53.
3. See Letter 18 and note 2.

LETTER 20

1. Quoted from memory from Adam Oehlenschläger, *Aladdin*, Act IV, end, *Poetiske Skrifter*, I–II (Copenhagen: 1805; *ASKB* 1597–98), II.

LETTER 21

1. See Letter 19, note 2.
2. Two musicians journeyed thither / From the woods so far away. / One of them is deeply in love, / The other would like to be so. In "Musikantengruss," Joachim von Eichendorff, *Dichter und Ihre Gesellen* (Berlin: 1834; *ASKB* 1633), p. 20. The quotation, slightly modified, is also used in *Either/Or, KW* III (*SV* I 326): Die eine ist verliebt gar sehr: / Die andre wäre es gerne.
3. See Matthew 13:46.
4. See Romans 8:38-39.
5. They stand there in the chilly wind / And sing beautifully and play: / Oh, that a child who has had sweet dreams / Might appear at the window. See note 2.

LETTER 22

1. Not preserved.

LETTER 23

1. St. Martin's Eve, November 11, is observed as a social occasion in Denmark. S. K.'s absence must have appeared discourteous to Regine.
2. A small town north of Copenhagen. See Map II. The literal meaning of the name is: the castle of peace.
3. See Psalms 85:10.

LETTER 24

1. The phrase employed by Michael Pedersen Kierkegaard in Letter 4.

LETTER 25

1. Not preserved.

LETTER 26

1. This letter is based entirely on Jens Baggesen's (1764–1826) romantic ballad, "Agnete fra Holmegaard," *Jens Baggesens danske Værker*, I–XI (Copenhagen: 1827-32; *ASKB* 1509–20), II, pp. 348-58. In folklore, any per-

son who hears sounds from above the ocean floor will be recalled to ordinary life (cf. T. S. Eliot's "Prufrock") and forfeit his enchanted life. See *Fear and Trembling*, *KW* VI (*SV* III 141-47).

LETTER 27

1. See Letter 18, note 2.

2. S. K. enclosed a colored print showing a young Turk with a lute beneath an open window where a woman sits holding a rose. The landscape in the background is oriental.

3. W. A. Schlegel lived at 5 Gammel Torv [Old Square]. Nytorv [New Square], where S. K. lived, forms part of the same square. See Map I.

4. No hour of the night passes / When my heart does not awaken / At the thought of you, / Who many thousand times over / Have bequeathed me your heart. From "Wenn ich ein Vöglein war" in *Des Knaben Wunderhorn*, ed. Achim von Arnim and Clemens Brentano, I-III (2 ed., Heidelberg: 1819; *ASKB* 1494-96), I, p. 232.

5. Johannes Ewald (1743-1881), *Fiskerne*, III, 4; *Johannes Ewalds samtlige Skrifter*, I-IV (Copenhagen: 1780-91; *ASKB* 1533-36), III, p. 234.

LETTER 28

1. Whatever passes, must come full circle, / Whatever understands itself must find itself, / Whatever is good must be committed, / Whatever loves must stay joined. / Whatever obstructs must yield, / Whatever is bent must straighten itself, / Whatever is distant must reach itself, / Whatever sprouts must thrive. Novalis, *Schriften*, ed. Ludwig Tieck and Friedrich Schlegel, I-II (4 ed., Berlin: 1826; *ASKB* 1776), II, p. 58.

LETTER 29

1. The visit was to Pastor P. D. Ibsen at Lyngby. See Map II, Letter 109, and *JP* V 5403 (*Pap.* II A 520, July 28, 1839).

2. Conradine C. Alberg (1786-1860), widow of Peter Alberg (1771-1831), and two sons.

LETTER 30

1. See Mark 12:42-44.

LETTER 31

1. Carl Bernhard (pseudonym of Andreas de Saint-Aubin, 1798-1865), *Gamle Minder* [Old Memories] (Copenhagen: 1840; *ASKB* 2194-95). Presumably a present to Regine Olsen.

2. An honorific title; literally, a minor servant of the Royal bed chamber.

3. See Exodus 16:3.

LETTER 32

1. See I Samuel 16:23.

LETTER 33

1. This stanza and the two lines quoted below are from "*Henrik og Else*," a romantic ballad by Christian Winther (1796-1876), *Digte* (3 ed., Copenhagen: 1839), p. 225. In the ballad, King Wolmer or Valdemar (1340-75), a national hero who defeated the Goths, attempts to seduce a young country girl, Else. Her virtuous refusal brings about the King's renunciation and her successful reunion with Henrik, her true love.

2. The action of the ballad takes place in a boggy area in southern Sjælland.

3. See I Kings 19:11-12.

LETTER 34

1. A colored print was enclosed with this letter. It shows a pair of lovers in Turkish costume. Cf. Letter 27, note 2.

2. I yours / You mine / You, my peace / Harmony in song / Comfort in suffering / The wellspring of all joy in life. Authorship unknown.

LETTER 35

1. The manuscript has not been identified.

2. Here S. K. adapts a free Danish translation of Thomas Moore's "Last Rose of Summer" by Steen Steensen Blicher (1782-1848). In a literal re-translation into English, Blicher says: I will not remind of the spring / Nor of the summer gone by. No! / But teach you how to find / The joy in your path. / —Do not lament the joys of spring! / Your harvest has its own flowers; / Even the tear that you shed / Is not without delight. From Blicher's *Samlede Noveller*, I-V (Copenhagen: 1834; *ASKB* 1521-23), IV, p. 160.

LETTER 36

1. From November 1840 to May 1841, S. K. was a student at the Pastoral Seminary, a training college for theological graduates planning for the ministry. This was one of S. K.'s assignments. See Document XIV.

2. Dr. Balthasar Münter (1794-1867), the principal of the Pastoral Seminary.

LETTER 37

1. See Ludvig Holberg, *Jacob von Tyboe*, III, 5.

2. The home of S. K.'s brother-in-law Johan Christian Lund. See Appendix I.

LETTER 38

1. From a poem by N.F.S. Grundtvig (1783-1872) in *Roskilde Rim* (Copenhagen: 1814).

2. See Luke 15:7.

LETTER 39

1. See *Repetition*, *KW* VI (*SV* III 173, 178); *Stages*, *KW* XI (*SV* VI 15-21).

LETTER 40

1. Thulstrup writes that this letter may be presumed to have been written as a thank-you note for the birthday present S. K. had received from Regine. However, the faded rose that is mentioned seems to bespeak a slightly later date.

2. *Tausend und eine Nacht*, I-IV, tr. Gustav Weil (Stuttgart, Pforzheim: 1838-41; *ASKB* 1414-17), III, p. 17.

LETTER 41

1. This note is dated one month after S. K. returned the engagement ring.

2. A village north of Copenhagen, now part of metropolitan Copenhagen. See Map II.

LETTER 42

1. See Letter 15.

LETTER 43

1. This note and the following three to Regine provide no clue to the dates. "From the tone one may perhaps conclude that they were written towards the conclusion of the engagement" (Thulstrup).

LETTER 46

1. It is possible that this note alludes to the visit to the theater referred to by S. K. in a concluding note to Letter 239.

LETTER 47

1. Hans Peter Kierkegaard (1815-62), a half-cousin, son of Michael Andersen Kierkegaard, who lived at Købmagergade 45. Hans Peter, although severely crippled from birth, was fine spirited and alert. Cousin Søren visited him from time to time. He most likely was the prototype for chapter vii, *Works of Love*, Part Two, *KW* XVI (*SV* IX 300-14).

2. Old family friends. Henning Fenger (see Letter 15, note 1) speculates that the famous Regina note (*JP* V 5368; *Pap.* II A 347, February 2, 1839) is addressed not to Regine Olsen, but to Bolette Rørdam, the youngest of the four Rørdam daughters. (See Fenger, *op. cit.*, pp. 14-15.) Fenger's argument is partly based on the fact that Regina is not the same as Regine, but this ignores S. K.'s own reference to Regine as Regina in Letter 236.

LETTER 48

1. See Letters 1 and 2. The title was honorific.

2. Probably *The Concept of Irony*, published September 16, 1841.

3. Michael Nielsen. See Document VI and note.

4. Standard classroom phrases employed by the teacher when calling on the next pupil to translate a text and comment upon it.

LETTER 49

1. S. K. arrived in Berlin, October 25, 1841, after a turbulent period in Copenhagen. On August 11, 1841, he returned the engagement ring to Regine Olsen, and on October 11 the final break took place. He remained in Copenhagen for two weeks after the final break and "flouted the town in all ways" (Letter 51). Ostensibly he was in Berlin to study and attend lectures, Schelling's in particular, but from this and the following letters we learn something about his private suffering. In his private journal, he toys with the idea of writing his Copenhagen relatives in such a style and with such "subtle suggestions" that she will find out that he still loves her. (See *JP* V 5530; *Pap.* III A 174.) Elsewhere he remarks: "My only desire was to remain with her, but from the moment I felt that it would inevitably come to grief, and unfortunately that moment came all too soon, I resolved to make her think that I did not love her; and now here I am, hated by everybody for my faithlessness, the apparent cause of her unhappiness, and yet I am faithful to her as ever. However painful it might be to my human pride, I would even rejoice to see her happy with another" (*JP* V 5515; *Pap.* III A 159). The letters to Emil Boesen from Berlin are our best source regarding S. K.'s agony, for "I confide in no one but you" (Letter 60). The charming letters to the Lund children are deliberately gay and carefree, lest Regine suspect his true feelings.

2. Or *nixus*: persistent pressure (used, for example, of the bearing down in childbirth).

3. Literally: "his face was bearing down." Adapted from Suetonius' portrayal of Vespasian in *De vita Caesarum*, VIII, 20.

4. Phillip Konrad Marheineke (1780-1846), who, with Carl Daub (1765-1836), was the founder of speculative theology. *Pap.* III C 26 comprises S. K.'s notes on Marnheineke's lectures on "Dogmatic Theology with Particular Reference to Daub's System."

5. F.W.J. Schelling's (1775-1854) first lecture was delivered on November 15, 1841, on *Die Philosophie der Offenbarung*. See *KW* II (*Pap.* III C 27-28).

6. See Document XVII, note 6.

7. Streets in Copenhagen. See Map I.

8. A coffee shop was located next to Regine's home, which was near the Stock Exchange on Børsgade. See Map I.

9. The refrain of a Danish ballad.

10. See Appendix I.

LETTER 50

1. See Letter 49. Perhaps S. K. thought of himself as a master spy as a result of his ferreting out his father's secret in 1834-35. See *JP* V 5430 (*Pap.* II A 805).

2. An eighteenth-century oath that occurs in comedies by Ludvig Holberg (1684-1754).

3. Johan Christian Lund, one of S. K.'s brothers-in-law. See Appendix I.

4. See Letter 46 and note; Letter 239 and note 6.

LETTER 51

1. Peter J. Spang (1796-1846), pastor of Helliggeistes Church, teacher of Latin and religion at Borgerdyds School, 1820-25.

2. A pillar of shame had been erected in 1662 in Copenhagen to commemorate the conviction for high treason of Corfitz Ulfeldt (1606-64), who died in exile. The pillar bore the quoted inscription.

3. See Document XVII and note 6.

4. C.F.J. Hiorthøy (1776-1848), a highly respected librarian. The title (Councillor of Justice) is honorific.

5. Henrich Steffens. See Letter 5 and note 4.

6. C. A. Reitzel. See Letter 12 and note 1.

7. See Letter 49 and note 5.

8. Karl Werder (1806-93), a German Hegelian philosopher, whose lectures "Logic and Metaphysics, with Special Consideration of the Prominent Systems in Ancient and Recent Philosophy" were attended by S. K. See *Pap.* III C 28-32.

9. Otto Friedrich Gruppe (1804-76), a German philosopher opposed to Hegelianism.

LETTER 52

1. See Appendix I.

LETTER 53

1. See Appendix I.

2. The Berlin opera, museum, and theater.

3. Troels Lund (1802-67), stage painter, *not* Kierkegaard's relative, Troels F. Lund, a brother of Henrik Ferdinand Lund.

4. See Appendix I.

LETTER 54

1. See Philippians 4:12.

2. E. D. Bærentzen (1799-1868), a portrait painter and Regine Olsen's neighbor, who painted a well-known portrait of her.

3. Emil Boesen, *En religiøs Livsudvikling i Breve fra Cornelius* (Copenhagen: 1845; *ASKB* 470).

4. See Letter 49 and note 5.

5. S. K.'s sarcasm is directed at Schelling's attempt to make revelation a proper field of inquiry for philosophy.

6. Eugène Scribe (1791-1861), *Les Premieres Amours*, one of Scribe's *Comedies Vaudeville* (Paris: 1825), tr. J. L. Heiberg (Copenhagen: 1832; *ASKB* U 98), the subject of extensive critical treatment in *Either/Or*, I, *KW* III (*SV* I 205-51). See also Letter 112 and note 1.

7. A Copenhagen bookseller.

8. A famous castrato singer at the court of Philip V of Spain and known for his ability to banish the King's melancholy. The protagonist in *Farinelli*, a vaudeville comedy (1835) by Georges-Henri Vernay de Saint-George (1799-

1875), tr. J. L. Heiberg (Copenhagen: 1837) and often performed at the Royal Theater. See *Repetition*, *KW* VI (*SV* III 176).

9. A character in Mozart's *Don Giovanni*. See "Silhouettes," *Either/Or*, I, *KW* III (*SV* I 167-79); *Repetition*, *KW* VI (*SV* III 184); *JP* V 5541 (*Pap.* III A 190).

LETTER 55

1. S. K.'s barely concealed irony in the opening paragraph may be explained by his remarks about Sibbern in Letter 49. On Sibbern, see Document XVII, note 6.

2. The philosopher and poet Poul Martin Møller had died on March 13, 1838. See Letter 17 and note 3.

3. See Letter 49 and notes 4-5.

4. H. Steffens, *Caricaturen des Heiligsten* (Leipzig: 1819-22; *ASKB* 793-94). See Letter 51 and note 5.

5. *Anthropologie*, I-II (Breslau: 1822; *ASKB* 795-96).

6. Karl Werder, *Logik als Commentar und Ergänzung zu Hegels Wissenschaft der Logik* (Berlin: 1841; *ASKB* 867). See Letter 51, note 8; *Pap.* III C 28-32.

7. See Letter 49 and note 5.

LETTER 56

1. Elise Dencker, housekeeper for Johan Christian Lund, one of S. K.'s brothers-in-law. See *JP* VI 6472 (*Pap.* X⁵ A 149).

2. An honorific title, privy councilor.

3. Henriette Lund's brothers and sisters.

LETTER 57

1. S. K. is correcting Wilhelm's spelling of "related."

LETTER 58

1. The young relatives.

2. Hunter Street, a pun.

3. See Exodus 10:1-20.

4. S. K. adds the Danish ending "t" to the German word.

LETTER 59

1. S. K. is correcting Carl Lund's spelling. *Brønd*: well. Close to Rosenborg Castle were some wells with uncontaminated drinking water. The Lund family lived on Kjøbermagergade nearby. See Map I.

2. See Letter 52.

3. See Letter 58.

LETTER 60

1. See Letter 54. Demoiselle Schultze.

2. In uncertainty.

3. See Map I. Today the street is Vestervoldgade.

LETTER 61

1. G.W.F. Hegel, *Vorlesungen über die Naturphilosophie*, ed. C. L. Michelet (Berlin: 1841; *ASKB* 555).

2. "*Verein von Freunden des Verewigten*" [The Society of Friends of the Immortal One], i.e., The Hegel Society.

3. The comic protagonist, a *miles gloriosus*, in Ludvig Holberg's *Jacob von Thyboe* (Copenhagen: 1725).

4. See Letter 55 and note 6.

5. By Karl Werder. First performed in January 1842.

LETTER 62

1. François Boieldieu's opera, *La dame blanche*, text by Eugène Scribe, tr. Thomas Overskou (Copenhagen: 1826), p. 12. See Letter 239; *Either/Or*, I, *KW* III (*SV* I, p. XIV).

LETTER 63

1. See Appendix I.

2. Emil Boesen.

3. See Letter 55.

LETTER 64

1. Letter 55.

LETTER 65

1. The letter is written on high quality stationery with a polychrome border.

LETTER 66

1. In writing this letter, Else Kierkegaard has apparently received outside assistance, as she did in Letter 10.

2. S. K.'s father, M.P.K., had left a family trust fund of 3000 *rdl*. The interest was to be given to M.P.K.'s mother and to his brothers and sisters. In 1842, Else Kierkegaard was the last surviving beneficiary.

3. Newly inducted army recruits who had been training in Jutland and had returned to Copenhagen.

4. P.C.K. was married in June 1841.

5. The public defense of S. K.'s dissertation, *The Concept of Irony*, took place in September 1841.

LETTER 67

1. Orla Lehmann (1810-70), a former schoolmate of S. K.'s at the Borgerdyds School. A Hegelian historian, he became one of the foremost agitators and orators advocating a free Constitution. The previous year, one speech had been so inflammatory that it resulted in his being jailed for three months. At least two broadside ballads about this incident are known.

2. Schelling. *Geheimeraad*, an honorific title, privy councilor.

LETTER 68

1. The microfilm text can be read as "storm" or "stream"; the context suggests the latter.
2. See Letters 62, 69, and 70.
3. See Letter 56 and note 1.
4. Not identified.
5. Published February 20, 1843.
6. Quoted from Holberg, *Den politiske Kandestøber* (Copenhagen, 1723).

LETTER 69

1. See Letter 68 and note 5.
2. S. K. was born on a Wednesday.
3. A nickname for the coachman of a carriage S. K. rented occasionally.
4. Refrain of a popular ballad. Also quoted in Letter 49.

LETTER 70

1. W. H. Rothe (1777-1857). His doctoral dissertation had been criticized by J. L. Heiberg in his journal *Perseus*, I, 1837.
2. J. Hornsyld (1757-1840).
3. The city of Copenhagen maintained a workhouse, Ladegaarden, for indigents, the homeless, and criminals.
4. Schelling defines potency as the particular relationship between the objective and the subjective, the real and the ideal, by means of which the absolute manifests itself in nature and in spirit.

LETTER 71

1. Danish for John Doe or Mr. X.

LETTER 72

1. The intended recipient of this draft may have been Emil Boesen.
2. See Septuagint, Job 15:11; *Either/Or*, I, *KW* III (*SV* I 9).
3. Erasmus, in *Apophthegmata*, III, 70, relates that Socrates was supposed to have said to a boy: "Loquere igitur, adulescens, ut te videam." See Letter 8.

LETTER 73

1. In the fall of 1842, P.C.K. was appointed pastor at Pedersborg near Sorø[e] (see Map II) and left the family house at 2 Nytorv (see Map I). In May 1843, S. K. bought his brother's share of the property (see Letters 77 and 149). The house was not sold until December 24, 1847, when papers were signed which stipulated that S. K. must vacate the premises by Easter 1848.
2. Johan Christian Lund. See Appendix I.
3. C. F. Mohr, a probate court copyist and tenant at 2 Nytorv.

LETTER 74

1. See Psalms 6:3.

LETTER 75

1. Bishop Mynster (see Appendix I). The disagreement concerned P.C.K.'s refusal to baptize the children of Baptists at a time when Church law demanded such conformity on the part of clergy and parents. The followers of Grundtvig—among them P.C.K.—refused to comply, and P.C.K.'s refusal became a test case. Bishop Mynster first requested and then in vain demanded compliance, whereupon he recommended to the Ministry for Church Affairs that P.C.K. be dismissed. But by virtue of the system, this was a complicated matter. A pastor was a civil servant, and hence his dismissal ultimately required the consent of the King. Even though the Ministry agreed with Bishop Mynster, royal consent was never granted. See also Letter 116.

2. The followers of Grundtvig.

LETTER 76

1. M. L. Nathanson (1780-1868). From 1838 to 1858 the editor of *Berlingske Tidende*, a Copenhagen newspaper. This letter was never sent. It was intended as a cover note to an elaborate hoax. Among S. K.'s papers found after his death is a letter to the editor in which S. K. urges Victor Eremita "to set aside his pseudonymity" and disclaims all responsibility for *Either/Or*. This disclaimer, now found as *Pap.* IV B 19 (February 22, 1843), was to be followed by a rejoinder to S. K. in *Fædrelandet*, another newspaper, in which Victor Eremita would protest his ignorance of the real identity of the author (*Pap.* IV B 20).

2. Kierkegaard's servant, Anders Westergaard Christensen.

LETTER 77

1. This letter constitutes S. K.'s account of the settlement of business affairs following his purchase of P.C.K.'s share of 2 Nytorv. See Letter 73 and note 1.

2. A tenant.

3. A tenant.

LETTER 78

1. The recipient has not been identified. H. P. Barfod, the first editor of Kierkegaard's papers, states that "one H., a student who ended his days as insane, had a very superficial acquaintance with S. K., but nevertheless he sent him (in 1843?) a philosophical dissertation and concluded with a fervent plea for financial aid. A couple of hours later, he received S. K.'s laconic reply." *Af Søren Kierkegaards Efterladte Papirer* [From S. K.'s Posthumous Papers], ed. H. P. Barfod and H. Gottsched, I-VIII (Copenhagen: 1869-81), II, p. 787.

LETTER 79

1. S. K. left Copenhagen for Berlin on May 8, 1843, and returned on May

30. He was apparently in a turbulent state of mind. On April 19 Regine Olsen nodded to him in church and "every Monday morning between 9 and 10" he met her (*JP* V 5653; *Pap.* IV A 97). See also *JP* V 5654 (*Pap.* IV A 101). Elsewhere he writes: "If I had had faith, then I would have stayed with Regine. Thanks to God, I now see that" (*JP* V 5664; *Pap.* IV A 107). See *Repetition, KW* VI (*SV* III 191-209) on the sojourn in Berlin.

LETTER 81

1. Andreas F. Krieger (1817-93), one-time pupil at Borgerdyds School, subsequently jurist and politician. The letter is Kierkegaard's account of his first train ride.

2. See Herodotus, I, 32; *Die Geschichten des Herodotos*, I-II tr. Friedrich Lange (Berlin: 1811; *ASKB* 1117), I, p. 19; *Either/Or*, I, *KW* III (*SV* I 195).

3. See Herodotus, I, 86; Lange tr. (see note 2), I, p. 49.

4. Carl L. Müller (1809-91), licensed to preach but unordained, subsequently numismatist and archeologist.

5. A railroad junction. Here is a concealed pun: *Angermünde* literally means "the mouth of repentance."

6. Prince Carl's, a restaurant, *Zum Prinzen Carl*, in Potsdam, the destination of a railway excursion by a group of Danes. Kierkegaard left without stopping at Prince Carl's and wrote his account of the return trip.

LETTER 82

1. See John 16:17.

2. Probably *Repetition* (published October 1843).

3. See *Repetition, KW* VI (*SV* III 254).

4. Ibid., 203.

LETTER 83

1. P.C.K.'s wife's maiden name was Glahn.

2. From "*Hic Rhodus, hic salta*," a challenge to a boaster who said he had made a mighty leap on the island of Rhodes: "This is Rhodes, leap here."

3. Adolph Peter Adler (1812-69), pastor of Rutsker and Hasle on the island of Bornholm, subsequently the subject of *The Book on Adler*, *KW* XXIV (*Pap.* VII² B 235).

4. A. P. Adler, *Nogle Prædikener af Magister Adolph Peter Adler, Sognepræst i Rutsker og Hasle Menigheder* (Copenhagen: 1843; *ASKB* U 9).

5. H. L. Martensen, *Den Christelige Daab betragtet med Hensyn paa det baptistiske Spørgsmaal* (Copenhagen: 1843; *ASKB* 652). See Letter 75 and note 1; *JP* 5710 (*Pap.* IV B 59); *Pap.* VI B 98:15. Hans Lassen Martensen (1808-84), born in Flensborg, Denmark. Greatly influenced by Hegel's philosophy, he became a popular lecturer and professor of theology at the University of Copenhagen. For a time he was S. K.'s private tutor. When Bishop Mynster died, Martensen succeeded him as Bishop of Sjælland and Primate of the Danish Church and became the object of S. K.'s attack upon the institutional Church ("Christendom").

LETTER 84

1. See Letter 77.

LETTER 86

1. Steen Steensen Blicher, *Samlede Noveller*, I–V (Copenhagen: 1833–36; *ASKB* 1521–23, I in 2 ed., 1833).

2. Presumably a reference to *Fear and Trembling*, published October 16, 1843.

3. See Letter 54 and note 8.

LETTER 88

1. The protagonist in Ludvig Holberg's comedy, *Geert Westphaler*, a rambling, babbling barber. See Letters 180–81.

2. Successor to Michael Nielsen (see Letter 1) as headmaster of the Borgerdyds School.

3. C. H. Visbye (1801–70) had been the assistant pastor at Christianshavn in Copenhagen. He was promoted to pastor of that parish in 1844, leaving the assistantship vacant.

LETTER 90

1. E. B. was then an instructor and occasional chaplain at the orthopedic school and clinic at Tuborg, a few miles north of Copenhagen.

LETTER 91

1. See I Corinthians 13:12.

2. See Matthew 25:31–46.

LETTER 92

1. See Letter 83 and note 2.

2. E. B.'s apartment at Tuborg. See Letter 90.

LETTER 93

1. Perhaps at some service conducted by Bishop Mynster in the Cathedral.

LETTER 96

1. A line by Nonpareil, a character in *Recensenten og Dyret*, a vaudeville comedy by J. L. Heiberg (Copenhagen: 1826).

2. A fancy grocery store.

LETTER 100

1. See I Corinthians 13:10.

LETTER 102

1. Possibly Edvard Smidt (b. St. Croix, ca. 1810).

2. Possibly a neighbor at Nytorv, C. F. Holm. See Map I.

3. One of S. K.'s brothers-in-law. See Appendix I.

LETTER 103

1. Carl U. Boesen (1801-68), Emil Boesen's brother, whom Kierkegaard visited on his Jutland journey (*JP* V 5451; *Pap*. III A 51).

LETTER 105

1. Bertel Thorvaldsen (1770-1844), the sculptor, had become a national hero. His funeral services (March 3, 1844) were conducted in the Cathedral, near S. K.'s apartment.
2. March 31.

LETTER 106

1. Probably E. B.'s *En religiøs Livsudvikling i Breve fra Cornelius*. See Letter 54, note 3.
2. Israel Salomon Levin (1810-83), well-known Danish philologist and man of letters, who served as S. K.'s amanuensis and proofreader for a number of years. See Letters 122-30.

LETTER 107

1. Not identified.
2. Cicero, *Epistulæ ad familiares*, V, XVI; *M. Tulli Ciceronis Opera omnia*, I-VI, ed., J. A. Ernesti (2 ed., Halis Saxonum: 1757, *ASKB* 1224-29).

LETTER 108

1. Northern or Western Gates. In S. K.'s time, the city of Copenhagen was still contained inside walls of fortification. There were three principal gates leading from the city: the Northern, Eastern, and Western. S. K. lived close to the Northern and Western gates and used them during his frequent walks. See Map I.
2. See Map II.
3. See Map II. P.C.K. lived at Pedersborg, a village near Sorø.
4. A street near Christiansborg in Copenhagen. See Map I.
5. *Politics*, I, 2 (1253 a 1).

LETTER 109

1. This is a draft for a letter of condolence. Pastor Ibsen's (see Letter 29 and note 1) wife had died July 8, 1844.

LETTER 110

1. See Appendix I.
2. Borrowers at the Royal Library must furnish such affidavits.

LETTER 111

1. J. F. Gi[j]ødwad (1811-91), editor of *Fædrelandet* 1840-45, Kierkegaard's middleman for the pseudonymous works until 1846 and one of the few he regarded as a "personal friend." See *JP* VI 6619 (*Pap*. X³ A 88).

2. Published August 31, 1844; *KW* V (*SV* V 75-144).
3. Israel Salomon Levin. See Letter 106 and note 2.

LETTER 112

1. *The First Love.* See Letter 54 and note 6. J. L. Phister played the part of Charles in the play.
2. This anecdote is related in greater detail in *Johannes Climacus, or De omnibus dubitandum est*, *KW* VII (*Pap.* IV B 1, pp. 106-7).
3. Triple punning. *Borg* means castle or fortress. P. C. Kierkegaard's home was in the parish of Petersborg, which thus literally is Peter's fortress. Petersborg is also the Danish name for Petrograd, today Leningrad. Poul Kierkegaard was Henriette and P.C.K.'s son. The harbor fortress of Petrograd was named Peter and Paul.
4. See Map II. Halfway to Copenhagen, where P.C.K. frequently had Church business.

LETTER 113

1. An allusion to *Repetition*, published October 16, 1843.

LETTER 115

1. A private library association and reading club.
2. Friends of P.C.K.
3. Thomas Colley Grattan (1792-1864), *Agnes de Mansfeldt* (London: 1835).
4. See Letter 8 and note 8.

LETTER 116

1. See Letter 75 and note 1.
2. S. K. guessed correctly. The King did not dismiss P.C.K.

LETTER 117

1. See Letters 75 and 116.
2. A variant of "Poul"; Kierkegaard's nephew.

LETTER 118

1. The Convent or The Roskilde Convention was an association of pastors adhering to Grundtvig. See Letters 75 and 116.
2. Like P.C.K., a Grundtvigian who refused to enforce compulsory baptism of Baptist children in the Danish Church.
3. See Letter 117, note 2.

LETTER 119

1. Christian Peter Bianco Luno (1795-1852), Copenhagen book printer, who printed most of Kierkegaard's works.
2. See Letter 152 and note 1.

LETTER 120

1. A character in J. L. Heiberg's *Aprilsnarrene*, a vaudeville from 1826. *Zierlich* means "tidy" or "neat"; *ziirligt* means "primly."

2. Farina was the manufacturer of a famous eau de Cologne. The reference is to the promises made on the label of the bottle.

LETTER 120a

1. Ole J. Kold, innkeeper at Fredensborg. See *JP* VI 6247 (IX A 262).

2. Presumably a play on one of the Grundtvigians' favorite phrases, "matchless discovery."

LETTER 121

1. P. L. Møller (see Letter 17 and note 3) published the first review of *Stages on Life's Way* (April 1845) on December 22, 1845, in his annual review, *Gæa*. This review, entitled "Et Besøg i Sorø" ["A Visit to Sorø"], was contemptuous of the style and themes of *Stages* (see *The Corsair Affair*, *KW* XIII, Part II). Møller may have had several axes to grind, among them that he himself and the literary world in general had assumed that Møller and his licentiousness had been the model for Johannes, the Seducer, in *Either/Or*. Apparently Møller, who at the same time was deeply involved in *The Corsair*, through Giødwad had offered Victor Eremita space for a rejoinder to the attack in "Et Besøg i Sorø." In order to help S. K. and his pseudonym, Giødwad wrote the following cover note to Letter 121:

"Some days ago Magister Kierkegaard sent me a sealed letter that had been delivered to his residence during his absence, even though it had been addressed to Victor Eremita. I forwarded the letter at once to the intended recipient and have received a note from him, a copy of which is herewith enclosed at his request.

Respectfully,   J. F. GIØDWAD."

Giødwad's note is dated December 27. On that day *Fædrelandet* published S. K.'s attack on Møller: "Om en omrejsende Æsthetikers Virksomhed" [Concerning the Activity of a Traveling Esthetician], in which he refers to Møller's relationship to *The Corsair* (see *KW* XIII; *SV* XIII-431). This relationship was already known in literary circles, not least through P. L. Møller's own sketch in Erslew's Author-Lexicon [*Forfatter-Lexicon*], II, K-R (title page dated 1847, but the fascicles had been appearing periodically since 1843), p. 406. S. K.'s article signaled the beginning of the war with the *Corsair*.

LETTER 122

1. The notes and letters to Israel S. Levin (see Letter 106, note 2) cannot be dated with certainty. They probably date from 1844-1846.

2. In February 1845, Levin invited some 130 people to submit specimens of their handwriting for a book, *Album af nulevende danske Mænds og Qvinders*

Haandskrifter [An Album of Specimens of the Handwriting of Contemporary Danish Men and Women] (Copenhagen: January 1846). The purpose was to provide *exempla* for the young. S. K. was probably asked to contribute. See *Stages*, *KW* XI (*SV* VI 8-9); Letter 123; *Pap*. VI B 7.

LETTER 123

1. See Letter 122 and note 1.
2. Ibid., note 2.

LETTER 124

1. See Letter 122 and note 1.
2. *KW* V (*SV* III 7-52, 267-315, IV 3-170, V 75-168).
3. Jacob Böhme (1575-1624), German pantheist and mystic visionary. His theories of contraries influenced Schelling.

LETTER 125

1. See Letter 122 and note 1.
2. Levin appears to have been litigious in public life, but no specific incident has been found.

LETTERS 126-30

1. See Letter 122 and note 1.

LETTER 131

1. This draft was written on the same sheet as S. K.'s note (*Pap*. X⁴ A 543) dealing with his personal friendship for Giødwad and dislike of Giødwad as editor of *Fædrelandet*. See Letter 111 and note 1.
2. See, for example, Letter 121 and note 1.

LETTER 132

1. The formal address to the *rector magnificus*, the Rector of the University of Copenhagen. Sibbern's term began in 1845.
2. *Concluding Unscientific Postscript* was published in February 1846.
3. Peder Blicher (1784-1864) was P.C.K.'s brother-in-law.
4. V. M. had been a University janitor.

LETTER 133

1. *Concluding Unscientific Postscript*, published February 28, 1846.
2. Cf. *Either/Or*, I, *KW* III (*SV* I 22-23).
3. CF. *Postscript*, *KW* XII (*SV* VII [545-47]0.
4. See Matthew 13:12.

LETTER 134

1. By Thomasine Gyllembourg (1773-1853), published anonymously by her son, Johan Ludvig Heiberg, in 1828. In 1845, Heiberg published her story *Two Ages*.

2. *Two Ages: the Present Age and the Age of Revolution. A Literary Review* (1846), *KW* XIV (*SV* VIII 3-105).

LETTER 135

1. *Concluding Unscientific Postscript* (February 1846), *KW* XII (*SV* VII), and *Two Ages* (March 1846), *KW* XIV (*SV* VIII 3-105).
2. See Letter 138.
3. A comedy, *Amors Genistreger* (1829), by Henrik Hertz (1797-1870).
4. In logic, the principle of excluded middle.
5. See title page of *Postscript*.

LETTER 136

1. Letter 135.
2. Petersborg, P.C.K.'s home.
3. Quoted from *Two Ages*, *KW* XIV (*SV* VIII 17).

LETTER 137

1. Henriette Lund was confirmed on April 26, 1846.
2. See James 1:17, Kierkegaard's favorite Biblical text. See *JP* VI 6965 (*Pap.* XI² B 291:4).

LETTER 138

1. The copy is in J. L. Heiberg's handwriting.
2. Cf. *Two Ages*, *KW* XIV (*SV* VIII 45).
3. *Two Ages*, *KW* XIV (*SV* VIII 27).
4. gentle as the eye of a friend / wander through the labyrinth of the heart in the night. Goethe, "An den Mond."

LETTER 139

1. P. P. Jørgensen, *H. P. Kofoed-Hansen* (Copenhagen: 1920), believes this letter was never sent. Hans Peter Kofoed-Hansen (1813-93), Danish pastor and writer, was one of the few contemporaries who had an insight into Kierkegaard's thought.
2. Kofoed-Hansen was then a teacher at a grammar school in Odense. See Map III.
3. A legendary medieval German prankster and mischief-maker.
4. A phrase used also in the preface to *Fragments*, *KW* VII (*SV* IV 175).
5. An allusion to a Danish ballad. See *Stages*, *KW* XI (*SV* VI 113).
6. Kofoed-Hansen's *Kjød og Aand* was favorably reviewed in *Nordisk Literatur-Tidende*, March 29, 1846.
7. Kofoed-Hansen had reviewed *Either/Or* in *For Literatur og Kritik: Et Fjerdingaarskkrift udgivet af Fyens Stifts literære Selskab*, I, 4 (October 1843).

LETTER 140

1. A line by Jeronimus (Kierkegaard uses a variant spelling), a character in Holberg's comedy *Jule-Stuen*,1724. This line is used again in Letters 186-87.
2. Henriette Lund's birthday was November 12. See Letter 71.

LETTER 142

1. Christiane Philipine Spang. See Letter 51.

LETTER 144

1. See I Timothy 5:3-5. Peter Johannes Spang had died on January 14, 1846.

LETTER 147

1. Carl Lund was born July 2, 1830. He was confirmed in 1845.
2. *Either/Or*, I, *KW* III (*SV* I, pp. vi–vii).

LETTER 148

1. Julie Augusta Thomsen (1810–84); her father, M. A. Kierkegaard, and S. K.'s father were first cousins. She became a widow in 1845.
2. Hans Brøchner (1820–75), a philosopher and S. K.'s distant relative. He studied in Berlin in 1846. Through Julie Thomsen he sent S. K. this newspaper advertisement:

Anfrage

Sollte es nicht zweckmassig sein, dass auch die Klempner sich assoziirten, um mit dem Zeitgeiste Schritt zu halten? [Query: Would it not be to some purpose to have the plumbers also form an association in order to keep up with the spirit of the times?] H. Brøchner, *Erindringer om Søren Kierkegaard* [Recollections of S.K.], ed. Steen Johansen (Copenhagen: 1953), pp. 42–43.

LETTER 149

1. See *JP* V 5999 (*Pap*. VIII[1] A 100).
2. See Letter 77.

LETTER 150

1. This letter appears to have been written shortly after one of the visits S. K. occasionally paid his brother, Peter Christian Kierkegaard, and his sister-in-law, Henriette, at Pedersborg near Sorø[e]. See Map II. There are records of visits in October 1846 and in April, June, and October 1847. See *Pap*. VII[1], p. xxv; VIII[1], pp. xvii–xix.
2. Presumably *Works of Love* (September 1847).
3. S. K.'s espousal of walking for curative purposes is a recurrent theme. See Letters 184, 186, 211.
4. This anecdote is also used in *Repetition*, *KW* VI (*SV* III 173). S. K.'s source was Hegel, *Vorlesungen über die Geschichte der Philosophie*, I–III (Berlin: 1833–36; *ASKB* 560–62), I, p. 314.

LETTER 151

1. See Letter 29 and note 1.
2. The "Scandinavians," a loosely organized pan-Scandinavian movement, sought the political union of Norway, Sweden, and Denmark. In

Denmark two of the leading spokesmen were H. N. Clausen (see Letters 158-59 and 287-88) and Orla Lehmann (see Letter 67). The Scandinavian movement, widely supported in the universities, was idealistic and liberal in content, but when Denmark found herself at war with Germany (1848-50 and 1864), Norway and Sweden failed to provide significant military support. Thus S. K.'s skepticism in this letter was justified.

3. The punning and the rhyme mentioned by S. K. in his footnote are scarcely translatable and lose their satirical force. The reference is to a Copenhagen juggler who earlier in the century had promised to enter a fiery furnace, as did the three men in Daniel 3:8-30. On the basis of that incident, the poet Jens Baggesen coined the phrase "tri-men" to satirize an opponent, T. C. Bruun, who replied with the phrase "topsy-turvy," which in Danish rhymes with Baggesen's. S. K. uses both phrases to imply that three men or nations can no more become one than one can become three. See "Til Herr Gely Latour," *Jens Baggesens danske Værker*, I-XII (Copenhagen: 1827-32; *ASKB* 1509-20), IV, p. 309.

4. See Map II. P. D. Ibsen lived at Lyngby.

5. The comic protagonist in *Den politiske Kandestøber* [The Tinker Turned Politician], by Ludvig Holberg (1648-1754).

6. King Christian VIII, who resided at Sorgenfri Castle near Lyngby. In fact, S. K. was summoned and presented himself. See *JP* V 6402, VI 6310 (*Pap.* VIII¹ A 249, X¹ A 42) and Letter 295.

LETTER 152

1. In the period from 1838 until 1847, S. K. was his own publisher and hence assumed all the financial risks. During this period, his works were offered for sale on a commission basis through C. A. Reitzel, a prominent Copenhagen bookseller and publisher. Letter 152 constitutes S. K.'s attempt to settle all accounts. With regard to comparative money values, see Letter 12, note 1. In the summer of 1847, he opened negotiations with another bookseller, P. G. Philipsen, according to which Philipsen would assume the role of publisher for a second edition of *Either/Or*. These failed. See Letters 153-56. In Letter 157, S. K. assigned to C. A. Reitzel the role of publisher, which he was to retain the rest of S. K.'s life. The second edition of *Either/Or* was published May 14, 1849.

2. See Letter 119 and note 1.

LETTER 153

1. See Letter 152 and note 1.

LETTER 154

1. See Letter 152 and note 1.

LETTER 155

1. See Letter 152 and note 1.

LETTER 156

1. See Letter 152 and note 1.

LETTER 157

1. See Letter 152 and note 1.

LETTER 158

1. Henrik Nicolai Clausen (1793-1877), theologian and politician, professor of theology in Copenhagen from 1822, and S. K.'s teacher.

LETTER 159

1. See Letter 158, note 1.
2. See Letter 152.
3. An honorific title, Councilor of Justice.

LETTER 160

1. Janus Lauritz Andreas Kolderup-Rosenvinge (1792-1850), prominent professor of law at the University of Copenhagen, developed the study of Danish legal history and published widely on old Danish jurisprudence. At his behest, he and S. K. would often take walks together on Monday afternoons. His title, *Conferentsraad*, which appears occasionally in the exchange of letters, is an honorific title.
2. *Works of Love* was published September 29, 1847.

LETTER 161

1. From Thomas Kingo's (1634-1703) hymn "Nu rinder Solen op" (1674), *Psalmer og aandelige Sange*, ed. P. A. Fenger (Copenhagen: 1827; *ASKB* 203), no. 187, p. 399.

LETTER 162

1. F. C. Petersen (1786-1859) was the provost of Regensen, a college residence of the University of Copenhagen. See Map I.
2. Presumably *Works of Love* (September 1847).

LETTER 163

1. Lorenz Krieger (1797-1838) was the vice-regent of Iceland (1829-37), and there he met Magnus Eiríksson (1806-81), whom he first employed as a secretary and subsequently helped to attend the University of Copenhagen. Eiríksson graduated in theology in 1837.
2. Magnus Eiríksson, *Om Baptister og Barnedaab, samt flere Momenter af den kirkelige og spekulative Christendom* (Copenhagen: 1844).
3. Bishop Hans L. Martensen. In 1846 Eiríksson had published a polemical pamphlet, *Dr. H. Martensens trykte moralske Paragrapher eller det saakaldte* "Grundrids til Moralphilosophiens System af Dr. Hans Martensen."

4. See Letter 162 and note 1.

LETTER 166

1. See Letter 149.

LETTER 168

1. C. T. Barfoed (1815-89), an instructor in chemistry and physics at the School of Veterinary Sciences.
2. See Matthew 21: 28-30.

LETTER 169

1. Christian Molbech (1783-1857), Danish historian and linguist, received the honorific title *Etatsraad* (Councilor of State) in 1845.
2. The opening of this letter is probably ironic. See *JP* V 5897 (*Pap.* VII¹ A 110), also 5997 (*Pap.* VIII¹ A 84).
3. Dr. Edmund Zoller of Stuttgart, to whom Molbech sent some Danish books in April 1847.
4. The first edition of *Either/Or* (February 1843) was sold out by 1845. The second edition was not published until 1849. See Letter 152 and note 1.

LETTER 170

1. See also Dedication 15 (b). N. P. Nielsen (1795-1860), an actor and director, was married to Anna H. D. Wexschall (1803-56), a famous actress.

LETTER 171

1. Julia Constantia Lütthans Werliin, who apparently had spoken to Kierkegaard about her forthcoming marriage to the poet Christian Winther, which took place on February 21, 1848.

LETTER 172

1. See Letter 160, note 1.

LETTER 173

1. In Denmark Shrove Monday is celebrated with games, practical jokes, tricks, and fool's errands.

LETTER 174

1. Frederik L. B. Zeuthen (1805-74), pastor in Tømmerup, near Kalundborg.
2. *Christian Discourses* (April 26, 1848), *KW* XVII (*SV* X).
3. An allusion to the Three-Year War with Germany (1848-50). See *JP* IV 4136-37 (*Pap.* VIII¹ A 608-609).
4. See *Christian Discourses*, *KW* XVII (*SV* X 19-28). There is an echo of Zeuthen's letter in *The Lily of the Field and the Bird of the Air*, *KW* XVIII (*SV* XI 41). In *Pap.* VIII¹ A 644, Kierkegaard observes: "The difficulty is to have the day today without presuppositions."

LETTER 176

1. Marcus Annaeus Seneca, *Excerpta Controversiarum*, III, 3.

LETTER 177

1. Rasmus Nielsen (1809-84), professor of moral philosophy at the University of Copenhagen from 1841, a position that had been left vacant by the death of Poul Møller, S. K.'s beloved teacher. In 1847, S. K. sought to establish a friendship of sorts with R. N. by introducing him to his pseudonymous works, but this attempt failed as S. K. became disappointed in R. N.'s indiscriminate adoption and use of his ideas. See, e.g., Letter 179 and note 1.

LETTER 178

1. In order to conform to the sequence of the Danish edition, this letter is retained as no. 178. However, the Thulstrup edition points out that Abelone Hedberg, a niece of S. K.'s father in his first marriage, did not become a widow until July 30, 1848. On Algreen-Ussing, see Letter 5, note 6. *Etatsraad* is an honorific title (Councilor of State).

LETTER 179

1. For an understanding of S. K.'s attitude toward any involvement with Rasmus Nielsen, see *JP* VI 6239-40, 6246 (*Pap.* IX A 229-230, 258). See Letter 177 and note 1.

2. A small fishing village on the Sound about 10 miles north of Copenhagen. Just west of it lies Dyrehaven [Deer Park]; see Letter 3 and note 11. The highway from Copenhagen to Elsinore passed through Taarbæk. See Map II.

3. The name of a house.

4. "Blessed": the first word in Psalm 1.

5. See Exodus 3. In Danish: *Tornebusk*; an allusion to the address at end of letter.

LETTER 180

1. See Letter 160, note 1.

2. Characters in *Geert Westphaler*, a comedy by Ludvig Holberg (1684-1754).

LETTER 181

1. A summer residence north of Copenhagen, which K.-R. had rented (see Map II).

2. Reference to "walking letter," no. 180.

3. Literally, free from care, the name of a castle near Lyngby (see Map II) belonging to the Royal Family. The name is a Danish version of "*Sans Souci.*"

4. Literally, the peace of grief, a pun alluding to the fact that King Christian VIII (1839-48) had died in January 1848. K.-R. was a guest of the

widowed Queen Caroline Amalie (1796-1881), who made Sorgenfri her permanent residence. See Letter 295.

5. See Letter 180 and note 2.

6. A quotation from Holberg's *Geert Westphaler*: Venetian noblemen from Harslev, a Danish village, i.e., an absurdity.

7. On May 18, 1848, the new German national assembly met for the first time in Frankfurt.

8. A machine gun.

9. From *Jacob von Tyboe*, a comedy by Ludvig Holberg (1684-1754).

10. See Horace, *Epistles*, I,I,15 [*Quo me cumque rapit tempestas*]; *Opera* (Leipzig: 1828; *ASKB* 1248).

11. From Schiller's "Der Antritt des neuen Jahrhunderts" [The Commencement of the New Century]. Schiller's stanza reads: In des Herzens heilig stille Räume / Muszt du fliehen aus des Lebens Drang! / Freiheit ist nur in dem Reich der Träume / Und das Schöne bluht nur im Gesang. [You must seek refuge in the holy, silent room of the heart from the stress of life. Freedom exists only in the realm of dreams, and the beautiful only blossoms in song.] *Samtliche Werke*, ed. Eduard von der Hellen (1904), I, 156.

12. Because Denmark was at war with Germany.

LETTER 182

1. See *JP* VI 6268 (*Pap*. IX A 375) and the following note.

2. S. K. moved to an apartment at the corner of Tornebuskegaden [Thornbush Street] and Rosengaarden [The Rose Court] in April 1848. See Map I.

LETTER 183

1. See I John 4:18.

LETTER 184

1. Reply to Letter 181. On Kolderup-Rosenvinge, see Letter 160, note 1.

2. The war between Denmark and Prussia broke out in Holsten [German: Holstein] on March 23, 1848. See Map III.

3. A playful allusion to the fact that German no longer was an acceptable language and a literal translation into German of *Nyboder*: the new cottages, a section of Copenhagen. See Map I.

4. Eugène Scribe, *Les Premieres Amours*. See Letter 54 and note 6.

LETTER 185

1. See Letter 181, note 1.

2. Properly, *post equitem sedet atra cura* (Horace, *Carmina*, III, 1, 40): somber care is seated behind the rider.

3. An allusion to the Holsten insurgents who had started the war but not yet been conquered.

4. See Map II.

5. Anders Sandøe Ørsted (1778-1860), brother of H. C. Ørsted, the physicist, was a well-known jurist and lawmaker. Productive in every department of the law, he founded Danish-Norwegian jurisprudence and led an active political life, becoming prime minister of Denmark in 1842 and bearing the title Privy Councilor.

6. A lodge located in Dyrehaven [Deer Park], belonging to the Royal Family. See Map II.

7. See Letter 184 and note 2.

LETTER 186

1. Reply to Letter 185. On Kolderup-Rosenvinge, see Letter 160, note 1.

2. See Document XVII and note 6.

3. See Letter 140 and note 1.

4. Throughout this letter, S. K. playfully puns on the two meanings of the Danish *Bremse*: (1) a brake, to brake, and (2) a gadfly or botfly. Socrates refers to himself as a gadfly. See note 9. See *Works of Love*, *KW* XVI (*SV* IX 124).

5. Such an account appears in *Berlingske Tidende*, August 9, 1848.

6. See *Either/Or*, I, *KW* III (*SV* I 9).

7. Alphonse de Lamartine (1790-1869), French author and politician. Following the Revolution of 1848, Lamartine became minister for foreign affairs. By 1847 he had published a historical work, *Histoire des Girondins*, which dealt with the events of the immediate past as well as with those contemporary occurrences that led to the revolution. In 1849 followed *Histoire de la Revolution de 1848*, translated into Danish and serialized in *Berlingske Tidende*, beginning July 27, 1849. See *JP* I 72 (*Pap.* X² A 79).

8. See *JP* VI 6255-56 (*Pap.* IX B 63:7; X⁶ B 40).

9. In the *Apology*, 30 e. See also *Works of Love*, *KW* XVI (*SV* IX 124).

LETTER 187

1. Reply to Letter 186.

2. *For Literatur og Kritik: Et Fjerdingaarsskrift udgivet af Fyens Stifts Literære Selskab*, 1848, pp. 146-190.

3. P. V. Christensen (1819-63) had been prepared for admission to the University of Copenhagen by P. C. Kierkegaard. Following his graduation in 1842, S. K. employed him as his secretary for some time. In 1846 he attacked S. K. in *Dansk Kirketidende*. See Letter 188.

4. See Letter 140 and note 1.

5. Louis Eugene Cavaignac (1802-57), French army officer who became head of the provisional government established after the Revolution of 1848. In the general elections in December 1848, he ran for President but lost to Louis Napoleon Bonaparte (1808-73). See Letter 186 and note 4.

6. From Jens Baggesen's (1764-1826) "Ja og Nej eller den hurtige Frier," *Jens Baggesens danske Værker*, I-XII (Copenhagen: 1827-32; *ASKB* 1509-20), I, p. 307.

7. Kolderup-Rosenvinge's Danish translation of this poem by Moritz Graf

Strachwitz also appears in his unpublished "Digte" (Royal Library, Copenhagen).

8. See Letter 108 and note 1. Both S. K. and K.-R. lived near the gates.

9. An allusion to *Barselstuen*, a comedy by Ludvig Holberg (1684-1754).

10. From Titus Livius, *Historia*, V, 37; *T. Livii Patavini Historiarum libri quæ supersunt omnes*, I-V (Leipzig: n.d.; *ASKB* 1251-55), I, p. 331.

11. Pomponius Mela, *De Chorographia*, III, 2.

12. I.e., *scilicet:* of course.

13. See Letter 186.

14. *Den politiske Kandestøber*, a comedy by Ludvig Holberg (1684-1754).

15. P. F. Lunde (1803-93), a prominent politician of liberal persuasion.

16. *Hexerie eller Blind Alarm*, a comedy by Ludvig Holberg (1684-1754). This play and *Den politiske Kandestøber* (note 14 above) are satires on the political and legal ambitions of vulgar and ignorant men.

LETTER 188

1. Jørgen Peter Frydendahl (1766-1836), a famous actor.

2. See Letter 187 and note 3.

3. A mythological figure of unlimited strength who will return to defend Denmark in times of need. Cf. *Holger Danske* (1837), a series of poems by B. S. Ingemann (1789-1862).

4. See *JP* III 2951 (*Pap.* X² A 383).

5. The Hippodrome in Copenhagen was the hall used by the advocates of a free constitution, and many turbulent meetings were held there in 1848.

6. Presumably a word-play on *Reguladetri*, "rule of three," a formula for finding the fourth term in a proportion when three terms are given.

7. Georg Christoph Lichtenberg (1742-99), German author of *Timorus, Vermischte Schriften*, I-IX (Gottingen: 1800-06; *ASKB* 1764-72), III, p. 98. Without hands . . . nothing can be tackled, yet the head is only a kind of hat which one does indeed wear now and then but which must be laid aside for the real gala events in our lives.

8. Knud Lyhne Rahbek (1760-1830), writer and for three generations a leading literary critic. Lars Mathiesen owned a popular restaurant at Frederiksberg.

9. See "The Gordian Knot," Letter 187 and note 7.

10. See Letter 187 and note 5.

11. Adolphe Thiers (1797-1877), President of France 1871-73. In 1848, Thiers was the anti-revolutionary leader of the supporters of the monarchy.

LETTER 189

1. *Don Ranudo de Colibrados*, a comedy about pretentious but impoverished nobility, by Ludvig Holberg (1684-1754).

2. Anders Sandøe Ørsted (1778-1860). See Letter 185 and note 5.

3. The war with Germany.

4. The newly elected National Assembly, the first democratically elected legislative body in Denmark, first assembled on October 23, 1848.

5. On March 22, 1848, the old ministry (including A. S. Ørsted) had been dismissed.

6. In 1813, the Kingdom of Denmark declared itself bankrupt, and the banks stopped payment. This was a national disaster.

7. The elections took place on October 5, 1848, and A. S. Ørsted was elected in Copenhagen's third precinct.

8. Negro slavery had been abolished on the Danish-owned Virgin Islands on July 3, 1848, in consequence of a slave rebellion.

9. See Map II. The railroad had opened the year before.

10. The West Gate of Copenhagen. See Map I.

LETTER 190

1. Not identified.

LETTER 191

1. "The gift" is not identified. N. Thulstrup speculates that it may have been either a sermon Mynster preached on the occasion of the opening of the National Assembly (October 23, 1848) or the funeral oration he delivered at the burial of J.L.A. Kolderup-Rosenvinge (autumn 1850). The icy formality of the note might favor the latter date. Twice in 1849 (see *JP* VI 6370, 6429; *Pap.* X^1 A 167, 497), S. K. attempted to speak with Mynster and was turned down. In 1850, they did meet and discussed *Practice in Christianity*, which had offended Mynster. See *JP* VI 6691-93 (*Pap.* X^3 A 563-65).

LETTER 192

1. This is a thank-you note to S. M. Trier, a physician, for having cured "my carpenter," F. C. Strube, who lived in S. K.'s household along with his family. See *JP* VI 6629, 6772 (*Pap.* X^3 A 144; X^4 A 299).

LETTER 193

1. "Hr. Phister som Captain Scipio" (*Pap.* IX B 67-73). Captain Scipio is a character in *Ludovic*, a comedy by Georges-Henri Vernay de Saint-George (1799-1875). Joachim Ludvig Phister (1807-96), philologist, lawyer, physicist, doctor, and celebrated actor respectively. See Dedication 18.

LETTER 194

1. Roskilde Convention; see Letter 118 and note 1. P.C.K.'s speech was delivered on October 12, 1848, and printed in *Dansk Kirketidende* on December 16, 1848.

LETTER 195

1. Nicolai Edinger Balle (1744-1816), *Lærebog* (Copenhagen: 1824; *ASKB* 183), Chapter One, paragraph 2: "By the world is usually understood both heaven and earth with everything therein contained."

2. "Sechse kommen durch die ganze Welt," *Kinder- und Haus-Märchen*, I-III (2 ed., Berlin: 1821; *ASKB*, 1425-27), no. 71, I, pp. 378-85.

LETTER 196

 1. See Letter 47, note 1.
 2. Cf. Ecclesiastes 12:13.

LETTER 197

 1. Quotation from a poem by Johan Herman Wessel (1742-85).

LETTER 198

 1. A village on the island of Als (see Map III), where H. L., a medical student, served as a subordinate physician with the army, then at war.

LETTER 199

 1. A village in northern Slesvig (see Map III). Like his brother Henrik, M. L. was a medical student and served as a subordinate physician with the army. See Letter 198 and note.
 2. See Map III.
 3. The war ended one year later. Although militarily victorious, Denmark had to accept the separation of Holsten [German: Holstein] from Denmark in 1851.

LETTER 200

 1. See Map II. The fire occurred on May 4.
 2. *Store Bededag.* From the middle of the sixteenth century, special days of penance and prayer were observed quarterly in the Danish Church and in some areas monthly or weekly. In 1686, the fourth Friday after Easter was declared the Great Day of Prayer.

LETTER 201

 1. See Letters 203-04 and note.

LETTER 203

 1. Frederika Bremer (1801-65), a Swedish author and a founder of the Swedish suffragette movement, who visited Copenhagen from the autumn of 1848 until May 1849.

LETTER 204

 1. See Letters 201-203 and note. In 1849, Frederika Bremer published her impressions of her recent stay in Copenhagen, entitled *Lif i Norden* (Stockholm: 1849), translated into Danish as *Liv i Norden, af Frederika Bremer, Forfatterinde til de svenske Hverdagshistorier* (Copenhagen: 1849). After praising Bishop Hans Martensen lavishly, she says: "While the richly talented Martensen enlightens the circumference of all existence and all the phenomena of life from his central point of view, Søren Kierkegaard stands like Simon Stylites on his lonely pillar with his eyes focused steadily on a single point. He holds the microscope over it, he scrutinizes it down to the least of its atoms,

he researches its most fugitive motions, its innermost alterations, he makes speeches about it, and again and again he writes endless folios about it. To him everything is found in this point. But that point is—the human heart. . . . Inasmuch as he does say divine things during his tiresome dialectical wanderings, he has gained a not inconsiderable audience, especially among the ladies in gay and merry Copenhagen. . . . He lives in solitude, this man who writes for 'that single individual,' inaccessible and really known by no one. During the day one sees him walking up and down the most heavily trafficked streets by the hour in the midst of the crowd; at night his lonely house is said to be shining with lights. It is not so much being rich and independent that makes him behave in this way as a sickly and irritable disposition that finds occasion to be annoyed with the sun itself when its rays fall in a direction other than that he might wish. . . ." S. K. reacted sarcastically (*Pap.* X¹ A 658) in commenting on F. B., who had had "legemlig omgang med notabiliteter" [sexual intercourse with famous people]. See also *JP* VI 6493 (*Pap* X² a 25).

LETTER 205

1. Frederik Paludan-Müller (1809-76), Danish poet, author of an epic poem *Adam Homo* (1841-48), which may well be read in connection with *Either/Or* and *Stages*, Goethe's *Faust*, and Byron's *Don Juan*.

2. The second edition was published on May 14, 1849. See *JP* VI 6413 (*Pap.* X¹ A 402).

LETTER 206

1. Andersen's surprise is presumably against the background of S. K.'s critical *From the Papers of One Still Living: On Andersen as a Novelist with Constant Reference to his Latest Work* "Only a Fiddler," *KW* I (*SV* XIII). See *JP* VI 6413 (*Pap.* X¹ A 402).

LETTER 207

1. See *JP* VI 6413 (*Pap.* X¹ A 407). Johannes Carsten Hauch (1790-1872), Danish poet and novelist, figured innocently in P. L. Møller's "A Visit to Sorø," which was the occasion of Kierkegaard's attack on *The Corsair* in 1845.

LETTER 208

1. This note may pertain to a disagreement between Rasmus Nielsen and S. K. Rasmus Nielsen published *Evangelietroen og den moderne Bevidsthed, Forelæsninger over Jesu Liv. 1. Deel* (Copenhagen: May 1849; *ASKB* 700). The book was advertised as published on May 19. S. K. felt himself plagiarized. See *JP* VI 6402 (*Pap.* X¹ A 343); Letter 252 and note.

LETTER 209

1. See Letter 208 and note.

2. *The Lily of the Field and the Bird of the Air, Three Devotional Discourses, KW* XVIII (*SV* XI 3-46), published May 14, 1849.

LETTER 210

1. Reply to Letter 209.

LETTER 211

1. Such an advertisement appeared in the *Adresse-Contoirs Efterretninger* (a paper specializing in announcements and advertisements), July 11, 1849.

2. The first free Danish Constitution (May 25, 1849) became effective on June 5, 1849. See Letter 189 and note 4.

3. The official government paper, which, like the *Congressional Record*, reports the proceedings in the Assembly, publishes notices and pending legislation, etc.

4. A mansion used for public assemblies. Today, the City Museum of Copenhagen, containing *inter alia* a number of S. K.'s personal effects.

5. See Letters 153-56 and 152 and note 1.

6. A reference to the principal character in J. L. Heiberg's vaudeville *Recensenten og Dyret* (1826).

7. Horace, *Epistles*, I, no. 1, 32; *Q. Horatii Flacci Opera* (Leipzig: 1828; *ASKB* 1248).

8. See James 1:19.

9. Barbara Abigail Rothe (1847-49).

LETTER 212

1. H. L. Martensen, *Den christelige Dogmatik* (Copenhagen: July 19, 1849).

2. See *Fear and Trembling*, *KW* VI (*SV* III 60).

3. There is a black smear on the back of the envelope.

LETTER 213

1. In this draft S. K. puns on *omnibus* as the public conveyance and the "system" for *omnibus* [everybody]: everything must be doubted, according to Descartes. See Letter 212 and note 2; *JP* V 5621 (*Pap.* IV B 1).

2. S. K.'s pseudonym in *Fear and Trembling* (October 16, 1843), *KW* VI (*SV* III).

3. *The Sickness unto Death*, by Anti-Climacus, *KW* XIX (*KW* XI 113-241), published July 30, 1849.

LETTER 214

1. Possible references: revolutionary movements of France and Germany reached Denmark: Christian VIII died, and thereafter a free constitution was adopted; Denmark was at war with Germany.

2. See Letter 186 and note 7.

3. See Letter 151 and note 3.

4. *Faust*, I, 1373; *Goethe's Werke* I-LIX (Stuttgart, Tübingen; *ASKB* 1641-68), XII, p. 72.

5. Marcus Aurelius, *Meditations; Marc. Aurel. Antonin's Unterhaltungen mit sich selbst*, tr. J. M. Schulz (Schleswig: 1799; *ASKB* 1219).

1. Reply to Letter 213.
2. See *Postscript, KW* XII (*SV* VII 349 FF.).
3. See *The Sickness unto Death* (July 1849), *KW* XIX (*SV* XI 195).
4. See Letter 213 and note 1.
5. See Letter 213. R. N. repeats S. K.'s pun: all those in the bus.

1. Reply to Letter 211.
2. Formerly the dwelling of K. L. Rahbek, in Frederiksberg, just west of Copenhagen. Kolderup-Rosenvinge moved there on May 29, 1849.
3. Master in the art of living—a pun on Magister *bibendi*, master in drinking.
4. A Danish proverb: *Den, som gemmner til Natten / Gemmer til Katten* [He who stores something away for the night stores it for the cat].
5. Each class or estate in society had held certain rights and privileges. Kolderup-Rosenvinge's comment satirizes the consequences of the recently effective Constitution (June 5, 1849), which cancelled the privileges but not the rank. As a *Conferentsraad*, Kolderup-Rosenvinge was near the top of the social pyramid, in the second class or estate.
6. See Letter 186 and note 7.
7. Alphonse de Lamartine, *Histoire de la Revolution de 1848* (Paris: 1849), p. 9.
8. See Letter 211.
9. A phrase alluding to the formal proceedings at the defense of doctoral dissertations.
10. An untranslatable Danish idiom. The King of Rats is a bunch of inextricably entwined rat tails.
11. Mineral water from Bad Kissingen in Bavaria.
12. *The Sickness unto Death* (July 29, 1849).
13. See note 5 above.
14. A. G. Sommer (1804-71), *Populære Forelæsninger over den asiatiske Cholera* (Copenhagen: 1849).
15. François-René de Chateaubriand (1768-1848). French author and politician. Kolderup-Rosenvinge was reading his *Mémoires d'outre-tombe* (Paris: 1849).
16. Concerning the motto on the overleaf of *The Sickness unto Death*, Kierkegaard had added in the ms.: A sermon by Bishop Albertini; cf. *Handbuch deutscher Beredsamkeit v*. Dr. O.L.B. Wolff, Leipzig 1845, I, p. 293 (*Pap.* VIII² B 171:6).
17. During the war (1848-50), there was constant talk of Scandinavian solidarity, and military assistance was expected from Sweden. See Letter 151 and note 2.
18. Pedro Calderon de la Barca (1600-81), *Gran ' Zenobia*. Kolderup-Rosenvinge published an anonymous translation of this tragedy (Copenhagen: 1849; *ASKB* 1934).

LETTER 217

1. K.-R. was staying at Frederiksberg, a walk of about half an hour.

2. Steen Bille, *Beretning om Corvetten Galatheas Reise omkring Jorden 1845, '46 og '47* [An Account of the Voyage Around the World on H.M.S. Galathea in 1845, '46, and '47] (Copenhagen: 1849).

3. Ibid., I, pp. 277-78.

4. Gerhard Tersteegen, *Auswahl aus Gerhard Tersteegens Schriften*, ed. G. Rapp (Essen: 1841; *ASKB* 729), p. 474. See *JP* IV 4751 (*Pap.* X¹ A 486).

LETTER 218

1. Carl E. Kiellerup (1822-1908), natural scientist who had sailed around the world on the light frigate *Galathea* in 1845-47.

2. See Letter 217 and note 2.

LETTER 219

1. See *JP* VI 6246 (*Pap.* IX A 258).

2. See Letter 177 and note 1.

3. See Letter 215.

4. The pseudonymous author of *The Sickness unto Death*. Johannes Climacus is the pseudonymous author of *Johannes Climacus*, *Fragments*, and *Postscript*.

5. A seminarian, someone attending a school of education.

6. From a seventeenth-century chapbook, Michael Saxe, *En liden aandelig Spørgsmaals Bog, sammendraget af den Hellige Scrifft etc. oversat ved Halvard Gunnersen*, published in 1602 and frequently thereafter until 1870.

7. See *KW* XIX (*SV* XI 118).

LETTER 220

1. The letter has not been found.

2. See I John 4:18.

LETTER 221

1. Letter 215.

2. See *The Sickness unto Death*, *KW* XIX (*SV* XI 196).

3. *KW* XII (*SV* VII 537).

4. See Map II.

LETTER 222

1. In *Pap.* X¹ A 636, S. K. writes: "In a note of August 10, R.N. has now discovered that the point of contact between Climacus and Anti-Climacus lies in despair, and apropos of that he quotes the closing words of Climacus, that he cannot call himself a Christian, which Anti-Climacus has to declare is despair.

"In an earlier note [i.e., Letter 215], R. Nielsen thought that the point of contact lay in offense. That was really far closer to the mark, and his new discovery is quite simply an anti-climax. For this is the scale: metaphysical *doubt* is ethically *despair* and *offense* in Christian terms.

"Anyway, insofar as there is truth in his discovery that the opposition indeed applies to the point of declaring oneself not to be a Christian—so there is this dubiousness in R. Nielsen's discovery that it had been written in my note to him that accompanied the book he has received."

LETTER 224

1. Reconciliation in the Hegelian system. Martensen was such a spokesman for "mediation." For S. K.'s opinion on mediation, see *Concluding Unscientific Postscript, KW* XII (*SV* VII 349).

LETTER 225

1. S. K. wrote an extensive comment on this letter; see *Pap.* X^1 A 674).
2. See Letter 224 and note.
3. Bishop Mynster. See Document IV and note 1.
4. Hans L. Martensen. See Letter 83, note 5.
5. Martensen.
6. *The Sickness unto Death, KW XIX* (*SV* XI 175, ll. 12-23): " 'It is . . . the self.' "

LETTER 226

1. Letter 219.

LETTER 227

1. S.A.V. Stein (1797-1868), a surgeon.

LETTER 228

1. King of Denmark (1808-39).
2. See II Corinthians 12:7; *JP* VI 6492 (*Pap.* X^2 A 20).
3. See Letter 227.

LETTER 229

1. An ironic reference to Martensen's system (see Letter 231 and note).
2. Pernille's remark in three languages, from *Jean de France*, a comedy by Ludvig Holberg (1684-1754).

LETTER 231

1. "The System" is Hans Martensen's *Den Christelige Dogmatic* (Copenhagen: 1849). In *JP* VI 6448 (*Pap.* X^1 A 553), S. K remarks: "While all existence is disintegrating, while anyone with eyes must see that all this about millions of Christians is a sham, indeed, that if anything Christianity has vanished from the world, Martensen sits and organizes a dogmatic system."

LETTER 232

1. See Letter 8, note 1.

LETTER 234

1. See Letter 162 and note 1.
2. *"The High Priest"*—*"The Publican"*—*"The Woman Who Was a Sinner,"* *Three Discourses at the Communion on Fridays* (published November 14, 1849), *KW* XVIII (*SV* XI 245-80).

LETTER 235

1. The reader who wishes to explore S. K.'s state of mind in Letters 235-239 is referred to the following entries: *JP* VI 6471-73, 6502, 6510, 6538-45, 6713 (*Pap.* X^5 A 148-50; X^2 A 68, 105, 210-17; X^3 A 769). These letters are in fact the drafts and final versions (the last two letters in no. 239) of letters intended for Regine Schlegel and her husband, J. F. Schlegel. The letters were sent on November 19, 1849. Schlegel returned unopened the sealed letter addressed to Regine. See *JP* VI 6538, 6472 (*Pap.* X^2 A 210; X^5 A 149). The drafts reveal the meticulous care with which S. K. revised and reworked his phrases.
2. Presumably a reference to *"The High Priest"* . . . *Three Discourses at the Communion on Fridays*; see Letter 234 and note. See *JP* VI 6545 (*Pap.* X^2 A 217).
3. See Ecclesiastes 3:7.
4. See note 2.
5. Regine Olsen had had an understanding with Johann Frederick Schlegel before her engagement to S. K. See *JP* VI 6472 (*Pap.* X^5 A 149:5). Their marriage took place November 3, 1847.

LETTER 236

1. See Letter 235 and note 1.
2. See Letter 47 and note.

LETTER 237

1. See Letter 235 and note 1.
2. Cf. Matthew, 5:25.

LETTER 238

1. See Letter 235 and note 1.
2. Terkild Olsen died on the night of June 25, 1849.

LETTER 239

1. See Letter 235 and note 1.
2. Ibid., note 2.
3. Ibid., note 5.
4. See *JP* VI 6713 (*Pap.* X^3 A 769): "At the time of her father's death, I wrote to Schlegel. He was furious and would in no way 'tolerate any intervention by another in the relationship between himself and his wife.' "

5. The date is assumed to be October 11, 1841. See *JP* VI 6472 (*Pap.* X⁵ A 149) and Letter 46, which conceivably might refer to one of the two theater performances mentioned below.

6. October 31 [1841], the date of Kierkegaard's first letter from Berlin.

7. See Letter 62 and note. This play was performed at the Royal Theater on October 12 and 18, 1841.

8. Alexandre Dumas, the Elder (1802-70), *Kean, ou Désordre et Génie* (Paris: 1836), performed at the Royal Theater on October 21, 1841.

9. Published as *JP* VI 6538 (*Pap.* X² A 210). NB¹⁴ refers to Kierkegaard's journal notebook no. 14.

LETTER 240

1. On October 30, 1849, P.C.K. addressed the Roskilde Convention and compared S. K. and Hans Martensen. P.C.K. praised Martensen at S. K.'s expense. The speech subsequently appeared in *Dansk Kirketidende*, December 16, 1849 (no. 219). S. K.'s indignation and deeply wounded feelings are also stated plainly in *JP* VI 6553-54 (*Pap.* X² A 273, 275). S. K. could never wholly forgive his brother and refused to receive him at Frederiks Hospital when he lay on his deathbed.

2. "A First and Last Declaration," *Concluding Unscientific Postscript, KW* XII (*SV* VII 545-49, unnumbered pages).

LETTER 241

1. Peter M. Stilling (1812-69), Danish philosopher.

2. *Om den indbildte Forsoning af Tro og—Viden, med særligt Hensyn til Professor Martensens "Christelige Dogmatik." Kritisk Polemisk Afhandling* (Copenhagen: 1850; advertised as published in *Berlingske Tidende*, December 22, 1849). See *Pap.* X² A 290, 303.

3. Stilling's wife had died two years earlier on December 22, 1847.

LETTER 242

1. Professor Oluf Lundt Bang (1788-1877) was Kierkegaard's physician.

2. Julie Thomsen (see Letter 148 and note 1).

3. Julie Thomsen was married to her cousin Hans Bentzen.

LETTER 243

1. Bishop J. P. Mynster published privately an essay, *"Om Hukommelsen, En psykologisk Undersøgelse"* (Copenhagen: 1849; *ASKB* 692), reprinted in *Blandede Skrifter* (Copenhagen: 1852; *ASKB* 358-63), I, pp. 203-49.

2. See *Stages on Life's Way, KW* XI (*SV* VI 15-21).

LETTER 244

1. An allusion to *Jeppe paa Bjerget*, a comedy by Ludvig Holberg (1648-1754).

2. Henrik Lund graduated from medical school in 1849 and served as a subordinate physician with the army.

LETTER 245

1. On December 22, 1849, Emil Boesen was installed as pastor in Horsens (see Map III).
2. Louise Caroline Holtermann (1815-79). They were married May 1, 1850. See Letter 265.

LETTER 246

1. An army hospital was established there during the war (1848-50); H. L.'s principal station. See Map III.

LETTER 248

1. See Letter 246 and note.
2. The Agerskov family was related to S. K.'s father by his first wife, Kristine Røyen. See Appendix I, Document II, and Letter 7.

LETTER 250

1. See Letter 245 and note 1.
2. See Letter 241 and note 2. In 1850 Stilling also published another pamphlet, *Et Par Spørgsmaal til Professor C. E. Scharling i Anleding af hans saakaldte Anmeldelse af Dr. Martensens Dogmatik* (Copenhagen: 1850). Emil Boesen could be referring to either work.
3. N. L. Helweg (1818-83), *"Professor Martensens Dogmatik og dens Angribere," Dansk Kirketidende*, V, col. 346-57, 369-73 (February and March 1850).
4. Peter Tetens (1791-1876).
5. See Letter 245 and note 2.
6. See Letter 263.

LETTER 251

1. See Letter 246 and note.
2. See Map III.
3. See Map II.

LETTER 252

1. Rasmus Nielsen dates this letter March 19, 1850, but in *Pap*. X³ A 2, S. K. states that he received the note on Thursday, April 18. S. K. assumes that the note is the consequence of a discussion they had had the previous Thursday, April 11, 1850, about Rasmus Nielsen's writing and his unacknowledged use of S. K.'s written work and private conversations. S. K.'s reproach caused Nielsen's indignation. Nielsen's published works were: *Evangelietroen og den moderne Bevidsthed* (Copenhagen: May 1849; *ASKB* 700); *Mag. S. Kierkegaard's "Johannes Climacus" og Dr. Martensens "Christelige Dogmatik" En undersøgende Anmeldelse* (Copenhagen: October 1849; *ASKB* 701); and *Evangelietroen og Theologien. Tolv Forelæsninger holdte ved Universitetet i Kjøbenhavn i Vinteren 1849-50* (Copenhagen: April 1850; *ASKB* 702). For S. K.'s private opinion of Nielsen and his work, see, for example, *Pap*. X³ A 2; *JP* VI 6607, 6610 (*Pap*. X³ A 3, 12).

LETTER 253

1. Letters 253-258 are drafts of Letter 259.

LETTER 259

1. *Pap.* X³ A 2; *JP* VI 6610 (*Pap.* X³ A 12). N.B.[14] refers to Kierkegaard's journal notebook no. 14.

LETTER 261

1. This note presumably predates Letter 252.

LETTER 262

1. In *JP* V 5761 (*Pap.* VI B 222), S. K. considers the idea of writing a book about migratory birds as a remedy for the melancholy of the times.
2. In Copenhagen. See Map I.

LETTER 263

1. Reply to Letter 250
2. See note 1.
3. Themes for sermons. See Letter 250.
4. E. B. graduated in 1834.
5. E. B. was planning to be married. See Letter 245 and note 2; Letter 265.

LETTER 264

1. Comprehensive written and oral examinations are given at the end of all studies at the University of Copenhagen. See Document XII. During the examination period, Kolderup-Rosenvinge would have a strenuous time.
2. *Om Kirkebestyrelse, Kirkeforfatning og Kirkens Ejendomsret* (Copenhagen: 1850).
3. See Letter 216.
4. K.-R.'s son, an officer and student at the Military Academy.

LETTER 265

1. The Cathedral of Copenhagen.

LETTER 267

1. The metrical arrangement of this epistolary poem is irregular, but the primary line seems to consist of five iambic feet, usually in rhymed couplets.
2. *Practice in Christianity*, *KW* XX (*SV* XII i-vii, 1-239), September 25, 1850.
3. O. L. Bang was a professor of medicine. See Letter 242 and note 1.
4. In addition to his physician's degree, Bang had written a post-graduate doctoral dissertation. University doctors in Denmark may wear a doctoral ring of gold with the seal of Minerva.
5. The post-graduate doctors of law, philosophy, and medicine place that title before their names. Bang's name would be "Dr. med. O. L. Bang."

6. All S. K.'s complimentary copies had gold edges and were bound in black leather.

7. *KW* XVI (*SV* IX).

8. Julie Thomsen (see Appendix I).

LETTER 269

1. Andreas Gottlob Rudelbach (1752-1862), from 1848 pastor of St. Mikkels Church in Slagelse on Sjælland.

2. *Practice in Christianity, KW* XX (*SV* XII, i-vii, 1-239).

3. Presumably A. G. Rudelbach, *Den Evangeliske Kirkeforfatnings Oprindelse og Princip* (Copenhagen: 1849; *ASKB* 171). See "An Open Letter . . . Dr. Rudelbach," *Prefaces and Newspaper Articles Related to the Writings, KW* IX (*SV* XIII 436-44).

LETTER 270

1. Fanny Lodovica le Normand de Bretteville (1827-59), daughter of Col. Louis le N. d. B and author of a work on the position of women in society, written under the pseudonym Sibylla.

2. H. C. Ørsted, *Aanden in Naturen*, I-II (Copenhagen: 1850; *ASKB* 945, Vol. I). A work on natural philosophy.

3.   Two buckets are seen to
      Be lowered and raised in the well,
      And if a full one hangs suspended above,
      Then the other must be below.
      Restlessly they travel back and forth
      Alternately full and now empty again,
      And when you bring this one to your mouth,
      Then that one hangs at the bottom.
      They can never with their gifts
      Refresh you at the same moment.

Friedrich Schiller, "Parabeln und Rätzel," *Schillers sämmtliche Werke*, I-XII (Stuttgart, Tübingen: 1838; *ASKB* 1804-15), I, pp. 349-50.

4.   But with your crown of victory
      You do still let your paternal eye light on me.
      Pray for me at the throne of Jehova
      And Jehova will hear you.

      Hover over me when the drop of time runs out
      Which God allowed me from his urn;
      When my death struggle begins,
      Hover by my deathbed.

Ludwig Hölty, "Elegi bei dem Grabe meines Vaters," *Der Göttinger Dichterbund*, ed. August Sauer, I-III (Stuttgart: *n.d.*), II, p. 35.

5. In Norse mythology, an ash whose branches encompass the world and extend to heaven and whose roots are in the depths of the earth.

LETTER 272

1. Published September 25, 1850, *KW* XX (*SV* XII).

2. Boesen must be referring to the attack on the Danish Church in *Practice in Christianity*, *KW* XX (*SV* XII 189-207).

3. In *Bemærkninger ved Skrivtet "Aanden i Naturen"* (Copenhagen, 1850), reprinted in J. P. Mynster, *Blandede Skrivter*, I-III (Copenhagen: 1853; *ASKB* 358-63), II, pp. 216-60. Here Mynster attacks Ørsted's work. See Letter 270 and note 2.

4. N. M. Spandet (1788-1858), a member of the National Assembly, introduced a law guaranteeing freedom of religion and abolishing mandatory baptisms and church weddings.

5. Gerhard Peter Brammer (1801-84), Bishop of Aarhus. See Map III. Horsens is in the Diocese of Aarhus.

6. In northern Jutland. See Map III.

LETTER 273

1. On the island of Als, near the battlefront. See Letter 246 and note.

LETTER 274

1. See Dedication 18; Letter 193 and note 1.

2. *Either/Or*, 2 ed. (May 1849).

3. *Either/Or*, I, *KW* III (*SV* I 214, 251).

4. Rosenborggade 156. On April 18, 1850, S. K. had moved to Nørregade 43. See Map I.

LETTER 275

1. S. K. might have thought so on reading Henrik Lund's letter (273).

LETTER 276

1. In Copenhagen. See Document XX.

LETTER 277

1. *Either/Or*, I, *KW* III (*SV* I 120).

2. The sermon "The Unchangeableness of God" (*KW* XXIII; *SV* XIV 276-94) was preached on May 18, 1851, and published in 1855.

3. See Matthew 25:45.

4. In April 1851, Kierkegaard moved from Nørregade 43 to Østerbro[e] 108 A.

LETTER 278

1. See Letter 186 and note 4; *Works of Love KW* XVI (*SV* IX 124).

2. See Letter 277 and note 2.

LETTER 279

1. H. P. Kofoed-Hansen had been appointed pastor at Haderslev in Jutland (see Map III) in December, 1850. At that time Haderslev was a difficult parish

with a congregation equally divided between Danish and German speaking members.

2. A review of *Practice in Christianity* by A. Lysander, *Tidsskrift för Literatur* (1851), pp. 227-52.

LETTER 280

1. P. C. Kierkegaard at Pedersborg near Sorø[e] (see Map II).

2. P.C.K.'s first wife, Marie Boisen (1806-37), daughter of Bishop P. O. Boisen (1762-1831).

3. Rasmus Møller (1763-1842).

4. Poul Martin Møller (1794-1838), a famous Danish poet. See Letter 17 and note 3.

5. Under Church auspices, a number of charitable establishments, referred to as convents, were maintained for ladies of the nobility. The Danish island Falster lies south of Sjælland.

6. See Document XVII and note 6.

7. Petronella Ross (1805-75), *Fortællinger for simple Læsere*, published occasionally between 1851 and 1867. P. Ross wrote a number of published works and carried on correspondence with the philosopher F. C. Sibbern.

8. See Map II.

9. Meaning that her brother lived in the same block as Kierkegaard.

10. *Christian Discourses*, III, *KW* XVII (*SV* X 42-51).

LETTER 281

1. This is a draft for a letter intended to accompany a complimentary copy of *On My Work as an Author* (August 7, 1851), *KW* XXII (*SV* XIII 489-509). See Letter 282.

LETTER 282

1. See Plato, *Phaedo*, 104-106.

2. I.e., Mr. Etatsraad (Councilor of State), the honorific title used in the salutation of the letter.

3. Presumably *Two Discourses at the Communion on Fridays*, published August 7, 1851.

4. *On My Work as an Author*, published August 7, 1851, in which S. K. acknowledges the authorship of *The Crisis and a Crisis in the Life of an Actress*, a work on Johanne Luise Heiberg, wife of J. L. Heiberg. See Letter 283.

LETTER 283

1. Johanne Luise Heiberg (1812-90), actress and wife of Johann Ludvig Heiberg, was a major factor in making the Royal Theater a center of Danish culture. Her sparkling performances captivated and inspired Danish theater-goers for a generation and generated a golden period in the history of Danish theater. She was much admired by the intelligentsia of her time, among them, S. K., who wrote *The Crisis and a Crisis in the Life of an Actress* in her honor.

2. *On My Work as an Author, KW* XXII (*SV* XIII 497). See Letter 282 and note 4.

3. *KW* XVII (*SV* X 319-44).

LETTER 284

1. In Danish, the verse is an eight-line stanza in lines alternating five iambic feet with five and one half feet, rhyming a b a b c d c d.

2. *Two Discourses at the Communion on Fridays, KW* XVIII (*SV* XII 263-90); *On My Work as an Author, KW* XXII (*SV* XIII 489-509).

3. O. L. Bang puns on Ki[e]rkegaard: cemetery. See Letter 10 and note 4.

4. Aalholm on Lolland (see Map III).

5. Sophie Bang (1801-78), wife of O. L. Bang.

6. O. L. Bang, *Eva Homo* (Copenhagen: 1851; *ASKB* 1532). This epic poem in fifteen cantos is a slavish but ludicrous imitation of Frederik Paludan-Müller's (1809-76) famous romantic epic *Adam Homo* (Copenhagen: 1842 and 1848).

7. Blanco Street, now part of Fredericiagade, near Amalienborg. See Map I.

8. An allusion to *Adam Homo*. See note 6 above.

9. See note 3 above.

LETTER 285

1. *An Upbuilding Discourse* (December 20, 1850), *KW* XVIII (*SV* XII 243-59). *On My Work as an Author* (August 7, 1851), *KW* XXII (*SV* XIII, 489-509). *Two Discourses at the Communion on Fridays* (August 7, 1851), *KW* XVIII (*SV* XII 263-290).

2. See Letter 272 and note 4.

3. *An Upbuilding Discourse* (December 20, 1850) deals with "what we may learn from the woman who was a sinner." With its warning against self-righteousness, it might be seen as relevant to the debate about Spandet's proposal.

4. "*Foranlediget ved en Yttring af Dr. Rudelbach mig betræffende,*" *Fædrelandet*, January 31, 1851, no. 26; "An Open Letter," *Prefaces and Articles, KW* IX, (*SV* XIII, 436-44). See Letter 269 and note 3.

5. Throughout *On My Work as an Author*, S. K. uses the past tense.

6. *For Self-Examination* (September 12, 1851), *KW* XXI (*SV* XII 293-370).

7. Mathias G. G. Steenstrup (1822-1904) lived in the same building as S. K. at Østerbrogade 108A. See Map I.

8. Johannes Boesen (1851-1909), who later became a pastor.

9. *For Self-Examination*. See note 6 above.

LETTER 286

1. Thulstrup assumes that this letter was never sent. This is supported by *Pap.* X⁵ A 60, where S. K. remarks that what had been written in the journals about Mynster, Goldschmidt, and the rural pastorate had not been used.

2. Anonymous [L. J. M. Gude (1820-95)], *Om Magister S. Kierkegaards Forfattervirksomhed, Iagttagelser af en Landsbypræst* (Copenhagen: October

1851). S. K.'s anger is apparent in *Pap*. X⁶ B 144-61. Gude was a follower of H. L. Martensen, with whom he carried on considerable correspondence.

3. In Gude's brochure (p. 42; see note 2 above), S. K. is reproached for allegedly having compared himself to the highest authorities in the Danish Church.

4. *KW* XXI (*SV* XII 311).

LETTER 287

1. Presumably *Den augsburgske Confession, oversat og belyst ved historisk-dogmatisk Udvikling*, tr. H. N. Clausen (Copenhagen: 1851; *ASKB* 387).

2. S. K.'s complimentary copies.

LETTER 288

1. Reply to Letter 287.

LETTER 289

1. Ilia Marie Fibiger (1817-67), Danish writer and philanthropist, became intensely interested in S. K.'s writings around 1852, especially *For Self-Examination*, which, she says, "surpasses everything she has ever read—apart from the New Testament, of course." In 1855, she served as head nurse at Frederiks Hospital and diligently tended to S. K. on his deathbed.

2. *Marsk Stig* was submitted to the Royal Theater and rejected in June 1851, with the comment that a tragedy with the same title, by Carsten Hauch, had been performed recently.

3. J. L. Heiberg (see Letter 3 and note 10), then Director of the Royal Theater, wrote to her: "In any event, this work deserves special attention." Later some of her writings were published, and the drama *Modsætninger* was presented by the Royal Theater.

4. *Et gammelt Eventyr*, submitted in July and rejected in October 1851.

5. *Hagbard og Signe, Tragedie i fem Akter*, submitted in January and rejected in April 1852.

6. I.e., than J. L. Heiberg's.

7. I. M. F.'s father had been a co-editor of *Maanedsskrift for Litteratur*.

LETTER 290

1. C. R. [Carl Reitzel?]. Carl F. T. Reitzel (1828-1906), son of C. A. Reitzel (see Letter 12 and note 1), lived at the address given in the letter, Kierkegaard's response is not known. In any case, there is no published commendatory preface as requested.

2. Presumably his father, C. A. Reitzel.

LETTER 292

1. *KW* XXI (*SV* XII 295-370); *KW* XX (*SV* XII 1-239).

2. *Three Discourses at the Communion on Fridays* (1849), *KW* XVIII (*SV* XI 245-59).

3. See II Samuel 12:7; *For Self-Examination*, *KW* XXI (*SV* XII 327).

4. The spelling suggests that the unknown writer was from Jutland.

LETTER 293

1. II Peter 2:22: "The dog turns back to his own vomit, and the sow is washed only to wallow in the mire."

2. See Letter 279.

3. Although the source of the quotation cannot be identified, the conclusion is known: ". . . , said the farmer as he sheared his pig."

4. F. Engelhardt Boisen (1808-82), brother of Marie, née Boisen, P. C. Kierkegaard's first wife.

5. See Map III.

6. Perhaps Kofoed-Hansen's *Det bør mig at være i min Faders Gerning* [Luke 2:49]. *Prædiken paa lste Søndag efter Helligtrekonger* (Odense: 1852).

7. When he became the pastor in Haderslev. See Map III.

8. See Letter 279 and note 1.

9. *Two Discourses at the Communion on Fridays*, *KW* XVIII (*SV* XII 263-90; see especially 273-78).

10. *KW* XXI (*SV* XII 293-370).

11. See *Danske Ordsprog og Mundheld, samlede og ordnede af N.F.S. Grundtvig* (Copenhagen: 1845; *ASKB* 1549), no. 3009. The Øresund is the sound between Sjælland and Sweden and was the scene of much strife, minor and major, between Danes and Swedes and of battles between fishermen and sailors. The Danish *slag* can mean both battle and blow. The proverb, as employed here, alludes to I Corinthians 9:26-27.

12. I.e., when Kofoed-Hansen quit schoolmastering at Odense and became a clergyman in Copenhagen.

13. The position as superintendent for Church Affairs in Southern Jutland and the Diocese of Slesvig was offered to Martensen in 1852. He considered it but declined.

14. Kofoed-Hansen's wife (1827-98) was born Sophie Isabella Lætitia Countess Moltke and was a cousin of Count Carl Moltke, in 1852 the Cabinet Minister for the Affairs of Slesvig.

15. S. K. had in fact moved to Østerbrogade 108A. See Map I.

16. See *JP* VI 6629 (*Pap.* X³ A 144).

17. *Preciosa* (1810), a German lyrical drama by P. A. Wolff (1782-1828), with a musical accompaniment by Carl Maria von Weber (1786-1826), translated by C. A. Boye. It was frequently performed at the Royal Theater in Copenhagen in the 1830s and 40s.

18. The source in Shakespeare has not been identified.

19. Cromwell is said to have used all fifteen bedrooms at Whitehall at one time or another.

20. Christoph Ernst Friedrich Weyse (1774-1842), a Danish composer, with whom K.-H. had lived in Copenhagen.

LETTER 294

1. This is the second of two extant drafts.

2. Jonas Collin (1776-1861), appointee to the Ministry of Finance and Privy Councilor, who served on the board of directors for the Royal Theater and was a patron of the arts.

3. The second edition of *Works of Love* (April 1852), *KW* XVI (*SV* IX).

LETTER 295

1. See especially *JP* VI 6310 (*Pap.* X¹ A 42). The meeting described in this letter to the Dowager Queen took place in 1849, when S. K. went to Sorgen-fri (see Letter 181 and note 3) to present *Works of Love* (September 29, 1849) to Christian VIII. See Letter 151.

2. King Christian VIII (1839-48).

LETTER 297

1. *Dannevirke*, a Danish newspaper in Slesvig. The article mentioned by Kofoed-Hansen appeared on October 1, 1851 (no. 176) and is signed "B" (perhaps Pastor U. S. Boesen). It praises S. K.'s *For Self-Examination* and goes on to compare S. K. and Grundtvig at the latter's expense. F. E. Boisen (see Letter 293 and note 4) replied to "B" two weeks later in *Dannevirke* (October 15), maintaining that praise of S. K. constituted no valid basis for criticism of Grundtvig.

2. Sophie Gyrithe Kofoed-Hansen (1852-99).

3. *Berlingske Tidende* (July 6, 1852): an advertisement for a meeting of "The Society for Truth in Religion."

4. A figure from *comedia dell'arte*.

5. See Letter 118 and note 1. The Roskilde Convention submitted a proposal for a new hymnal for the Danish Church in 1850. In the Diocese of Slesvig two hymnals were in use: one authorized in 1844 and E. Pontoppidan's of 1740.

6. Count Otto Joachim Moltke (1770-1853), Danish statesman and owner of the Espe estate on Sjælland.

7. A private library association. See Letter 115.

LETTER 298

1. The date is uncertain. Iversen was Rudelbach's publisher from 1852 onwards. See Letter 269 and note 3.

LETTER 299

1. F. J. Mynster (1816-57) may have sent S. K. a copy of his father's (see Appendix I) *Meddelelser om mit Liv* (Copenhagen: 1854). On Bishop J. P. Mynster, see Document IV and note 1.

2. S. K. subsequently wrote explicitly about Mynster. See, for example, *KW* XXIII (*SV* XIV 5-10, 15-35).

LETTER 299a

1. See Letter 13 and note 1. Letter 299a is the latest dated personal letter from Kierkegaard's hand. The text is in H. P. Rohde, *Gaadefulde Stadier paa*

Kierkegaards Vej (Copenhagen: Rosenkilde og Bagger, 1974), pp. 115-16. Concerning the date, see Letter 200, note 2.

2. The undertaker was making preparations for the funeral of Øllegaard Baggesen Kierkegaard (1782-May 2, 1855), wife of M. A. Kierkegaard.

3. Karen Jørgensen Kierkegaard (1770-January 1, 1844), wife of Anders Andersen Kierkegaard (1767-1816), a brother of M. A. Kierkegaard.

4. Andreas Kierkegaard (1799-August 28, 1853), son of Anders A. Kierkegaard and Karen J. Kierkegaard. See note 3 above.

5. Hans Peter Kierkegaard. See Letter 47 and note 1.

LETTER 300

1. *KW* XXIII (*SV* XIV 116-38), published June 4, 1855. From 1847 on, S. K. would sell rights to the first edition to C. A. Reitzel and renegotiate sales of subsequent editions. See Letter 152 and note 1.

LETTER 301

1. Adam Oehlenschläger (1779-1850), *Erindringer*, I-IV (Copenhagen: 1850-51).

LETTER 303

1. N. C. Møller, bookbinder at Graabrødretorv 97.

LETTER 306

1. G. Stephanie, *Apothekeren og Doctoren*, a musical drama from 1789.

LETTER 307

1. Goethe, *Aus meinen Leben* [From My Life], *Goethe's Werke, vollstandiger Ausgabe letzer Hand*, I-LV (Stuttgart, Tübingen: 1828-33; *ASKB* 1641-68).

LETTER 308

1. Not identified.

LETTER 311

1. This anonymous letter contains the misspellings and awkward syntax of a poorly educated person.

DEDICATIONS

1. See Letter 83 and note 5.
2. Hans Peter Holst (1811-93), Danish poet.
3. See Letter 3 and note 10.
4. See Document VI and note 1.
5. See Letter 3 and note 10.

6. Johan Nikolai Madvig (1804-86), professor of philology in Copenhagen from 1829 and S. K.'s teacher.

7. See Letter 185 and note 5.

8. Jens Olaus Hansen (1795-1854), respected jurist and Councilor of State and a member of the board of directors, University of Copenhagen.

9. See note 6 above.

10. See Letter 3 and note 10.

11. See Document IV and note 1.

12. See Letter 3 and note 10.

13. See note 8 above.

14. See Document IV and note 1.

15. Rasmus Villads Christian Winther (1796-1876), Danish poet.

16. Henrik Hertz (1797-1870), Danish poet and esthetician. He and S. K. moved in the same cultural circles.

17. See Letter 3 and note 10.

18. See Document IV and note 1.

19. See Letter 269 and note 1.

20. See Letter 185 and note 5.

21. See Letter 3 and note 10.

22. See Letter 158 and note 1.

23. Wilhelmine Susanne Rothe, b. Kolderup-Rosenvinge (1823-88), was married to P. C. Rothe (1811-1902), pastor at Frue Church. He and S. K. occasionally saw each other during S. K.'s first visit to Berlin (1841-42).

24. See Letter 269 and note 1.

25. See Letter 158 and note 1.

26. Miss Rosenvinge was the unmarried daughter, Sophie Wilhelmina Bertha Kolderup-Rosenvinge, who kept house for her father (see Letter 160 and note 1).

27. A. G. Rudelbach was Superintendent in Glaucha, Saxony, 1829-45. See Letter 269 and note 1.

28. See Letter 294 and note 2.

29. See Letter 283 and note 1.

30. See Letter 170 and note 1.

31. See Letter 177 and note 1.

32. See Document IV and note 1.

33. See Letter 111 and note 1.

34. See Letter 193 and note 1.

35. Christen Nieman Rosenkilde (1786-1861), Danish actor and father of Adolf Marius R., also an actor.

36. See Letter 134 and note 1, and the introduction to *Two Ages, KW* XIV, by Howard and Edna Hong.

Kierkegaard Family

Michael Pedersen Kierkegaard, born in Sæding, December 12, 1756, died in Copenhagen, August 9, 1838; he was married twice. His first wife, Kirstine Nielsdatter Røyen, died March 23, 1796. They had been married two years; no children.

M.P.K.'s second marriage to Ane Sørensdatter Lund (June 18, 1768–July 7, 1834) took place April 26, 1797. There were seven children in this marriage:

1. Maren Kirstine K., Copenhagen. September 7, 1797–March 15, 1822; unmarried.

2. Nicoline Christine K., Copenhagen. October 10, 1799–September 10, 1832. Married to clothier Johan Christian Lund, Copenhagen. February 5, 1799–July 10, 1875. 5 children:
Henrik Sigvard Lund. July 18, 1825–February 26, 1889.[1]
Michael Frederik Christian Lund. September 2, 1826–July 6, 1907.[2]
Sofie Vilhelmine Lund. November 28, 1827–March 12, 1875.
Carl Ferdinand Lund. July 2, 1830–January 21, 1912.[3]
Stillborn son.

3. Petrea Severine K., Copenhagen. September 7, 1801–December 29, 1834. Married to the head of Nationalbanken (the National Bank) Henrik Ferdinand Lund (the brother of Nicoline K's husband),[4] Copenhagen, March 15, 1803–August 24, 1875. 4 children:
Anna Henriette Lund. November 11, 1829–May 16, 1909.[5]
Vilhelm Nicolaj Lund. March 23, 1831–July 18, 1902.[6]
Peter Christian Lund. July 4, 1833–September 6, 1904.[7]
Peter Severin Lund. December 13, 1834–July 18, 1864.[8]

4. Peter Christian K., Hillerød. July 6, 1805–February 24, 1888.[9]
First marriage: Elise Marie Boisen. January 31, 1806–July 18, 1837.
Second marriage: Sophie Henriette Glahn. May 14, 1809–June 1, 1881. 1 child:
Pascal Michael Poul Egede K. March 27, 1842–February 28, 1915;[10] unmarried.

5. Søren Michael K., Copenhagen. March 23, 1807–September 14, 1819.

6. Niels Andreas K., Copenhagen. April 4, 1809–September 21, 1833 (in Paterson, New Jersey); unmarried.

7. Søren Aabye Kierkegaard, Copenhagen. May 5, 1813–November 11, 1855; unmarried.

NOTES TO KIERKEGAARD FAMILY

1. Physician and gentleman farmer; had close connections with S. K. and was an intern at Frederiks Hospital during S. K.'s terminal illness. Attracted attention at S. K.'s funeral by a speech attacking the institutional church.

2. Physician and surgeon, later district medical officer in Copenhagen; Knight of *Dannebrog*.

3. Owner of *"Aldersro,"* a freehold farm in Værslev parish.

4. Henrik Ferdinand Lund had two brothers. Christian Lund (1799–1875) was married to Nicoline K. The other brother was Professor Vilhelm Lund (1801–80), biologist and scientist who lived in Lagoa Santa, Brazil, from 1832 until his death. After the death of his first wife he married his cousin Cathrine L. (1800–59), whose brother was Professor Troels Lund (1802–67), a member of the Danish Academy of Arts.

5. Henriette Lund wrote *Mit Forhold til hende* (1904) (My Relationship to Her) and *Erindringer fra Hjemmet* (Memories from My Home).

6. Titular Councillor of State and Knight of *Dannebrog*; freehold farmer-owner of *"Anissegaard."*

7. Captain of the cavalry and gentleman farmer.

8. B. D., teacher of history and Danish language; died as a volunteer in Schleswig-Holstein, 1864.

9. Th. M., 1836; pastor in Petersborg-Kinderstofte, 1842–56; Bishop of Aalborg, 1856–75; Minister of Education and Ecclesiastical Affairs in Count Frij's government, 1867–68; knighted.

10. B. D., librarian in Aalborg.

Maps of Copenhagen, North Sjælland, and Jylland

Appendices

Map I: Copenhagen

1. Østerbrogade 108A (razed)	15. University
2. Nyboder	16. Løvstræde 7
3. Frederiks Hospital	17. Trinitatis Church and Round Tower,
4. Østergade	Kjøbmagergade
5. Holmens Church	18. Nørregade 43 (now 35), 230A
6. Børsgade	(now 38)
7. Knippelsbro	19. Kultorvet 132 (now 11)
8. Railway Station	20. Tornebuskegade and
9. Tivoli	Rosenborggade 156A (now 7)
10. Philosophgangen	21. Nørreport
11. Vesterport	22. Assistents Cemetery (outside city)
12. Nytorv 2 (now 27)	23. Royal Theater
13. Klædeboderne 5-6 (now 11)	24. Regensen
14. Vor Frue Church	25. Helligaands (Helliggeistes) Church

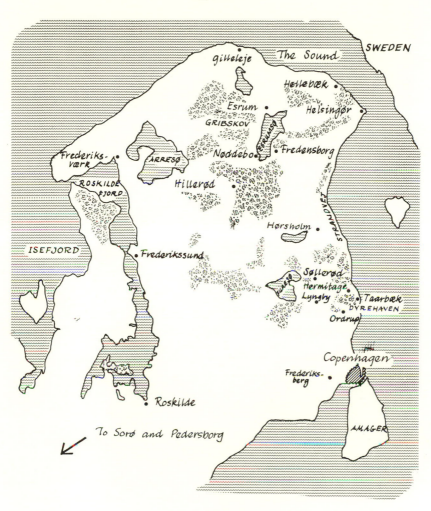

MAP II: North Sjælland

MAP III: Jylland

BIBLIOGRAPHICAL NOTE

For·general bibliographies of Kierkegaard studies, see:

Jens Himmelstrup, *Søren Kierkegaard International Bibliografi*. Copenhagen: Nyt Nordisk Forlag Arnold Busck, 1962.
Aage Jørgensen, *Søren Kierkegaard-litteratur 1961-1970*. Aarhus: Akademisk Boghandel, 1971.
Kierkegaard: A Collection of Critical Essays, ed. Josiah Thompson. New York: Doubleday (Anchor Books), 1972.
Søren Kierkegaard's Journals and Papers, ed. and tr. Howard V. Hong and Edna H. Hong, assisted by Gregor Malantschuk, I. Bloomington, Indiana: Indiana University Press, 1967.

For topical bibliographies of Kierkegaard studies, see ibid., I, II (1970), III-IV (1975).

ADVISORY BOARD

KIERKEGAARD'S WRITINGS

Howard V. Hong, General Editor, *St. Olaf College, 1972-*

Robert L. Perkins, *University of South Alabama, 1972-76.*

Niels Thulstrup, *University of Copenhagen, 1972-76.*

John W. Elrod, *Iowa State University, 1977-*

Per Lønning, *University of Oslo, 1977-*

Gregor Malantschuk, *University of Copenhagen, 1977-*

INDEX

(The references are to the page numbers in the text and notes.)

Aabye, Abelone, 3
Aabye, Niels, 3
Aabye, Peter, 3
Adler, Adolph Peter, 23, 156, 448, 466
Agerskov, Christian, 3, 51, 452, 454
Agerskov, Niels, 343, 490
Algreen-Ussing, Tage, 50, 244, 452, 477
Andersen, Hans Christian, 289, 483
Anger, Edvard Julius, 5, 445
anonymous, 365, 366, 379, 381, 398, 400, 401, 425, 493, 496, 499
Aquinas, St. Thomas, 107
Aristotle, 170, 468
Arnim, L. A. von, 64, 455; *Des Knaben Wunderhorn*, 457
Aurelius, Marcus, 484

Baggesen, Jens, 265, 474, 479; *Danske Værker*, 456
Balle, N. E., *Lærebog* [Catechism], 278, 481
Bang, Ole Lundt, 339, 360, 390, 489, 491, 495
baptism of infants, 147–48, 176–78, 180, 229, 465, 466, 469, 475. *See also* Martensen, H. L.; Kierkegaard, Peter Christian
Barfod, Hans Peter, 465
Barfoed, Chresten Thomsen, 237, 476
Bentzen, H., 339, 489
Bernhard, Carl (pseudonym for Andreas de St. Aubin), 457; *Old Memories*, 77, 457
Bille, Steen, 308, 486

Blicher, Steen Steensen, 159, 467
Boesen, C. U., 468
Boesen, Emil, 51, 89, 92, 101, 110, 113, 120, 127, 133, 139, 143, 150, 151, 154, 159, 160, 161, 162, 163, 164, 165, 166, 167, 243, 321, 341, 344, 357, 359, 372, 393, 449, 453, 460, 461, 463, 464, 467, 468, 490, 491, 492
Boisen, Frederik Engelhardt, 405, 407, 415
Bojesen, Ernst Frederik Christian, 38, 89
Borgerdyds School, 7, 9, 17, 24, 25, 37, 38, 39, 40, 89, 159, 168, 429, 445, 447, 450, 461, 466
Böhme, Jacob, 184, 471
Brammer, Gerhard Peter, 373, 493
Bremer, Frederika, 286, 287, 288, 482
Bretteville, Fanny Lodovica le Norman de, 366, 371, 492
Brorson, Hans Adolf, 27, 449
Bruun, T. C., 216, 474
Brøchner, Hans, 210, 473
Bærentzen, E. D., 102, 461

Caesar, Julius, 5
Calderon de la Barca, Pedro, 307, 359, 485
Caroline Amalie, Dowager Queen of Denmark, 412, 478, 498
Cavaignac, L. E., 265, 266, 270, 271, 471
Chateaubriand, François-René de, 306, 485

Chievitz, Joachim Christian, 21, 447
Christian VIII, King of Denmark,
23, 25, 218-19, 412-14, 447, 474,
477, 484, 498
Christensen, P. V., 264, 265, 268,
269, 479
Cicero, Marcus Tullius, 5
Clausen, Emil, 180, 469
Clausen, Henrik Nicolai, 224, 225,
396, 397, 433, 434, 452, 473, 475,
496
Collin, Jonas, 225, 410, 435, 497
confirmation, 4, 195, 207, 208, 445
contemporary politics, 255, 260-61,
262, 265, 266, 268, 270, 271, 273,
274, 277, 292, 293, 294, 295, 299,
300, 305, 405, 450, 451, 474, 478,
481, 484, 485
Corsair affair, 470, 483. *See also*
newspapers, periodicals, and
journals

Dannebrog, Order of, 448
Daub, Carl, 58, 454, 460
Dencker, Elise, 136, 462
Don Juan, 43, 451, 483
Dumas, Alexandre, the Elder, 337;
Kean, ou Dèsordre et Genie, 337,
489

Eichendorff, Joachim von, 67, 456
Eiríksson, Magnus, 228, 231, 475
Engelstoft, Christian Thorning, 12,
447
Till Eulenspiegel, 199, 472
Ewald, Johannes, 73, 457

Fabricius, Frederik, 58, 454
Farinelli, 105, 461
Fenger, Carl Emil, 37, 450
Fenger, Henning, 455, 459
Fenger, Johannes Ferdinand, 37, 450
Fenger, N. H., 41, 451
Fenger, Peter Andreas, 37, 450

Fenger, Rasmus Theodor, 19, 20,
37, 447, 450
Fibiger, Ilia Marie, 398, 496
Frederik VI, King of Denmark, 3,
317, 487
Frederiks Hospital, 28, 449, 453,
489, 496
Frydendahl, Jørgen Peter, 267, 268,
480

Giødwad, Jens Finsteen, 172, 183,
187, 225, 236, 468, 470, 471
Goethe, Johann Wolfgang von, 198,
472; *Faust*, 43, 300, 483, 484; *Die
Wahlverwandtschaften*, 350; *Aus
meinem Leben*, 423, 499
Goldschmidt, Meïr Aron, 495
Grimm, J. L. C. and W. C., *Kinder-
und Hausï-Märchen*, 278-79, 481
Grundtvig, Nikolai Frederik Severin, 402, 458, 465, 497, 498
Grundtvigianism, 148, 176-78, 180,
402-3, 465, 469, 470, 475
Gruppe, Otto Friedrich, 98, 461
Gude, Ludvig Jacob Mendel, 395,
396; *Om Magister S. Kierkegaards
Forfattervirksomhed, Iagttagelser af
en Landsbypræst* [On Magister
S. K.'s Work as an Author: Observations by a Village Parson],
396-98, 495, 496
Gyllembourg, Thomasine, 191-95,
196-98, 437, 471; *A Story of Everyday Life*, 191, 192, 194, 196-98,
437. *See also* Kierkegaard, Søren
Aabye, *works: Two Ages* (*KW* XIV)

Haase, Karl, 57, 454
Hald, Peter Tetens, 41
Hammerich, Martin Johannes, 23,
448, 453
Hansen, Jens Olaus, 430, 431
Hauch, Carsten, 289, 483
Hedberg, Abelone, 245, 477
Hegel, Georg Wilhelm Friedrich,

Logik, 107; *Encyclopaedie*, 118, 463; *Vorlesungen über die Geschichte der Philosophie*, 215, 473
Hegelianism, 42, 104, 107, 118, 156, 251, 252, 337, 452, 461, 463, 466, 486, 487
Heiberg, Johan Ludvig, 46, 51, 54-55, 105, 191, 192, 193, 294, 388, 399, 429, 430, 431, 432, 433, 451, 452, 453, 461, 464, 467, 471, 494, 496, 499; *Recensenten og Dyret* [The Critic and the Beast], 467, 484; *Aprilsnarrene* [April's Fools], 470
Heiberg, Johanne Luise, 389, 435, 452, 494
Helweg, Nicolaus Ludvig, 344, 490
Herodotus, 5
Hertz, Henrik, 432, 472
Hirsch, Emanuel, 455
Hjorthøy, C. F. J., 97, 461
Hoffman, E. T. A., 53, 453
Hohlenberg, Matthias Hagen, 14, 57, 447, 454
Holberg, Ludvig, 93, 460; *Jacob von Thyboe*, 83, 118, 249, 458, 463, 478; *Den politiske Kandestøber* [The Tinker Turned Politician], 137, 216, 267, 464, 474, 480; *Geert Westphaler*, 159, 246-49, 467, 477, 478; *Julestuen* [The Chistmas Parlor], 201, 259, 262, 265, 472; *Barselsstuen* [The Borning Room], 266, 480; *Hexerie eller Blind Alarm* [Witchcraft or False Alarm], 267, 480; *Don Ranudo de Colibrados*, 271, 272, 480; *Jean de France*, 319, 487; *Jeppe paa Bjerget* [Jeppe of the Hill], 340, 489
Holst, Hans Peter, 429, 500
Holtermann, Louise Caroline, 342, 346, 357, 359, 374, 394, 490
Homer, 5
Horace, 5, 256, 478, 484
Hornemann, Jens Wilken, 8, 45, 446, 451

Hornsyld, Jens, 141, 464
Hölty, Ludwig, 369, 492

Ibsen, Peter Diderik, 171, 216, 457, 468
Ingemann, Bernhard Severin, 480
Iversen, A. C. D. F. G., 417, 498

Kiellerup, C. E., 309, 486
Kierkegaard, Anders, 3, 59
Kierkegaard, Ane Sørensdatter, 3, 27, 130, 449
Kierkegaard, Else Pedersdatter, 55, 56, 59, 130, 454, 463
Kierkegaard, Hans Peter, 88, 175, 280, 286, 418, 459
Kierkegaard, Henriette, 148, 150, 156, 173, 179, 190, 191, 214, 226, 235, 466, 469, 473
Kierkegaard, Maren Kirstine, 449
Kierkegaard, Marie Boisen, 387
Kierkegaard, Michael Andersen, 59, 60, 418, 454, 459, 473, 498
Kierkegaard, Michael Pedersen, 3, 9, 10, 27, 39, 47, 55, 59, 130, 174, 211, 327, 396, 417, 445, 449, 451, 452, 453, 454, 456, 463, 490
Kierkegaard, Peter Christian, 5, 37, 55, 59, 90, 110, 127, 130, 138, 141, 144, 146, 149, 155, 157, 169, 173, 174, 175, 176, 178, 180, 189, 193, 211, 227, 228, 233, 277, 337, 387, 445, 449, 450, 454, 463, 464, 465, 468, 469, 471, 472, 473, 479, 489, 494
Kierkegaard, Poul, 174, 179, 180, 190, 191, 228, 469
KIERKEGAARD, SØREN AABYE,
  academic record: 7, 9, 10-28, 40, 46, 445-49, 450, 458
  baptism: 3
  burial plot: 26-27, 449
  confirmation: 4
  engagement to *Regine Olsen*: 61-88, 89-91, 92-95, 101-5, 113-

Kierkegaard, Søren Aabye (*cont.*)
16, 120-26, 133-38, 455-59, 461-
62, 463, 464
  final approach to Regine Schlegel:
  322-37, 488-89
  money matters: 144-45, 149-50,
  157, 211-13, 220-24, 233-34, 474
  pseudonyms: 338, 382, 468, 478;
  Anti-Climacus, 299, 303, 310,
  312, 316, 360, 454, 484, 486;
  Climacus, 193, 221, 294, 303, 310,
  312, 454, 469, 484, 486; Inter et
  Inter, 389; Victor Eremita, 183,
  207, 286, 376-77, 432, 465, 470,
  500
  sermons: 17-22, 346, 357, 379-
  80, 381-84, 385, 388, 394, 405,
  406, 447-49, 493
  sickness and death: 28-32, 449
  will: 33, 337, 450, 489
  works: *From the Papers of One
  Still Living* (1838) (*KW* I), 55, 58,
  453, 454, 483; *The Concept of Irony*
  (1841) (*KW* II), 23-25, 89, 429,
  447, 448, 451, 459, 463; *Johannes
  Climacus, or De omnibus dubitandum
  est* (1842) (*KW* VII), 469, 484, 486;
  Either/Or (1843 and 1849) (*KW* III
  IV), 123, 137, 138, 139, 173, 200,
  206, 207, 220, 222, 223, 224, 225,
  237, 238, 268, 288, 289, 290, 341,
  344, 376-77, 379, 382, 431, 432,
  453, 454, 456, 461, 462, 463, 464,
  465, 466, 470, 471, 472, 473, 474,
  476, 479, 483, 493; *Repetition*
  (1843) (*KW* VI), 150, 151, 154,
  175, 215, 221, 455, 458, 462, 466,
  469, 473; *Fear and Trembling* (1843)
  (*KW* VI), 221, 298, 457, 467, 484;
  Four Upbuilding Discourses (1843)
  (*KW* V), 429; *Philosophical Fragments* (1844) (*KW* VII), 200, 221,
  451, 454, 472, 486; *The Concept of
  Anxiety* (1844) (*KW* VIII), 221,
  455; *Prefaces* (1844) (*KW* IX), 221;
  Four Upbuilding Discourses (1844)

(*KW* V), 173, 469; *Three Discourses
  on Imagined Occasions* (1845) (*KW*
  X), 221, 430; *Stages on Life's Way*
  (1845) (*KW* XI), 221, 286, 339-40,
  454, 458, 470, 471, 483, 489;
  Eighteen Upbuilding Discourses
  (1845) (*KW* V), 181, 183, 184,
  185, 338; *Concluding Unscientific
  Postcript* (1846) (*KW* XII), 188,
  189, 220, 221, 303, 312, 430, 471,
  472, 485, 486, 487, 489; *Two Ages:
  The Age of Revolution and the Present Age. A Literary Review* (1846)
  (*KW* XIV), 191-94, 196-98, 220,
  221, 472; *The Book on Adler*
  (1846-47) (*KW* XXIV), 466; *Upbuilding Discourses in Various Spirits*
  (1847) (*KW* XV), 220, 221, 430;
  Works of Love (1847) (*KW* XVI),
  214, 226, 228, 229, 363, 383, 410,
  411, 412-14, 430, 431, 459, 473,
  475, 479, 492, 493, 494, 497, 498;
  Christian Discourses (1848) (*KW*
  XVII), 241, 242, 379, 387, 431,
  476; *The Crisis and a Crisis in the
  Life of an Actress* (1848) (*KW*
  XVII), 389, 390, 494; *The Lily of
  the Field and the Bird of the Air.
  Three Devotional Discourses* (1849)
  (*KW* XVIII), 291, 431, 476, 483;
  The Sickness Unto Death (1849)
  (*KW* XIX), 303, 306, 311, 313,
  432, 484, 485, 486, 487; *The High
  Priest—The Publican—The Woman
  Who Was a Sinner, Three Discourses
  at the Communion on Fridays* (1849)
  (*KW* XVIII), 322, 325, 326, 393,
  394, 402, 432, 488, 494, 496; *An
  Upbuilding Discourse* (1850) (*KW*
  XVIII), 393, 434, 435, 494; "*An
  Open Letter*" (1851) (*KW* IX),
  394, 495; *Two Discourses at the
  Communion on Fridays* (1851) (*KW*
  XVIII), 389, 390, 406, 494, 495,
  497; *On My Work as an Author*
  (1851) (*KW* XXII), 388, 389, 390,

393, 394, 395, 435, 494, 495; *For Self-Examination* (1851) (*KW* XXI), 394, 401, 403, 407, 415, 495, 496, 497; *The Unchangeableness of God. A Discourse* (1855) (*KW* XXII), 379, 493; *The Moment* (1855) (*KW* XXIII), 418
Journals and Papers: 449, 451, 454, 455, 457, 459, 460, 462, 466, 468, 470, 472, 473, 474, 476, 477, 478, 479, 480, 481, 483, 484, 486, 487, 488, 489, 490, 491, 497, 498

Kierkegaard, Søren Michael, 41, 446, 449

Kingo, Thomas, 227, 475

Kofoed-Hansen, Hans Peter, 199, 200, 384, 404, 414, 472, 493, 497

Kold, Ole J., 182, 470

Kolderup-Rosenvinge, Janus Lauritz Andreas, 226, 240, 241, 246, 248, 252, 255, 259, 264, 267, 271, 274, 292, 299, 304, 307, 358, 475, 478, 479, 480, 481, 485, 486, 491, 500

Kolderup-Rosenvinge, Sophie Wilhelmina Bertha, 434, 500

Kolderup-Rosenvinge, Valdemar, 359

Krieger, Andreas F., 152, 466

Krieger, Lorentz, 229, 475

Lamartine, Alphonse de, 261, 299, 305, 306; *Histoire des Girondins*, 479; *Histoire de la Revolution de 1848*, 261, 305, 479, 485

Lange, Frederik Olaus, 40, 451

Lehmann, Orla, 132, 463, 474

Levin, Israel Salomon, 173, 183, 184, 185, 186, 187, 449, 468, 469, 470, 471

Licht, Hans Henrik, 21, 447

Lichtenberg, Georg Christoph, 269, 480

Lind, Peter Engel, 48, 452

Linnemann, Ingvar Henrik, 19, 447

Livius, Titus, 5, 266, 480

Louis Philippe, 305

Lund, Carl, 98, 112, 129, 130, 207, 422, 462, 473, 499

Lund, Christian, 144, 145, 146

Lund, Henriette, 108, 109, 127, 142, 157, 181, 195, 201, 202, 231, 423, 424, 462, 472, 499

Lund, Henrik, 106, 172, 283, 284, 340, 342, 343, 346, 355, 360, 375, 377, 378, 422, 482, 489, 490, 491, 493, 494

Lund, Henrik Ferdinand, 39, 41, 451, 461

Lund, Johan Christian, 203, 458, 460, 462, 464

Lund, Michael, 109, 110, 111, 112, 127, 131, 284, 482

Lund, Peter Wilhelm, 41, 451

Lund, Sophie, 128, 129, 423, 424

Lund, Troels, 461

Lund, Wilhelm, 109, 237, 462

Lunde, Peter Frederik, 267, 480

Luno, Christian Peter Bianco, 181, 220, 221, 222, 469

Madvig, Johan Nikolai, 430, 499, 500

Malantschuk, Gregor, 452

Marheineke, Phillip Konrad, 90, 106, 460

Martensen, Hans Lassen, 311, 315, 316, 320-21, 337, 344, 348, 395, 408, 429, 482, 487, 495, 497, 499; *Grundrids til Moralfilosofiens System* [Principal Characteristics of the System of Moral Philosophy] (1841), 156, 230, 466, 475; *Den Christelige Dogmatik* [Christian Dogmatics] (1844), 298, 299, 303, 310, 315, 319, 320-21, 337, 338, 484, 487, 489

Mathiesen, Lars, 269, 480

mediation, 312, 313, 314, 315, 316, 338, 486, 487, 489. *See also* reconciliation

Mela, Pomponius, 266, 480

Merimée, Prosper, *Les Âmes du Pur-gatoire*, 43, 451
Michelet, C. L., 118, 463
Molbech, Christian, 237, 476
Moltke, O. J., 416
monetary system in Denmark in 19th century, 450, 454
Moore, Thomas, 458
Mozart, W. A. von, *Don Giovanni*, 462; *Marriage of Figaro*, 499
Müller, Carl L., 152, 466
Münter, Balthasar, 21, 22, 82, 447, 458
Mynster, Frederik Joachim, 417, 498
Mynster, Jakob Peter, 4, 147, 162, 177, 178, 179, 180, 275, 315, 339, 367, 373, 395, 417, 431, 432, 436, 445, 465, 466, 467, 481, 487, 489, 493, 495, 498, 500
Møller, N. C., 422, 499
Møller, Peter Ludvig, 183, 470, 483
Møller, Poul Martin, 63, 66, 105, 106, 387, 455, 462, 477, 494
Møller, Rasmus, 387, 494

Napoleon Bonaparte, 265, 479
Nathanson, Mendel Levin, 149, 465
National Assembly, 45, 272, 293, 373, 451, 480, 481, 484
Nepos, Cornelius, 5
newspapers, periodicals, and jour-nals, *Adresse-Avisen*, 17, 292, 293, 484; *Aftenbladet*, 218; *Berlingske Tidende*, 149, 218, 259, 270, 415, 465, 479, 489, 498; *The Corsair*, 183, 470, 483; *Dannevirke*, 415, 498; *Dansk Kirketidende*, 268, 337, 344, 479, 481, 489, 490; *For Literatur og Kritik*, 264, 479; *Fædre-landet*, 173, 187, 188, 216, 270, 336, 390, 394, 452, 465, 468, 470, 471, 495; *Gæa*, 470; *Kjøbenhavns Flyvende Post*, 51, 452; *Maanedsskrift for Litteratur*, 496; *Nordisk Literaturtidende*, 472; *Per-seus*, 453, 464; *Rigsdagstidende*, 293, 359, 484; *Tidsskrift för Literatur*,

386, 493; *Videnskabsskriftet*, 367
Nielsen, Michael, 7, 16, 24, 25, 37, 89, 168, 429, 445, 450, 459, 476, 499
Nielsen, Nikolai Peter, 238, 435, 476, 500
Nielsen, Rasmus, 244, 245, 249, 251, 258, 290, 291, 298, 303, 310, 311, 312, 313, 314, 315, 316, 317, 319, 320, 342, 344, 348, 349, 350, 351, 352, 353, 354, 400, 414, 436, 477, 486, 490; *Evangelietroen og den moderne Bevidsthed, Forelæsninger over Jesu Liv* [Gospel Faith and the Modern Consciousness, Lectures on the Life of Jesus], 483, 490
Novalis, *Schriften*, 74, 457

Oehlenschläger, Adam, *Aladdin*, 66, 456; *Sct. Hansaftens-Spil* [A Play for Midsummer's Eve], 54, 453; *Erindringer* [Memoirs], 421, 499
Oldenburg, Theodor Vilhelm, 37, 450
Olsen, Jonas, 63, 455
Olsen, Regine, 33, 61-88, 90, 91, 92, 93, 94, 96, 102, 103, 114-16, 120-24, 126, 133-38, 455-61, 466. *See also* Schlegel, Regine
Olsen, Terkild, 333, 335, 356, 488

Paludan-Müller, Frederik, 288; *Adam Homo*, 483, 495
Paulli, Just Henrik, 26, 449
Petersen, Frederik Christian, 228, 322, 475
Philipsen, Philip Gerson, 181, 222, 223, 294, 474
Phister, Joachim Ludvig, 276, 376, 437, 469, 481, 493, 500
Plato, 5; *Symposium*, 66-67, 456; *Phaedo*, 389, 494

Rahbek, Knud Lyhne, 269, 480, 485
reconciliation, 310-18, 338, 486, 489. *See also* Hegelianism
Reitzel, Carl, 400

Reitzel, Carl Andreas, 97, 220, 221, 223, 400, 418, 454, 461, 474, 496, 499

Rosenkilde, Christen Nieman, 437, 500

Roskilde Convention, 180, 277, 416, 449, 469, 481, 498

Ross, Petronella, 387, 494

Rothe, Barbara Abigail, 296, 484

Rothe, Wilhelm, 141, 464

Rothe, Wilhelmine Susanne, 433, 500

Rudelbach, Andreas Gottlob, 363, 374, 417, 432, 434, 435, 492, 498, 500.

Rørdam, Bolette, 459

Røyen (Røjen), Kirstine Nielsdatter, 26, 245, 449, 454, 490

Sallust, 5

Scandinavianism, 216-19, 224, 225, 306, 473, 474, 485

Scharling, Carl Emil, 10, 26, 447, 490

Schelling, Friedrich Wilhelm Joseph von, 90, 97, 98, 104, 106, 107, 109, 118-19, 125, 127, 132, 135, 136, 138, 139, 141, 460, 461, 463, 464, 471

Schiller, Johann Christoph Friedrich von, 249, 368, 492; *Der Antritt des neuen Jahrhunderts*, 478

Schlegel, Johan Frederik, 322-37, 450, 488

Schlegel, Regine, 322-37, 450, 488-89. *See also* Olsen, Regine

Schlegel, W. A., 73, 457

Schmidt, A. T., 285

Schouw, Joachim Frederik, 45, 451

Schubert, G. H. von, 451

Schubothe, Johann Jürgen Heinrich, 105, 461

Schultze, Hedwig, 105, 113, 461, 462

Scribe, Eugène, 105, 173, 254, 336; *Les Premieres Amours*, 461, 469, 478; *La Dame Blanche*, 463, 489

Sibbern, Frederik Christian, 25, 90, 91, 96, 106, 127, 128, 188, 259, 387, 448, 462, 471, 494

Socrates, 117, 259, 260, 262, 263, 350, 383, 388, 479

Sommer, Andreas Gartner, 485

Sophism, 262, 263

Spandet, Niels Møller, 373, 393, 493, 495

Spang, Christiane Philipine, 203-6, 421, 473

Spang, Peter Johannes, 95, 117, 461, 473

Steenstrup, Mathias G. G., 495

Steffens, Henrik, 97, 106, 452, 461, 462; *Caricaturen des Heiligsten*, 106; *Anthropologie*, 107

Stein, Sophus August Vilhelm, 487

Stilling, Peter Michael, 338, 489; *Om den indbildte Forsoning af Tro og— Viden, med særligt Hensyn til Professor Martensens Christelige Dogmatik. Kritisk Polemisk Afhandling* [On the Imagined Reconciliation of Faith and—Knowledge with Specific Application to Professor Martensen's "Christian Dogmatics." A Critical Polemical Essay] (1849), 338, 344, 489; *Et Par Spørgsmaal til Professor C. E. Scharling i Anledning af hans saakaldte Anmeldelse af Dr. Martensens Dogmatik* [Some Questions to Professor C. E. S. Occasioned by His So-called Review of Dr. Martensen's *Dogmatics*] (1850), 490

Strachwitz, Moritz von, 265, 480

Strøm, Gollich Frederik Peter, 17, 447

Terence, 5

Tersteegen, Gerhard, 486

Tetens, Peter, 490

Thiers, Adolphe, 271, 480

Thomsen, Jacob Nicolai Theodor, 20, 21, 447

Thomsen, Julie Augusta, 208, 278, 281, 339, 363, 473, 489, 492
Thorvaldsen, Bertel, 167, 468
Trier, Seligmann Meyer, 276, 481

Vergil, 5
Visbye, C. H., 467
Volkslieder der Deutchen, ed. von Erlach, 453

Wad, Mattias, 19, 447
walking, 214-15, 241, 247, 248, 254, 255, 256, 257, 260, 263, 264, 266, 267, 268, 272, 274, 290, 291, 294, 297, 298, 300, 301, 308, 342, 344, 348, 349, 350, 351, 353, 354, 400, 414, 449, 473, 475
war with Germany (1848-50), 242, 253, 254, 257, 258, 272, 283, 284, 300, 343, 375, 378, 386, 474, 476, 478, 480, 482, 484
Werder, Carl, 98, 106, 107, 119, 461,

462, 463; *Christopher Columbus*, 119
Werliin, Julia, 240, 476
Wessel, Johan Herman, 282, 482
Wexschall, Anna H. D., 238, 435, 476, 500
Winther, Christian, 431, 456, 458, 476, 500
Wittrock, Johan Georg, 17, 447

Xenophon, 5

Zeuthen, Frederik Ludvig Bang, 241-43, 476

Ørsted, Anders Sandøe, 257, 272, 273, 274, 430, 432, 479, 480, 481, 500
Ørsted, Hans Christian, 25, 44, 253, 448, 451, 479; *Aanden i Naturen* [Spirit in Nature], 367, 492

Library of Congress Cataloging in Publication Data

Kierkegaard, Søren Aabye, 1813-1855.
  Letters and documents.

  (Kierkegaard's writings; 25)
  Translation of Breve og aktstykker.
  Bibliography: p.
  Includes index.
    1. Kierkegaard, Søren Aabye, 1813-1855.
  2. Philosophers—Denmark—Correspondence.   3. Philosophers—
  Denmark—Biography.   I. Rosenmeier, Henrik, 1931-
  II. Series: Kierkegaard, Søren Aabye, 1813-1855.
  Works. English. 1977- ; 25.
  B4376.A3313   198'.9 [B]   77-85897
  ISBN 0-691ᴥ7228-0